PREDICTING RELIGION

Religion in the contemporary west is undergoing rapid change. In *Predicting Religion* twenty experts in the study of religion present their predictions about the future of religion in the 21st century – predictions based on careful analysis of the contemporary religious scene from traditional forms of Christianity to new spiritualities. The range of predictions is broad. A number predict further secularization – with religion in the west seen as being in a state of terminal decline. Others question this approach and suggest that we are witnessing not decline but transformation understood in different ways: a shift from theism to pantheism, from outer to inner authority, from God to self-as-god, and above all from religion to spirituality.

T. accessible book on the contemporary religious scene offers students and scholars of the sociology of religion and theology, as well as interested general readers, fresh insights into the future of religion and spirituality in the west.

THEOLOGY AND RELIGION IN INTERDISCIPLINARY PERSPECTIVE SERIES

Published in association with the BSA Study of Religion group as part of the Ashgate *Theology and Religion in Interdisciplinary Perspective Series*

Series Editors

Professor Douglas Davies, University of Durham, UK
Professor Richard Fenn, Princeton Theological Seminary, New Jersey, USA

Publications Officer, BSA Sociology of Religion Study Group
Pink Dandelion, Woodbrooke Quaker Study Centre
and the University of Birmingham

Creativity through shared perspectives lies at the heart of Ashgate's new series on *Theology and Religion in Interdisciplinary Perspective*. Central religious and theological topics can be raised to a higher order of expression and clarity when approached through interdisciplinary perspectives; this new series aims to provide a pool of potential theories and worked out examples as a resource for ongoing debate, fostering intellectual curiosity rather than guarding traditional academic boundaries and extending, rather than acting as a simple guide to, an already well-defined field. Major theological issues of contemporary society and thought, as well as some long established ideas, are explored in terms of current research across appropriate disciplines and with an international compass. The books in the series will prove of particular value to students, academics, and others who see the benefit to be derived from bringing together ideas and information that often exist in relative isolation.

Also in the series

The Return of the Primitive
A New Sociological Theory of Religion
Richard K. Fenn
ISBN 0 7546 0419 5 (HBK)
ISBN 0 7546 0420 9 (PBK)

Christian Language and its Mutations
Essays in Sociological Understanding
David Martin
ISBN 0 7546 0739 9 (HBK)
ISBN 0 7546 0740 2 (PBK)

Predicting Religion

Christian, Secular and Alternative Futures

Edited by

GRACE DAVIE
University of Exeter, UK

PAUL HEELAS
Lancaster University, UK

LINDA WOODHEAD
Lancaster University, UK

ASHGATE

Published by
Ashgate Publishing Limited
Gower House
Croft Road
Aldershot
Hampshire GU11 3HR
England

Ashgate Publishing Company
Suite 420
101 Cherry Street
Burlington, VT 05401–4405
USA

Ashgate website: http://www.ashgate.com

British Library Cataloguing in Publication Data
Predicting religion : Christian, secular and alternative
    futures. – (BSA sub-series of religion and theology in
    interdisciplinary perspectives)
    1. Religion and sociology 2. Secularization (Theology)
    3. Christianity – Great Britain – Forecasting
    I. Davie, Grace II. Heelas, Paul III. Woodhead, Linda
    IV. British Sociological Association
    306.6

Library of Congress Cataloging-in-Publication Data
Predicting religion : Christian, secular and alternative futures / edited by Grace Davie, Linda Woodhead, and Paul Heelas.
        p. cm. – (Religion and theology in interdisciplinary perspective series)
    Includes bibliographical references.
    ISBN 0-7546-3009-9 (alk. paper) – ISBN 0-7546-3010-2 (pbk. : alk. paper)
        1. Religion–Forecasting. 2. Christianity–Forecasting. 3. Twenty-first
    century–Forecasts. I. Davie, Grace II. Woodhead, Linda. III. Heelas, Paul. IV. Series.

    BL48 .P74 2002
    200'.1'12–dc21   2002026286

ISBN 0 7546 3009 9 (HBK)
ISBN 0 7546 3010 2 (PBK)

Printed and bound in Great Britain by MPG Books Ltd, Bodmin, Cornwall

Contents

III PREDICTING ALTERNATIVES

Acknowledgments

This volume reflects the vitality of the sociology of religion in the UK today, a vitality that is institutionally reinforced by the Sociology of Religion Study Group of the British Sociological Association. It is to those who founded, supported and sustain this group that we owe our first debt of gratitude. In particular we would like to acknowledge two of its founding fathers, Bryan Wilson and David Martin. The meeting of the Study Group from which many of the contributions in this volume are drawn was convened in their honour and in recognition of their huge contribution to the discipline.

We would also like to express our thanks to the officers of the Study Group who encouraged us in organizing a meeting on 'Prophets and Predictions' and gave us their full support throughout. These included Kieran Flanagan, Sophie Gilliat-Ray and David Herbert. Acknowledgment is also due to Steve Bruce, who first had the idea of asking sociologists to predict the future of religion, and who secured funding from the University of Aberdeen. Further funding was supplied by the University of Exeter and Lancaster University, and by a generous grant from the British Academy. The meeting was held at the University of Exeter in the Spring of 2001. We are particularly grateful to Sandra Hogan for her help in the smooth running of the event.

We are also grateful to Sarah Lloyd at Ashgate Publishing, who has been supportive of the project throughout, and to Robert Segal, who encouraged us to publish a number of papers in a special section of the journal *Religion* (2002), Volume 32.

As editors we have found it particularly rewarding to be able to present the work of scholars in this lively field, and have deliberately selected contributions from across the generations – from the newest scholars just starting to make their mark, to those whose reputation is already firmly established. We have also included contributions by colleagues from outside the UK, in order to achieve a wider perspective. It has been a pleasure and a privilege to be part of this body of national and international scholarly endeavour and to engage with colleagues at home and abroad in the task of predicting religion.

List of Contributors

Steve Bruce is Professor of Sociology at the University of Aberdeen, Scotland. From 1978 to 1991 he taught at The Queen's University of Belfast. His main research interest is the fate of religion in modern Western democracies. Recent works include *Conservative Protestant Politics* (1998), *Choice and Religion: a Critique of Rational Choice Theory* (2000) and *God is Dead: Secularization in the West* (2002).

Helen Cameron is a Visiting Fellow at the Centre for Civil Society, London School of Economics, and a tutor on courses in Practical Theology for the Westminster Institute of Education, Oxford Brookes University. Her current research interests concern understanding membership as a means of social engagement and the congregation as an actor in the local voluntary sector. Recent publications include 'Are Members Volunteers? An Exploration of the Concept of Membership drawing upon Studies of the Local Church', in *Voluntary Action* (1999) and 'Colleagues or Clients? The Relationship between Clergy and Church Members', in Nigel Malin (ed.), *Professionalism, Boundaries and the Workplace* (2000).

José Casanova is Professor in the Department of Sociology at The Graduate Faculty of the New School for Social Research, New York. He is currently directing a three-year research project on Religion and Immigrant Incorporation in New York (RIINY). His publications include *Public Religions in the Modern World* (1994).

Paul Chambers lectures in sociology at the University of Glamorgan, Wales, and is currently working on a research project examining the interaction between political devolution, religious institutions and civil society in Wales. He was previously at the University of Wales, Swansea, where he completed his doctoral thesis, 'Factors in Church Growth and Decline', in 2000. His research interests centre on religion and identity in modern Wales. He is currently writing *Religion, Secularization and Social Change in Wales*. Previous publications include work on Neo-Pentecostalism and patterns of participation in adult education in Wales. He has a number of forthcoming journal articles and publications on subjects as diverse as religious change in Wales, church growth and decline, religious identity and sacred architecture. Chambers is also engaged on a research project with Andrew Thompson investigating political devolution, religion and civil society in Wales.

Grace Davie is a Professor of Sociology of Religion at the University of Exeter. Recent publications include *Religion in Britain since 1945: Believing Without*

Belonging (1994), *Religion in Modern Europe: a Memory Mutates* (2000) and *Europe: The Exceptional Case. Parameters of Faith in the Modern World* (2002). In 2000–2001 she held the Kerstin-Hesselgren Professorship in the University of Uppsala.

S.J.D. Green is Fellow of All Souls College, Oxford and Senior Lecturer in Modern History at the University of Leeds. He is interested in both the social history of religion and the intellectual debates about the future of religion since *c.*1850. His publications include *Religion in the Age of Decline* (1996).

Paul Heelas is Professor in Religion and Modernity in the Department of Religious Studies, Lancaster University. He has spent all his career, over a quarter of a century, at Lancaster. His current research (and teaching) interests are very much focused on whether or not a 'spiritual revolution' is under way: a shift from 'religion' to 'spirituality'. Recent publications have paved the way for finding out whether this 'revolution' is in evidence. The present Kendal Project, involving five researchers including Heelas, should provide some answers, which will be published shortly.

Rob Hirst is currently a freelance social and market research consultant, based in Southampton, having previously worked as a social researcher for the Department of Culture, Media and Sport. He took his PhD in the Sociology of Religion at the University of Surrey in 2000, having previously been a Research Fellow at the University of Southampton. His research interests include the sociology of religion, social networks, gerontology, housing and community care, homelessness, sport and leisure, and counselling. Publications include *Now or Never: Older People's Decisions About Housing* (1995, with Graham Allan and Lynn Watson), 'Care in the Original Home or a Housing Move?', in *Community Care* (1995), 'Nature or Nurture', in *Quadrant* (2000), and 'Nature or Nurture', in *Research* (Aotearoa, New Zealand, 2000).

Kate Hunt works as a qualitative research consultant for Riley Consulting. Her previous position was as a research associate in the Centre for the Study of Human Relations, the School of Education, University of Nottingham. Her key research interests have to do with non-institutional forms of spirituality and women's spirituality.

Anastasia Karaflogka is a PhD candidate, sponsored by AHRB, in the Study of Religions Department, at the School of Oriental and African Studies. She was a part-time lecturer in the Study of Religions department at Bath Spa University College. Her research interests are religion and advanced information technologies; religion and robotics; and theory and method of cyberreligious discourse. Publications include *The Soul and its Continuity in Tibetan Buddhism and in Pythagorian Greek Philosophy*, (1997), 'Orthodoxy and Society in Contemporary

Greece', in *Man and the Universe* (1998; Ukrainian translation), 'Religion, Church and the State in Contemporary Greece: A People's Perspective', in Irena Borowik (ed.), *Church–State Relations in Central and Eastern Europe* (1999) and '2002 Religious Discourse and Cyberspace', *Religion*, vol. 32, 4, pp.279–91.

David Martin retired as Professor at the London School of Economics in 1989 and has since then been attached to Southern Methodist University, Dallas (1986–91), Boston University as continuing international research fellow at the Institute for the Study of Economic Culture (from 1990), and the Department of Religious Studies, Lancaster University (from 1993). His first book was on pacifism (1965) and he has since produced some 24 volumes (10 of them edited collections). Over the last 15 years he has focused on the growth of Pentecostalism in the developing world, following on his earlier studies of secularization. His continuing interests have been peace and war (*Does Christianity Cause War?*, 1997) and the relation of sociology to theology (*Reflections on Theology and Sociology*, 1997). He latest book, *Pentecostalism: The World their Parish* (2002), offers an overview of the global charismatic upsurge.

Jo Pearson is a Lecturer in the Department of Religious Studies at the Open University, with research interests in Wicca, magic and religion, women in 'alternative' spiritualities, and film. She has recently completed *A Popular Dictionary of Paganism* (2002) and is currently working on a book on Wicca.

The Revd Canon Dr Martyn Percy is Director of the Lincoln Theological Institute for Religion and Society at the University of Sheffield. Formerly he was Chaplain and Director of Studies at Christ's College, Cambridge. His research interests lie in modern religion: ecclesiology, church–state relations, revivalism and new religious movements. Publications include *Power and the Church: Ecclesiology in an Age of Transition* (1997) and *Salt of the Earth: Religious Resilience in a Secular Age* (2001).

Gay Pilgrim is currently a PhD student in the Department of Theology, Birmingham University. She has previously been a part-time lecturer in Sociology and Social Policy at Wolverhampton University, and is currently an external tutor at Woodbrooke Quaker Studies Centre, Birmingham. Her research interests include religion and identity, religious/faith community, alternative spiritualities and pilgrimage.

Benjamin Seel is a Research Associate in Religious Studies at the Institute for the Environment, Public Policy and Philosophy at Lancaster University. Before this he worked at the University of Kent on an EC-funded cross-national project looking at 'The Transformation of Environmental Activism'. His PhD, 'Strategic Identities: Strategy, Culture and Consciousness in the Road Protest and New Age Movements', was awarded by Keele University in 1999. He is co-editor of *Direct Action in British Environmentalism* (2000). His research interests are social and religious movements, New Age and expressive spiritualities, Tibetan Buddhism, and more broadly the assumptions and submerged encodings that underlie people's pursuit of happiness.

Ulf Sjödin is an Associate Professor at the Turkku Academy, Finland. He has previously been a Lecturer at Umea University, Sweden, and a Researcher at Uppsala University. His key research interests include the study of non-organized religion, youth studies, values, value changes, and religious education. His key publications, all in Swedish, include *Invisible Religion. Theory and Method* (1987), *Flying Saucers, Ghosts, and True Dreams. Young Swede's Belief in Paranormal Phenomena* (1994), *One School – Several Worlds. Teachers' and Students' Values* (1995), *More Between Heaven and Earth? Young Swede's Views on Proven Experience* (2001). His ongoing and planned research include projects on 'Young People's Views on the Sacred, especially Church-related and Spontaneous Rites', and 'Popular Music and Life Interpretations'.

Wayne Spencer is a British civil servant who works in the field of social security law. Alongside his professional work, he amuses himself as a private researcher in sociology and psychology. He is currently working on a social psychological model of the consequences of exposure to racist material on the World Wide Web. His recent publications include a paper on spiritualism and New Age channelling and a co-authored article on the cult archaeology of the popular author Graham Hancock.

Jenny Taylor is a freelance writer and media consultant and a member of the Management Council of the Gospel and Our Culture. She is a qualified journalist and has written for the London *Evening Standard*, the *Times*, the *Guardian* and the European press. Her research interests include inter-faith relations, secularization and power. She has co-authored *Faith and Power. Christianity and Islam in 'Secular' Britain* with Lesslie Newbigin and Lamin Sanneh (1998), and has recently completed a doctorate at the School of Oriental and African Studies on the Inner Cities Religious Council.

Olivier Tschannen teaches sociology at the Universities of Neuchâtel, Fribourg and Lausanne (Switzerland). His key research interests are the sociology of religion, the history of sociology and sociological theory. Publications include 'The Secularization Paradigm: A Systematization', in the *Journal for the Scientific Study of Religion* (1991), *Les Théories de la Sécularisation* (1992) and chapters in Rudi Laermans, Bryan Wilson and Jaak Billiet (eds), *Secularization and Social Integration: Papers in Honour of Karel Dobbelaere* (1998) and Jean-Pierre Bastian (ed.), *La Modernité Religieuse en Perspective Comparée: Europe Latine – Amérique Latine* (2001).

Bryan Wilson FBA is Reader Emeritus in Sociology at the University of Oxford where he taught for over 30 years, and Emeritus Fellow of All Souls. His work has largely been devoted to the study of sects and new movements, and to the development of secularization theory. His principal publications include *Sects and Society* (1961), *Religion in Secular Society* (1966), *Patterns of Sectarianism* (ed., 1967), *Religious Sects* (1970), *Magic and the Millennium* (1973), *Religion in Sociological Perspective* (1982), *The Social Dimensions of Sectarianism* (1990), *A Time to Chant* (with Karel Dobbelaere, 1994) and *New Religious Movements: Challenge and Response* (ed. with Jamie Cresswell, 1999).

Linda Woodhead is Senior Lecturer in Christian Studies at Lancaster University. Her research is focused on Christianity and its transformations in the modern world. A co-director of 'the Kendal Project', she is currently collaborating on a book summarizing its findings on the state of religion and spirituality in the UK today. Recent edited and co-edited books include *Religion in Modern Times: An Interpretive Anthology* (2000), *Reinventing Christianity: Nineteenth-Century Contexts* (2000), *Peter Berger and the Study of Religion* (2001), *Religions in the Modern World: Traditions and Transformations* (2002). She has recently completed an *Introduction to Christianity* for Cambridge University Press.

Andrew K.T. Yip is Senior Lecturer in Sociology at the Department of Social Sciences, Nottingham Trent University. He is currently involved in two ESRC-funded research projects: 'British Non-heterosexual Muslims' and 'Social and Policy Implications of Non-heterosexual Ageing'. He is the author of *Gay Male Christian Couples: Life Stories* (1997) and of articles in, among others, the *British Journal of Sociology*, *Sociology of Religion*, *Sociology* and the *Journal for the Scientific Study of Religion*.

Introduction

Linda Woodhead, Paul Heelas and Grace Davie

On the Importance of Looking to the Future: Prophets and Predictions

In the press as well as in ordinary conversation, speculation about the future of religion is widespread. In the academy, however, the topic is often evaded. It has not always been so: Freud wrote about 'the end of an illusion', Comte anticipated the demise of traditional religion and magic, and Durkheim predicted that a religion of individual consciousness would develop. Such forecasts (and we could add many more) have since fallen from favour, the very enterprise of futurology having become suspect. In a considerably chastened post-colonial and post-modern climate, academics have come to favour the particular over the general, thick description over grand theory, and close attention to the present rather than speculation about the future, particularly when the latter carries the hidden assumption that Western societies are at the leading edge of an almost evolutionary progress. Against this background, the contributors to this volume were bold enough to accept an unfashionable challenge: *make a prediction about the state of religion in 30 to 50 years from now and to be as bold and as concrete in the prediction as you can.*

This unfashionable enterprise was deemed worthwhile for a number of reasons, some theoretical, some empirical, and some more practical. At the theoretical level, the continuing hold of the secularization paradigm in the sociology of religion means that scholars in this field are unable to abandon the business of prediction entirely. Secularization names a trend, evident in the past and the present and generalizable into the future. Even where the paradigm is challenged – as it increasingly is by those who point to the rude health of religion in many parts of the world – theorists tend to imagine alternative futures rather than concentrating on the past or present alone. Thus theories of 'sacralization' carry just as strong a predictive element as those they seek to replace. Indeed, to the extent that social science seeks to generalize about social processes and to identify regular connections between them, the element of prediction may be integral to the enterprise of sociology itself.

Together with such theoretical considerations, there is the simple empirical fact that religion/spirituality keeps unfolding, in the process opening up vistas onto the future. The 20th and 21st centuries have witnessed not only the decline but also the reinvention and resurgence of traditional religions alongside the rise of new forms of religion and spirituality. Some of the resurgence has been dramatic both in its nature and in its political consequences: the Islamic-backed Iranian Revolution of

1979; the role of Christianity in the overthrow of communism in the former USSR in the late 1980s and early 1990s; the rise of militant Hinduism in India; the reassertion of religio-ethnic identities in the former Yugoslavia; the impact of Islamic activity during and since 11 September 2001 – to mention only a few examples. Less immediately visible or controversial, but of considerable numerical significance, has been the rise of new, more amorphous, forms of spirituality in the West and beyond. Religion might be in decline, but spirituality – perceived to be less dogmatic, more tolerant and flexible, and better suited to the pursuit of personal inner quests – is waxing. At one extreme such spirituality has given rise to new movements such as those called New Age; at the other it shades off into a quest for the healing and energization of body and mind which is catered for on the high street rather than in designated sacred spaces. If some of those who contribute chapters to this volume are to be believed, all of this is set to grow.

Turning to more practical considerations, prediction seems possible for the simple reason that much that is underway in the religious realm is relentlessly regular. In many Western settings there are constant trends: total church attendance in nearly every part of Europe declines year in and year out, whilst spirituality grows in its appeal, again year in and year out, both in Europe and in North America. And not only is prediction possible, it is also useful. People want to know what might happen next, and with good reason. Well-researched predictions may be useful to religious professionals, educationalists, politicians, local government community officers, journalists and opinion formers, development personnel, management trainers, market researchers, retailers, doctors, nurses, counsellors, teachers and parents. Many in the public world need to know what is likely to happen in order to plan, make decisions and frame policies. Christian leaders, for example, may need to understand secularization trends in order to plan the future of their churches and their personnel. Those capitalizing on the growth of alternative forms of spirituality can take advantage of predictions which speculate about future directions in this realm. Politicians, community leaders and educationalists need to know as much as possible about developments in, for example, ethnic or immigrant religion. And educationalists can benefit from knowing that increasing pluralization is highly likely, making it ever more difficult to teach one particular religious tradition in schools to the exclusion of others, with ever more profound consequences for the teaching of Religious Education or Religious Studies.

To develop the last point a little more, it is likely that the trend towards experiential RE or RS which focuses on a universalist spirituality that unites rather than divides people of different faiths and cultures will retain its momentum, because of its ability to handle, or rather bypass, differences between traditions. It is also highly likely that the development of a similarly universalist spirituality within another major sector of public life – health care – will accelerate, with health professionals (doctors, nurses, counsellors, those working in hospices) responding to the increasing demand for spiritual care by referring patients to spiritual practitioners (in the case of GPs) or learning about spiritual care during their training (in the case of nurses). Even in the realm of consumer culture and spirituality there is no doubting the fact that professionals in the worlds of marketing, branding, advertising, store operation and high street provision are increasingly operating in terms of what they take to be a growing cultural concern with spirituality-cum-well-being (for example, the 'well-being' zones now found in Sainsbury's food and Boot's chemist shops in the UK).

How religion and spirituality are likely to fare in the future is also of concern to those concerned with the fate of Western societies more generally. Some argue that the decline of religion is a major factor in the 'demoralization' of society and the creation of a 'naked public square'; they work with the prediction that things will only get worse. Others, especially in North America, argue that religion is an effective bulwark against the forces of individualization and the 'bowling alone' society; they work with the prediction that things will probably not get worse. And yet others argue that the decline of traditional forms of religion is a condition for the creation of an open, tolerant and pluralistic society; their prediction is that continued decline will see things getting better.

In short, there is no harm in being brave and attending to the future. Far from it. Theory calls for it; so do developments on the ground; and so do the needs of those who have to look into the future for practical reasons. And, as the postscript to this Introduction also suggests, there is a further pressing practical reason which impels us to gaze into the future and make predictions on the basis of what we know of the past and the present.

On Specific Predictions

Christian ... or Secular

The dominance of secularization theory within the sociology of religion means that the most common way in which questions about the future of religion are posed is in terms of the polarity between religion and secularity. Is religion growing or declining? Are we becoming a religious society or a secular one? The options are starkly posed: religion or lack of religion?

Despite its general formulation in terms of 'religion' and 'secularity' and its universal claims, secularization theory has tended (at least implicitly) to focus upon the Christian religion and European societies. As the opening chapters of this book by José Casanova (Chapter 1) and David Martin (Chapter 2) point out, theories and predictions about religion have always been shaped by the contexts from which they derive. Since the founding fathers of sociology and the sociology of religion were European, their predictions about the future of religion were inevitably influenced by the progressive decline of church-based religion in the countries in which they lived. The result, as David Martin comments, was that secularization was 'problematically incorporated as a closely associated trend, and indeed a major defining characteristic of the modern'. Comte, Durkheim, Marx and Weber all developed some form of secularization theory, arguing that there was a causal link between modernization and the decline of traditional religion. They differed only with respect to the nature of this link: for Durkheim, for example, it was located in the breakdown of traditional forms of community, for Weber in the process of rationalization.

Since the majority of contributors to this volume are also European, it may not be surprising to find that many of them continue to predict the decline of traditional (Christian) religion. If anything, the influential European experience of change from a point in the past where religion was all-pervasive to one of rapidly declining influence has been even more dramatic in the last few decades. Despite significant variation across Europe (as Casanova explains here; see also Davie, 2000), the rate of Christian decline has generally accelerated since the 1970s. In Britain, for example, church attendance has declined from 19 per cent in 1903 to 15 per cent in 1951, to 12 per cent in 1979, to 10 per cent in 1989 and to an estimated 8 per cent in 2000 (Wraight and Brierley, 1999, p.26). Steve Bruce (Chapter 4) rams these 'facts' home, marshalling a whole range of indicators that point to accelerating decline: church attendance and membership, changing religious beliefs, numbers of clergy, Sunday School attendance, participation in Christian rites of passage. As both he and Bryan Wilson (Chapter 5) argue, however, decline at the level of individual belief and participation may be a less significant feature of secularization than the declining social, political and economic role of religion in European societies. Where once churches and clergy would have had a central role in (for example) education, welfare, moral regulation and political legitimation, such functions have now largely been taken over by the state, the market or voluntary agencies. Neither author sees any real hope for Christianity in the future, either for the churches or for 'harder' cultic and sectarian forms of religion. Bruce is the most dramatic in his prediction, nailing his colours to the mast by predicting that 'thirty years from now, Christianity in Britain will have largely disappeared ... In 2031, if it has not by then merged with the Church of England, British Methodism will die and other denominations will be close behind'.

Whilst Bruce explains secularization in terms of a range of processes of modernization, including pluralization and individualization, Wilson favours a more Durkheimian explanation which focuses on the way in which the decline of traditional forms of close-knit community goes hand in hand with that of the religion which sustained them and undergirded their moral and social economy. Both Paul Chambers (Chapter 6) and Rob Hirst (Chapter 7) put the latter theory to the test in relation to detailed historical and empirical research. Analysing the growth and subsequent decline of church and chapel in Wales, Chambers finds much to support theories which link secularization to the collapse of old-established localized forms of community. He shows how the growth of an indigenous form of Welsh Christianity centred upon the local chapel and expressed in the Welsh language helped create and sustain a distinctive national identity over against a potentially hegemonic English culture. Such religion was, however, 'essentially a localized phenomenon referentially tied to the communitarian and solidaristic networks surrounding individual chapels. It was only "national" in the sense that these localized conditions were repeated in many locations'. Thus the collapse of these networks under the pressure of forces of modernization has led inexorably to the collapse of Welsh Christianity. Hirst's detailed research on the links between religious transmission and social networks puts further flesh on Durkheimian bones, not least in its finding that it is predominantly those individuals whose parents were regular church attenders who will themselves attend church, though some opt not to. As the numbers who attend church diminish generation by generation, so the speed of decline accelerates (with a smaller and smaller pool from which to recruit). Given that intimate social networks are so decisive for church attendance, and given that the mass media, advertising or other 'impersonal' means of communication seem to have little or no impact on religious recruitment, Hirst too offers a gloomy prognosis for the churches.

Even those who are most forceful in their prediction of Christian decline are often willing to admit that some forms of Christianity are doing better than others. Dean Kelley first drew widespread attention to the growth of 'strict' forms of Christianity at the expense of more liberal forms in his book, *Why the Conservative Churches are Growing* (1977). In this volume, Steve Bruce develops Kelley's thesis by arguing that it is liberal Christianity which will collapse first owing to its inability to articulate, police and transmit its beliefs with clarity and conviction. The statistics are on his side. Yet the growth of 'hard' or sectarian forms of Christianity (in the UK at least) appears to be slowing, and such religion in any case still attracts only a relatively small minority of churchgoers. Where there appears to have been most significant growth since the early part of the 20th century is in the realm of charismatic Christianity, and this has been true not only in the UK or Europe but dramatically so worldwide (see, for example, Martin, 2002). Such growth is evident not only in the rise of new Pentecostal churches and denominations, but in the influence of charismatic revival within existing churches. Yet Martyn Percy's contribution (Chapter 8) on charismatic Christianity suggests that even this most apparently vibrant and growing movement may be on the cusp of significant decline, in the UK at least. 'Like all revivals,' he argues, charismatic Christianity 'seeks to exchange the perceived absence of God for a new sense of presence.' As such, it is pre-eminently a religion of experience and affect – and as such highly vulnerable. For not only do revivals by their very nature have a limited lifespan, but those like the charismatic movement which fail to develop any clear theology or ecclesiology are even more vulnerable because of their lack of any serious intellectual and institutional underpinning. Looking at the British scene, Percy already finds signs of the decline he predicts.

Not all are quite so gloomy about Christianity's present and future. One of the editors of the volume, Grace Davie, has argued elsewhere that the institutional decline of the churches in Britain has not necessarily been accompanied by a decline in belief (Davie, 1994). One of her supporting arguments is that decline in church membership and belief needs to be seen in a wider context, since it is paralleled by a decline in many other voluntary membership organizations, ranging from trades unions to political parties. In this volume Helen Cameron (Chapter 9) contributes to this debate by considering churches as local membership organizations and seeking to identify the pressures and competition faced by all such bodies. While she foresees continuing decline in church membership and attendance, she suggests that alternative forms of Christian affiliation may become increasingly important, such as affiliation to para-church leisure and heritage services, to small face-to-face groups, and to Christian campaigning organizations. Jenny Taylor (Chapter 10) considers the observation about the growth of new forms of political involvement by the churches in more detail, through her extensive research on a British government initiative, the Inner Cities Religious Council, a forum for the leaders of five faiths, which she shows to have had considerable direct political influence. Taylor theorizes this phenomenon in terms of the 'dedifferentiation' of the spheres of state and religion (Casanova, 1994) which, according to much secularization theory, should by now have disengaged from one another.

In their predictions about the future of Christianity both Cameron and Taylor focus attention not so much on decline as on transformation. Like the other contributors to this volume, however, neither expects a revival of the churches in anything like their traditional form. While they might suggest the refinement and revision of some aspects of secularization theory, none of those who attempt to characterize the present and future of Christianity in this volume seriously challenges its fundamental premises. The key question raised by both Casanova and Martin, however, is whether the European experience on which these authors base their work should be regarded as exceptional or normative. Is secularization a universal process or one peculiar to the unique historical experience of a particular part of the globe? The tendency in classical sociology and sociology of religion has been to assume that Europe was to be understood as the 'lead society', and where Europe travelled other societies would, in time, inevitably follow. As Olivier Tschannen (Chapter 3) argues, such an 'evolutionary' assumption is still present in much modern sociology – he uncovers it in the work of Bryan Wilson as well as Anthony Giddens. As Tschannen argues (and as Bryan Wilson's chapter illustrates), both theorists draw a clear distinction between modern and pre-modern (or traditional) societies in which both rationalization (or reflexivity) and societalization are identified as markers of modernization. Given that both these processes are understood as inevitable concomitants of industrialization and the spread of technology, and that both are seen as inherently corrosive of religion, it is hard to avoid the conclusion that a fate similar to that of Europe eventually awaits every part of the globe.

While it may be implicit in their work, Tschannen argues that Giddens draws back from drawing this conclusion explicitly, while Wilson only hints at it. Both Martin and Casanova question it, radically so (see also Davie, 2002). In their view the evidence points the other way. Far from being typical, Europe may be exceptional, an island of secularity in an ocean of vibrant religiosity. What is more, there is no good reason to believe that such secularity awaits all societies as they modernize. Assumption of secularity, for example, shaped early studies of charismatic upsurge in Latin America and other parts of the southern hemisphere (indeed the lack of such studies). Martin argues, however, that this does little justice to what has manifestly happened and is still unfolding. Serious attention to religious life in the non-Western world suggests something quite different: that different parts of the globe are experiencing different forms of modernity and modernization than those experienced by Europe, forms in which religion plays an integral and central role. To raise one's sights from the European context is thus to see and predict a very different future for religion, a future which undermines the claims of secularization theory to have universal explanatory power. Casanova makes the same point in relation to the USA. The American experience defies the predictions of classical (European) secularization theory both because of the continuing vitality of the churches and because this vitality occurs within the context of a highly modernized society in which religion has been cut loose from the state and lost many of its traditional sociopolitical roles. Rather than speak of 'European exceptionalism' or 'North American exceptionalism', Casanova argues that it would be better to abandon monolithic theories of religious decline (to which certain societies might be an exception) altogether and look instead at the specificities of each particular case.

Once the universal claims of a Europe-based secularization theory are refused a new vision of the religious present and future of the world opens up: a vision in which the coexistence of secularization and sacralization can at least be entertained. Such processes may not only be operative in different societies in different parts of the globe, but may be taking place simultaneously within a single society. A number of the contributors to this volume entertain this possibility, even in relation to so-called secular European society. They do so by focusing, not so much on Christianity and its decline, as on new or altered forms of religion and spirituality in which growth and vitality may be evident. In doing so they reject the assumption that the decline of traditional forms of Christianity necessarily implies the wholesale secularization of Western society. This approach implies a distinction, not only between different forms of society, but between different forms of religion within them. The distinction may be drawn in different ways. Following Weber and Troeltsch, Casanova suggests a distinction between religions which operate at the societal level, the group level and the individual level. At any one time, one or two of these may be in decline, whilst the other is growing – or vice versa. For example, many of the contributions to this volume (particularly when taken in aggregate) suggest that societal forms of religion (for example, politically established forms of Christianity such as the Church of England or the Church of Sweden) are doing particularly badly, whereas churches which operate as close-knit groups (for example, many evangelical–charismatic churches) are doing relatively well, whilst those forms of Christian and especially post-Christian spirituality which lend themselves to appropriation by individuals as part of a personal spiritual/self-developmental quest are positively flourishing.

Alternative ... or Complementary

The observation that 'soft' or subjectivized forms of religion and spirituality, both Christian and non-Christian or post-Christian, are doing relatively well in the West and can be expected to continue to do well, begins to undermine the very distinction between Christian and alternative forms of religion (and spirituality). Just as the simple dichotomy between religion and secularity may artificially constrain and distort our vision of the future, so too may that between Christian and alternative.

Both Andrew Yip (Chapter 11) and Gay Pilgrim (Chapter 12) provide evidence of the softening of Christianity, and predict the continued success of its softened forms. Yip's research amongst gay and lesbian men and women who continue to identify themselves as Christian and to attend Christian churches shows how Christianity can be successfully subjectivized or turned into a resource for the enrichment of individual life. Despite, as well as because of, the hostility of much 'traditional' Christian teaching to homosexuality and homosexual lifestyles, over 80 per cent of those questioned by Yip believe personal experience to be the most important basis of their faith and church authority to be the least. What is more, 91 per cent of his sample draw a distinction between religiosity and spirituality and favour the latter over the former. Respondents claim that 'exploring the inner self' and 'meditating' are the most important aspects of their spirituality, and reject a religiosity which is defined in terms of external rather than inner practices (participating in rituals, studying the Bible, and so on). Yip argues that tradition is not abandoned by gay and lesbian Christians, but is made subject to the authority of the individual rather than vice versa. His prediction is not religious decline but 'the growth of self-based spirituality which selectively draws upon broad religious themes and values and adapts them in accordance with the individual's salient personal circumstances'. Working on a broader canvas, Pilgrim traces the softening of an entire denomination – British Friends. Noting the 'hardening' of Quakerism in the 19th century under the influence of Evangelical Christianity, Pilgrim explores the way in which Quakerism subsequently softened both by returning to the past (recovering traditions of personal inspiration and the 'inner light') and by embracing the future (the new sciences and the advent of pluralism). Her characterization of the current Quaker scene in the UK notes the rise of an increasingly open and tolerant form of 'syncretic' Quakerism which is defined by nothing but its tolerance and openness, and which may be becoming increasingly detached from both more traditional and more 'inclusivistic' Quakerism.

From a starting point outside rather than within Christianity, Kate Hunt's research (Chapter 13) amongst those who do not attend church but nevertheless identify themselves as 'spiritual' also problematizes a hard and fast distinction between 'Christian' and 'alternative' forms of religiosity. Focus groups and interviews elicited evidence of a rich though largely invisible pool of personal spirituality which is rarely articulated in public. Whilst interviewees appeared highly appreciative of the chance to speak about their spiritual experiences, their enthusiasm was tempered by a fear that making such things public would lead to ridicule, and they often prefaced spiritual confessions with comments such as 'You may think I'm crazy, but ...'. Hunt notes that a further factor here appears to be the lack of a vocabulary in which to articulate spiritual beliefs and experiences. One of the most common statements she encountered when asking people about their spirituality was simply: 'I believe in something.' Such vagueness may appear apt for a spirituality which is tolerant, personalized/subjectivized, anti-dogmatic and has much more to do with *life* than with *belief*. As Hunt notes, however, it may also indicate the lack of a traditional reservoir of language, beliefs and symbols on which to draw. Insofar as such a resource is still available, however, Hunt notes that it is predominantly Christian. Despite displaying some hostility to church-based forms of Christianity, Hunt's respondents continued to draw upon Christian language and imagery, and to express a profound appreciation of the (spiritual) significance of Christian buildings.

This picture of the boundaries between Christian religion and alternative spirituality breaking down, and of interchange between what have previously been considered separate realms, is interestingly confirmed from the so-called alternative side by Jo Pearson (Chapter 14). In her discussion of the course of Wicca she notes how the lines between witchcraft, Wicca and neopaganism are becoming increasingly blurred (though she predicts that retrenchments on the part of those involved in initiatory witchcraft may increasingly take place in response to the spread of 'popular' witchcraft within the general culture). Similarly, she notes how 'pagan' hostility to the Judaeo-Christian tradition seems to be breaking down as men and women draw on both traditions. So we find 'Jewitches' and 'Judaeo-Pagans' proclaiming their existence, and note the emergence of 'Christo-Pagans' in North America. Against Steve Bruce, Pearson suggests that, far from being a weakness which leads to inevitable decline, it is precisely the softness of much Wicca (as well as more liberal forms of Christianity) which may secure their continued existence in a culture which shares so many of their values.

S.J.D. Green (Chapter 15) moves the discussion of the growth of subjectivized forms of religion beyond Europe as he considers the rise of pantheism in North America, as seen through the eyes of Alexis de Tocqueville. Whereas other major theorists of secularization have fixed upon the associated processes of urbanization, industrialization, rationalization and societalization as the aspects of modernization most corrosive of religion, de Tocqueville singled out democratization as the single most salient factor. He also differed in predicting not so much decline as transformation of religion. In particular, he believed that just as democracy levelled the social order, so it levelled the hierarchical orders of traditional Christianity (both in the heavens and on earth). Thus an authoritative religion which could safeguard individuality (and superiority?) was destined to give way to a bland pantheism which would abolish difference in favour of homogeneity.

In his discussion of de Tocqueville, Green notes the active alarm with which this great social commentator made his predictions about the future of religion. Far from straining at detachment, many of the great sociologists of religion have faced the future with open alarm or optimism. Bryan Wilson's clear-sighted predictions of the collapse of religion have, for example, always been tinged with melancholy at what he foretells and dislike of what he foresees. In making her predictions about the important impact which the growth of the Internet and World Wide Web is having on religion and spirituality, Anastasia Karaflogka (Chapter 16) seems, in contrast, markedly enthusiastic about what she believes to be in train. She argues that this new mode of instant and egalitarian communication is not only reshaping traditional forms of religion, but enabling the creation of entirely new ones. If she is right about the importance of this development, we see yet another instance of how the distinction between traditional and alternative modes of religion may collapse, for it is hard to maintain the natural authority of, say, Roman Catholicism, when the Vatican Home Page shares the same (cyber)space with any number of other religious sites, and when any individual or group can present their religion in the same way.

Not all of those who write about the future of subjectivized and alternative forms of spirituality are as sanguine about their future or their importance. While not disputing growth of alternative forms of religiosity in recent decades (particularly since the 1970s – interestingly coincident with the decline of the churches), defenders of secularization theory like Steve Bruce argue that this is wholly insignificant at every one of the levels at which religion may operate: in society, in group formation and in the living of individual lives. Unlike traditional religion, it is a shallow leisure activity, a distraction from real life and a mere entertainment. On the basis of their empirical research, both Ulf Sjödin (Chapter 17) and Wayne Spencer (Chapter 18) seem inclined to agree. Both consider the significance of what appears (on the basis of polls) to be a growing belief in the paranormal, particularly amongst young people. Sjödin's own research amongst Swedish youth confirms this trend, but also casts serious doubt upon the salience of their belief in the paranormal within their lives. Sjödin speculates that such belief may simply be occupying a space opened up by their corresponding lack of belief in traditional Christian doctrines, but that it is held with little real conviction. He makes the interesting observation that Swedish youth seem both *more* interested in metaphysical exploration and *less* interested in definitive answers. 'In relation to their quest,' he says, 'we seem to find both a shrinking *and* an expanding transcendence'. Spencer takes a complementary approach to the same issue by exploring not the individual but the social salience of astrology. His investigation into its role and significance in a range of primary institutions in modern Western society yields the conclusive finding that it has none. Contrary to those who claim that the authority of science is diminishing, Spencer notes its continuing prestige and the importance of rationalized processes in the exclusion of astrology from the public realm. His conclusion is that the significance of the latter is confined almost exclusively to the individual level and the private sphere, that even there it is 'broad but shallow', and that there is no reason to think that this situation will change in the coming decades.

In 'An Ageing New Age?' (Chapter 19), Paul Heelas and Benjamin Seel also begin by pouring cold water on more enthusiastic and extravagant claims about the growth of alternative spirituality and its ability to reverse secularizing trends in the West. Focusing on what is perhaps the most influential movement within alternative spirituality to date, Heelas and Seel amass evidence that suggests that New Age was a product of the counter-cultural revolution of the 1960s and that it serves the particular needs, anxieties and dreams of the cohort shaped by that decisive decade and its immediate aftermath. The prediction would seem to be that baby boom religion will die out along with the baby-boomers. Yet Heelas and Seel go on to show that the counter-culture has not so much died as become diffused into mainstream culture. What was previously alternative is now easily available over the counter in the high street, taught in the classroom, and on the referral list of many GPs. It is quite possible, therefore, that there will continue to be a ready supply of both practitioners and clients of an alternative spirituality which is rapidly becoming mainstream.

On Predicting Danger: a Short Reflection Provoked by 11 September 2002

The events of 11 September cut across our preparation of this volume, and stood before us as a particularly unwelcome test of what we had just written about the importance of predicting religion. They prompted two main reflections: firstly, that while we had largely restricted ourselves to reflection on religion in the West, particularly in Europe, the events in New York and Washington served as a reminder of how foolish it really is to think that the West can be understood in total isolation from 'the rest' (or at least key aspects of 'the rest'). The aeroplanes which flew into the Twin Towers and Pentagon symbolized in a powerful way how aspects of one culture and territory may enter into another.

The second reflection points to the fact that, if anything, we might have *underestimated* the growing importance of the task of predicting the conditions under which religion can become dangerous: dangerous not only for the West, but for the other countries and societies in which 'dangerous' religion may have its immediate origins. What follows is no more than a tentative suggestion about how such an endeavour might proceed. It is offered not so much as an addition to this volume as a suggestion about priorities for future volumes and research, and as an underlining of our claim that there are very practical reasons why predicting the future of religion is such an important task.

Two books, above all others, summarize two radically contrasting ways of envisaging the direction in which the world is travelling: Francis Fukuyama's *The*

End of History and the Last Man (1992) and Samuel Huntington's *The Clash of Civilizations and the Remaking of World Order* (1998). The former paints a picture of a world becoming ever-increasingly homogenized, with the interrelated forces of a globalizing capitalism and a universalizing, dedifferentiating ethic of humanity resulting in the progressive eradication, or 'softening' of difference. The latter, in contrast, paints a picture of a world being ever-increasingly rent asunder, with the forces of resurgent or 'hardening' traditions ensuring the progressive enhancement of conflict and difference.

Both pictures are true, not least in the realm of religion. What can be thought of as religions of humanity (for which humanity and a shared human nature have transcendent value) and spiritualities of life (which identify the divine with the spirit and energies of life, particularly personal, subjective life) are very much bound up with the first, softening, process. What on the other hand can be thought of as religions of difference (which articulate the divine in terms of divine–human as well as sociocultural difference) are bound up with the second, hardening, process. The first is thus threatened by the second; the second by the first.

Processes of homogenization (bound up with the forces of globalizing capitalism, the spread of the ethic of humanity and the development of inclusivistic forms of religion and spirituality) tend to be associated with the West and, at least from the point of view of those who favour the inclusivistic ethos, are 'safe'. They bring about 'the same', a sameness which renders no (differentiated) challenges to those who belong to the same. However, processes of differentiation (bound up with traditionalization) are – primarily – to be found among 'the rest'. Again from the point of view of the West as well as those who are inclusivistic elsewhere, such processes are 'unsafe', for they encourage difference and exclusivism ('my tradition is the only true one') and challenge those who belong to other forms of life or tradition.

But some forms of hard, strongly differentiated, religion are much more dangerous than others. Attention to the key beliefs of the Taliban/al-Qa'eda helps us see which factors are most salient in this respect. One is the way in which great importance is attached to the difference between 'us' and 'them' (we are right, you are wrong). Things are black and white. There is only one truth, and the 'mission of our Prophet Muhammad' (Bin Laden) is to spread it: all the more so given the belief that all that does not belong to the truth brings 'evil' to those who seek to 'purify [one's] heart and clean it from all earthly matters' (we are on the path, you are dangerous, your destruction can only be good).[1] Another factor is the belief that if one should die in the process of spreading the truth, this will only hasten salvation (one's own and the world's). Furthermore, the Taliban/al-Qa'eda believe that the life of the true believer is part and parcel of the life of Allah (as Atta wrote, 'My prayer, my sacrifice and my life and my death belong to Allah, the Lord of the Worlds'). This entails (a) that the life in and of this world is 'meaningless' (Bin Laden), which means that the death of the true believer is of little ultimate consequence; and (b) that the lives of those who are not true believers are also meaningless (or dangerous). When life-itself only becomes true-life within a tradition, the lives of others are dismissed – as untrue, if not evil.

Such are some of the key aspects of what we might call 'the dynamics of danger' of this particular form of Islam. So the multi-million dollar question has to be: *why do hard, really hard, religions of difference, with their ability to make a real and dangerous difference, flourish under particular circumstances, and particularly outside the West? More specifically, what encourages the development and operationalizationing of the kind of meaning dynamics found among the Taliban?* And the key answer has to be that such forms of religion thrive under conditions of suffering and abject poverty, especially when these are believed to be imposed upon one people by the oppression and injustice of another. Thus life within a very hard Islamic tradition serves to redress life lived by the wretched of the earth: what is promised is both victory within this world and paradise within the next. And, in any case, for the truly wretched, what is there to lose?

Islam is by no means the only example here. Certain forms of hard, exclusivistic Christianity (for example) operate in much the same fashion. Thus in sub-Saharan Africa, in the extremely impoverished regions of southern Sudan and northern Uganda, we find movements such as Joseph Kony's Lord's Resistance Army teaching that lives lived in and through the Holy Spirit by the 'born again' will bring victory, both within this world (for the Holy Spirit ensures that you cannot be killed when fighting the enemy) and in the next. But sub-Saharan movements as yet lack the knowledge, skills and technology to be dangerous on an international scale. Throw in what was available to the Taliban/al-Qa'eda, however, and the prediction is that they will become correspondingly more dangerous.

As leading politicians in Europe have been pointing out, the dynamics of danger are increasingly likely to be developed as the gulf between the West and the rest grows ever greater. And their epicentre is most likely to be the world's most impoverished region: sub-Saharan Africa. The Pentagon and the White House might not like this prediction. But that may be just one of the reasons why it is so important for academics to engage in a serious study of the future.

Note

1 Material is gathered here from a variety of newspaper reports.

References

Casanova, José 1994: *Public Religions in the Modern World.* Chicago and London: University of Chicago Press.

Davie, Grace 1994: *Religion in Modern Britain: Believing without Belonging.* Oxford, UK and Malden, USA: Blackwell.

Davie, Grace 2000: *Religion in Modern Europe: a Memory Mutates.* Oxford: Oxford University Press.

Davie, Grace 2002: *Europe: the Exceptional Case. Parameters of Faith in the Modern World.* London: Darton, Longman and Todd.

Fukuyama, Francis 1992: *The End of History and the Last Man.* London: Penguin.

Huntington, Samuel 1998: *The Clash of Civilizations and the Remaking of World Order.* London: Touchstone.

Kelley, Dean 1977: *Why the Conservative Churches are Growing.* 2nd edn. San Francisco: Harper and Row.

Martin, David 2002: *Pentecostalism. The World Their Parish.* Oxford: Blackwell.

Wraight, Heather and Brierley, Peter (eds) 1999: *UK Christian Handbook 2000/01. Millennium Edition.* London: Christian Research/Harper Collins Religious.

I
SECULARIZATION THEORY RE-EXAMINED

CHAPTER 1

Beyond European and American Exceptionalisms: towards a Global Perspective

José Casanova

We have reached an impasse in the secularization debate between European and American sociologists of religion (Swatos, 1999). The traditional European theory of secularization, the 'inherited' (Wilson, 1985) or 'orthodox' (Bruce, 2000) model, offers a relatively plausible account of European developments, but is unable or unwilling to take seriously, much less to explain, the surprising vitality and extreme pluralism of denominational forms of salvation religion in America. The emerging American paradigm (Warner, 1993) offers a convincing explanation of the US religious market, but is unable to account for the significant internal variations within Europe. Hence the impasse. The orthodox model works relatively well for Europe but not for America, the American paradigm works for USA but not for Europe. In order to overcome the impasse and surmount the fruitless debate, we first of all need to make clear the relative agreements and disagreements between the European and American positions.[1] But, more importantly, we need to refocus our attention beyond Europe and the West, historicize and contextualize our categories, and adopt a more global perspective.

The European–American Secularization Debate

Terminological Disagreements

The first and most basic disagreement is terminological. Europeans tend to use the term 'secularization' in a double sense, constantly switching back and forth between two related meanings. There is, firstly, secularization in the broader sense of the secularization of societal structures or the diminution of the social significance of religion. There is, secondly, secularization in the narrower sense of decline of religious beliefs and practices among individuals. The broad meaning of social secularization is related to the long-term historical processes of social differentiation and the emancipation of the secular spheres (state, capitalist economy, science, and so on) from religious institutions and norms; and the concomitant relegation of religion to its own greatly reduced and delimited sphere.

This has always been the traditional meaning of secularization, a term which derives etymologically from the mediaeval Latin word *saeculum*, with its dual temporal–spatial connotation of a secular *age* and a secular *world* counterposed to the religious age and the religious world (Casanova, 2001). As the dictionary of any Western European language will show, to secularize means 'to make worldly', to convert or transfer persons, things, meanings, and so on, from religious or ecclesiastical to secular or civil use. In the European context, therefore, secularization is a concept overloaded with multiple historically sedimented meanings which simply point to the ubiquitous and undeniable long-term historical shrinkage of the size, power and functions of ecclesiastical institutions *vis-à-vis* other secular institutions. The second, narrower meaning of the term, the decline of religious beliefs and practices among individuals, is secondary, posterior and mainly derivative from the primary meaning. Europeans, however, see the two meanings of the term as intrinsically related: for they view the two realities, the decline in the societal significance of religious institutions and the decline of religious beliefs and practices, as structurally related. Supposedly, one necessarily leads to the other.

Americans tend to view things differently and practically restrict the use of the term 'secularization' to its secondary and narrower meaning, to the progressive decline of religious beliefs and practices among individuals. It is not so much that they question the secularization of society, but simply that they take it for granted as an unremarkable fact, as a *fait accompli*. The USA, they assume, has always been, at least constitutionally since independence, a secular society, as secular, if not more so, as any European society. Yet they see no evidence that this unquestionable fact of the *desacralization* of society has led to a progressive decline in religious beliefs and practices among Americans. If anything, the historical evidence, as historians and sociologists of American religion have amply documented (Butler, 1990; Finke and Stark, 1992; Greeley, 1989), points in the opposite direction: to the progressive growth in religious beliefs and practices and the progressive *churching* of the American population since independence. Consequently, many American sociologists of religion tend to discard the theory of secularization, or at least its postulate of the progressive decline of religious beliefs and practices, as a European myth (Stark, 1999; Stark and Bainbridge, 1985).

Factual Agreements: Relative Consensus

Despite some lingering disagreements concerning the factual evidence of the extent of religious vitality on both sides of the Atlantic, there is a relative consensus that religion, in its institutional as well as in its individual manifestations, is generally doing much better in America than throughout most of Europe. Even after discounting the tendency of Americans to inflate their rates of church attendance (Hadaway *et al.*, 1993) and to exaggerate the depth and seriousness of their religious beliefs, the fact remains that Americans are generally more religious than most Europeans, with the possible exception of the Irish and the Poles. Moreover, the very tendency of the Americans to exaggerate their religiousness, in contrast to the opposite tendency of Europeans to discount and undercount their own persistent religiosity, tendencies which are evident among ordinary people as well as scholars, are themselves part of the very different and consequential definitions of the situation in both places. Americans think that they are supposed to be religious, while Europeans think that they are supposed to be irreligious.

The progressive, though highly uneven, secularization of Europe is an undeniable social fact (Martin, 1978). An increasing majority of the European population has ceased participating in traditional religious practices, at least on a regular basis, while still maintaining relatively high levels of private individual religious beliefs. In this respect, one should perhaps talk of the *unchurching* of the European population, rather than of secularization. Grace Davie (1994; 2000) has characterized this general European situation as 'believing without belonging'. A majority of the European population in every European country, except the Czech Republic and East Germany, still affirms 'belief in God', and the proportion of those who declare themselves to be 'not atheist or agnostic' is consistently even larger. Only in East Germany do 'atheists' constitute a majority of the population (51 per cent). In every other European country 'atheists' remain below 20 per cent of the population.[2]

Moreover, the rates of religiosity vary significantly across Europe. East Germany is by far the least religious country of Europe by any measure, followed at a long distance by the Czech Republic and the Scandinavian countries. At the other extreme, Ireland and Poland are by far the most religious countries of Europe with rates comparable to those of the USA. In general, with the significant exception of France and the Czech Republic, Catholic countries tend to be more religious than Protestant or mixed countries (West Germany, Netherlands), although Switzerland (a mixed and traditionally pillarized country comparable to Holland) stands at the high end of the European religious scale, with rates similar to those of Catholic Austria and Spain. In general, former communist countries in East and Central Europe have rates of religiosity lower than the European average, but many of them, most notably Russia, have experienced remarkable religious growth since 1989 (Greeley, 1994).

Theoretical Disagreements: Competing Analytical Frameworks

European social scientists tend to view these European facts through the analytical lenses of the inherited theory of secularization (Wilson, 1966). According to the orthodox model of secularization, most forcefully restated by Steve Bruce (1992; 1996; 2000; 2002), secularization is intrinsically and structurally linked to general processes of modernization. Social differentiation, and other components of modernization like societalization and rationalization, lead to a decline in the societal significance of religious institutions, which in turn leads eventually to the decline of religious beliefs and practices. As a general rule the theory postulates that the more modern a society the less religious will be its population.

Generally, the theory holds well against the European evidence. The core European countries – Great Britain, France, Holland and Germany – the ones which have led the processes of European modernization, fit well the orthodox model. The theory is less able to account for the significant internal European variations, particularly at the extremes. Some countries, particularly East Germany, the Czech Republic and the Scandinavian countries, are relatively oversecularized. The higher levels of secularization of East Germany simply cannot be explained in terms of higher levels of modernization. At the other extreme, countries like Italy, and particularly Poland and Ireland, are relatively, almost absolutely, undersecularized. The assumption that it is only a matter of time before they more closely follow the general European rule is highly questionable. Moreover, traditional explanations of European secularization in terms of general theories of modernization, by reference to either increasing institutional differentiation, increasing rationality or increasing individualism, become even less persuasive when confronted with the evidence from other equally modern societies, like the USA, which do not manifest comparable levels of religious decline.

When faced with any internal or external counter-evidence, however, European defenders of the orthodox model tend to offer *ad hoc* historicist explanations of the deviations from the norm, rather than to question or revise the general rule itself. Bruce (1996) exemplifies such an analytical strategy when he argues that generally 'modernity undermines religion except when it finds some major social role to play'(p.96) or 'work to do' other than relating individuals to supernatural powers. Bruce offers as examples the work of cultural defence and the social role of ethnic and national collective identity production and reproduction. Although theoretically problematic, as will be pointed out later, Bruce's strategy may seem plausible in accounting for the inordinate religiosity of Ireland or Poland, but is less helpful in accounting for the American deviation from the European rule.

European visitors have always been struck by the vitality of American 'salvational' religion. In comparison with Europe, at least since the early 19th century, the USA appeared simultaneously as the land of 'perfect disestablishment' and as 'the land of religiosity *par excellence*' (Marx, 1975, p.217) Yet until very recently Europeans rarely felt compelled to call into question the thesis of the general decline of religion in view of the American counter-evidence. Progressive religious decline was so much taken for granted that what required an explanation was the American 'deviation' from the European 'norm'. The standard explanations have been either the expedient appeal to 'American exceptionalism', which conveniently does not require questioning the European rule, or the casuistic strategy to rule out the American evidence as irrelevant, because American religion is supposed to have become so 'secular', so 'commercialized' or so 'privatized' that it should no longer count as authentic religion (Weber, 1946a; Luckmann, 1967; Wilson, 1979).

It is in reaction to the European failure to confront seriously the evidence of American religious vitality that a new American paradigm has emerged offering an alternative explanation of the American religious dynamics; a paradigm which challenges the basic premises of the European theory of secularization. In and of itself, the explanation of religious vitality in terms of the beneficial effects of the dual clause of the First Amendment to the US Constitution, 'no establishment' and 'free exercise' of religion, is not novel. Tocqueville (1990), and Marx (1975) following him, had already maintained this basic insight. The combination of high secularization in the broad primary sense of social differentiation ('perfect disestablishment') and low secularization in the narrower secondary sense of religious decline ('land of religiosity *par excellence*') already call into question the alleged structural relationship between the two dimensions of secularization in the orthodox model. Tocqueville (1990, vol. 1, p.308), moreover, had already used the American evidence to question two basic premises of modern theories of secularization which, as he pointed out, had their origins in the Enlightenment critique of religion under the *ancien régime*: that the advancement of rationalism (education and scientific knowledge) and individualism (liberal democracy and individual freedoms) would necessarily lead to the decline of religion.

What is refreshingly new in the American paradigm is the move to turn the European 'orthodox' model of secularization on its head and to use the American evidence to postulate an equally general structural relationship between disestablishment or state deregulation, open, free, competitive and pluralistic religious markets, and high levels of individual religiosity. With this reversal what was until now the American exception attains normative status, while the previous European rule is now demoted to being a deviation from the American norm. But it is this very move to turn what is a highly illuminating account of the exceptionally pluralistic and competitive American religious market into a universal general theory of religious economies that is problematic. The perils are precisely the same as those which led the European theory astray by turning a plausible account of the exceptional European historical pattern of secularization into a general theory of modern development. A peculiar fusion of ethnocentrism and scientism leads in both cases to the fallacy of misplaced concreteness.

According to the American paradigm, the low levels of religiosity in Europe ought to be explained by the persistence either of establishment or of highly regulated monopolistic or oligopolistic religious markets (Caplow, 1985; Stark and Iannaccone, 1994; Finke, 1997). As a general point indicating the crucial relevance of church–state relations in accounting for differential patterns of secularization within Europe as well as between Europe and the USA, this is an important insight much neglected by the orthodox model of secularization. But as Bruce (2000) has convincingly shown, internal comparative evidence within Europe simply does not support the basic tenets of the American theory. Monopolistic situations in Poland and Ireland are linked to persistently high levels of religiosity, while increasing liberalization and state deregulation elsewhere are often accompanied by persistent rates of religious decline. Hence the impasse. The orthodox model works relatively well for Europe but not for America, the American paradigm works for the USA, but not for Europe. Neither can offer a plausible account of the internal deviations within Europe. Most importantly, neither works very well for other world religions and other parts of the world.

Towards a Global Perspective

In order to move beyond the fruitless secularization debate between the 'European' and the 'American' positions we need to adopt a global perspective. Such a perspective should help to historicize our categories, our theories and the stories we tell about religious change. From a global historical perspective the series of changes we call secularization evince an internal dynamic unique to a particular form of religious regime, Western Christendom and its Catholic and Protestant derivatives, which has very few parallels in other world religions, or even in the oldest and most traditional forms of Christianity, the Eastern Churches. In order to facilitate genuine comparative historical analyses, we need to dissociate the historical theory of European secularization from general theories of modernization. The secularization of Europe is a particular, unique and 'exceptional' historical process, not a universal teleological model of development which shows the future to the rest of the world.

But the same can be said about the historically unique and 'exceptional' American religious market. It owes its existence to a series of peculiar historical circumstances that are unlikely to be repeated elsewhere.[3] There are, no doubt, important lessons to be learned from the American story of denominationalism. And there are important insights to be gained from the analogical discourse of religious economies. But we need to dissociate the historical lesson of the benefits of no establishment and free exercise of religion from specious general supply-side theories of religious economies. Above all, the American sociology of religion should refrain from imperialist attempts to impose the 'American way' of religion upon the rest of the world, in the name of spurious scientific claims.

It is time to abandon the universal general claims of both theories and accept the fact that from a global perspective both the European and the American experiences are exceptional and unique, and neither serves as a model of development for other parts of the world which also follow their own exceptional and unique paths. Indeed, one could expand almost endlessly the model of exceptionalism. Ernest Gellner (1992), for instance, while basically upholding the European orthodox model of secularization, has formulated a theory of Islamic exceptionalism, according to which Islam (thanks to a combination of factors which it is not pertinent to analyse here) has been uniquely immune to modern processes of secularization. Islamic countries, one could add, are not only exceptions to the orthodox model of secularization insofar as processes of modernization there are accompanied by religious revivals and religious growth rather than by religious decline, something which a Tocquevillian theory of democratization may have anticipated; they are also clearly deviations from the American supply-side model of religious economies since their high levels of religiosity are linked, not to free competitive religious markets, but to monopolistic conditions even in the absence of state churches.

Surely, scholars of Hinduism could easily develop similar theories of Hindu exceptionalism to explain the current 'saffron revival' in India; students of Japanese religion could readily stress the unique developments of modern Japan; and so on. Indeed, when faced with such a proliferation of exceptionalisms not much is left of the rule of secularization. It is now Europe and European settler colonies which appear as the exception to the global rule of religious vitality. The new concept of 'European exceptionalism' (Davie, 1999), which I myself have promoted (Casanova, 1994), while helpful in undermining the old universal claims of European secularization, becomes problematic and misleading if it is meant to imply that there is some general global pattern or rule of religious development or resurgence, be it the American paradigm or 'the desecularization of the world' (Berger, 1999), to which Europe would be the exception.

Indeed, we need to go beyond exceptionalisms as much as against invidious misleading contrasts between the secular liberal West and the religious fundamentalist 'Rest' (Juergensmeyer, 1993). It is not proposed here, however, that we altogether abandon the concept or the theory of secularization as meaningless. The theory of secularization is still useful, not only as a way of reconstructing analytically the transformations of modern European societies, but also as an analytical framework for a comparative research agenda which aims to examine the historical transformation of all world religions under conditions of modern structural differentiation, as long as the outcome of this transformation is not predetermined by the theory, and as long as we do not label as religious fundamentalism any counter-secularization, or any religious transformation which does not follow the prescribed model.

The story of secularization is primarily a story of the tensions, conflicts and patterns of differentiation between religious and worldly regimes. The European concept of secularization refers to a particular historical process of transformation of Western Christendom and might not be directly applicable to other world religions with very different modes of structuration of the sacred and profane realms. It could hardly be applicable, for instance, to such 'religions' as Confucianism or Taoism, insofar as they are not characterized by high tension with 'the world' and have no ecclesiastical organization. In a sense, those religions which have always been 'worldly' and 'lay' do not need to undergo a process of secularization. To secularize, that is, 'to make worldly' or 'to transfer from ecclesiastical to civil use', are processes which do not make much sense in such a civilizational context. But to ask how 'religions' like Confucianism, Taoism or any other religion for that matter respond to the imposition of the new global worldly regime of Western modernity becomes a very relevant question.

In such a context, the study of modern secularism (Asad, 1999) as an ideology, as a generalized world view and as a social movement, and regarding its role as a crucial carrier of processes of secularization and as a catalyst for counter-secularization responses, should be high on the agenda of a self-reflexive comparative historical sociology of secularization. Otherwise, teleological theories of secularization themselves become conscious or unconscious vehicles for the transmission of secularist ideologies and world views. What makes the European situation unique and exceptional when compared with the rest of the world is precisely the triumph of secularism as a teleological theory of religious development. The ideological critique of religion developed by the Enlightenment and carried out by a series of sociopolitical movements throughout Europe from the 18th to the 20th century has informed European theories of secularization in such a way that these theories have came to function, not only as descriptive theories of social processes, but also, and more significantly, as critical–genealogical theories of religion and as normative–teleological theories of religious development which presupposed religious decline as the telos of history.

Three dimensions of the Enlightenment critique have been particularly relevant: the cognitive critique of religion as a primitive, pre-rational world view to be superseded by the advancement of science and rational thought; the political critique of ecclesiastical religion as a conspiracy of rulers and priests to keep the people ignorant and oppressed, a condition to be superseded by the advancement of popular sovereignty and democratic freedoms; and the humanist critique of the very idea of God as human self-alienation and as a self-denying other-worldly projection of human aspirations and desires, a critique which postulated the death of God as the premise of human emancipation. Although the prominence and pertinence of each of these three critiques may have changed from place to place, each of them to varying degrees has come to inform most modern European social movements, the political parties associated with them, and European theories of secularization (Casanova, 1994).

In this respect, theories of secularization in Europe have functioned as self-fulfilling prophecies to the extent that a majority of the population in Europe has come to accept the premises of those theories as a depiction of the normal state of affairs and as a projection of future developments. The premise that the more modern and progressive a society becomes the more religion tends to decline has assumed in Europe the character of a taken-for-granted belief widely shared not only by sociologists of religion but by a majority of the population. The postulate of progressive religious decline has become part of the European definition of the modern situation, with real consequences for church religiosity. It is the assumed normality of this state of affairs, accepted even by the main religious institutions, which points to the exceptional character of the European situation, a situation which tends to reproduce itself and to appear increasingly irreversible, in the absence of either a general religious revival or a radical change in the European *Zeitgeist*.

Bruce (2000) is correct when he implies that this 'secularization of demand' imposes almost insurmountable constraints on 'supply-siders' (p.40). These constraints work upon both the many new and unsuccessful religious entrepreneurs in Europe supplying 'supernatural compensators' for which there is apparently little religious need, and supply-side theories of religion which assume that there is a universal constant demand for supernatural compensators and that one only needs to liberalize religious markets in order to generate supply, competitive pluralism and religious growth (Stark and Bainbridge, 1985; Finke, 1997). The notion of a constant demand for supernatural compensators is ahistorical, asociological and flies in the face of European facts.

It may be instructive to return to Bruce's (1996) attempt to offer an explanation for the Polish and Irish 'deviations', in terms of the proposition that modernization undermines religion *except* in situations where religion finds or retains 'work to do' other than relating individuals to supernatural powers. The proposition seems paradoxical in that, despite the radically different conclusions they draw from it, Bruce seems to share with his theoretical opponents – the supply-siders – a definition of religion which may be part of the problem in trying to grasp the European religious situation. Implied in Bruce's formulation is the assumption that the essence or primary function of religion is to offer salvation or supernatural goods to the individual. However, for Bruce it is this very function of individual supernatural mediation which alone cannot withstand the corrosive forces of modernization. Rodney Stark and William Bainbridge (1985), by contrast, might share this definition of religion but insist that only the proper discharging of this function makes religion immune to forces of secularization, and that in the long term supernatural compensators will always prove superior to any secular equivalent because of their unfalsifiability.

But at times religions can also assume the additional, apparently non-essential, function of societal integration of imagined communities, that is, collective identity formation, particularly in conflictive situations. It is this secondary work of 'cultural defence' which paradoxically explains the resilience of some religions in the face of secularizing trends. What seems surprising, if not ironic, in such a formulation is that what appears for Bruce to be only additional non-essential work is precisely what Durkheim's (1995) sociological theory of religion defines as the essence of religion. It is worth noting here that Bruce's explanation of Irish and Polish 'exceptionalism' is almost identical to Gellner's (1992) explanation of Islamic 'exceptionalism'. In both cases religion becomes apparently immune to secularization because it serves as carrier of nationalism. What is remarkable is not the parallelism but the fact that an anthropologist of Islam and a student of European nationalism like Gellner could make the claim that there is something unique about this Islamic 'exceptionalism', when similar fusions appear repeatedly throughout modern European history and indeed throughout the world today (van der Veer and Lehmann, 1999; Juergensmeyer, 1993).

What if we were to invert the order of the question and see the Irish and Polish cases as confirmations of Durkheim's theory of religion: to ask ourselves why other religions in Western Europe have apparently lost their ability to function as 'churches' which unite individuals into a single moral community, hence serving to create and recreate the bonds of social solidarity? It is our tendency to link processes of secularization to processes of modernization, rather than to the patterns of fusion and dissolution of religious, political and societal communities, that is of churches, states and nations, that is at the root of our theoretical impasse. The Christian church and the Islamic *umma* are particular historical fusions of two types of religion which, following Weber (1946b), we should distinguish analytically: the community cult and salvation religions (Casanova, 1994, pp.45–8). Not every salvation religion functions as a community cult, that is, is coextensive with a territorial political community or plays the Durkheimian function of societal integration – think of the many denominations, sects or cults in America which function primarily as religions of individual salvation. Nor does every community cult function as a religion of individual salvation offering the individual *qua* individual salvation from sickness, poverty and all sorts of distress and danger. Think of state Confucianism in China, Shintoism in Japan, or most caesaro-papist imperial cults. Individual healing in those contexts is supplied by lesser forms of 'folk' religion (Sharot, 2001).

The truly puzzling question in Europe, and the explanatory key in accounting for the exceptional character of European secularization, is why churches and ecclesiastical institutions, once they ceded to the secular nation-state their traditional historical function as community cults, that is, as collective representations of the imagined national communities (Anderson, 1991) and carriers of the collective memory (Hervieu-Léger, 2000), also lost in the process their ability to function as religions of individual salvation. The issue of greater or lesser monopoly is relevant, but not the most crucial one. We could rephrase the question and ask: why is it that individuals in Europe, once they lose faith in their national churches, do not bother to look for, or actually look disdainfully upon, alternative salvation religions? Such a kind of brand loyalty is hard to imagine in other commodity markets. Why does religion today in Europe remain 'implicit', instead of taking more explicit institutional forms? It is this peculiar situation that explains the absence of a truly competitive religious market in Europe. The culprit is not so much the monopolistic laziness of the churches protected by state regulation, but the lack of demand for alternative salvation religions among the unchurched, even in the face of new, enterprising yet generally unsuccessful, religious suppliers.

Weber's (1946b) distinction between 'community cults' and 'salvation religious communities' is primarily analytical, pointing more to two crucial dimensions of religion than to two different separate types of religion. But any sociological theory of religion that emphasizes exclusively one of these two dimensions, the communal or the individual, dismissing the latter (for example) as 'magic' (Durkheim, 1995) because it is too individualistic and does not produce community, or as an inauthentic secularized substitute because its does not cater to the individual's need for supernatural compensators (Stark and Bainbridge, 1985), is necessarily a partial and incomplete theory of religion. Actually, any theory that claims to be a 'general' theory of religion ought to function simultaneously at three analytical levels: at the individual level, at the group level and at the societal level. In a certain sense, Troeltsch's (1931) three types of religion – 'individual mysticism', 'sect' and 'church' – correspond to these three levels of analysis. It is true that Troeltsch in typically Hegelian fashion constructed his theory as progressive stages in the development of Christian religion from church, to sect, to individual mysticism. But one does not need to share this teleological vision, or Bruce's (1996) gloomy reformulation 'from cathedrals to cults'. Nor does one need to share Stark and Bainbridge's (1985) reformulation of 'cult', 'sect' and 'church', as three stages in an ever-recurring cyclical process of secularization and resacralization, a new myth of eternal return. One can also view them as three types of religion coexisting in many societies, indeed in the global village today, and more importantly as three dimensions coexisting within the same religions.

The sociology of religion should be less obsessed with the decline of religion and more attuned to the new forms which religion assumes at all three levels in all world religions: to new forms of individual mysticism, 'invisible religion' and cults of the individual; to new forms of congregational religion, from new religious movements to the global expansion of Pentecostalism and charismatic communities in all world religions; and to the re-emergence of the world religions as transnational imagined communities, vying with if not replacing the nation-state for a prominent role on the global stage.

Current patterns of globalization force us to rethink our secularization stories and the criteria we should use to measure the declining or ascending significance of religion. At a time when processes of globalization are leading to new transformations of worldly and religious regimes, and the Weberian definition of both states and churches as territorial monopolistic institutions is becoming less and less relevant, it may also be time to look for evidence of the social significance of religion in the emerging world order, not so much in national settings but elsewhere: in the re-emergence of the transnational dimensions of religious regimes, in new civilizational and intercivilizational dynamics, and in the formation of a global civil society (Casanova, 1997; 2001). Sociologists of secularization may be able to predict with exact accuracy the hour of death of Christianity in Britain in 2030 (Bruce, 2001; see also his chapter in this volume), only to find out that the Anglican Communion thrives globally and that other world religions are growing in Britain. Like the death of Mark Twain, the repeated announcement of the death of religion may turn out to have been greatly exaggerated.

Notes

1   I call them 'European' and 'American' not so much because of the place of origin of their proponents, but because of the place of origin of the evidence for both theories. Not every European holds the European position. David Martin, for instance, has been a prominent critic of the orthodox model of secularization. Most American sociologists, by contrast, at least outside the field of religion, tend to share the inherited model.

2   The figures are based on four general European surveys – the European Values Studies (EVS) of
     1981, the EVS of 1990, the International Social Survey Programme (ISSP) of 1991 and the ISSP of
     1998, as provided by Andrew Greeley (unpublished manuscript). The data from EVS 1981/1990 and
     ISSP 1991/1998 can be obtained from Zentralarchiv fuer empirische Sozialforschung an der
     Universitaet zu Koeln (www.za.uni-koeln.de). The home page of the EVS is http://
     cwis.kub.nl/~fsw_2/evs/info.htm and of ISSP www.issp.org.
3   Although the current situation of competing national churches in independent Ukraine resembles the
     structural situation in the USA at the time of independence (Casanova, 1998).

References

Anderson, Benedict 1991: *Imagined Communities*. London: Verso.
Asad, Talal 1999: Religion, Nation-State, Secularism. In Peter van der Veer and Hartmut Lehmann (eds),
     Nation and Religion: Perspectives on Europe and Asia. Princeton: Princeton University Press,
     pp.178–96.
Berger, Peter L. (ed.) 1999: *The Desecularization of the World*. Washington, DC: Ethics and Public
     Policy Center.
Bruce, Steve (ed.) 1992: *Religion and Modernization: Sociologists and Historians Debate the
     Secularization Thesis*. Oxford: Clarendon Press.
Bruce, Steve 1996: *Religion in the Modern World: From Cathedrals to Cults*. Oxford: Oxford University
     Press.
Bruce, Steve 2000: The Supply-Side Model of Religion: The Nordic and Baltic States. *Journal for the
     Scientific Study of Religion*, 39 (1), pp.32–46.
Bruce, Steve 2001: Christianity in Britain, R.I.P. *Sociology of Religion*, 62 (2), pp.191–203.
Bruce, Steve 2002: *God is Dead. Explaining Secularization*. Oxford: Blackwell.
Butler, Jon 1990: *Awash in a Sea of Faith: Christianizing the American People*. Cambridge, MA: Harvard
     University Press.
Caplow, Theodore 1985: Contrasting Trends in European and American Religion. *Sociological Analysis,*
     46 (2) pp.101–8.
Casanova, José 1994: *Public Religions in the Modern World*. Chicago: University of Chicago Press.
Casanova, José 1997: Globalizing Catholicism and the Return to a 'Universal Church'. In Susanne
     Rudolph and James Piscatori (eds), *Transnational Religion and Fading States*. Boulder, CO:
     Westview Press, pp.121–43.
Casanova, José 1998: Between Nation and Civil Society: Ethno-Linguistic and Religious Pluralism in
     Ukraine. In Robert Heffner (ed.), *Democratic Civility*. New Brunswick, NJ: Transaction Books,
     pp.203–28.
Casanova, José 2001: Religion, the New Millennium and Globalization. *Sociology of Religion*, 62 (4),
     pp.415–41.
Casanova, José 2001: Secularization. In Neil J. Smelser and Paul B. Baltes (eds), *The International
     Encyclopedia of Social and Behavioral Sciences*. Oxford: Elsevier, pp.13786–91.
Davie, Grace 1994: *Religion in Britain Since 1945: Believing Without Belonging*. Oxford: Blackwell.
Davie, Grace 1999: Europe: The Exception That Proves the Rule? In Peter Berger (ed.), *The
     Desecularization of the World*. Washington, DC: Ethics and Public Policy Center, pp.65–83.
Davie, Grace 2000: *Religion in Modern Europe*. Oxford: Oxford University Press.
Durkheim, Émile 1995 : *The Elementary Forms of the Religious Life*. New York: Free Press.
Finke, Roger 1997: The Consequences of Religious Competition: Supply-side Explanations for
     Religious Change. In Lawrence A. Young (ed.), *Rational Choice Theory and Religion*. London and
     New York: Routledge, pp.45–65.
Finke, Roger and Stark, Rodney 1992: *The Churching of America, 1776–1990: Winners and Losers in
     Our Religious Economy*. New Brunswick: Rutgers University Press.

Gellner, Ernest 1992: *Postmodernism, Reason and Religion*. London and New York: Routledge.

Greeley, Andrew 1989: *Religious Change in America*. Cambridge, MA: Harvard University Press.

Greeley, Andrew 1994: A Religion Revival in Russia. *Journal for the Scientific Study of Religion*, 33 (3), pp.253–72.

Greeley, Andrew (unpublished): Religion in Europe at the End of the Second Millennium. A Sociological Profile.

Hadaway, Kirk, Marler, Penny Long and Chaves, Mark 1993: What the Polls Don't Show: A Closer Look at U.S. Church Attendance. *American Sociological Review*, 58, pp.741–52.

Hervieu-Léger, Danièle 2000: *Religion as a Chain of Memory*. New Brunswick, NJ: Transaction Books.

Juergensmeyer, Mark 1993: *The New Cold War? Religious Nationalism Confronts the Secular State*. Berkeley: University of California Press.

Luckmann, Thomas 1967: *Invisible Religion*. New York: Macmillan.

Martin, David 1978: *A General Theory of Secularization*. Oxford: Basil Blackwell.

Marx, Karl 1975: On the Jewish Question. In *Early Writings*. New York: Vintage, pp.211–41.

Sharot, Stephen 2001: *A Comparative Sociology of World Religions*. New York: New York University Press.

Stark, Rodney 1999: Secularization RIP. *Sociology of Religion*, 60 (3), pp.249–73.

Stark, Rodney and Bainbridge, William S. 1985: *The Future of Religion*. Berkeley: University of California Press.

Stark, Rodney and Iannaccone, Laurence 1994: A Supply-side Interpretation of the 'Secularization' of Europe. *Journal for the Scientific Study of Religion*, 33, pp.230–52.

Swatos Jr., William H. (ed.) 1999: The Secularization Debate. Special Issue, *Sociology of Religion*, 60 (3), pp.203–33.

Tocqueville, Alexis de 1990: *Democracy in America*. 2 vols, New York: Vintage.

Troeltsch, Ernst 1931: *The Social Teaching of the Christian Churches*. 2 vols, New York: Macmillan.

Veer, Peter van der and Lehmann, Hartmut (eds) 1999: *Nation and Religion: Perspective on Europe and Asia*. Princeton: Princeton University Press.

Warner, R. Stephen 1993: Work in Progress Toward a New Paradigm for the Sociological Study of Religion in the United States. *American Journal of Sociology*, 98 (5), pp.1044–93.

Weber, Max 1946a: The Protestant Sects and the Spirit of Capitalism. In H.H. Gerth and C.W. Mills (eds), *From Max Weber: Essays in Sociology*. Oxford and New York: Oxford University Press, pp.302–22.

Weber, Max 1946b: The Social Psychology of the World Religions. In H.H. Gerth and C.W. Mills (eds), *From Max Weber: Essays in Sociology*. Oxford and New York: Oxford University Press, pp.267–301.

Wilson, Bryan 1966: *Religion in Secular Society*. London: C.A. Watts.

Wilson, Bryan 1979: *Contemporary Transformations of Religion*. Oxford: Clarendon Press.

Wilson, Bryan 1985: Secularization: The Inherited Model. In Philip Hammond (ed.), *The Sacred in a Secular Age*. Berkeley: University of California Press, pp.9–20.

CHAPTER 2

On Secularization and its Prediction: a Self-examination

David Martin

Secularization is a type of concept which looks back over a series of trends and links them together in a view of the broad movement of history and its likely future development. The trends it brings together are likewise understood as major historical shifts in their own right, such as individualization, modernization and urbanization, though a trend like individualization resembles secularization in including several others, secularization being one of them. Indeed, it may be that modernization is the master concept, with secularization problematically incorporated as a closely associated trend, and a major defining characteristic of the modern.

What matters, apart from these problems with respect to the nature of concepts, is how far secularization is really a trend so closely associated with modernization that it can be treated as a defining characteristic. It is here that one has to take into account the extent to which secularization carries ideological loadings derived from the specifically European experience, and moreover loadings which identify a point in the past where religion was powerful and all-pervasive and a point in the future where it is weak and a mere leisure pursuit. Such a polarity between powerful past and weak future also has its companion concepts such as community and association or tradition and detraditionalization. Given the complexity of the problems, perhaps secularization is most easily and economically regarded as part of the organizing rhetoric of the sociology of religion and a dramatic shorthand for referring to the course and future of religion in the sometime Christian world. Moreover, if secularization carries ideological loadings, it helps if those who write about it give some indication of their stance, both in terms of their own commitments and in terms of autobiography, as is done in what follows.

Let me offer an example before proceeding. If you understand religion as a single and distinct class characterized essentially by empirical mistakes and implausible speculations then you will tend to focus for the most part on how far these have undergone cumulative public discredit. If, however, you understand some religions as sets of apprehensions or sightings or languages expressing alternative logics then you will tend more to trace their modes and mutations. Thus those who take the latter view might pursue accounts of secularization (in the plural) through changes in music or architecture, or (as in the conclusion of this chapter) through changes in the distribution of sacred space in the city.

Ambiguous Terms

My own (1965a) first encounter with secularization came through my initial study of war, religion and peace, more especially pacifism, over the past several centuries. That immediately set me thinking in a long-term historical perspective, with all that implied for the complex and changing meanings of notions like secular, worldly, mundane, natural and so on. Some ancillary studies in the history of art compounded the complexity with terms like realism, naturalism, modernism and humanism. (Here I think I suffered certain advantages, first by doing a degree through private study, so that I was undersocialized by the culture of sociology, and second by being supervised by Donald MacRae, the maverick polymath of the London School of Economics. Hence the stimulation of a contrary imagination fostered by reading off-piste.)

Perhaps I might briefly illustrate the implications of an historical perspective acquired through the study of pacifism. It seemed to me perfectly clear that attempts to inaugurate a kingdom of peace in the early modernity of the Renaissance and the Reformation meant bringing heaven down to earth, even if protected in a communal capsule, and rejecting the worldly assimilation of Christianity to the profane dynamism of power and raison d'état. You will already have noticed that I have built several partially cognate terms for secular into that sentence, such as 'earth', 'worldly' and 'profane', in order to show how earthy is the intense faith of some sectarians, and how worldly the dominance of the all-inclusive Church. The governing paradox here is that this-worldly aspirations for peace are utopian in a 'religious' mode, and yet, as Schmuel Eisenstadt (1999) has recently argued, these translations of transcendence have laid the foundations for our secular utopianism, including our radical politics, as well as the communal experiments so influential up to the present day.

Of course, this aspiration to peace might also be a motivation for social scientific enquiry, and you might judge that a proper context for yet another deployment of 'secularization'. But I also draw a more general inference, which is this: I find it characteristic of a Christian engagement with culture to germinate in part outside the boundaries of the Church. Certainly you cannot estimate the power and influence of the Christian repertoire, such as the meanings attached to 'the body of Christ', embodied and re-presented, by counting, but by tracing extramural mutations. Only in this way can the singular oddity of Christian civilization be properly exposed. An example of this would be Marcel Gauchet's *The Disenchantment of the World* (1997), where he claims Christianity fulfilled itself in the first 18 centuries by its destruction of religion. There's secularization for you!

Forward Movement and/or Oscillation

Like Peter Berger, then, I saw the roots of secularity bound up in the highly specific character of Judaism and Christianity, and secularization as internal to their working-out, given what Weber argued with regard to their approach to 'the world'. Unlike Ernest Gellner, I was critical of historical schemata which dug too deep a ditch between the pre-modern and the industrial or post-industrial present. Not only did continuities strike me as forcibly as discontinuities, but oscillations seemed as important as persistent forward movement.

Oscillation is perhaps not quite the right word, but what I have in mind has to do with the persistent reappearance not only of a 'realized eschatology' of the Kingdom but the humanization of divinity: the image of Christ so sensitively analysed by Neil MacGregor in the National Gallery Exhibition 'Seeing Salvation' (2000). Supposing we consider three successive movements of Christianization, the Franciscan, the Reformed and the Evangelical, and the way they commingled with the 'secular' movements of urbanization, nationalization, individualization and industrialization. These movements not only left deep deposits before they went into partial recession (which, again, I take to be rather characteristic of the Christian engagement with culture) but played out a counterpoint with contrary 'secular' tendencies, absorbing, reflecting and deflecting them.

Appearances deceive, and if that sounds rather gnomic let me take the relation between Reformation and Nationalism, first as Sacred Monarchy and then as Sacred Peoplehood. Arguably, the nationalization of Christianity (whether Reformed or Counter-Reformed) is *the* major secularization of modernity, culminating in claims by nations like Britain and the USA to an Elect or Messianic role, and in the ethnoreligiosity of Ireland and Eastern Europe. The local collectivity acquired sovereign status contrary to Christian universalism, in that respect reverting to a version of Judaism. Yet the initial thrust of the Reformation countermanded the claims of collective solidarity and sovereignty by affirming the perspicuity of scripture to individual scrutiny and the priesthood of all believers, principles which helped set in motion a prolonged crisis of legitimation. It follows that the histories of the sacred and of functional solidarity are very different from the history of Christianization. That is presumably the context in which to view the complaints about the dysfunctionality of Christianity from the viewpoint of republican 'virtue' by Machiavelli, Mandeville and Rousseau.

The bridge between Sacred Monarchy and Sacred Peoplehood is perhaps Napoleon I, as symbolized in Ingres' famous picture (and we can perhaps imagine a Sociology of Religion comprising in part exemplary sacred icons between Holbein's Henry VIII and Ingres' Napoleon). The era of Napoleon is precisely coincident with the nadir of the papacy, when Rome could even have been deported to Paris. Yet, as Eamon Duffy (1997) has shown, the two centuries since then have seen a remarkable recovery of papal influence. As José Casanova argues in his remarkable book, *Public Religions in the Modern World* (1994), the Roman Church has been freed (or discharged) as a subordinate adjunct of secular power to become a major player in debate in the public square, including incitement to revolution. The trajectory of 1789 concluded in 1989.

Considerations of this kind would be consonant with the critique I began with the publication in 1965 of my essay on the ideological sources and inflections of secularization, and with the essays immediately following on the range of its meanings, their relation to Utopia, and their incoherence (Martin, 1965b; 1969a). In writing those essays I was not all that aware of a body of literature articulating secularization, even though a soft and benign variant in terms of the functional specialization of religion to play its proper role was available in Talcott Parsons. Rather, I was reacting to an atmospheric, above all at the LSE. That atmospheric derived from the classics of the subject as well as from its cultural location, including the Jewish escape from a Christian to an enlightened universalism, though it was also Jews like Gould, Shils, Lipset and Bell who over time encouraged me in a critical response.

I was also responding to what was then known as a 'secular theology' which deployed sociology for its own purposes, a late and brilliant offshoot of which is Richard Fenn's study of idolatry, *Beyond Idols* (2001). Another stimulus came from pioneering sociohistorical and ethnographic work by Pickering and Wickham, too often ignored, and represented today by Simon Green (1996) and Timothy Jenkins (1999). But that kind of analysis simply took secularization into account, rather than propagating a world-historical trend.

Differentiation as a Guiding Concept

However, an articulation of the theory of secularization was not long delayed in the development of the magisterial work of Bryan Wilson, which provided a benchmark for the decades following. As José Casanova (1994) has rightly argued, functional differentiation represents shared ground between Wilson and myself, and it is extensive. For my part, I found differentiation superbly deployed in Parsons' article on Christianity in the 1968 *International Encyclopedia of the Social Sciences* and I used it as a basis for a decade of empirical enquiry in order to produce *A General Theory of Secularization* (1978).

Before turning to that perhaps I might interpolate a rueful warning about the importance of edited volumes on contentious subjects like secularization, such as Phillip Hammond's edited volume, *The Sacred in a Secular Age* (1985) and Steve Bruce's edited volume *Religion and Modernization* (1992), which, among their many merits, recruited social historians like Hugh McLeod and Callum Brown to the debate. Unfortunately, in this second instance I was unable to respond to the invitation, and in consequence found that for quite a number of people my initial critique had slipped from view. It was one thing to be evaluated by some commentators unaware of my critique as a straightforward theorist of secularization, but quite another (when giving a paper on secularization in Canada) to undergo reproof for not acknowledging the prior critical claims of Rodney Stark. At that moment I confess I felt mortification had set in before the fact, as well as realizing where and how it is students acquire what counts as common knowledge. Rodney Stark and Roger Finke's critique (2000) is, of course, otherwise based than my own, though with areas of interesting consonance.

It was through the accident of being told to invent a paper on the spot in a seminar run by Ernest Gellner that I actually began my empirical decade by devising nearly all the necessary categories. As usual our ends are implicit in our beginnings. The result was published in 1969 in *The European Journal of Sociology* (1969b). The scope of enquiry was restricted to changes in practice and belief in industrializing society, a prolonged process in Britain and one barely begun in Albania. *A General Theory of Secularization* (1978) incorporated my 1969 article as its first chapter and brought together empirical trends, especially as researched in France and the Low Countries, and set them in the frame of functional differentiation as modified by historical filters.

Such filters related to a standard contrast between northern and southern Europe, as well as to the very distinctive experiences of the USA and of eastern Europe under communism. This is where the problematic of a 'lead society' emerges: if Europe was markedly different from the USA, was the USA the lead society, or (say) post-Protestant Sweden or post-Catholic France? Was the USA exceptional merely in being not urbanized until 1920, as Bruce contends, or in being internally secularized, as Luckmann and Wilson have contended? (A further issue emerged. In the construction of general theory I began an attempt to include Kemalist Turkey, for example the separation of church and state, religion and education, but the range of differences made it clear just how distinctive is the dynamic of a Christian compared to an Islamic civilization, or indeed compared to anything else whatever.)

The trends charted in *A General Theory of Secularization* (1978) were nearly all downward, and the downward movement has continued. That is not in dispute, though differently contextualized by Steve Bruce (2002) and Grace Davie (2000). Work by Inglehart (1990) shows a steep decline, age group by age group, in western Europe, especially in Germany, which is very much less evident in the USA, though present even there. Without entering into close debate here, I would say that Bruce's stress on individualization (in which I include the declining role of authorization and canonicity) seems to me to have more explanatory purchase than generalized notions like 'Rationalization' or the impact of the technical replication of identical units. Rationalization is a process, like the effect of increasing anomie, which is clamped down on data by a kind of thought experiment rather than genuinely inferred. But how does it explain the seemingly unimpaired capacity of people to accept non-empirical assertions of all kinds from Nostradamus to channelling? As Davie (2000) has argued, what does a specifically religious decline *mean* where the reproductive capacities of so many kinds of institution are reduced, and where – as Inglehart (1990) indicates – public institutions *as such* fail to elicit respect and commitment? Even individualization has its problems as an explanation, given that Britain and America are both highly individualized, the latter most of all, and yet the vitality of religious institutions remains so much higher in the USA than in Britain.

Extrapolation or Contingency and Narrative

Prediction in the sense of extrapolation from these trends is, of course, easy. Other things being equal, they will continue, but as I said in introductory comments to my 'general theory' things rarely are equal. Indeed, correct prediction will probably be right only by accident and we do well to remember Von Hayek's and J.S. Mill's warnings about impenetrability. Clearly, we are making our way at unprecedented speed through serious turbulence for most kinds of institution and these may be exposed to even greater volatility when bobbing about on the sea of post-modernity. Sociology has proved vastly better at retrospective understanding than prospective anticipation, and three epochal events central to our topic were entirely unexpected: the cultural mutation of the 1960s, the collapse of Soviet Marxism, and the rise of Islam and Pentecostalism.

That is hardly to our discredit, given the number of our variables and their porous boundaries, but there is a further problem that maybe has rather more to do with methodological inhibition. It is the extent to which we have discounted either the flux of open-ended and eventful narrative, such as the effects of war or loss of national status and confidence, or the ebb and flow of ideas. It could be that one of the major differences between the USA and Europe has to do with the varied impact of the war and destruction, and consequent loss of confidence.

Idea and Process

Looking specifically at the poor integration of idea and process, I only became aware of how circumscribed our work can be when R.K. Webb, the historian of early modern religion, told me (in a personal communication) that I had managed to write *A General Theory of Secularization* while referring only once to Unitarianism (and that in Romania). This lack is the obverse of what we find in Owen Chadwick's (1975) splendid history of secularization, where it is the sociology that is pigeonholed. (A remarkable and ignored exception is Harvie Ferguson's *Religious Transformation in Western Society*, 1992.) I tried later to repair that particular omission but if we take the comment seriously it radically broadens the critique of secularization. Already in the 1960s I had suggested (1969a, ch. 7) we were too much influenced by paradigms of secular process derived from the history of art and science by comparison with (say) music. After all, modern serious music is religious to a quite astonishing degree, from Britten to Macmillan, Poulenc to Messiaen – or someone like Penderecki. But the effect of

Webb's commment has been to alert me to any number of possible secularizations, perhaps seriously athwart the histories of religious beliefs and institutions. For example, if we consider the cultural shift in England from about 1870 to 1914, marked say by the transition from Gaskell and Dickens to Hardy, Kipling and Wells, it raises the question as to how far that runs parallel to the developments analysed by Simon Green in *Religion in the Age of Decline* (1996) as well as further questions about the intellectual avant garde and the existence of a lead stratum as well as a lead society. Many other cognate questions immediately follow, such as whether seeming major shifts, such as the New Age sensibility analysed by Paul Heelas (1996), presage the future. Or are they the last gasps of spiritual animation doomed to the irrelevance of private fantasy? The same question arises in relation to the much smaller phenomenon of new religious movements. Granted these movements in no way balance losses in the mainstream, are they a significant forward indicator or a *cul de sac*?

An Interim Division: Us or Them?

So we return to the idea of a leading edge or lead society and the sheer variety of historical filters which bear on what we take to be general processes like differentiation and pluralism. I take my own experience with regard to the rise of Pentecostalism as minatory. After reading Emilio Willems (1967) and Lalive D'Epinay (1969) I remember briefly entertaining the idea that maybe Pentecostalism in Latin America might be analogous to Methodism in North America because it ran parallel to the modernization of a continent. But, guided by the controlling assumptions of sociology, I foreclosed on this, supposing Latin America would largely repeat the experience of Latin Europe in generating large secularist political parties. Like the fall of Marxism, the rise of Pentecostalism was forbidden by theory. Hence my little book, *Forbidden Revolutions* (1996), discussing the two together as different instances of the caving in of ideological monopoly, whether religious or secular and enlightened.

When, at Peter Berger's suggestion, I turned in 1985 to the study of Pentecostalism, certain options (predictions if you like) presented themselves. One was to fit Pentecostalism into the prevailing secularization paradigm, rather in the Kuhnian manner. That was, and still is, a viable option, with the argument running like this. Pentecostalism is an instalment of secularization in that it represents the advent of pluralism in Catholic Latin America, and its version of the Protestant Ethic will be eroded as Pentecostals better themselves and go to school. Given the effect of the revolving door, ex-Pentecostals will be harbingers of secularity.

This is the 'interim diversion' theory of Pentecostalism, consigning it to a phase of modernization and using the history of American Methodism to predict its upper limit and eventual decline. Such an approach can be backed up by its relative confinement to developing societies and the fact that in the USA (and the middle classes of the third world) Pentecost mostly mutates into the charismatic movement, while in Europe it makes scant impact in the secular heartlands by comparison with marginal areas in Portugal and Romania.

However, there is another variant of the 'interim diversion' approach, sketched in my *Pentecostalism: The World their Parish* (2001a) which turns on who or what needs 'explaining'. Perhaps it is not so much 'fundamentalism' in the third world, constructed and construed according to a liberal moral panic, which needs explanation, as the exceptional state of Europe.

That at least has to be explored as part of a proper social scientific tactic. The first move might be to suggest that what is happening today in the third world implies that the USA is the lead society rather than France or Sweden, but one might go on to suggest that the sheer multiplicity of cultural modes opening on to modernity in global society throws the whole idea of lead society into doubt and, in addition, maybe the whole notion of 'exceptionalism'. The trouble is that we veer between the concepts of difference on the one hand and of the natural or expectable way on the other. Ontology haunts our thinking where we least expect it.

It could be that Pentecostalism, as analysed in different contexts by Rowan Ireland, David Lehmann, André Corten, Paul Freston, David Maxwell, Birgit Meyer *et al.*, is one of the main global options before us. Having been generated in the experimental matrix of the USA outside any cultural or clerical sponsorship out of a fusion of the faith of poor blacks and poor whites, and uniting elements of the expressive revolution with Protestant discipline and the deep structure of shamanism, it may be capable of crossing any number of cultural species barriers. The evidence makes that a viable hypothesis and so the question then becomes whether there still remains a necessary trajectory leading to liberal Protestantism.

Here we arrive at the core of this alternative variant of the 'interim diversion' approach, since it picks up the by now standard query as to whether the intensity of the pressure of enlightened reason against alternative logics during the last quarter of a millennium has been a permanent development or a necessary but temporary rigour. The question is how far the carriers of modernity along with the more restrictive protocols of rationality, positivist sociology included, will dominate the cultural reproduction of the future.

Of course, analysis needs to examine North America and Europe in turn. In the USA, it would need to ask why Pentecostalism mainly yields social space to a more staid evangelicalism or to old and new forms of charismatic movement. In Europe, it would need to ask how the control of the older monopolistic or semi-monopolistic establishments, especially in media and education, switched hands in favour of secular or secularist elites, how religion was discredited by close involvement in dying social systems and hierarchies, and how it lay athwart most of the national projects of the continent as it did not in the USA. The way nationalism either coopts religion or treats it as a barrier to advance is crucial.

Zero-sum or Expanding Social Space?

All that is eminently debateable and therefore renders vulnerable any predictions along the lines of secularization theory, especially given the genesis of that theory out of the European situation. What seems to me important is to treat the polarity of religion and secular and the zero-sum relation between them with greater agnosticism.

What then, finally, of that zero-sum relation? I, for one, am attempting now to explore the notion of expanding universes as embodied in the expansions of urban space (Martin, 2003). If we think back to the early mediaeval nucleus, religion and power coinhere, so that bishop and potentate are literally related, and the church is often a fortress. In the Renaissance the nexus of power, religion and wealth remained in place in spite of the clash of civic and ecclesiastical, so that the papacy itself could be a bauble fought over by great families. If the religious protest this engendered in turn leads to a commercial society in Amsterdam choked by the embarrassment of riches, with its individualized portraiture and sober domestic interiors, that in itself suggests just how nuanced is the dynamic of religion and the secular.

We need to recollect that as we look first at the emergence of rival spaces, Duomo and Signoria, and at how that led on to churches cast as temples like San Lorenzo, as well as to the idealization of the city, until by one mutation after another we arrive at the evocative landscapes of a Wordsworth or Corot, and at a disposition of urban space where the gallery, the theatre and the concert hall are fresh foci of high seriousness and contemplation.

Yet that is not necessarily a zero-sum spatial relationship between religious emplacements and others, and in the same way the temporal transitions and periods we mark out are not necessarily the straightforward displacement of one modality by another, but rather include counterpoint and accumulation. To exemplify the counterpoint, Art Nouveau is a secular style (Gaudi apart) but the roughly contemporary Symbolist movement has rather different potentials, including Neo-Platonism.

The development of Boston might simultaneously exemplify secularization, counterpoint and accumulation. At the heart of the various galleries, theatres, stadia and concert halls one finds the idealized 'City set on a hill' in the Promised Land, constantly invoked, and the civic faith ritually recollected in the awareness of the freedom trail. There are also the ethnoreligions of the Irish, Italians, Armenians and Jews, and the niche-markets of the voluntary denominations, including dozens of Pentecostal churches and megachurches offering comprehensive environments to tens of thousands. If differentiation is secularization then this is certainly secularization, though I do not know whether it is also the future for Calcutta or Islamabad, or just how far secularization is also privatization or rationalization. On such matters I think the jury stays out. It could be that the sociologist of religion is an academic deviant tracing the evanescence of an epiphenomenon, or the one who enquires into the phenomenology and precipitating circumstances of our most fundamental transformations.

References

Bruce, Steve (ed.) 1992: *Religion and Modernization*. Oxford: Clarendon Press.

Bruce, Steve 2002: *God is Dead*. Oxford: Blackwell.

Casanova, José 1994: *Public Religions in the Modern World*. Chicago: University of Chicago Press.

Chadwick, Owen 1975: *The Secularization of the European Mind*. Cambridge: Cambridge University Press.

Davie, Grace 2000: *Religion in Europe. A Memory Mutates*. Oxford: Oxford University Press.

Duffy, Eamon 1997: *Saints and Sinners. A History of the Popes*. New Haven: Yale University Press.

Eisenstadt, Schmuel 1999: *Fundamentalism, Sectarianism and Revolution*. Cambridge: Cambridge University Press.

Fenn, Richard K. 2001: *Beyond Idols. The Shape of a Secular Society*. Oxford: Oxford University Press.

Ferguson, Harvie 1992: *Religious Transformation in Western Society*. London: Routledge.

Gauchet, Marcel 1997: *The Disenchantment of the World*. Princeton: Princeton University Press.

Green, Simon 1996: *Religion in the Age of Decline*. Cambridge: Cambridge University Press.

Hammond, Phillip E. (ed.) 1985: *The Sacred in a Secular Age*. Berkeley: University of California Press.

Heelas, Paul 1996: *The New Age Movement*. Oxford: Blackwell.

Inglehart, Ronald 1990: *Culture Shift in Advanced Industrial Society*. Princeton: Princeton University Press.

Jenkins, Timothy 1999: *Religion in English Everyday Life*. Oxford: Berghahn.

Lalive D'Epinay, Christian 1969: *Haven of the Masses*. London: Lutterworth.

Martin, David 1965a: *Pacifism*. London: Routledge.

Martin, David 1965b: Towards Eliminating the Concept of Secularization. In Julius Gould (ed.) *Penguin Survey of the Social Sciences*. Harmondsworth: Penguin.

Martin, David 1969a: *The Religious and the Secular*. London: Routledge.

Martin, David 1969b: Notes towards a General Theory of Secularization. *European Journal of Sociology*, X, December, pp.192–201.

Martin, David 1978: *A General Theory of Secularization*. Oxford: Blackwell.

Martin, David 1996: *Forbidden Revolutions*. London: SPCK.

Martin, David 2001a: *Pentecostalism: The World Their Parish*. Oxford: Blackwell.

Martin, David 2003: Changing your Holy Ground. In Stephen Barton (ed.), *Holiness Past and Present*. Edinburgh: T. and T. Clark.

Stark, Rodney and Finke, Roger 2000: *Acts of Faith*. Berkeley: University of California Press.

Willems, Emilio 1967: *Followers of the New Faith*. Nashville: Vanderbilt University Press.

CHAPTER 3

The Evolutionary Principle in the Study of Religion and Society

Olivier Tschannen

Introduction

The main purpose of this chapter is to attempt to clarify a notion which I take to be central in the work of Bryan Wilson: the notion of 'evolution'. Such clarification seems necessary because of certain ambiguities in his writings. However, I also think that these ambiguities are representative of certain contradictions within modern sociology with regard to the notion of evolution. This is why I propose to resituate Wilson's work within this broader context and, most notably, to compare his work with that of Anthony Giddens.

The chapter is organized in three parts. This introduction will briefly expose the problem, by showing, through a few examples, the types of ambiguities we have in mind. The next section proposes some reflections on evolutionist thinking in contemporary sociology. The third section proposes a detailed exegesis of the work of Wilson, in order to try to clear up the ambiguities.

The first point which needs to be made is that Wilson (1976a) indeed presents secularization as an evolutionary process: 'The context of my discussion is the process of secularisation, which I believe can be shown to be a broad, if albeit uneven, evolutionary process' (p.vii). Furthermore, it is clear for Wilson (1987) that this evolutionary process possesses a universal validity: 'The process of secularisation, whilst it has gone much further in the West, is likely to occur in greater or lesser measure and at locally determined rates of social change, throughout human society' (p.170).

So much for the 'positive' side of the argument. But there is also the 'negative' side, which raises the ambiguity. Thus, in some places, Wilson (1998) qualifies the universality of the secularization thesis. As he puts it, 'It is to [developed countries] that the secularisation thesis is specifically applied' (p. 59). Furthermore, he sometimes explicitly underscores the fact that secularization is a complex process, which does not unfold in a mechanical and deterministic way: 'These phenomena are likely to be causally linked, and yet they occur in varying order, and with different degrees of rapidity. In what measure, or in what priority they occur, is an empirical question for each specific case, and cannot be settled *a priori*' (1982, p.149). Indeed, sometimes Wilson (1985b) even seems to waver in his convictions, to accept that secularization is not an evolutionary process: 'Certainly, it is an open question whether secularisation is reversible' (p.17).

'Evolution' in Contemporary Sociology

It is proposed to define evolution, in very broad terms, as a deterministic process which gives a definite direction to human history. Within present-day sociology, evolutionism appears to be definitely discredited – at least officially: to the best of my knowledge, no first-order sociologist claims to be an evolutionist. However, at the same time, there is an extraordinary growth of theories which explain the transition from 'pre-modern' to 'modern' and, very often, to 'post-modern' societies. Giddens' theory of 'late modernity' is representative of this trend. And, as this chapter will try to show, this theory, like all the other theories of which it is representative, does not entirely escape a mode of thinking which strongly resembles evolutionism.

In the theory of modernity proposed by Giddens, the notion of *complexity*, whose central role in classical evolutionary theory is well known, has been replaced by *time–space distanciation*. According to Spencer, evolution is the product of increasing complexity. The more complex a society is, the higher it is situated on the scale of evolution. However, it is now widely recognized that the notion of complexity is ambiguous: societies which appear to be simple with regard to their level of technology and their level of division of labour can be very complex with regard, for example, to kinship rules (Giddens, 1981, p.90). Time–space distanciation, on the other hand, appears to be quite unequivocal as a criterion of classification.

Thus the extension of societies in time–space constitutes one criterion for the understanding of history. The second criterion, quite different in nature, is the classification of types of societies (hunter-gatherers/class-divided societies/class societies). This classification presents the appearance of an evolutionary scheme, in that it looks like the typologies of Comte, Durkheim or Parsons. However, Giddens insists that this resemblance is only superficial: his typology is nothing but a *classification* of types of societies, which have very often coexisted in human history. There is no necessary transition from one type to the other.

This coexistence of two criteria, the first of which (extension in time–space) is continuist, while the second (the typology) is discontinuist, raises some problems. For example, it appears that the *quantitative* progression of distanciation is one of the factors explaining the *qualitative* jump from one type of society to another. Thus, at the beginning of *The Consequences of Modernity* (1990), Giddens argues that, in order to understand modernity, we must use a discontinuist approach. Modernity is radically different from the preceding types of societies. But then, without transition or justification, he goes on to argue that this radical break can be explained by the *acceleration of the rhythm of change* and by an *increase in the magnitude of change* (p.6), both of which are clearly continuist criteria. On the other hand, a few lines further on, he also mentions other types of changes, most notably the appearance of the state, whose discontinuist character is quite apparent at first sight. However, elsewhere, he explains that it is the extension of societies in time–space which raises the need for a new type of integration, which he calls 'system integration' as opposed to social integration (1979, pp.77–9), and that it is precisely the state which is the main instrument of system integration (1981, p.159). So there is a tension in his theory between continuist criteria (which appears to constitute an unrecognized evolutionist heritage) and discontinuist criteria (which are the result of his effort to break free from evolutionist thinking). The tension between these two approaches can even be seen as a contradiction. At any rate, the relationship between these two approaches is nowhere explicitly spelled out and analysed in Giddens' work. So we cannot be quite certain what all this means. But if indeed, as all appearances indicate, discontinuity can be shown to be a consequence of continuity, we must conclude that Giddens' effort to escape evolutionism has failed. For time–space distanciation clearly *is* an evolutionist criterion – although Giddens never says so – if only because distanciation in space is subordinated to technological progress (improvement in transport and communication means), and distanciation in time depends mainly on the invention of writing, whose character of 'evolutionary universal' in Parsons' sense can hardly be denied.

Of course, Giddens is not the only one, among contemporary sociologists, to propose a theory of modernity that attempts to go beyond evolutionism. But, as if to highlight their difficulties in handling the evolutionist heritage, these theories largely rely on the prefix 'post-'. This is the case, most notably, for 'post-industrialism' and for 'post-modernism'. Giddens himself, in a later phase, rebaptized his theory, inventing the term 'post-traditionalism' (Beck *et al.*, 1994). This incapacity to give a name to the basic principle undergirding the new order, which must also be considered an incapacity to give a name to the principle having historically given rise to this order, is symptomatic of modern sociology's difficulties with the notion of evolution.

The main problem contemporary sociology has with evolutionism is that it seems to imply the superiority of Western civilization and also, quite logically, a certain vision of 'development', both of which are no longer fashionable, or politically defensible. This has been highlighted in particular by Robin Horton. For example, this is how Horton (1993) explains the success of what he calls 'symbolist' explanations of traditional religious beliefs:

> If we are wrong-headed enough to treat [religious beliefs] as explanations, we have to admit that traditional religious beliefs are mistaken. And the only possible interpretation of such mistakes is that they are the product of childish ignorance. Neo-Tylorians who take traditional beliefs at their face value therefore subscribe to the stereotype of the 'ignorant savage' and are illiberal racists. If on the other hand we treat them as having intentions which, despite appearances, are quite other than explanatory, we no longer have to evaluate traditional beliefs in the light of the canons of adequacy current in the sciences. Anthropologists who take this line are therefore not committed to the 'ignorant savage' stereotype. They are good liberals. (Horton, 1993, p.58)

And, according to Horton, if contemporary anthropologists reject evolutionism with such unanimity, it is not for objective but for ideological reasons:

> It is true, of course, that no British anthropologist returning from two years of participant observation in an African or Polynesian village can ever again give serious consideration to Victorian theories that rest ultimately on a thesis of the childishness and stupidity of non-western people. And thus far, facts *have* swept away ideology. ... However ... whilst facts have helped to sweep away the ideologically based theories of the nineteenth century, they have been overwhelmed again by ideology in the present century. For in Western ideology ethnocentrism and arrogance have given way to collective pessimism and self-questioning; and these are equally powerful and equally distorting in their influence on the study of man. ... The key to this ideology is given by its attitude to the notion of progress. Of all the guiding notions of the nineteenth century, this is the one that has come in for the most ridicule. (Ibid., pp.89, 91)

Are we really sure that the ridicule that has been heaped on the idea of evolution is justified? Intellectual honesty should compel us to recognize the fact that, at least with regard to technological and economic change, there are tendencies which it is hard indeed to interpret in non-evolutionist terms. This fact helps account for the stubborn persistence of continuist factors within all the theories of modernity that claim to be post-evolutionist, even though, at the same time, in order to be consonant with the contemporary intellectual climate, these theories must give pride of place to discontinuist factors.

Back to Wilson: an Exegesis

With this context in mind, let us now turn to the work of Wilson on secularization and try to understand the ambiguities presented earlier.

Strength of the Claim about Secularization

The first thing that needs to be underscored with regard to Wilson's position on evolution is the strength of his claims about secularization. Indeed, it is fair to say that, among contemporary sociologists of religion, he is the foremost representative of those who are convinced that secularization has indeed taken place:

> All the evidence from our own times suggests that, at least in the western world, Christian faith is in serious decline. What is true of the institutions of the Church appears also to be true of the belief and the practice of the majority of men. ... Most modern men, for most of their time, in most of their activities, are very little touched – if they are touched at all – by any direct religious intimations. (Wilson, 1976a, p.6; see also 1976b, p.259)

Furthermore, he takes the secularization thesis to have a universal validity.

> It is not ... to be assumed that the secularisation thesis is merely a commentary specifically on Christian history. The model is intended to have general validity. Were it to be stated in sufficiently abstract terms, there would be no reason why it should not be applied in any context. (Wilson, 1985b, p.16)

One of the signs of the strength of his interpretation is that he considers all signs that could be taken as proofs of a revival of religion as precisely the opposite, namely signs of the reality of secularization (1976a, p.96; see also 1998, p.60).

To conclude, Wilson clearly concurs with Giddens on the idea that modernity has consequences that cannot be repealed. It remains to be seen more precisely what these consequences are.

Absence of any Trace of Optimism about Secularization

From 19th-century evolutionism, we have inherited a tradition which associates two factors in its view of evolution: a decline of religion on the one hand, associated with an enhanced role for science, in social life in particular, on the other. Both of these factors have been viewed with optimism. Such is not Wilson's point of view:

> Within the Comtean, Marxist, and Freudian approaches ... the science of society was regarded as emerging in order to dislodge the religious conceptions. ... As sociologists became more circumspect in their claims, and as they came increasingly to document the decline of religion as a purely sociological process (and not as a declaration of a sociological manifesto), so they ceased to present sociology as itself an alternative source of prescription for social order. (Wilson, 1982, p.5)

Indeed, as Roy Wallis and Steve Bruce (1989) put it, 'some critics have argued along with Martin that the secularisation thesis is ineluctably *ideological*, a plank of secularist ideology; as it was in the work of Marx, Freud and other avowed secularists' (1989, pp.493–520). But this is explicitly refused by Wilson (1982, p.148). Far from being optimistic, Wilson's view of secularization is radically pessimistic. Not only is secularization causing human distress (1976a, p.vii), but it is socially corrosive, putting the very survival of society at risk:

> The questions remaining are whether a society which has lost its value consensus and relinquished common morality can be held together and whether there are alternative agencies of social integration. [If] civic space is peopled by those whose emotions are uneducated, who are fed on hedonism and cynicism, and who are untrammelled by inner restraints, shall we escape new forms of oppressive social control to contain the latent hostilities between a people which does not trust the system and a system which cannot trust the people? (Wilson, 1985a, p.332)

On this point, Wilson is much more pessimistic than Giddens. Of course, Giddens does refer to the 'discontents of modernity', but, as is well known, he has also proposed an optimistic political programme that should enable 'advanced modernity' to yield positive results. Without knowing anything in detail about

Wilson's political position, it is very unlikely that this programme would appeal to him.

Absence of any Claim to Originality

Another important point is the fact that Wilson does not claim to have invented a new theory. Quite the contrary. He always presents his work as modest, as for example when he writes that 'I seek only to add a tentative footnote ... to the task which, in *Morals in Evolution*, Hobhouse set himself' (1985a, p.315). And the title of one of his papers is 'Secularisation: The Inherited Model' (1985b). Of the many names he quotes in this paper, whose heir he claims to be, one could argue that the most important is Tönnies, since, as we will see, Wilson's theory is based on the fundamental dichotomy between community and society. However, in using this dichotomy, it is not directly to Tönnies that Wilson refers, but rather to a broad tradition, encompassing many authors, all of whom Wilson considers to have contributed to a single thesis, which he even calls the 'central thesis of sociology': 'My argument ... is an elaboration, from the perspective of religion, of the central thesis of sociology – the shift from *Gemeinschaft* to *Gesellschaft*. ... The community is essentially religious; the society is essentially secular' (1976b, p.261; see also 1998, p.45).

In comparison with Giddens, Wilson presents himself as a much more modest thinker. However, in terms of content, Giddens does not appear much more innovative. Indeed, Giddens strikes one as someone who is very skilful at synthesizing the works of his predecessors and contemporaries, without adding much to them, while also presenting this synthesis as something new and personal. So we may concur with Wilson that most of what is presented as radical and innovative in contemporary sociological theory is very much in line with what we rightly call 'classical' sociological thought.

After all these preliminary points, it is time to come to the heart of the matter: to a detailed exposition of Wilson's secularization theory.

The Conceptual Base: the Community/Society Dichotomy

Compared with other secularization theories (especially those of Peter Berger, Thomas Luckmann and Richard Fenn), Wilson's theory is not highly theoretical: it does not rest on a grand theoretical scheme, but rather results from the patient combination of a multitude of strands of argument weaved together in a complex manner. However, behind this complexity lies at least one broad theoretical generalization, the idea of the historical transition from community to society. In other words, Wilson's theory is decidedly based on the idea that it is structural factors that are determining the course of evolution: 'It is not the "age" which is secular, in the sense that earlier sociologists and philosophers sometimes spoke of a cycle of ages. Rather, it is the structure of modern society that is secular' (1976b, p.259; see also 1981, p.358).

These structural transformations have direct consequences at the individual level, which Wilson (1982) states as follows: 'The societal system relies less on people being good (according to the lights of the local community), and more on their being calculable, according to the requirements of the developing rational order' (p.165). We can, in very rough terms, compare this position of Wilson's with that of Giddens: the opposition between community and society is the equivalent of the opposition between social integration and system integration.

Evolution as a General Trend (or the Necessity of Secularization)

As mentioned earlier, there are two tendencies, which may appear to be contradictory, in Wilson's argument: on the one hand, he seems to argue that evolution is a general trend, and that, as a consequence, secularization is inevitable, but, on the other hand, he seems to argue that evolution is a complex process, largely unpredictable, and that, concomitantly, secularization may not be necessary. Let us look at these two lines of analysis in some detail, starting with the first.

The root of the argument for the necessity of evolution and, more precisely, for the inevitability of the decline of community, seems to lie in the fact of technical progress: 'The development of new means of communication, new forms of energy, new techniques of control, and a new rationalisation of labour have all led to the breakdown of effective community life' (Wilson, 1976b, p.264; see also 1976a, p.25). Technical progress, in Wilson's view, 'encapsulates rationality'. But rationality does not remain encapsulated: it 'overflows', so to speak, and diffuses itself in social life, thus giving birth to *Gesellschaft*:

> Societal organisation is itself the result of processes of rationalisation .... The system becomes more effectively rationalised as new techniques and planned procedures are adopted and institutionalised. Technology, indeed, encapsulates rationality. ... In any human society, the idea of the supernatural (in whatever form it takes) is an arbitrary presupposition. A wholly rational social structure would dispense, wherever possible, with items of this kind, since the implication of such a structure is that it should be internally coherent and self-sustaining, making no recourse to any external source of legitimation. (Wilson, 1982, pp.156, 158)

It seems clear that Wilson's notion of 'a structure that is internally coherent and self-sustaining' is the parallel of Giddens' notion of 'internally referential systems', and that what Wilson calls 'rationality' is very close to what Giddens calls 'reflexivity'. Thus, according to Wilson, there is an incompatibility between rationality and superstition, a permanent tension which keeps pushing societies forward on the path of social evolution (1976a, p.11).

Rationalization must thus be considered as a causal factor in the process of social evolution. The changes initiated by this cause can roughly be described as a succession of phases, which clearly resembles the schemes of 19th-century evolutionism:

Permit me, for the sake of brevity, to collapse the long process of social evolution, into a crude and simple model useful for my argument. Let me postulate three broad phases, overlapping but loosely associated with patterns of socio-economic organisation. The first phase coincides with communal organisation. ... This phase embraces tribalism, feudalism, and such communal organisation as persisted in to the early phases of industrialism (and perhaps beyond). ... Second, there is the period of industrialisation, with intensified division of labour, new techniques, and sources of power. The third phase has emerged in very recent times, in post-industrial society largely based on the communications revolution. (Wilson, 1985a, p.317)

Or, in Giddens' terms, we have class-divided societies, followed by class societies, followed by advanced modernity. On a more analytical level, according to Wilson, social change can be described mainly as a process of differentiation, along a line which will be familiar to anyone who has read the functionalist literature (1976b, p.272).

According to Wilson, religion as a social phenomenon is a normal correlate of community life, which can survive in society only in an artificial form: 'Religion functions in communities. ... Sometimes religion has been functional for societies, of course, but where that has been so, the function has been political. ... The basic functions of religion, and the locus of its operation, exist in the community' (ibid., p.265). In the following quotation, Wilson quite clearly sets forth the nature of this relationship:

Societal systems have evolved alternative and *more conscious* mechanisms to fulfil [the functions that used to be fulfilled by religion]. The process of societalisation is the process by which once latent functions are made manifest. It is the process by which the apparently 'accidental' effects of particular social arrangements, which remained undiscovered until sociologists discovered them, are subject to rational thought and deliberative action. (1976b, p.268)

Again, we are very close to Giddens, according to whom modern society is highly reflexive, which means nothing but what Wilson says when he asserts that the 'apparently accidental effects of particular social arrangements' have become 'subject to rational thought and deliberative action'.

Evolution as a Complex Process (or the Weight of Historical Factors)

Let us now turn to the second line of argument, in which Wilson seems to introduce a number of qualifications to his evolutionary thesis. Maybe the first point that needs to be mentioned is that in some places he plays down the importance of the incompatibility between rationality and science, on the one hand, and religion and magic, on the other: 'All this is not to suggest that the confrontation of science and religion ... was in itself essentially harmful to religion, or even that there was an incompatibility between them. Indeed, religion and science can coexist as alternative orientations to the world' (1966, p.43). Now, it is not quite clear what exactly this means. If religion and science indeed can coexist as alternative orientations to the world, how is this possible? We can understand this if we come back to Wilson's definition of secularization, which he considers to be a structural process. As he repeatedly asserts, it is the social structure, not the individual, that has been secularized. Not only does religion remain alive in the heart of individuals, it also remains alive wherever there is a survival of the communal form of life, as today in sects. We must understand secularization, not as an automatic process, but as the outcome of historical struggles between local communities and centralized social forms of organization:

> During the course of history there have been, from time to time, occasional, spasmodic, and unsustained tendencies toward a societal form of organisation. This occurred with the development of ancient empires, but in every case the attempt to establish centralised control was jeopardised by the powerful claims of local leaders and by the limited vision of men in their allegiance to essentially local goals and relationships. (Wilson, 1976b, p.262)

Again, this historical reconstruction is quite close to the one offered by Giddens in *The Nation-State and Violence* (1985). According to Wilson, the outcome of this historical struggle is never determined in advance, as the case of present-day Japan illustrates:

> The relation of morality to economy is subtle and must vary in accordance with divergent factors in each society and its culture and history. For example, the modernisation of Japan has clearly involved quite different patterns of moral change, and it is obvious that, despite the deliberate cultivation of the most advanced technology, a moral system prevails which still draws considerably on localised sentiment ... The homogeneous ethnic base of Japanese society – perhaps less racially and culturally mixed than any other in the world – probably facilitates the maintenance of a moralised social order that has not been abandoned in spite of the expansion of technological procedures and controls. (Wilson, 1981, pp.345, 346)

Conclusion

We may summarize the model proposed by Wilson in the following terms. Social evolution includes at least one deterministic factor: technical evolution. Once this evolution has started, it has social consequences. One of these consequences is the weakening of community, and the construction of society. Since religion is incompatible with society, it will survive (at the structural level) only insofar as the communal form of organization survives. However, for the social consequences of technology to unfold completely, certain conditions must be met. One cannot predict *a priori*, in a theoretical vacuum, what these conditions must be. The case of Japan illustrates one of the circumstances under which the communal form of organization can resist the transforming impetus of a deep technological revolution. But other such circumstances can be imagined and are possible.

As far as developed countries are concerned, the predictive implications of this analysis seem relatively clear, at least in abstract terms. On the one hand, it seems obvious that, once they have unfolded, the social consequences of technological evolution cannot be repealed. Dreams of a reawakening of community can never become true: 'Religion in secular society will remain peripheral, relatively weak, providing comfort for men in the interstices of a soulless social system of which men are the half-willing, half-restless prisoners' (Wilson, 1976b, p.276). On the other hand, there is no way of telling how many new communal organizations might be created within the rational structure of society. Nor is it possible to guess what type of influence these communities could be able to exert in the future. As for non-Western countries, predictions seem more difficult to make. Some strong cultures might be able, as the case of Japan illustrates, to adapt to the technological revolution while preserving communal forms of life. So, if we follow Wilson, religion might be able to survive in the future – perhaps indefinitely – in two types of locations within the world system: in communal organizations embedded within modern, rationalized societies, and in countries where communal forms of life have established a form of successful adaptation to technological change.

This position seems to be in line with the reflections on contemporary society proposed outside the sociology of religion by theorists like Giddens. Unlike many other theorists in the sociology of religion, who seem to have worked from a narrower perspective, it is one of the merits of Bryan Wilson to have proposed, under a modest disguise, a theory of religion in modern society that contributes to breaking down the barriers between general sociology and the sociology of religion.

References

Beck, Ulrich, Giddens, Anthony and Lash, Scott 1994: *Reflexive Modernization: Politics, Tradition and Aesthetics in the Modern Social Order*. Cambridge: Polity Press.

Giddens, Anthony 1979: *Central Problems in Social Theory: Action, Structure and Contradiction in Social Analysis*. London: Macmillan.

Giddens, Anthony 1981: *A Contemporary Critique of Historical Materialism: Vol. 1, Power, Property and the State*. Berkeley: University of California Press.

Giddens, Anthony 1985: *The Nation-state and Violence* (Volume 2 of *A Contemporary Critique of Historical Materialism*). Cambridge: Polity Press.

Giddens, Anthony 1990: *The Consequences of Modernity*. Cambridge: Polity Press.

Horton, Robin 1993: *Patterns of Thought in Africa and the West: Essays on Magic, Religion and Science*. Cambridge: Cambridge University Press.

Wallis, Roy and Bruce, Steve 1989: Religion: The British Contribution. *The British Journal of Sociology*, 40 (3), pp.493–520.

Wilson, Bryan R. 1966: *Religion in Secular Society: A Sociological Comment*. London: C.A. Watts.

Wilson, Bryan R. 1976a: *Contemporary Transformations of Religion*. Oxford: Clarendon Press.

Wilson, Bryan R. 1976b: Aspects of Secularisation in the West. *Japanese Journal of Religious Studies*, 3–4, pp.259–79.

Wilson, Bryan R. 1981: Morality and the Modern Social System. *Religions, Valeurs et Vie Quotidienne* (Actes de la 16e Conférence Internationale de Sociologie des Religions, Lausanne). Lausanne: CISR, pp.339–60.

Wilson, Bryan R. 1982: *Religion in Sociological Perspective*. Oxford: Oxford University Press.

Wilson, Bryan R. 1985a: Morality in the Evolution of the Social System. *The British Journal of Sociology*, 36 (3), pp. 315-32.

Wilson, Bryan R. 1985b: Secularization: The Inherited Model. In Phillip Hammond (ed.), *The Sacred in a Secular Age*. Berkeley: University of California Press, pp.9–20.

Wilson, Bryan R. 1987: Secularization in the Non-western World: A Response. *Secularization and Religion: The Persisting Tension* (Acts of the 19th International Conference for the Sociology of Religion, Tübingen). Lausanne: CISR, pp.169–75.

Wilson, Bryan R. 1998: The Secularization Thesis: Criticisms and Rebuttals. In Rudi Laermans, Bryan Wilson and Jaak Billiet (eds), *Secularization and Social Integration: Papers in Honor of Karel Dobbelaere*. Louvain: Leuven University Press, pp.45–65.

II
PREDICTING CHRISTIANITY

CHAPTER 4

The Demise of Christianity in Britain

Steve Bruce

Introduction

When Bryan Wilson (1966) first began to write about the 'secularization' of Britain, it was possible to be sceptical about his assertion that religion was declining in social significance. David Martin (1969) warned against exaggerating the piety of the Middle Ages. Glassner (1975) questioned the contemporary evidence. Some 30 years on there can be no doubt. A vast body of detailed historical research has confirmed that pre-industrial Britain was indeed a religious society.[1] The culture was thoroughly pervaded by a Christian world view. The life cycle of the individual and the community was glossed by religious ritual. To safeguard their souls, rich and poor gave generously to the Church. Everyday interaction constantly reaffirmed the power of the supernatural and the efficacy of the Church's control over it. Despite the practical difficulties of attending church, most people did so periodically and at least half the people did so routinely. Christianity now is but a pale shadow of its former self. Rural churches are converted to houses; city churches become night clubs and carpet warehouses; church commissions examine the entrails for signs of hope; and sympathetic commentators publish studies with titles such as *The Tide is Running Out* (Brierley, 2000). One of Britain's leading social historians of religion, who has repeatedly criticized Wilson's sociological treatment of secularization, nonetheless accepts his description and titles his book *The Death of Christian Britain* (Brown, 2001). Elsewhere I have presented detailed accounts and explanations of the decline of religion in Britain (Bruce, 1996; 2002). Here I will cite just some of the data that explain why Peter Brierley thinks the tide is running out, sketch my explanation of one central part of that phenomenon, and conclude with a number of predictions.

The Facts

Assessing the power, popularity and prestige of Christianity, even in one country over a relatively short time span, is not easy. It is always possible to contest any particular index. However, when every measure points so clearly and so consistently in the same direction, such technical reservations need not distract us from the obvious conclusion.

Church Attendance

In 1851, between 40 and 60 per cent of the population of Great Britain attended church (Bruce, 1999, pp.65–9). In 1979, the figure was around 12 per cent; in 1989 10 per cent; in 1999, under 8 per cent (Brierley, 2000). In the 1980s, the Church of England lost 24 per cent of its attenders; the Methodists almost half. In 1997, Anglican church attendance fell below one million for the first time since records began and that is in the context of a population that has more than trebled between 1850 and 2000. Catholic church attendance remained high longer (largely because it was topped up with migrants from more religious Ireland) but in the 1980s and 1990s declined rapidly towards the British norm (Hornsby-Smith, 1999).

The gross figures hide a more worrying trend for the churches: age bias. Between 1979 and 1999, some 15 per cent of the population was aged 65 and over but, for all the major churches, the comparable figure was markedly higher and growing. For example, in 1979, 18 per cent of Anglicans were over 65, and by 1999 the proportion had risen to 25 per cent. For the Methodist and United Reformed Churches, the proportion over retirement age rose from 25 to 38 per cent. This is not growth caused by religion being particularly attractive to the elderly; it is a result of young people abandoning Christianity. Or, to put it another way, had life expectancy not increased so much in the last 30 years, the decline of the churches would have been even more dramatic.

Church Membership

The Church of the Middle Ages did not have members. It placated God on behalf of the entire people and expected to be supported and obeyed by the entire people. When, in the centuries after the Reformation, the single national church faced increasing competition from a variety of dissenting organizations, it became possible to talk about 'membership'. Especially when, as with the Free Church schism in Scotland in 1843, rivalries became intense, many people who would previously have regularly attended a particular place of worship started to think of themselves as belonging to this or that organization. But even at the end of the 19th century, attendance was higher than membership because many regular attenders, for reasons of social class or piety, felt they were unworthy of full membership. In 1900 when half the population regularly attended church, about 27 per cent were members. This fell to 10 per cent in 2000, but the relationship between attendance and membership switched. In 1900, not all who went were members. In 2000, not all members went.

Sunday Schools

One way in which the British churches dominated the culture and society was through education. Until the middle of the 19th century (and later in many places) most formal schooling was provided by the churches. The desire for secular education explains much of the initial popularity of Sunday schools. Even after state primary schooling became universal, the habit of non-churchgoing parents to send their children to Sunday schools spread basic knowledge of the Christian faith beyond the church members. In 1900, half of Britain's children attended Sunday school; in 1998, the figure was 4 per cent (Brierley, 1999, table 2.15).

Religious Professionals

Full-time clergy may be paid either from public taxation or from the donations of the congregants. In the first case, their number is a good indicator of the social power of religion; in the second, a good sign of its popularity. Counting clergy is easier than counting adherents: religious organizations keep better records of their staff than their members and national surveys of occupations tend to be more accurate than surveys of beliefs or behaviour. In 1900, there were about 45 400 clergy in the UK. In 2000, there were some 34 160. That is a fall of 25 per cent over a century when the population nearly doubled. Or, to put it in relative terms, had the Christian churches been relatively as powerful or as popular at the end of the century as at the start, there would have been 80 000 clerics.

Rites of Passage

While the proportion of people coming to church to be married, baptized and buried remains higher than the number of members or regular attenders, the trends are moving in the same direction. At the start of the 20th century, more than 80 per cent of marriages in England and Wales were solemnized in church; at the end of the century, the figure was less than 40 per cent (Brown, 2001, p.167).

Religious Beliefs

The above data would permit the suggestion that it is faith in religious institutions rather than faith per se that has declined: the case made by Grace Davie (1994) with her depiction of Britons as 'believing without belonging'. But there is plenty of evidence that Christian beliefs are declining behind, but in step with, institutional decline. In the 1950s, 43 per cent of the population said they believed in a personal God. In the 1990s, the figure was 31 per cent. In a May 2000 survey, it was 26 per cent (Opinion Research Business, 2000). In an extensive review of a half-century of Scottish survey data, Clive Field (2001) comes to the same conclusion as Robin Gill, Kirk Hadaway and Penny Marler (1998) in their review of almost 100 British surveys carried out between 1939 and 1996: 'These surveys show a significant erosion of belief in God ... the most serious decline occurred in specifically Christian beliefs including belief in a personal God and belief in Jesus as the Son of God as well as traditional Christian teaching about the afterlife and the Bible' (p.514).

Politics

Religion no longer plays any major part in British identity; that died with the Empire. Around the middle of the 19th century, the fact that the peripheries were more religious than the centre gave Presbyterianism in Scotland and Methodism in Wales (on which, see Chambers in this volume) some salience as a mark of distinctiveness *vis-à-vis* England. But the debates about identity that accompanied devolution in 1997 were significant for their lack of reference to religion. And current debates about immigration show that, whatever hostility there is in Britain to foreigners and to 'foreign' institutions such as the European Union, religion plays little or no part in it. Apart from the prurient tabloid interest in vicars-and-choirboys and insufficiently celibate priests, religion is rarely now of public interest. When it does become news, as in the case of the Iranian government's offer of a reward for the murder of author Salman Rushdie (because he blasphemed in *The Satanic Verses*), it is generally because we object to some religious minority taking its religion too seriously. Those who supported the *fatwa* were criticized, not because they were heathen but because they were bigots (or, as we say in Scotland, 'religious o'ermuch'). Since Scientology, the Moonies and the like attracted attention in the 1970s, new religious movements have been criticized, not for ensuring damnation, but for encouraging fanaticism.

Indifference

It is worth stressing that the demise of Christianity in Britain owes very little to active opposition. Unlike the situation in Catholic countries, there is almost no anti-clericalism. The number of people willing to describe themselves in surveys as atheists or agnostics is rising steadily. In 1965 only 2.9 per cent answered 'atheist, agnostic or no religion' when asked 'What is your religion?' (Foster 1972, p.159). In 2000, 18 per cent chose 'a convinced atheist' or 'an agnostic person' in preference to 'religious' or 'spiritual' (Opinion Research Business, 2000). But we remain content to allow clerics privileged access to the airwaves, have little objection to religious services in schools, and generally suppose religion to be a 'good thing'. An interesting observation from recent surveys is that we are more tolerant of church leaders pronouncing on abstract issues that come within the remit of governments (such as world poverty or education) than speaking out on personal matters of behaviour (such as sexuality). We seem quite happy to allow religious leaders to act as spokesmen for general values, provided they do not tell us how to behave.

I could go on, but the point is clear. Christianity in Britain is in serious decline. To that gross fact may be added this subsidiary one: liberal versions have been declining faster than conservative ones. If we compare the membership figures of the four largest Presbyterian churches in Scotland, we find that, between 1956 and 1995, those for the most liberal (the United Free Church) fell by 72 per cent. The Church of Scotland declined by 47 per cent. The two conservative churches (The Free Presbyterian Church and the Free Church) lost respectively 24 and 12 per cent of their members (Bruce, 1999, pp.130–34). The same pattern can be found among US churches. In Holland, the liberal Lutheran Church in the Kingdom of the Netherlands lost 39.5 per cent of its members in the decade 1990–2000. The mainstream Dutch Reformed Church lost 22.8 per cent of its members. But seven small conservative Protestant churches remained stable and there was even some growth among evangelical and charismatic groups (Krol, 2001).

Ideological Diffuseness and Organizational Precariousness

We can fruitfully use the language of church, sect, denomination and cult to describe economically the evolution of religion in many modern democracies. The notion of a single religious organization encompassing an entire nation or state – a church – is undermined by a number of common features of industrialization: increasing structural and social differentiation, cultural diversity, egalitarianism and individual autonomy.[2] The sect can survive in regional pockets and to the extent that the state permits sub-cultures to form their own sub-societies: a circumstance more common in the USA than in the overcrowded and centralized polities of western Europe. But many sects become denominations as they come to terms with their enduring minority status, and churches become denominations as they come to terms with their failure to retain the loyalty of the bulk of the population.

While much distinguishes the denomination and the cult, they are similar in what may be regarded as the primary determinant of their fate: their epistemology. The typical Methodist may not worry about her epistemology but the trouble starts there. The church and the sect have in common that they believe there is one truth and that they, and pretty well they alone, have it. In contrast, the denomination and the cult share an open epistemology. They suppose either that there is more than one truth or that the truth is broad and wide. Either way, access to it is widely available and no single embodiment of it can be treated as finally authoritative. From that basic epistemological difference all sorts of organizational consequences follow. In brief, diffuse, tolerant and liberal belief systems are difficult to sustain and reproduce. Lack of obedience to a central authority (be that an organization as in Catholicism, a text as in Protestantism, or a body of religiously sanctioned law as in Islam) produces three closely related problems of social organization. It makes consensus on details of belief impossible, it weakens individual commitment, and it reduces the need and the ability to evangelise.[3] Elsewhere I have considered the implications of this for the cultic religion of the New Age (Bruce, 2002, ch.4). Here I will concentrate on denominational Christianity.

Consensus and Commitment

Most religions, for most of their history, have supposed that we the believers are subordinate to the God or Gods in whom we believe. In Judaism, Christianity, Islam,

Hinduism and the more theistic versions of Buddhism, there is a God (or Gods) who tells us what to do. Although all these religions have produced deviant strands in which the believer to varying extents may manipulate the deity, essentially we worship and obey the deity, not the other way round. Liberal religion reverses that relationship and in so doing loses its power to shape us.

Getting people to agree (especially about making sacrifices) is always difficult. Consensus is not the default position, even for people who inhabit similar social circumstances. It must be engineered. For any belief system to survive intact there must be control mechanisms. These may be formal and bureaucratic, as they are in the Catholic Church, where officials deliberate slowly before announcing the Church's position. They may be informal and 'charismatic', as they are in many branches of Protestantism: the minister who preaches a gospel unacceptable to the audience finds himself without an audience. But in either case there are controls. To put it starkly, consensus requires coercion. In the church and sect types of religion, coercion is possible. It is legitimated by the claim to have unique access to the will of God. As the denomination does not claim a monopoly of salvational knowledge, it is severely constrained in what it can do to maintain discipline. Indeed, the individual's right to choose what to believe is so elevated that the idea of discipline is largely absent from liberal religion. The result has been a gradual loss of cohesion and identity.

The increasing power given to the individual has important social psychological consequences. It is unlikely that such a religion will attract the high levels of commitment found in other forms of religion. The willingness to embody a certain ideology depends on maintaining negative evaluations of alternatives. Given that such evaluations must entail some degree of sacrifice (if only the sacrifice of positive social relationships with those from whom we differ), they are most likely sustained when there is a strong community of like-minded believers to provide alternative rewards to those available elsewhere and to stiffen the resolve of the believer in the face of subtle pressure to abandon anything that is distinctive in belief or behaviour. Consider the example of financial sacrifice. Sectarian Protestants often give a tenth or more of their income to religious activities. The 'liberality' of liberals is rarely above 1 per cent. The reason for the difference is obvious. If you believe that your religion is especially pleasing to God and especially effective in ensuring access to salvation, then it is worth the earth. If it is merely one of many equally valid expressions of an innate human desire for answers to questions of ultimate significance (or some such), there is no pressing reason to put yourself out much to maintain it.

This has implications for recruitment. Either in socializing your own children to follow in your faith or in recruiting outsiders, a necessary element is the certainty that your beliefs are superior and that bad things will happen to those who do not share them. Despite being an elected member of three parliaments, the leader of a political party and the head of an organization with over 100 congregations, Ian Paisley finds time to stand on a Belfast street corner every Wednesday afternoon and preach at the passing multitudes. He does this because he believes that those who are not saved will go to hell. Liberal Christians altogether lack that drive, and its absence is visible not just in the lack of effort that is put into recruiting outsiders but also in their practical attitude towards their children. Whereas evangelicals indoctrinate their children, liberals help their children to 'think for themselves'. The net result is agreement on matters of procedure ('no-one has the right to tell others what to think') and diversity on matters of substance. Hence, even if liberals could discover a desire to evangelize and indoctrinate, they would be unable to agree on a simple message to be transmitted. An ecumenical evangelistic mission is an organizational absurdity because the various parties that might cooperate could not agree on who should be converted or to what they should convert.

Wasting Assets

The fragility of liberal Christianity was disguised for a large part of the 20th century because it benefited in three ways from a more conservative past. So long as there were very large numbers of Roman Catholics, Free Church Presbyterians, Primitive Methodists and the like, the liberal version of Christianity had a large pool of recruits: people who were attracted by the idea of being able to retain some of their religious heritage while abandoning the most stifling, sacrificial and socially marginalizing elements. Becoming increasingly liberal and ecumenical allowed people raised in a conservative Christian tradition to enjoy some of the psychological benefits of the individual autonomy and freedom of conscience that non-religious people enjoyed while still thinking of themselves as Christians.

What was not often noticed was that very few people outside the churches were attracted to liberal religion. And why should they be? Non-believers already had liberty of conscience.

Denominational Christianity was also parasitic in the sense of enjoying residual cohesion. The sectarian past provided the first few generations of liberals with a basic grounding in a shared set of dogmas and thus ensured some degree of shared identity. It is fascinating to go back to 1900 and read the debates in the Student Christian Movement between those who pioneered ecumenism and those who stayed conservative (Tatlow, 1933; Johnson, 1979). The liberals argued against dogmatic tests of membership on the grounds, first, that they hampered missionary work and, second, that they were unnecessary because Christians knew what they believed. Of course, they only knew what they believed because they had been raised in a more conservative tradition. As that sectarian past faded, so what was acceptable expanded. The pioneers of ecumenism took it for granted that only Protestants would qualify; they never imagined the modern ecumenical movement's stance of complete inclusion.

The third sense in which liberal Christianity depends on its past is financial. Whether it is the Church of England and its capitalized taxes or the Methodists and their invested inheritances, British denominations rely heavily on capital acquired in a more powerful or popular past.[4]

The first two bequests – recruits from conservative religion and ideological cohesion – are wasting assets. The fate of the third is not so clear. Most denominations have not been able to make enough profit on their investments to keep abreast of costs, but the age profile of members is now producing some windfalls as elderly women bequeath their property to shrinking congregations.

To these three senses of parasitism we may add a fourth. The absence of anti-clericalism has meant that religious leaders have for the last 50 years enjoyed a prominence not justified by the numbers of people they can claim to represent. That prominence too is a wasting asset. Although there is little desire to downgrade Christianity, changes in social institutions made for quite other reasons have caused its status to be reviewed, and the end result is usually secularization. For example, the privileged position of the Church of England bishops in the House of Lords has not been recreated in any of the devolved political assemblies. Every reform of broadcasting legislation has weakened the requirement to produce religious broadcasting. The BBC regions no longer have religion departments staffed by clerics chosen in proportion to the size of the major churches. The last ordained Head of Religious Programmes resigned in 2000 when the remit of his department was radically altered. His successor was an agnostic. Schools have responded to increased cultural diversity either by reducing the space and time given to religion or by treating all religions as if they were equally plausible. That some politicians see religious groups as an important thread in the fabric of civil society (see Taylor in this volume) should not blind us to the fact that such groups only have any input to public policy provided they avoid religion as such[5] and that much of current political rhetoric about community is just that: rhetoric.

Predictions

Although little has been said here about the church, sect or cult types of religion, I will add them to my predictions. They are of a piece with my expectations for denominational religion and will allow the future reader greater opportunity to test my prescience and by implication the value of my general perspective on religion in liberal democracies.

1   The church form of religion cannot return. There will be no national revival of shared religious identity. Even in Scotland and Wales there is insufficient consensus to permit any more than the most vacuous religious expressions a place in the public square, and we are too wedded to individualism to accept any overarching belief system. That many of us may rue the consequences of individualism and yearn for a return to 'community' does not of itself create the social conditions for consensus.

2   The sect form of religion will decline slowly. As we saw in the 1980s, with the shift from the classic Pentecostal sects, independent evangelical congregations and the conservative wing of the Baptist movement to the softer, less dogmatic, charismatic 'new churches', there will be a steady drift from more conservative to more liberal positions. There is no evidence in any modern society of a significant number of people moving from denominations to sects.

3   The cultic religion of New Age spirituality will become ever more diffuse and ever less significant. Eastern religious traditions will be trivialized as they are looted for interior decor fashions and beauty therapies. As with the diffuse religion of denominational Christianity, the New Age as an organized movement will die out as it fails to recruit the next generation (see Heelas and Seel in this volume).

4   Three decades from now, Christianity in Britain will have largely disappeared. Total Christian church membership will be below 5 per cent, as will church attendance. In 2031, if it has not by then merged with the Church of England, British Methodism will die and other denominations will be close behind. The demand for some sort of ritual to accompany death will ensure that perhaps 50 per cent of funerals will be glossed with some sort of vaguely religious ceremony, but fewer than 10 per cent of babies will be baptized or marriages celebrated in church. The proportion of people describing themselves as Christian will have fallen to below 20 per cent of the population.[6] In attitude surveys, only the vaguest possible affirmations (such as 'There is something there' in answer to 'Do you believe in God?') will attract even half the responses. The general cultural capital of Christian language and ritual will be so attenuated that the vast majority of the population will be utterly ignorant of the beliefs and values that once shaped their world.

It is worth stressing that in making these predictions I am doing nothing more than continuing the trends that have been clear and stable for 50 years. When I say this sort of thing in public, a member of the audience will retort along the lines that it is unscientific to assume the future will be like the past. Of course, descriptions of the past and the extrapolation of those differences into the future have a very different status: the latter is a forecast and forecasts vary in their reliability. But we have to ask ourselves if we can imagine a different future for organized religion in Britain. There are no signs that the ethnic minority religions have recruited native Britons in significant numbers in the last three decades: can we imagine it occurring in the next three? There has been no significant shift from the unchurched to the churched in the last 150 years: can we imagine it occurring in the next 50? Those who argue against extending trend lines must explain why they think the future will be unlike the past.

In conclusion I would like to return to my main theme. What separates me from many of my colleagues is my attempt to bring the sociology of organizations to bear on the sociology of religion. Beliefs, ideology and culture do not float in the ether. They need to be 'carried'. They must be maintained, policed, controlled, tended and propagated. In the 1980s, Peter Berger recanted some of his earlier contributions to the secularization debate (see Woodhead *et al.*, 2001). He has not altered his assessment of the consequences of social diversity and its attendant cultural pluralism: all beliefs must now be held with less conviction, dogmatism and certainty than was possible in societies that enjoyed an ideological consensus. In that sense all believers are now 'heretics' (Berger, 1980). What has changed is that he no longer believes lightly-held, tolerant, liberal, privatized and compartmentalized beliefs to be precarious. In his view, the US experience shows liberalism can endure. Time will settle that argument. Here I have given my reasons for supposing that liberal religion is precarious. Elsewhere I have argued that the British pattern is now becoming evident in the USA (Bruce, 2002): conservative sects are becoming more liberal and liberal denominations are declining. But let us confine ourselves to Britain. If it is possible, as Berger believes, for liberal religion to endure, the technique has to date eluded the British denominations.

So the last word: Britain in 2030 will be a secular society.

Notes

1   Critics of the secularization paradigm often distort the argument by imputing to the secularizationists the view that the pre-industrial past was a 'golden age of faith' and then citing historians such as Keith Thomas (1978) who show considerable dereliction, heresy and deviation. They thus miss the two crucial points. Even by the evidence of Thomas, the people of the Middle Ages were far more likely than us to be orthodox Christians and, when they were not, they were still profoundly religious. The case is argued in detail in Bruce (2002, ch.2).

2   My explanation of secularization is given in detail in Bruce (2002, ch.1). On the debate between Wilson and Martin presented in this volume, I agree with much said by both! I accept that industrialization, when, as in the First World, it is 'naturally occurring' and its economic benefits are widespread, has a secularizing effect. However, I also believe that modernization, when externally imposed, can produce the traditionalist reactions we commonly describe as 'fundamentalist' (see Bruce, 2000). What does set western Europe apart is the pervasive egalitarianism that forces us to respond to increasing diversity by becoming ever more liberal in the public sphere and tolerant about the private world. In the absence of egalitarianism, a more common response to diversity is repression and a heightened sense of communal identity.

3   This case is similar in some respects to Dean Kelley's arguments about the greater resilience of what he calls 'strong' religion (1972; 1978) but there are important differences (see Bruce, 2002).

4   Even in the USA the proportion of available wealth being given to religious activities and institutions is declining, which explains the new movement among right-wing religious groups to persuade the state to fund 'faith-based' social welfare programmes. (On this decline, see Barna Research Online, 2001.)

5   Because this point is often overlooked, it is worth stressing that this is the case even in the USA. New Christian right groups have been forced by the functional prerequisites of a culturally diverse state to promote their agenda on secular and not religious grounds. Thus abortion infringes the basic right to life, divorce and homosexuality are socially dysfunctional, and creationism should be taught because it is good science.

6   In line with the remit of the original conference to concentrate on one's area of expertise and in order to be brief, I have not considered the fate of non-Christian religions. I will simply say that I expect these also to decline: it is more likely that non-Christian immigrants and their descendants will conform to the native British norm than the other way round.

References

Barna Research Online 2001: Churches Lose Financial Ground in 2000. 5 June, *www.Barna.org*.

Berger, Peter L. 1980: *The Heretical Imperative: Contemporary Possibilities of Religious Affirmations*. London: Collins.

Brierley, Peter 1999: *UK Christian Handbook Religious Trends 2000/01 No. 2*. London: Christian Research Association.

Brierley, Peter 2000: *The Tide is Running Out*. London: Christian Research Association.

Brown, Callum 2001: *The Death of Christian Britain*. London: Routledge.

Bruce, Steve 1996: *Religion in the Modern World: From Cathedrals to Cults*. Oxford: Oxford University Press.

Bruce, Steve 1999: *Choice and Religion: a Critique of Rational Choice Theory*. Oxford: Oxford University Press.

Bruce, Steve 2000: *Fundamentalism*. Cambridge: Polity Press.

Bruce, Steve 2002: *God is Dead: Secularization in the West*. Oxford: Blackwell.

Davie, Grace 1994: *Religion in Britain since 1945: Believing without Belonging*. Oxford: Blackwell.

Field, Clive 2001: 'The Haemorrhage of Faith'? Opinion Polls as Sources for Religious Practices, Beliefs and Attitudes in Scotland since the 1970s. *Journal of Contemporary Religion*, 16, pp.157–75.

Foster, Peter G. 1972: Secularization in the English Context. *Sociological Review*, 20, pp.153–68.

Gill, Robin, Hadaway, C. Kirk and Marler, Penny Long 1998: Is Religious Belief Declining in Britain?, *Journal for the Scientific Study of Religion*, 37, pp.507–16.

Glassner, P. 1975: Idealisation and the Social Myth of Secularization. In Michael Hill (ed.), *Sociological Yearbook of Religion Vol. 8*. London: SCM Press, pp.7–14.

Hamilton, Bernard 1986: *Religion in the Medieval West*. London: Edward Arnold.

Hornsby-Smith, Michael P. 1999: English Catholics at the New Millennium. In Michael P. Hornsby-Smith (ed.), *Catholics in England 1950–2000: Historical and Sociological Perspectives*. London: Cassell, pp.291–306.

Johnson, Douglas 1979: *Contending for the Faith: a History of the Evangelical Movement in the Universities and Colleges*. Leicester: Inter-Varsity Press.

Kelley, Dean 1972: *Why the Conservative Churches Are Growing*. New York: Harper and Row.

Kelley, Dean 1978: Why the Conservative Churches are still Growing. *Journal for the Scientific Study of Religion*, 17, pp.129–37.

Krol, Arbam J. 2001: Developments in the Dutch Churches. *Quadrant*, March, pp.1, 6.

Martin, David 1965: Towards Eliminating the Concept of Secularization. In Julius Gould (ed.), *The Penguin Survey of the Social Sciences*. Harmondsworth: Penguin, pp.169–82.

Martin, David 1969: *The Religious and the Secular*. London: Routledge and Kegan Paul.

Marsh, Christopher 1998: *Popular Religion in Sixteenth-Century England*. London: Macmillan.

Opinion Research Business 2000: *The Soul of Britain Survey*. London: Opinion Research Business.

Tatlow, Tissington 1933: *The Story of the Student Christian Movement*. London: SCM Press.

Thomas, Keith 1978: *Religion and the Decline of Magic*. Harmondsworth: Penguin.

Wilson, Bryan 1966: *Religion in Secular Society*. London: C.A. Watts.

Woodhead, Linda, with Heelas, Paul and Martin, David (eds) 2001: *Peter Berger and the Study of Religion*. London: Routledge.

CHAPTER 5

Prediction and Prophecy in the Future of Religion

Bryan Wilson

Prophecy and Prediction Distinguished

Prediction has not had a good track record in sociology: prophecy even less so. Durkheim put his futuristic faith in the diffusion throughout society of the professional ethic: we have lived to see how Mrs Thatcher put the last nails into that coffin. Hobhouse took optimistic refuge in endorsing belief in an inevitable law of progress that would usher in an epoch in which a universalistic rational ethic would prevail. Who now believes that? Karl Marx may have demonstrated prescience in averring that California would become the economic centre of the world, but he predicted such a destiny for the wrong reasons – the discovery of gold rather than the exploitation of glitter. Max Weber pinned his hope for German destiny on the emergence of an informed charismatic leader controlling a democracy: what we got, at least in the short run, was Hitler. When the future expectations and predictions of sociological giants like these go so far astray, what chance, even when standing on their shoulders, has a dwarf to see 'beyond the blue horizon' or 'somewhere over the rainbow'?

Perhaps it should be said of all these forecasts that they embraced something more of prophecy than of prediction. Prediction is dependent on explanation, is indeed a form of explanation projected forward. In turn, explanation relies on replication of experimental method. However, despite the clarion call for method, with which Auguste Comte enunciated his new discipline, the rigour of its methodology cannot be said to be sociology's strongest suit. It is less strong, say, than the methodology of economics, in which the variables, numerous as they are, are more manageable. Economic categories are more readily quantified and, in that discipline, human motivations are traditionally assumed to operate according to the set psychological principles incorporated in economic theory. Given this weakness of methodology combined with the desire of sociologists to develop theories that explain the totality of social phenomena, and the hubris implicit in their belief that they are capable of formulating universally valid propositions – a goal which is a chimera – is it surprising that they so lightly confuse prediction with prophecy, and patch up the lacuna of calculation by recourse to speculation?

And what form does prophecy usually take? Often it professes to reveal the (as yet) unforeseen consequences of particular courses of action or inaction, or of failure to abide by rules or to meet obligation. Further, unlike prediction, prophecy is not neutral: it not infrequently takes the form of a warning, almost of a threat. Thus it embodies, overtly or covertly, specific value judgments. The legitimization which it claims also differs: whereas prediction is justified as being the result of consciously applied rational procedures, prophecy invokes mystic power, supernatural revelation or special inspiration. It invokes knowledge of the hitherto undisclosed purposes of a god, a universal law or a force of destiny. Prophecy is often relative, in that it frequently allows for the circumvention of prophesied events if particular prescribed courses of action are pursued. Whereas prediction is generally consonant with – indeed, is an extrapolation of – contemporary states of affairs, what prophecy claims is foreknowledge of the adventitious, the radical and, literally, the altogether unexpected.

Given this character of prophecies, it should not be surprising that particular prophecies usually fail to be fulfilled. So much is this the case that even individuals and organizations that are committed to the idea of prophecy, and believe themselves specially anointed for prophetic utterance, not infrequently dilute their claims, not only by introducing qualifying circumstances, but more generally by declaring that prophecy is rightly seen, not as foretelling, but rather as forthtelling, that is, as telling the people rather than telling the future. Thus prophecy – celebrated by St Paul as a God-given gift to Christians for the benefit of the Church – is watered down to accommodate the much attenuated expectations of the faithful, even the faithful who populate those churches which retain the most fundamentalist interpretations of Pauline claims and prophecies.

Prophetism as a Social Phenomenon

In what has been suggested thus far, there is an implication that is worth drawing out: that, as one legitimate exercise within the discipline, the sociologist may apply predictive competence to the phenomenon of prophecy itself. In generalizing about the circumstances in which prophecy is evinced, is heeded or becomes a stimulus for action, the sociologist is implicitly applying the standards of – may we say, 'scientific' – method to an *a*rational expression of response to some measure of social anguish. The sociologist is typifying a species of social action, and locating it in a particular set of social relationships; may, indeed, be said to be categorizing a distinctive genre of utterance, or even depicting a virtually institutionalized phenomenon, recognizable in certain societies in the recurrent incidence of prophetic visions and warnings (as occurred, to give but three examples, among the Ancient Israelites, among the Utes in late 19th century Utah[1] and among the 20th century natives of Biak, New Guinea[2]) and which we may legitimately designate as 'prophetism'. The sociologist may then appropriately ask whether and, if so, under what conditions, prophetism is predictable. The obverse case is less than entirely symmetrical – a prophet explaining the prospect of an outcrop of social scientific predictions. Perhaps the nearest we come to such a case – and it might be a curate's egg of an example – are the utopias and distopias of science fiction, from the excursuses of Samuel Butler and William Morris to those of L. Ron Hubbard.

The Predictability of Persisting Trends

After this disquisition on prediction and prophecy, it will come as no surprise when it is made clear that this chapter has neither well-founded predictions nor resounding prophecies to produce respecting the prospects of religion in the 21st century. At most it will venture to suggest that certain existing trends are likely to persist, and that some of these will bring about consequences of their own.

Secularization: the Realization of a Man-made World

Secularization has been the single most important feature of the religious condition of advanced societies in the 20th century. It appears that, in those societies, the belief (conscious or unconscious) has been induced that humans control their own destiny, and that society (including all its sub-systems from the family to the state) is a product of human organization and not a God-given structure. Such an assumption permeates people's thinking, their relationships and their role performances. It is at the very foundation of their corporate endeavours, an unstated (unstated because it is taken for granted) constitutional principle of political, economic, judicial and scientific institutions and organizations. It increasingly characterizes educational provision, and invades even the intimacies of marital and familial life (as evident in family planning and contraception).

Community and Communication

This unsung tenet, that we live in a man-made world, is attributable to the increase of technical knowledge. It reflects the mounting dependence on an ever more refined division of labour and hence of professional specialization. The motor in the machine has been the increased dependence on technology. If technical innovation has had this consequence in the 20th century, there is every reason to suppose that the much more rapid process of social change prompted by the electronics revolution will have yet more profound secularizing effects in the 21st. The increased articulation of role performances implies a depersonalization of activities, even indeed of the human element in social interaction, and that process is likely to be further enhanced by information technology, as the Archbishop of Canterbury noted in a lecture on Christianity and citizenship in early 2000.[3] The decay of community induces reliance on its substitute – communication. That process represents a shift of dependence from the inchoate, pervasive shared emotional apprehensions in which a (necessarily local) population is immersed, to reliance on articulate, increasingly precise, and quantifiable instructions and injunctions. The growing assumption that we live in a man-made world entails the replacement of moral commitment and common *mentalité* by technical regulation.

Further, as modernization affects less developed parts of the world, comparable processes of secularization, albeit varying in speed and incidence in accordance with specific traditions and circumstances, will, we may predict, occur there too. Eventually, again allowing for some diversity in subsidiary causes and effects, there are likely to be consequences for the traditional religious beliefs of the general populace, and in the behaviour which may be predicated on those beliefs. In the 20th century, crossing oneself and confession declined among Catholics. The utterance of 'grace' before and after meals came to be virtually confined to public occasions, its function ceasing to be so much to thank God for food as to be a more decorous version of a starting pistol. Cremation, once seen as almost sacrilegious, became steadily more widespread. Where there were weddings, they were increasingly likely to be secular weddings, and that against a background in which marriage of any kind, with all its moral and religious vows, promises and imputations, has withered as an institution. All of these small changes have, of course, been no more than straws in the secularizing wind, but as such they allow us to see which way the wind is blowing, and they also indicate that over the course of the 20th century that wind has not been losing strength. It is likely to continue to blow in the 21st.

Structural Change and Individual Behaviour

If the trend of voluntary choice in all these – and many other – small matters has been towards a preference for secular models, that trend amounts to a response to the structural process of secularization, the process in which secular agencies have taken over functions once fulfilled by religion. The behaviour of individuals is not the substance of secularization, but is, at most, an indication that the crucial relationships between the institutions of society no longer operate under the presidency of religion. Falling church attendance, or the declining incidence of other forms of religious action, such as those to which allusion has just been made (and including baptism, confirmation, Sunday school enrolment and church attendance) are not the kernel of secularization: they are merely an epiphenomenal reaction to it. Popular mentality does indeed manifest secularizing trends, but it does so principally in reflection of the prevailing social structure.

The evacuation of religious dispositions from other institutional contexts does not lead to a prediction – or a prophecy – of the total disappearance of religion. It merely suggests that religious belief and behaviour will become more and more confined to its own specialized activities, hence of less significance for the social system and its operation. In the process, religious agents may acquire enhanced autonomy – for instance in the disestablishment of state churches (as has recently occurred in Sweden) and greater freedom to act – but a freedom confined to religion's own preserved social space. That space may include the possibility of forming new, or sustaining old, voluntary welfare agencies, or of attaining recognition as NGOs — non-governmental organizations. Such agencies may continue to be anchored in churches or religious movements, (places where there may be surplus plant, office space or personnel). The likelihood, however, is that they will operate only at the margins of the social system, or that their religious inspiration will be very much attenuated as they are bought into necessary conformity with increasingly technical (hence increasingly secular) standards: church schools in England and Catholic hospitals in Belgium illustrate the trend.

Do these considerations imply that the religious commitment of individuals, no matter how widely diffused within a given population, has no prospect of influencing the prevailing degree of secularity of a society or of affecting a current process of secularization?

Residual Reservations: Revivals and Renewals

In modern societies, societies in which freedom of religion is secured, designated social space is officially allocated and generally protected as space in which vent to religious feeling and the expression of belief and belonging may be manifested. In a sense, although this has not been an explicitly stated social or political purpose, or perhaps even an intended purpose, religious action has been insulated from most operations of the institutional framework of the social system. Like recreational activity, religion is acknowledged as a legitimate pursuit to which individuals may, if they so wish, give their time, energy, income and talents. Religious believers may also canvass their concerns in the public square, and claim the relevance of their commitment to various social activities, such as the maintenance of values or the socialization of the young: but they may not assume any special privileges in so doing. The claim of the religiously committed thus takes its place as one propagandist voice among others.

The recent evidence suggests that that voice is not particularly widely regarded in modern societies, except on rare occasions when an issue arises in which religious predilections coincide with goals pursued by other agencies. Calls for religious revival, which had a certain measure of success in the 18th and 19th centuries, particularly in America, faded away in the 20th, or have become diluted into television chat shows and money-raising programmes – in those societies which accord freedom of the airwaves to religious sponsors. Official endeavours to regalvanize church activity, successively attempted by Catholic and Anglican churches, such as the decade of evangelism, just ended, have been largely ineffectual. Charismatic renewal – itself a relatively spontaneous resurgence of religious emotion gathering momentum in the 1960s and 1970s – appears now to be socially inconsequential and of little significance. One may tentatively suggest that there is no substantial evidence that even a widespread and well-organized campaign for the increase of religious influence in matters of social organization has much chance of success in the coming years.

From Public Worship to Minority Cult: from Church to Sect?

The growing impersonality of modern society, contingent upon the growth of role-articulated work systems, information technology, mass communication, electronic media, commuting and the breakdown of local community structures has implications for churches. The worshipping community, if community it may still be called, becomes increasingly anonymous, at least in urban centres. With that is sundered one of the vital links of religious performance. Religion was strong when worship was one facet of a more diversified but integrated community life. Today, it brings together not the natural community (as if that still existed) but a self-selected coterie of aficionados, many of whom are unacquainted except as their shared religious impulses demand. Some church involvement becomes more of a cultic activity, with those who are smitten often travelling far out of their own vicinal religious context to worship in a distant place which offers what is for them a more congenial style of churchmanship and religious performance. Believers are sufficiently few, and worship styles sufficiently diverse, that in some circumstances one may, without impropriety, begin to talk of churches as sects, and some species of supposed orthodoxy as emphatically cult-like.

It is possible that the churches, fixated as they are with moral apprehensions that were evolved in (and that had their greatest purchase in) old-style local communities, may take on new life as oases in the desiccated context of modern life. When new techniques have depersonalized and *de*moralized social life beyond a certain point, there may be a search for defences against the signs of the times and even the attempt at resistance to what those signs portend. In such circumstances, the churches – unless they themselves have sold out to the new order – may come to be seen as the appropriate agencies to mobilize those disenchanted with the brave new world. How effective they might be, and to what extent they might survive in such a role, is not easy to foretell. Like the churches in Poland during the years in which that country struggled under the hegemony of Russian communism in Eastern Europe, they might enjoy success as an opposition, as a focal point for traditional religious values, as long as oppression persisted. But what would be their role once external circumstances had changed? Just as the religious resilience of Poland wobbled once the Church was no longer the agency of resistance, symbolizing Polish identity against this latest of the several aggressors who, over a long history, had sought to submerge it, so the Church as a moral bastion might find that its celebrity as a subversive movement afforded few advantages once subversion was no longer the name of the game.

Of course, the institutional churches have a sizeable investment in the existing social structure: plant, clergy, training facilities for intending clerics, pension schemes, hierarchic status systems and numerous ancillary agencies. All of these amount to bulwarks, not only against change, but also against decay. There are many people with significant vested interests embowelled in church structures, and they constitute a rearguard fending off whatever secularizing forces threaten the attrition of church status and power. Even if the erosion of local community life has debilitated much of the erstwhile religious ethos, the institutional presence persists, albeit sometimes as little more than a hollow shell from which the formerly encapsulated life form has largely escaped. Yet, as the state subvents their income, cathedrals may persist as tourist attractions, as museums or, for some modern men, almost as 'follies' which evoke wonder at the social and fiscal priorities of past ages. Parish churches may continue as a local resource for people who may still respond, at moments of crisis or collective anguish, to the need for symbolic expression.

The Persistence of Sects

If this is a likely future for the major churches, what of the missions and minority conventicles? Nineteenth-century sects have shown a considerable capacity to persist, as they have brought into service the competencies of a better-educated public. Literacy among the rank and file, more systematic education of the leadership, or the cadres from which leaders might be drawn, and modern organizational structures have secured a durability for some sects which contrasts sharply with the volatility of many of the transitory sects of earlier centuries (allowing, in passing, for a few distinguished exceptions, among which it is necessary to mention as examples only the Waldensians, the Hutterians, the Amish Mennonites, the Quakers and the Moravians).[4] Some more modern sects – Jehovah's Witnesses, Seventh-day Adventists, Mormons and some Pentecostal sects – have in place systems of management which rival, where they do not outclass, the efficiency of comparable bureaucracies in the major churches. As with the churches, such facilities militate against decay, although they do not guarantee survival, as the decline of another 19th-century American sect, Christian Science, illustrates.[5]

If, in their concern to sustain and expand their following, sects arising in the 19th and early 20th centuries were able to exploit newly emerging facilities, such as mass literacy and bureaucratic organization, it does not follow that they will continue to be able to make use of comparable secular innovations in the 21st. In contrast to churches, hidebound by their own traditional procedures, 19th-century sects had the advantage of beginning *de novo*. But by now, at the beginning of a new millennium, they have experienced the accretion of traditions of their own, have accumulated their own historically prescribed cultural baggage. The traditional rigidities, once confined to the old churches, are now no less evident among the old sects. We must then expect tensions within these sects as reformers vie with conservatives on a number of issues respecting the extent of innovation which the sect can tolerate: consider the current schism in the Free Church of Scotland.[6]

Some of these issues will be contingent on external circumstances: the use of information technology, the Internet, the increasing secularity of the mass media – all threaten lingering religious values. The cultural heroes – the role models – of modern society do not present to the young a coherent curriculum of Christian values. Even sectarians, despite their conscious endeavour to insulate their members from the influences of secularized society, are faced, willy-nilly, with the prospect of ever more extensive involvement with the alien world without. If worldliness was once the threat, globalism challenges the very circumstances which made possible the maintenance of a separated distinctive corporate culture. If education begins to erode the deposit of fundamentalism which, though diminished, still persists within the mainstream denominations and churches, the effect may no less be felt within many fundamentalist sects.

Corporate Life Style and Internal Recruitment

Apart from the influence of the increasing secularity of the external culture, there may also be internal processes of structural change affecting sects. Hitherto, many sects have been able to maintain their own corporate way of life, and a collective culture of their own, transmitted from one generation to the next. For many of the sects formed in the 19th century, induction of the inborn has been the increasingly normal source of recruitment. It has been an important factor in ensuring the preservation of group culture and the maintenance of sectarian identity and allegiance. But as the gap in the social experience of successive generations widens – and this may inevitably occur even among the most cloistered of sects – the likelihood of their being able to continue this pattern of endogenous growth may weaken.

At the same time, the received mind-set of these sects is likely to become more and more remote from that of the younger generation of the wider public, and hence the prospect of winning recruits from among that public may be expected to diminish. In their own way, but somewhat retarded, the sects face a problem already evident in multiple ways in the major denominations. The dilemma is whether, on the one hand, to embrace and adapt to the secular culture, adjusting its mores to some sort of identifiable sectarian requirements; or, on the other hand, to stand firm in accordance with received sect principles, rejecting entirely the values canvassed in and by the secular agencies of society and by those churches which have in some measure compromised and 'gone over'. The position is entirely analogous, if less pointed, to that of those other voluntary associations, political parties: should the party organize and persist in presenting a platform of enduring values, principles and commitments, no matter whether these are popular or not; or should it be prepared to trim original beliefs and values in order to attract and retain a following?

Third World Influences

Globalization does, however, present some opportunities for sectarian growth. The older Protestant denominations, and even the Catholic Church, long ago traversed the apogee of missionary endeavour. The recruitment of missionaries will become increasingly difficult, and those recruited have long been, and continue to be, among the more conservative and fundamentalist votaries of the faith – in short, to have a literalist perspective closer to that of most sectarians. Since sects often seek converts from those already Christianized (however lightly) they are likely, in the third world, to sustain their growth at the expense of (formerly mainstream) Christians. One further consequence of such a process is the increase of internal divisions and disagreements within both the burgeoning Christian sects and the established mission churches. Already today, there are pronounced differences between the first world, home-base congregations of such sects and their third world contingents. The same rift is evident within the major churches: when the Catholic Church has to sequestrate the one-time Archbishop of Lusaka for illicit healing practices, and Church of England delegates are outvoted on moral teachings at the worldwide Lambeth Conference, it is not surprising that smaller religious bodies, such as the Seventh-day Adventists, with a membership overwhelmingly based in the third world, should experience difficulty in maintaining authority for Western principles of faith and order, and licence for the (relatively) more liberal opinions of their Western ministry. Such persisting cross-currents may lead to eventual schism, or more likely to the attrition of the more liberally-minded Western membership, and, in third world countries, once Western subventions diminished or were withdrawn, to indigenization as missions are transmogrified as independent churches.

Predictable Prophetism: Unpredictable Prophets?

Of course, the social scientist cannot rule out the possibility that, in some remote place, there might not arise a convincing prophet, healing the sick, raising the dead, and casting out demons, and thereby winning a mass following. We should all hear of such a prophet on the Internet, and see him or her on television. Would such advanced technical means of communication facilitate dissemination of the prophet's message or subvert it, enhance his or her career or undermine it? Evidence to test such propositions may already exist, out there, since, in the last few decades, there have been well-publicized and well-documented prophets aplenty, from Alice Lenshina to Sun Myung Moon. They have come and, at least in their more trenchant mode, have gone, demonstrating recurrently the ephemeral nature of prophets and prophecies, even if testifying to the somewhat more enduring capability of prophetism. Prophetism is, of course, a constructed category of the social scientist, not the self-acclaimed commitment of prophets, who generally regard each other as, at best irrelevant, and at worst, as fraudulent rivals. The concept of prophetism does, however, permit us to stabilize our definition of the phenomenon, enabling us, as ultimately it might enable everyone, all the better to identify prophets and to appraise their social functions – always allowing that, if we can see them, perhaps we may also see through them.

Notes

1 The *locus classicus* for prophetism among the Utes is James Mooney (1896).
2 For prophetism among the people of Biak, see F.C. Kamma (1954). A condensed account is to be found in Peter Worsley (1957, pp.126–30).
3 The Archbishop told an audience in Liverpool, 'Increasingly, we are not only citizens of the world, but also citizens of the World Wide Web. Clearly the access to information and the ability to tap resources not otherwise available can be a potent tool of empowerment. But it can also be exclusive and isolating.' He said that people deluded themselves that they were 'connecting' with others through e-mail when there was no real relationship between correspondents. 'Yes, we have to make contact but it is the quality of that contact that matters. We must be sure that the virtual community is at the service of real communities, not a substitute for them.'
4 Three of the four great heresies of mediaeval Europe, the Lollards, Hussites and Cathars (as designated by M.D. Lambert, 1992) failed to survive into post-Reformation times. The fourth, the Waldensians, still has congregations in the Alpine regions.
5 For an account of the decline of Christian Science, see Rodney Stark (1998).
6 From the mid-1980s, Donald McLeod, editor of the *Free Church Monthly Record* and Professor of Systematic Theology at the Free Church College, had been questioning the church's distinctive theological, liturgical and social positions. Unable to muster support for a heresy trial, his opponents orchestrated a campaign of claims of sexual harassment which, when they were finally tested in court in 1996, were dismissed by the Sheriff as a conspiracy. When the majority of the General Assembly in January 2000 censured the conservatives for maintaining their Free Church Defence Association, 32 ministers (out of 160) withdrew to form the Free Church (Continuing). The smaller Free Presbyterian Church had split a decade earlier along similar lines, the trigger there being the decision of a leading elder, Lord McKay of Clashfern, the Lord Chancellor, to attend the funeral of a Catholic colleague.

References

Kamma, F.C. 1954: *De Messiaanse Koreri-bewegingen in het Biaks-Noemfoorse Culturgebied*. The Hague: J.N. Voorhoeve.
Lambert, M.D. 1992: *Mediaeval Heresy*. Oxford: Blackwell.
Mooney, James 1896: *The Ghost Dance Religion and the Sioux Outbreak of 1890*. Fourteenth Annual Report of the Bureau of Ethnology to the Secretary of the Smithsonian Institution, Washington, DC: Government Printing Office.
Stark, Rodney 1998: The Rise and Fall of Christian Science. *Journal of Contemporary Religion*, 13 (2), pp.189–214.
Worsley, Peter 1957: *The Trumpet Shall Sound*. London: McGibbon & Kee.

CHAPTER 6

Social Networks and Religious Identity: An Historical Example from Wales

Paul Chambers

Introduction

Protestant Nonconformity has traditionally been seen as an important carrier of Welsh cultural and social identity (Williams, 1991; Davie, 1994), but religious practice in Wales is now declining at a faster rate than anywhere else in the UK (Gallacher, 1997). This raises questions, not only about the future of religious institutions in Wales but also about the survival of traditional ways of formulating Welsh cultural and social identity.

In *Public Religions in the Modern World* (1994), José Casanova suggests that within the social sciences there has been a tendency to dichotomize culture into sacred and secular spheres and to read off 'culture' as exclusively 'secular', ignoring religion altogether. Conversely, sociologists of religion have tended to focus either on the internal characteristics of religious organizations or on external forces and trends emanating from the 'secular' sphere and 'acting' upon the religious sphere.

In truth, the relationship between religion, culture and modernity has always been more ambiguous. This truism has been highlighted in recent years with the emergence of sociologies of post-modern culture, nationalism and globalization that explicitly recognize the inseparability of religion and sociopolitical factors, especially in the formation of national identities and the life politics of cultural resistance (Robertson, 1992; Casanova, 1994; Calhoun, 1997; McCrone, 1998). Religion certainly shaped modern Wales and, for a time, the Welsh saw themselves, and were seen by others, as 'wedded to the chapel'. Adopting an eclectic theoretical rationale, the following discussion seeks to account for the rise of Nonconformity as a significant force in Welsh life and self-understanding, and its subsequent decline, examining the historically contingent relationships between religious institutions, society, culture and national identity and the implications of continued religious decline for future Welsh self-identities.

Nonconformity and Welsh Identity

Both the Welsh reputation for piety and a distinctive sense of national identity are relatively recent phenomena, emerging in the late 18th and early 19th centuries.

While it is reasonable to speculate that from early times, something approaching a distinctive Welsh culture, based on shared language, custom and practice was in place (Davies, 1996), it could not yet constitute a sense of 'national' identity (Smith, 1999).[1] The Anglo-Norman conquest of Wales and the imposition of new ecclesiastical structures marked the marginalization of vernacular expressions of religious practice, and the scant evidence we have about pre-modern religious life suggests a superstitious rather than a religious population (Thomas, 1971; Williams, 1994). The Reformation in Wales was met with general indifference, merely marking the replacement of one alien liturgical language, Latin, with another, English (Harris, 1990). Parallel political developments had seen the incorporation of Wales into England and the progressive anglicization of the Welsh gentry, with elite and folk cultures becoming distinct from each other (Aull Davies, 1983). Increasingly, indigenous Welsh culture was effectively marginalized into peasant culture (Jenkins, 1978; Evans, 1988) as 'Welsh ceased to be an official language and retreated into the kitchen' (Williams, 1985, p.121).

Benedict Anderson (1991) has emphasized the importance of the written and particularly, the printed word in forging a collective sense of 'national' identity.[2] Given the growing ascendancy of English as the language of the gentry in Wales, the creation of a vernacular Welsh literature, which might act as a carrier for Welsh culture and identity, initially appeared an unlikely project (Jenkins, 1978). It was the perceived irreligion of the Welsh people (Hill, 1964; Thomas, 1971) that fortuitously provided the impetus for printing religious texts in the Welsh language (Jenkins, 1978; Williams, 1994).

Puritanism in Wales was initially an anglicizing movement (Owen, 1960; Williams, 1985), but English and Welsh puritans, concerned at the lack of impact of the Reformation in Wales, began to sponsor the translation and printing of religious texts in Welsh.[3] This publishing activity was seen largely as a short-term expedient geared towards revitalizing religious life (Williams, 1985; Jenkins, 1988) and of the 545 books printed in Welsh between 1660 and 1730, 322 had an overtly religious theme (Jenkins, 1978). The creation of a Welsh literati was seen as the first stage of the eventual adoption of English as the primary literary medium, but as Glanmor Williams (1994) comments, an unintended consequence of this publishing activity by the Reformers was that 'they accomplished more than any other single factor in keeping the [Welsh] language alive and vigorous into the twentieth century' (p.98).

As a result of this activity in the religious sphere, a body of texts in a uniform fixed version of the Welsh language was established (Childs, 1962), creating the conditions for a 'national consciousness' to emerge (Anderson, 1991, p.46). Given the nature of this publishing activity, this emerging consciousness was also firmly Protestant in character, and the link between nascent Welsh identity and Protestantism at the literary level was firmly established by the 18th century (Jenkins, 1978; Williams, 1985). Geraint Jenkins (1978) suggests that many of these vernacular texts were produced for family devotions, but that this readership would have only included those classes of people who could both read and afford to buy books, which were still relatively expensive commodities.[4] At the lowest levels of society, folk religion 'owing little or nothing to creed, conviction or spiritual commitment' (Jenkins, 1978, p.49) was still the norm.

Popular assumptions about Welsh religiosity draw much of their strength from the series of religious revivals that took place in Wales from 1649 to 1905. The phenomenon of religious revival itself contains a paradox. It might be seen as a reflection of an inate religiosity among the participating population or as a response to widespread irreligiosity. Contemporary accounts (Saunders, 1949; Macmillan, 1989) reflect the then widespread belief that the Welsh were largely ignorant of religion, but modern historians are rather more circumspect about this picture, suggesting as it does an incremental spread of Nonconformity. Gwyn Alf Williams (1985) suggests that it was that intermediate class of persons – lesser gentry, yeoman farmers, tradesmen and craftsmen and their families – who constituted the bedrock of dissent and that it was within this relatively marginalized interstitial section of the population that Nonconformity initially prospered.[5] What is certain is that the period from the passing of the 1662 Act of Uniformity to the mid-18th century saw much activity by itinerant Welsh speaking preachers and the growth of many small independent worshipping communities meeting in private houses and barns (Macmillan, 1989). By 1794, 300 religious societies were meeting in this way, and there was a growing need to establish places of public worship. These new chapels were predominately situated in rural locations, drawing their congregations from a widely dispersed population.

A parallel development was the establishment of Welsh medium circulating schools (based within the new chapels) teaching basic literacy to the peasantry in order that they could understand the rudimentary principles of religion. It follows that, as Williams (1988) has argued, 'the Welsh people ... learned to read in terms of the Bible and Protestant sectarianism' (p.121). Thus the transformation of the status of the spoken Welsh language into a 'national print language' (Anderson, 1991, p.46) went hand in hand with both a burgeoning subjective 'national' consciousness and a burgeoning religious consciousness that was distinctively 'Welsh' (Jenkins, 1988). Nonconformist religion and Welsh cultural identity were becoming increasingly inseparable as the growth of literacy fuelled religious piety, which in turn transformed the status of the language, giving it a sacral character.[6]

In applying Benedict Anderson's line of argument to the Welsh case, it can be demonstrated that the increasingly widespread supply of cheap reading matter in the Welsh language was a necessary precursor to the possibility of the creation of a new form of 'imagined community', in this case, Williams' (1985) 'People of the Book' (p.131), 'which in its basic morphology set the stage for the modern [Welsh] nation' (Anderson, 1991, p.46). It is ironic, therefore, that what began in 1588 (the translation and publication of the Welsh Bible) as a move to incorporate the Welsh into a dominant English hegemonic structure was to provide the basis for the formulation of a distinctive oppositional cultural identity driven forward by periodic religious revivals and grounded in religious dissent.[7]

The Chapel as a Moral Property

This process of discourse formation originating in the effects of religious revival was to reach its zenith during the 19th century after the rapid changes initiated by the agricultural and industrial revolutions. The effects of religious revival can be overstated (Davies, 1981; Jenkins, 1988), but there is little doubt that by the mid-19th century Nonconformity appeared to have swept all before it, and 'one of the most remarkable transformations in the history of any people' had taken place (Williams, 1988, p.121) as Nonconformism became both 'the national creed and the national practice' (Lambert, 1988, p.97).

In a similar vein, E.T. Davies (1981) suggests that 'The Welsh language, industrialism and Welsh nonconformity were the triple foundations of a way of life that was to dominate Wales into the twentieth century' (p.61). The new chapels, organized and controlled by the people and utilizing the language of the people, constituted sites of resistance to English cultural and religious hegemony. Drawing from the work of Stuart Hall (1976, 1977) we might see the emergent chapels as providing a competing set of oppositional ideological and cultural meanings to that of the dominant religious system (Anglicanism), and as paving the way for the creation of a distinctively Welsh religious and cultural identity. Furthermore, it allows us to understand the transition from the subjective idea of a Welsh nation (Anderson, 1991) into something more concrete: particular sets of social relations predicated on the organization of cultural and social life and in opposition to a dominant hegemonic structure (Hall, 1977; Williams, 1985).[8]

The growth and consolidation of chapel culture cannot be seen outside of the context of mass migration to the new centres of industrial activity. It was within this context that, as Lambert (1988) succinctly notes, 'the chapel, a "moral property" in Thomas and Znaniecki's (1988) excellent phrase, was [to become] the very emblem of the community's collective existence' (p.103). Whereas, in geographical terms, religious provision had been relatively sparse – reflecting the general distribution of a numerically small, predominately rural population – this mass migration was accompanied by an accelerated programme of chapel building in the new areas of industrial activity. Some of these new chapels were paid for by local magnates eager to instil in their new workforces a sense of probity and discipline. But many were built and paid for by the working people themselves.[9]

Evidence from one such industrial area (Chambers, 1999) reveals a common pattern of inward migration, followed by the almost immediate organization of religious societies and subsequent chapel building, with migrants drawing on their prior experience of chapel life elsewhere to create new community structures and public amenities in areas where there were none. That religion should constitute the organizing principle is unsurprising given that the chapel was the one independent and established area of associational life that was the common property of the new Welsh working class (Davies, 1981; Lambert, 1988). And, as Hall (1985) suggests, 'Religious ideologies, however "other worldly" they appear, inform social practices and have a mobilising "practical" impact on society' (p.273). While the presence of an ideology, or the institution that carries it, is not in itself a sufficient condition for religious allegiance, if we add the presence of local social networks to the equation, then we can begin to see how the chapels became the focal points of communities.

Kinship networks were crucial to the establishment and maintenance of the life of chapels. To these were added networks derived from working and living in close proximity, and these established strong social and cultural linkages between chapels and their surrounding populations. The strength of the chapel was derived from a particular form of local social structure, while, at the same time, it increasingly informed local social practices. This dialectical relationship, driven along concrete social networks, was increasingly to establish the chapel as the institutional expression of local community life.

By the late 19th century, the individual Welsh chapel had become transformed into a form of public religion, the concrete expression of communities that lived, worked, worshipped and died in tightly circumscribed locales. People 'lived their lives within the orbit of, or in reaction to the chapels' (Williams, 1985, p.206). The chapel was the voice that claimed to encapsulate the public social, political and economic life of the community, the totalizing expression of habitus, both derived from and informing community life (Durkheim, 1995). Chapels were variously labour exchanges, marriage bureaux, schools, social clubs and, most importantly, agencies of social control. Nonconformity cast a long shadow over Welsh society, and whether within or outside the family of the chapel, to transgress against the strict moral codes of the chapel (even as late as the 1920s) was to be placed outside respectable society (Welsby, 1995; Chambers, 1999).[10]

The chapel also constituted the only centre of cultural activity in many communities. As Lambert (1988) notes, this cultural activity was not merely religious and, importantly, in most chapels it was mediated through the medium of the Welsh language. By the late 19th century, in many chapels the *cymanfa ganu* (singing festival) or *Eisteddfod* was an established part of chapel life. Even where such 'worldly' activities were frowned upon, religious life was distinctively 'Welsh', as is reflected in the number and variety of contemporary Welsh language periodicals devoted to religion (Robbins, 1994). These had a wide readership among chapelgoers, not least because, in a climate of strict Sabbatarianism, the only leisure pursuit permissible on a Sunday was the reading of religious literature. E.T. Davies (1981) also notes that the secular vernacular press was increasingly controlled, either directly or indirectly, by Welsh Nonconformity. However, from 1804 onwards, the English language was increasingly making inroads, particularly in the commercial sphere and this was reflected in the trend towards building 'English' chapels for the emerging anglicized middle class (Davies, 1981). By 1880, it was increasingly apparent that the use of the English language in chapel services was becoming commonplace in urban areas; and by 1895 the 'English' chapels were organized enough to hold their own separate conferences (Lambert, 1988).

The 1904–5 Revival: a Question of Language?

By the turn of the century, influential writers such as J. Vyrnwy Morgan (1909, pp.254–5) were lamenting the spread of the English language into chapel culture. At the heart of this lament was the perception that the privileged position of Welsh Nonconformity as a cultural carrier of Welsh national identity was under threat from creeping anglicization. The 1904–5 Revival has been seen variously as either a reaction to the emergence of secularizing forces within Welsh society and the resultant diminuation of the hegemonic power of the chapels (Lambert, 1988; Robbins, 1994), or the point at which a genuine Welsh working class emerged from out of the shadow of the chapel as a class for itself (Williams, 1985), or as a struggle between youthful iconaclasts and the entrenched conservatism of the chapel establishment (Jones, 1995). While the Revival was all this and more, contemporaneous accounts of this social movement suggest that language was also a key issue (Morgan, 1909; Philips, 1923).

The followers of Evan Roberts, 'The Great Revivalist', were engaged in breaking down the institutional structures of the chapels while simultaneously reaffirming the centrality of the Welsh language within the religious sphere. The failure of the religious establishment to halt the encroachment of the English language into the religious sphere was seen as part and parcel of a generalized capitulation within Welsh society to the growing hegemony of English culture and values, epitomized in the religious sphere by the growing professionalization of the ministerial function (Jones, 1995).[11]

The 1904–5 Revival can be seen as a prime example of a social movement acting as a vehicle for cultural resistance (Hall, 1985), articulating the concerns of many Welsh people about the growing hegemony of English culture in both the religious and secular spheres of Welsh society. Underpinning the rhetoric of salvation was the belief that the Welsh possessed a distinctive religious culture and 'national' identity, predicated on the belief that the Welsh 'nation' was more religious than surrounding nations (Lambert, 1988, pp.99–100) and that only a mass return to the principles and practice of Welsh Nonconformity could halt and reverse the tide of anglicization and save the soul of the nation.

Despite massive publicity, the impressive manifestations of religious fervour and the power of revivalist preaching to change radically individual lives (Jones, 1995), in retrospect the 1904–5 Revival must be adjudged a failure. It failed to halt (or even slow) the increasing hegemony of the English language in both the religious and secular spheres. It also marked the end of a 100-year period of intermittent religious revivals and so represents a watershed in the secularization of Welsh society.

The Decline of Public Religion

The 20th century has seen a radical shift in the relationship between Nonconformity and the Welsh people, reflecting the fragmentation of the cultural sphere and marked transformations within the social, political and economic domains. The century can be characterized as a progressive disengagement or uncoupling of religious institutions from their surrounding populations and the increasing differentiation of the religious and secular spheres. The status of religion in Wales has progressively reverted to a private religion of individual salvation rather than a public religion of social control, reflecting an axial shift from public to private religion (Casanova, 1994) which is more typical of the religious situation elsewhere in Europe.

In rural Wales, Nonconformity largely retained its social and cultural significance for half a century. While the proportion of active worshippers as a percentage of the population remains much higher than in the industrialized areas, continuing rural depopulation means that individual congregations are small and growing smaller (Gallacher, 1997). The trajectory of the decline of public religion in the industrial areas is more marked and the reasons behind this decline more complex, reflecting a move from a 'closed' to an 'open' society (Davies, 1981). While evidence suggests that secularizing forces were already in play in the late 19th century (Williams, 1985; Harris, 1990), the pattern of religious decline in urban and industrialized areas is strongly related to social, cultural and economic transformations going on within the communities that had formerly sustained the chapels (Chambers, 1999).

Chapel life was part of a complex system of local social networks. As the ties that held these networks together unravelled, visible religious decline followed. Factors such as the decline in general usage of the Welsh language and the emergence of competing cultural and recreational attractions, the collapse of the Liberal-Nonconformist consensus and the rise of socialism as an alternative ideology, the decline of traditional industries and increased social and geographical mobility, all undermined the previously homogenous nature of working-class communities. The chapels were faced with both an increasingly secularized social and cultural environment and a parallel fragmentation of community life, undercutting the foundations upon which religious praxis was based (Rosser and Harris, 1965).

This transformation of solidaristic communities into locales, based on nothing but common residence, has, in most cases, left the chapels high and dry (Chambers, 1999). Their modes of organization, activities and modes of expression; the interpretive framework that structured human experience and made sense of the self and the world, are all based on a notion of habitus that is no longer relevant to many Welsh people. The notion that Welsh Nonconformity still represents the public face, or *ysbryd* (spirit), of Welsh culture and national identity appears increasingly contestable in the face of many competing discourses (Thompson and Day, 1999).

Facing the Future

Bare statistical facts leave little doubt that organized religion in Wales has experienced a marked decline in the 20th century and that this decline has been most apparent within Welsh Nonconformity (Gallacher, 1997). Currently, 8.7 per cent of Welsh people still regularly attend a place of worship. It is now evident that religion and religious observance is a minority interest that increasingly goes on behind closed doors, separate from the mainstream affairs of the majority of Welsh people. It is clear that the Welsh reputation for collective piety, a marker which distinguished them from, above all, the English, is no longer sustainable. The picture of the decline of public religion is further complicated by fragmentation within the religious sphere. Changes in the occupational sphere have fuelled the expansion of a middle class, and within the religious sphere this has been reflected in a shift towards anglicized middle class patterns of religious observance (Harris, 1990; Gallacher, 1997). Outside the rural heartlands, and with a few exceptions in urban areas, religious praxis is no longer distinctively 'Welsh'.

Facing the 21st century, it is apparent that the Welsh are no longer 'wedded to the chapel'. Mass participation in Welsh Nonconformity was a fairly short-lived experience, specific to a particular set of social, cultural and economic conditions. The 'myth' of Welsh religiosity rests entirely on the fact that a burgeoning 'national' consciousness and a burgeoning Nonconformist consciousness emerged at roughly the same time. However, it was the mass migrations associated with industrialization that created the new community structures which proved conducive to the expansion of Nonconformity. Despite its claims to be the 'national religion', Welsh Nonconformity was essentially a localized phenomenon referentially tied to the communitarian and solidaristic networks surrounding individual chapels. It was only 'national' in the sense that these localized conditions were repeated in many locations. It was strong because it was the symbolic mirror of the communities from which it derived its life. But it was always vunerable because it was highly dependent on these community structures remaining intact.

The decline of the social significance of organized religion in urban areas, the rise of new political parties (both socialist and nationalist), the creation of a national secular education system, sport and new leisure activities, changing employment patterns – all have undermined the traditional constituency of Welsh Nonconformity while at the same time offering new bases of self understanding for the Welsh people. Most importantly, the now almost complete anglicization of industrial Wales, the continuing contested status of the Welsh language, and the growing recognition that Wales must secure its place in an increasingly Europeanized and globalized landscape, have all contributed to an increasingly fragmented national consciousness. This has been reflected in current debates about Welsh identity; a growing recognition that it is only possible to talk of a multiplicity of Welsh identities (Williams, 1985; Smith, 1999; Thompson, 1999). The extent to which the production of a collective sense of national identity remains problematic is well illustrated by the lukewarm reception of the Welsh electorate to their new National Assembly.

There is now a growing recognition among the religious denominations that they need to readdress the public dimension of religion. The Welsh-speaking denominations have attempted to reconcile their differences (as yet unsuccessfully) in order to create an umbrella 'Free Church of Wales' which might give them a united voice in the public arena. In an ecumenical spirit, the churches have appointed a liasion officer to the new Welsh Assembly. The Church in Wales now has a charismatic and internationally respected scholar as its leader: Rowan Williams regularly contributes to public debates in Wales.[12] Locally, religious organizations have increasingly made a significant contribution to community regeneration projects. However, these moves are being played out in a social and cultural environment where church and chapel attendance continues to decline rapidly, and where the rate of chapel closures shows no signs of abating. Public indifference to religion in Wales has never appeared greater, which must raise questions for the future of religion. Specifically, 'Welsh' Nonconformity is hardest hit in terms of numerical decline. What limited congregational growth there is, is now most likely to be found either within Anglican congregations or among the 'new churches' (Gallacher, 1997). This suggests that the future of organized religion in Wales is likely to be in a mainly anglicized cultural form.

The connection between religion and national identity has now been largely relegated to the past. It is difficult to see how it might be revived for the future. Unlike the situation in Northern Ireland or Eastern Europe, religious organizations in Wales have not been able to connect with nationalist politics in the 20th century, reflecting the secularized constitution of Plaid Cymru. The recent political successes of Plaid Cymru have been built on a deliberate policy of inclusivism, together with an implicit recognition that there are now a plurality of Welsh identities. If the Welsh are abandoning their old gods and, as Durkheim (1995) argues, a human institution that endures must be founded on some sort of collective representation, the crucial question in terms of a national identity is: what form should this collective representation take? Dai Smith (1999, p.205) suggests that the only viable discourse left is 'the language of citizenship'. It is, perhaps, the improbable (but not impossible) new institution of the Welsh Assembly that may yet provide a new totemic principle signifying 'Welshness'.

Notes

1   As Dai Smith (1999) suggests, a distinctly Welsh sense of *national* identity was, as elsewhere in Europe, a relatively new phenomenon, emerging with modernity. He writes, 'the words in Welsh for "nationalism", "national" and "nationality" appear for the first time in the late eighteenth century ... [and prior to this] ... there was no use for a widespread, embracing concept like "nation". Loyalties and organising principles were based on more immediate concerns for most people' (pp.83–4).

2   The presence of a fixed print language allows people to imagine themselves as one community, united by a common standard literary form, whereas, when the common language of European elites had been Latin, this had allowed readers to imagine themselves as located within 'Christendom', an abstraction given concrete reality through the medium of language (Mehl, 1970; Kung, 1995), the dissemination of books in vernacular languages created 'national' reading publics. The move from printing books in Latin to the printing of vernacular texts was a by-product of the relentless search for new markets by the emerging protocapitalists of the printing trade (Anderson, 1991).

3   In 1588 the first Welsh Bible was produced. This has been described as both 'the model for all subsequent prose writers in Welsh' (Jones, 1988, p.55) and 'the sheet anchor of a threatened language' (Williams, 1985, p.121).

4   Glyn Alf Williams (1985) notes the importance of the 1640 publication of the Beibl Bach, costing five shillings and designed for family consumption. The relatively modest cost of this edition meant that it was disseminated widely among the more prosperous farming classes.

5   Marginalized both in terms of political power from that class above them and socially and culturally from the mass of peasantry below them. In Marxian terms (Marx, 1969, pp.126–8) these groups might be characterized as an emergent proto-bourgeoisie and, as such, constitute a definite (if essentially transitory) force for ideological change (Engels, 1969, pp.158–68).

6   Gwyn Alf Williams comments that, 'In the world of the popular language, it was an intensely religious, devotional and, increasingly, a doctrinal and disputive culture, that a sophisticated and high quality Welsh registered. Welsh became peculiarly a sacral language with less and less secular purchase of intellectual substance. In the end, as that people and its religion took over the cultural identity of Wales, they emerged as a People of the Book – and of a Book which was Holy. It stamped an identity on this people which proved tenacious' (1985, p.131).

7   While this process of discourse formation was largely unself-conscious, it had very real (if unforeseen) effects. It can be seen to constitute the beginnings of a 'myth' of Welshness, in which religion itself is merely a contingent factor. The myth, however, is a convenient vehicle creating the possibility of a new form of imagined community. And as both Barthes (1973) and Gellner (1983) suggest, 'mythology' is only one step away from 'history'.

8   Williams (1985) sees the creation of what he terms this 'alternative society' as a reaction to the effects of social and economic change in the late 18th century. These changes had created a power vacuum and increasingly the dissenting chapels provided 'an alternative local leadership in a time of abrupt change'. Furthermore, this alternative society 'was being offered a new Welsh national ideology of radical temper and some new Welsh institutions to serve it' (pp.161–7).

9   A Gramscian interpretation of the cultural politics of class would suggest that this does not necessarily entail a simplistic oppositional reading and may represent a process whereby elites can avoid confrontation (Gramsci, 1971). In the case of the chapels, while the working class were able to organize themselves socially, in cultural terms the values of discipline and moral probity that were preached from the pulpit were precisely the same values that employers sought in their new workforces. Indeed, the class composition of chapels was never entirely homogenous and the emphasis on the other world can be seen as defusing any potential confontation pertaining to these worldly matters (Williams, 1983; Harris, 1990).

10 The distinction between 'pub' and 'chapel' was an important one, particularly as a significant section of the Welsh population never darkened the doors of the chapels. However, the irreligious were still constrained by the ethical climate of Nonconformity.

11 A vigorous campaign against the Revd Peter Price, a prominent Congregationalist minister from Dowlais, by Roberts' supporters in the letters pages of the *Western Mail*, indicates the strength of feeling against university-educated ministers. Price's negative comments on some aspects of the Revival were interpreted as the product of his Oxford education, and the anglicized, educated Price was compared unfavourably to the peasant naïf Roberts. 'Creeping anglicization' was perhaps most apparent among the Congregationalist chapels which were viewed with suspicion by the more 'Welsh' chapels. Anglicization was equated with theological 'liberalism', which in turn was seen as diluting and enervating the traditional Protestant truths as understood by the Welsh chapels (Morgan, 1909).

12 Since writing this, Rowan Williams is now Archbishop of Canterbury designate, with Bishop Barry Morgan, an able cleric and communicator, likely to succeed him as Primate of Wales.

References

Anderson, Benedict 1991: *Imagined Communities*. London: Verso.

Aull Davies, Charlotte 1983: Welsh Nationalism and the British State. In Glyn Williams (ed.), *Crisis of Economy and Ideology: Essays on Welsh Society, 1840–1980*. Bangor: BSA Sociology of Wales Study Group, pp.201–13.

Barthes, Roland 1973: *Mythologies*. London: Paladin.

Calhoun, Craig 1997: *Nationalism*. Buckingham: Open University Press.

Casanova, José 1994: *Public Religions in the Modern World*. Chicago: University of Chicago Press.

Chambers, Paul 1999: Factors in Church Growth and Decline. PhD thesis, University of Wales.

Childs, Derrick G. 1962: The Age of the Reformation. In Edward T. Davies (ed.), *The Story of the Church in Glamorgan*. London: SPCK, pp.49–66.

Davie, Grace 1994: *Religion in Britain Since 1945*. Oxford: Blackwell.

Davies, Edward T. 1981: *Religion and Society in the Nineteenth Century*. Llandybie: Christopher Davies.

Davies, Oliver 1996: *Celtic Christianity in Early Medieval Wales*. Cardiff: University of Wales Press.

Durkheim, Emile 1995: *The Elementary Forms of the Religious Life*. New York: Free Press.

Engels, Frederick 1969: Preface to the Peasant War in Germany. In Karl Marx and Frederick Engels, *Selected Works Vol. 2*. Moscow: Progress Publishers, pp.158–65.

Evans, R. Paul 1988: Mythology and Tradition. In Trevor Herbert and Gareth Elwyn Jones (eds), *The Remaking of Wales in the Eighteenth Century*. Cardiff: University of Wales Press, pp.149–73.

Gallacher, John 1997: *Challenge to Change: The Results of the 1995 Welsh Churches Survey*. Swindon: British & Foreign Bible Society.

Gellner, Ernest 1983: *Nations and Nationalism*. Oxford: Blackwell.

Gramsci, Antonio 1971: *Selections From the Prison Notebooks*. London: Lawrence & Wishart.

Hall, Stuart 1976: Subculture, Culture and Class. In Stuart Hall, John Clarke, Tony Jefferson and Brian Roberts (eds), *Resistance Through Rituals*. London: Hutchinson, pp.9–74.

Hall, Stuart 1977: Culture, the Media and the 'Ideological Effect'. In James Curran, Michael Gurevitch and Janet Woolacott (eds), *Mass Communication and Society*. London: Edward Arnold, pp.315–48.

Hall, Stuart 1985: Religious Ideologies and Social Movements in Jamaica. In Robert Bocock and Kenneth Thompson (eds), *Religion and Ideology*. Manchester: Manchester University Press, pp.269–96.

Harris, Chris C. 1990: Religion. In Richard Jenkins and Arwel Edwards (eds), *One Step Forward? *Llandysul: Gomer Press, pp.49–59.

Hill, Christopher 1964: *Society and Puritanism in Pre-Revolutionary England*. Harmondsworth: Penguin.

Jenkins, Geraint H. 1978: *Literature, Religion and Society in Wales*. Cardiff: University of Wales Press.

Jenkins, Geraint H. 1988: The New Enthusiasts. In Trevor Herbert and Gareth Elwyn Jones (eds), *The Remaking of Wales*. Cardiff: University of Wales Press, pp.43–76.

Jones, Brian P. (ed.) 1995: *Voices From The Welsh Revival: An Anthology of Testimonies, Reports and Eyewitness Statements From Wales' Year of Blessing, 1904–5*. Bridgend: Evangelical Press of Wales.

Jones, Emrys 1960: Tregaron: The Sociology of a Market Town in Central Cardiganshire. In Elwyn Davies and Alwyn D. Rees (eds), *Welsh Rural Communities*. Cardiff: University of Wales Press, pp.67–117.

Jones, G. 1998: *A Pocket Guide to the History of Wales*. Cardiff: Western Mail/University of Wales Press.

Kung, Hans 1995: *Christianity: The Religious Situation Of Our Time*. London: SCM.

Lambert, William R. 1988: Some Working Class Attitudes Towards Organised Religion in Nineteenth Century Wales. In Gerald Parsons (ed.), *Religion in Victorian Britain. Vol IV, Interpretations*. Manchester: Manchester University Press, pp.96–114.

Macmillan, John D. (ed.) 1989: *Restoration in the Church: Reports of Revivals 1625–1839*. Belfast: Ambassador.

Marx, Karl 1969: Genesis of the Capitalist Farmer. In Karl Marx and Frederick Engels, *Selected Works Vol. 2*. Moscow: Progress Publishers, pp.126–7.

McCrone, David 1998: *The Sociology of Nationalism*. London: Routledge.

Mehl, Roger 1970: *The Sociology of Protestantism*. London: SCM.

Morgan, J.Vyrnwy 1909: *The Welsh Religious Revival 1904–5: A Retrospect and Criticism*. London: Chapman Hall.

Owen, Trefor M. 1960: Chapel and Community in Glan-Llyn, Merioneth. In Elwyn Davies and Alwyn D. Rees (eds), *Welsh Rural Communities*. Cardiff: University of Wales Press, pp.185–248.

Philips, D.M. 1923: *Evan Roberts: The Great Welsh Revivalist and His Work*. London: Marshall.

Robbins, Keith 1994: Religion and Community in Scotland and Wales since 1800. In Sheridan Gilley and William J. Sheils (eds), *A History of Religion in Britain*. Oxford: Blackwell, pp.363–80.

Robertson, Roland 1992: *Globalization: Social Theory and Global Culture*. London: Sage.

Rosser, Colin and Harris, Christopher C. 1965: *The Family and Social Change: A Study of Family and Kinship in a South Wales Town*. London: Routledge.

Saunders, Erasmus 1949: *A View of the State of Religion in the Diocese of St David's*. Cardiff: University of Wales Press.

Smith, Dai 1999: *Wales: A Question for History*. Bridgend: Seren.

Thomas, Keith 1971: *Religion and the Decline of Magic*. Harmondsworth: Penguin.

Thompson, Andrew 1999: Nation, Identity and Social Theory. In Ralph Fevre and Andrew Thompson (eds), *Nation, Identity and Social Theory – Perspectives from Wales*. Cardiff: University of Wales Press.

Thompson, Andrew and Day, Graham 1999: Situating Welshness: 'Local' Experience and National Identity. In Ralph Fevre and Andrew Thompson (eds), *Nation, Identity and Social Theory Perspectives From Wales*. Cardiff: University of Wales Press, pp.27–47.

Welsby, Catherine 1995: 'Warning Her as to Her Future Behaviour': The Lives of the Widows of the Senghenydd Mining Disaster of 1913. *Llafur: Journal of Welsh Labour History*, 6 (4), pp.93–109.

Williams, Glanmor 1991: *The Welsh and Their Religion*. Cardiff: University of Wales Press.

Williams, Glanmor 1994: Medieval Wales and the Reformation. In Sheridan Gilley and William J. Sheils (eds), *A History of Religion in Britain*. Oxford: Blackwell, pp.77–98.

Williams, Glyn 1983: On Class and Status Groups in Welsh Rural Society. In Glyn Williams (ed.), *Crisis of Economy and Ideology: Essays on Welsh Society, 1840–1980*. Bangor: BSA Sociology of Wales Study Group, pp.134–49.

Williams, Gwyn Alf 1985: *When Was Wales?* Harmondsworth: Penguin.

Williams, Gwyn Alf 1988: Beginnings of Radicalism. In Trevor Herbert and Gareth Elwyn Jones (eds), *The Remaking of Wales in the Eighteenth Century*. Cardiff: University of Wales Press.

CHAPTER 7

Social Networks and Personal Beliefs: An Example from Modern Britain

Rob Hirst

This chapter will consider the effects of modernization on personal religious beliefs from a social network perspective. It will briefly explain social network analysis, explore a network theory of religion, examine recent empirical data and finally attempt to predict the likely state of religion in Britain in 50 years' time in the light of this discussion.

Social Network Analysis

The social anthropologist John Barnes (1954) was the first to examine informal social relationships using the concept of a 'net'. His idea was that the lines of the net represent individual relationships whilst the points where the lines intersect (the nodes) represent the individuals involved. Barnes realized that these network connections hold social life together and help to explain it. For several reasons, this approach to analysing personal relationships soon captured the imagination of sociologists. Network analysis facilitates the detailed examination of network connections through the 'mapping' of relationships. The approach also enables sociologists to move away from traditional notions of 'community' because social connections are clearly no longer restricted to a particular locality. More sophisticated analyses of community are thereby made possible.

Recent theorists such as John Law (1991; 1992) have argued that social networks ought to be the *starting point* of an analysis of social life:

> It is important not to start out *assuming* whatever we wish to explain ... Instead, we should start with a clean slate. For instance, we might start with interaction and assume that interaction is all that there is. Then we might ask how some kinds of interactions more or less succeed in stabilizing and reproducing themselves: how it is that they overcome resistance and seem to become 'macrosocial'; how it is that they seem to generate the effects such as power, fame, size, scope or organisation with which we are all familiar. (Law, 1992, p.380)

Claude Fischer (1982) mirrors this emphasis: 'We cannot exaggerate, however, the overall importance of networks. It is through personal connections that society is structured and the individual integrated into society' (p.3). Social network analysis is therefore fundamental to gaining a clearer understanding of social life, and can help to explain a range of other social phenomena, including present-day religion.

The Effects of Modernization

If the effects of modernization are examined from a social network perspective it is clear that certain changes have occurred in the structures of personal network relationships between pre-modern and modern societies. There is, however, an immediate danger of oversimplifying these differences. The few sociologists who have specialized in the study of kinship and friendship relationships are right to be cautious about using sweeping generalizations concerning differences between pre-modern and modern societies. Graham Allan (1996) argues that the history of personal relationships is essentially unknowable in sociological terms, for lack of appropriate data. And a number of studies have been carried out which question some of the assumptions of Ferdinand Tonnies' *Gemeinschaft* and *Gesellschaft* model, which postulates a transition from a pre-modern communal society to a modern associational society (Bottomore and Nisbet, 1979). For example, it has been demonstrated that it is simply not true that in urban societies people have fewer ties with one another.

Bearing these points in mind, there are certain differences which *can* be identified with reference to historical evidence. It is clear, for example, that personal relationships are now less localized and have tended to become more geographically dispersed. Significant changes have also occurred to the links between the general population and the Christian Church in England over the past few centuries. In the context of modernity the Christian Church is no longer directly integrated with the majority of the surrounding population, and controls over church attendance have been lost. This is not to suggest there was a religious 'Golden Age' but merely that, in the past, there was a higher likelihood people would have had some sort of network connection with the Church or with church attenders. Even as late as 1851, the first religious census completed in that year revealed that out of a total population of 15 million living in England and Wales, two-thirds still attended church on a regular basis (Thomas, 1988, pp.19–20). So links between church attenders and non-church attenders were still prolific and the chances of not having religious others in one's immediate social network were minimal.

Nevertheless, during the 18th and 19th centuries the Church of England's parish structure was unable to cope with the migration of the population from the countryside to the towns and cities. The Roman Catholic Church likewise struggled to cope with the influx of starving Irish migrants from famine (Beck, 1950). Owing to the process of differentiation, the Church was also unable to retain control over several key areas of social life. These factors have been highlighted by theorists such as Peter Berger (1969) and Bryan Wilson (1982). The emphasis of Wilson's thesis is clearly placed on a loss of community – and thereby a concomitant loss of a collective, single, overarching world view held by the members of such communities – rather than on the damage incurred by personal network links with religious organizations.

In the light of the work of theorists such as Berger and Wilson, one might well ask if the argument about population migration and redistribution already pre-empts my own thesis concerning the effects of personal network relationships. The answer to that question is a resounding 'no'. The Wilsonian approach implies that a collective overarching religious world view is heavily dependent upon the existence of small communities, whereas my own thesis argues that overarching religious world views may be held and maintained by the members of *discrete networks* which need not be local. James Beckford (1989) shares a similar reservation about the Wilsonian view of a necessary connection between religion and community when he states: 'In my view, the connection between religion, obligatory beliefs and community may be an historical contingency ... there is no *necessary* connection between religion and local community' (p.110).

The decline of religious belief is therefore not inevitable just because the majority of people now live in huge conurbations. If *network links* exist, or become established, between religious individuals and other types of individuals, traditional religious beliefs, or any other types of religious belief, at the very least, have an *opportunity* to flourish. It is the damage which has been incurred by network links with church attenders which has arguably been a major cause of the undermining of traditional religious beliefs in Britain. A lack of exposure of the majority of the population to traditional religious networks in the private sphere may well help to account for the decline in *traditional* religious beliefs and practice.

Empirical Evidence

The empirical data obtained from a quantitative 500 questionnaire survey of a middle class suburb in the south of England, followed by 39 qualitative semi-structured interviews with selected respondents, provided strong evidence in support of a network dependency hypothesis derived from this social network theory of religion (Hirst, 1999). The hypothesis stated that personal social networks are intrinsically associated with the content and expression of each individual's system of religious belief or unbelief, and form the primary social arena wherein religious belief or unbelief is formulated, maintained, modified and transmitted. In order to test this hypothesis, in addition to a survey question on religious upbringing the 39 selected informants were asked very detailed and extensive questions about their former and current social networks, together with in-depth questions about their beliefs and about the beliefs held by those within their social networks.

In terms of the key findings of the research, it is clearly evident that the people with whom each informant interacted during early life had a profound effect upon what the informants believed in later life (that is, either religious or secular belief).

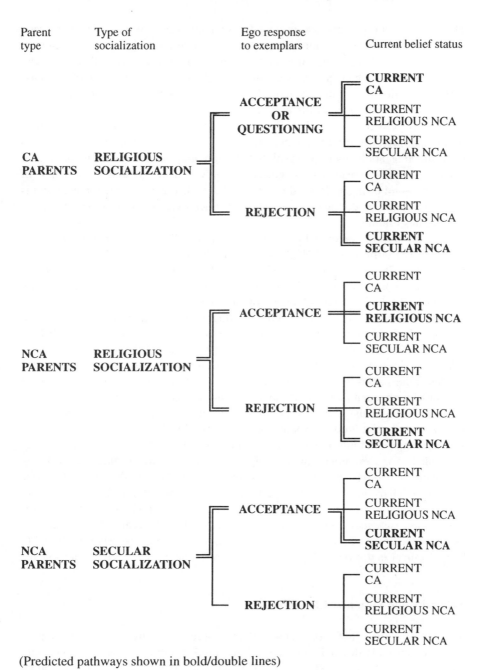

(Predicted pathways shown in bold/double lines)

Figure 7.1 Pathways to current religious or secular beliefs

This socialization process also provided a foundation for the type of persons each informant was prepared to admit into his or her social network in later life. In their current social networks the informants tended to associate only with others who shared like-minded beliefs. If they did *not* share like-minded beliefs, the informants' colleagues, friends, neighbours and relatives were kept at a greater social distance from them. Moreover, with the exception of religious converts, the beliefs of the informants formed during early childhood and adolescence tended to be maintained throughout life. The informants demonstrated a need to maintain a consistency in their thinking about their personal beliefs and they tended to avoid people or situations which threatened to undermine or to challenge that consistency of thought. Leon Festinger (1985) describes and demonstrates this phenomenon in his theory of cognitive dissonance, and there is much evidence from other studies to support this finding.

Figure 7.1 shows predicted pathways to current beliefs based upon the research findings. The terms CA and NCA denote church attender and non-church attender respectively. The term 'ego' refers to any individual at the centre of a social network. So 'ego response to exemplars' refers to the way in which an individual generally reacted to the beliefs and behaviour of the members within his or her personal network. Predicted pathways are shown in double lines. The figure shows that the current beliefs of an individual were not necessarily a reflection of the beliefs held by the parents but were determined more by whether those beliefs were accepted or rejected. This reaction then tended to be carried over into adulthood. The bottom of the figure does show, however, a direct association between the secular beliefs held by non-church attending parents and the current secular beliefs of non-church attending individuals. This was due to the fact that a secular socialization process was *invariably* met with a response of acceptance by these particular informants. Also the majority of informants whose primary socialization was religious generally responded to the exemplars of the religious individuals within their networks by accepting their religious belief systems. One final finding is that the social base through which the informants' beliefs were maintained was not the local community and surprisingly it was not the local church either. Church attenders' relationships with church attenders outside their own church had a greater bearing on the maintenance of their beliefs. So, to summarize, most people's beliefs were found to be maintained in discrete, geographically dispersed networks in the private sphere.

Networks and Organized Religion

So how have these network factors affected organized religion? It is no longer virtually inevitable that individuals will have a link either to a local church or with others who attend a church. The only likely way, therefore, that a non-church attender will be influenced by the beliefs of organized religion is through some kind of network connection, either with church attenders or with those involved in some other form of organized religion. Likewise, my research shows that this principle applies to church attenders in the sense that it is highly likely that they will have had some form of network connection with other church attenders at some time during their past experience. Conversely, if network connections with church attenders are absent and individuals only have network connections with people who have no religious beliefs, it is almost inevitable that such individuals will not develop religious beliefs themselves. And even when contact *is* established between church attenders and non-church attenders, the situation is exacerbated by certain aspects of our culture, which will be outlined in a moment, which inhibit the transmission of religious belief.

Most of the informants were engaged in maintaining an established response to primary socialization, hence no further belief changes or modifications generally took place in their lives. In *all* cases, the overall orientation of the informants was either in a permanently religious or a permanently secular direction. This even applied to the religious converts in the sample. The religious converts generally questioned the religious beliefs of people in their earlier networks until these beliefs were consolidated at a later date. This consolidation or 'conversion' usually took place through interaction with religious individuals who managed to penetrate the social networks of the potential converts. These religious individuals who were able to reach the informants may be described as 'effective agents'. Effective agents were characterized by a high level of relational proximity to each informant. In other words, they were people who tended to have been known by the informants for some time; they tended to be in frequent contact with the informants, usually face-to-face; they tended to be of equal status; and they had much in common with the informants. Effective agents were also characterized by a consistency of life style and beliefs; an ability to establish trust and respect in relationships; and the willingness to allow each of the informants to take the initiative in conversations about religious belief.

But for the majority of informants, the following factors greatly inhibited any transmission of religious belief from taking place.

1 Religious individuals within the informants' networks often inadvertently reinforced the secular beliefs held by the informants through hypocrisy, dogmatism and/or excessive force when communicating their religious beliefs.
2 The informants had a tendency to restrict access to their close social networks of individuals holding different beliefs.
3 Discussion of religion tended to be avoided, particularly by non-church attenders, owing to its sensitivity as a topic of conversation in modern Britain. Avoidance of religious discussion often functioned as a means to avoid conflict in relationships if the beliefs in question were not shared between the two parties involved.
4 The social and geographical mobility of some of the informants had a detrimental effect on their religious practice, with housing moves resulting in the

termination of church attendance and thereby the termination of any further transmission of church religion.

All of these factors greatly inhibit the transmission of church religion in the context of modernity.

Networks and Marginal Religion

But how have these network factors affected personal religious beliefs outside organized religion? My study revealed little evidence that traditional religion is being replaced by New Age beliefs, apart from some rather vague notions of spirituality or yogic beliefs held by a few of the informants. The interview stage of the research, with 39 informants, revealed that a third of the 30 non-church attenders held religious beliefs which were customary or traditional. Customary beliefs are those characterized by conventionality. They are derived from official religion but are not subject to continued control by the churches. These beliefs are subject to trivialization, apathy, convenience and self-interest (Hornsby-Smith *et al.*, 1985). A further six informants from the 30 non-church attenders were categorized as 'active customary' since their beliefs were similarly derived from official religion. But these informants tended to be actively and regularly engaged in prayer, Bible study and religious discussions with others, even though they were non-church attenders. But why were these people non-church attenders, particularly when some of them professed to hold strong religious beliefs? As with the church attenders in the sample, these non-church attenders were likewise brought up religiously. But there were four major differences between the church attenders and the religious non-church attenders. With regard to the church attenders: (a) their parents generally considered church attendance to be essential; (b) these informants were immersed in the life of the church at an early age; (c) they attended church on a voluntary basis; and (d) they had positive church-attending role models who espoused traditional religious beliefs requiring commitment to the Church. None of these factors tended to characterize the religious non-church attenders. Most of their role models emphasized the importance of a Christian way of life in preference to church attendance, and these role models often drew attention to the hypocritical life styles of church attenders. The pattern mentioned earlier, of primary socialization followed by belief maintenance in later life, seems to be very evident here, and it extends to religious practice as well as belief.

Implications of Social Network Theory

So, in conclusion, what are the implications of my social network theory for the future of religion in Britain? The Christian Church in Britain certainly has an established place in society based upon many years of tradition: in fact, centuries of tradition in terms of the Roman Catholic Church and the Church of England. People often turn to the church in times of trouble and crisis. For many, it is still a focus of celebration for key festivals throughout the year and, again, for many the church still provides rites of passage at birth, marriage and death. Owing to these factors alone, the church is unlikely to suffer an excessively rapid erosion. But it would be foolish not to acknowledge that it does face the danger of a slow, continuous overall decline in Britain unless it does something to encourage growth amongst its ranks. Church growth is arguably the most pressing requirement that the church faces today. It is not sufficient to rely on the recruitment of the children of existing members of the church. Decline is virtually inevitable unless an effective strategy of evangelism can be devised. That strategy must include creating personal relationships between the church and those who are outside it. Modern methods of communication through the media might be regarded as an opportunity for church growth, but studies have shown that the media are vastly overrated in that respect. Moreover, none of the converts from my own study became involved with the church through the media. They only used religious media to support their beliefs after they became converts. It appears that, unless the church pays attention to the social network factors outlined in this chapter and abandons its tendency to be inward-looking, gradual overall decline is inevitable.

Given these observations, I will now throw all caution to the wind and make a couple of simplistic predictions based upon the overall figures for active church membership in Britain since 1975. These figures show the following decline in the percentage of the adult population claiming active membership: 1975, 18.5 per cent; 1980, 16.8 per cent; 1985, 15.6 per cent; 1990, 14.9 per cent; 1992, 14.4 per cent (Davie, 1994, p.46). I would predict that by the year 2050 only 3 to 5 per cent of the total population of Britain will be active church members. This allows for an average decline of 1 per cent every five years. Admittedly this is a very pessimistic view, but it is nevertheless likely, based upon current overall rates of decline.

As for the future of personal religious belief outside organized religion, given my findings about the customary or traditional nature of religious belief held by those outside organized religion, religious belief among members of the general population is equally under threat. It hangs on the precarious thread of the necessary religious socialization of the offspring of these non-church attenders. Unless the Church becomes involved in that socialization process, religious belief is likely to decline among non-church attenders. After all, the church generally had some original involvement in the socialization of religious non-church attenders in my sample of informants. It is not possible to quantify this decline since we do not have sufficient data concerning the current (and past) state of belief without belonging, but my research findings suggest that religious belief outside organized religion is likely to diminish unless the Church begins to forge network links with the unchurched, particularly among the young.

References

Allan, Graham 1996: *Kinship and Friendship in Modern Britain*. Oxford: Oxford University Press.

Barnes, John 1954: Class and Committees in a Norwegian Island Parish. *Human Relations*, 7, pp.39–58.

Beck, George Andrew (ed.) 1950: *The English Catholics: 1850–1950*. London: Burns and Oates.

Beckford, James 1989: *Religion and Advanced Industrial Society*. London: Unwin Hyman.

Berger, Peter 1963: *Invitation to Sociology*. Harmondsworth: Penguin.

Berger, Peter 1969: *The Social Reality of Religion*. London: Faber & Faber. (Formerly published under the title of *The Sacred Canopy*.)

Bottomore, Tom and Nisbet, Robert (eds) 1979: *A History of Sociological Analysis*. London: Heinemann Educational.

Davie, Grace 1994: *Religion in Britain Since 1945*. Oxford: Blackwell.

Festinger, Leon 1985: *A Theory of Cognitive Dissonance*. California: Stanford University Press.

Fischer, Claude 1982: *To Dwell Among Friends*. Chicago: University of Chicago Press.

Hirst, Robert 1999: 'The Network Dependency of Religious and Secular Belief', University of Surrey (unpublished PhD thesis).

Hornsby-Smith, Michael, Lee, Raymond and Reilly, Peter 1985: Common Religion and Customary Religion: A Critique and a Proposal. *Review of Religious Research*, 26 (3), pp.244–52.

Law, John (ed.) 1991: *A Sociology of Monsters: Essays on Power, Technology and Domination*. London: Routledge.

Law, John 1992: *Notes on the Theory of the Actor-Network: Ordering, Strategy and Heterogeneity*. London: Plenum Publishing.

Thomas, Terence (ed.) 1988: *The British: Their Religious Beliefs and Practices, 1800–1986*. London: Routledge.

Wilson, Bryan 1982: *Religion in Sociological Perspective*. Oxford: Oxford University Press.

CHAPTER 8

A Place at High Table? Assessing the Future of Charismatic Christianity

Martyn Percy

Some time during January 1936, the Pentecostal preacher and revivalist Smith Wigglesworth, from Bradford, Yorkshire, spoke to a young man named David Du Plessis, a fellow Pentecostal minister from the USA. According to Peter Hocken (1986), Du Plessis immediately knew that the words spoken to him were a 'prophecy':

> There is a revival coming that at present the world knows nothing about. It will come through the churches. It will come in a fresh way. When you see what God does in this revival you will then have to admit that all you have seen previously is a mere nothing in comparison to what is to come. It will eclipse anything that has been known in history. Empty churches, empty cathedrals, will be packed again with worshippers. Buildings will not be able to accommodate the multitudes. Then you will see fields of people worshipping and praising together ... the Lord will use you if you remain faithful and humble – you will see the greatest events in Church history. (Hocken, 1986, p.19)

Startling prophecies about the impact of revival are not new. Indeed, the latter half of the 20th century may be said, in some sense, to have borne out the predictions and prophecies of Pentecostals, Revivalists and Charismatics, who have seen their numbers steadily rise on a global scale. Estimates of numbers vary, but, taken as a whole, the number of Christians *influenced* by charismatic renewal, Pentecostalism or its variants (which is not to say that being influenced by these movements means that individuals identify themselves as being inside or part of any one movement) may run to some 400 million people or more, which is something like 20 per cent of the world's Christian population. Charismatic Christianity has touched every part of the world and has significantly affected virtually every Christian denomination, as well as spawning its own seminaries, churches and exponents.

Broader than Pentecostalism, Charismatic Christianity has spread to the 'mainline churches' and the 'middle-class churches', and is allegedly 'flourishing in the contemporary world ... a fluid culture that is seeping into numerous social contexts' (Coleman, 2000, pp.22, 49). Whereas Pentecostalism is a distinctive culture with a recognizable ecclesiology and doctrines (for example, affirming the necessity of a 'second baptism' of the Holy Spirit, which may lead to a phenomenon such as the individual speaking in tongues), Charismatic Renewal is more of a hybrid. It takes insights from revivals of previous eras, stresses the Pentecostal theme of empowerment through the Holy Spirit, but at the same time tends to influence and feed off mainstream denominations rather than creating its own.

Assessing the relative strength of Charismatic Christianity – and thereby testing the veracity of the prophecy – is a complex business. For example, do Roman Catholics or Anglicans, influenced by the teaching and ministry of recent exponents of revivalism such as John Wimber, count as 'charismatic'? Some may, but many choose to remain within their own denomination, and relate to an influential movement rather than joining it. Equally, Restorationists may not see themselves as 'renewing' churches in the sense that Du Plessis meant, but rather as a movement – not a church or new denomination – that is restoring God's kingdom and power in 'the last days' (Walker, 1985; 1998). Then there are the Pentecostals themselves, an established denomination (or rather federation of denominations, bound together by their cultural morphology rather than any formal concordat) that is committed to maintaining and proclaiming the immanence of God, the gifts of the Spirit and the continuity of the miraculous.

To speak of Charismatic Christianity is to deploy an umbrella term that covers many different churches, movements, theologies, expressions of belief and modes of behaviour. It is impossible to generalize. For example, not all Charismatics speak in tongues. For some, if not many, this is a Pentecostal distinctive, as is the theology and epiphenomenon of 'baptism in the Spirit'. Some Charismatics believe that the spiritual renewal they strive for will be reified in the churches; others, that it can only be truly manifested in movements that are beyond any recognized type of ecclesial structure. Some stress spiritual warfare – combating demons, principalities and powers – whilst others stress physical or 'inner' healing. For still others, the combination of a conservative theological outlook and a strong emphasis on the immediacy of spiritual encounter, provides a powerful type of belief: 'fundamentalistic ... not just a noetic phenomenon, but also a way of being in the world' (Coleman, 2000, p.27; Percy, 1998, pp.62–6). For many, the major characteristic of Charismatic Christianity is its exuberant and dynamic worship, with many new songs written, a number of which have been adopted by historic denominations. It is now almost impossible to purchase a hymnal of any kind that does not contain several 'choruses': short, pithy and affective worship songs tend to be more expressive of sentiment to or from God than they are didactic.

Surveying the achievements of Charismatic Christianity over the last 50 years can leave the onlooker feeling a little breathless. The movement seems to have swept all before it. For many Charismatics, it seems that the mighty river of God's revival is flowing, and it looks to be unstoppable. But rivers have to flow somewhere, and indeed, they also have to be fed – by streams. And this simple observation, albeit based on a metaphor, raises some interesting questions. Are all the tributaries that have fed Charismatic Christianity sustainable as sources? And what of the river itself? Is it still flowing thick and fast, or has it now spread out so much into the wide compass of the denominationalist delta that its once intense and concentrated power has given way to an extensive but dissipated influence?

The signs point in somewhat different directions. We have already alluded to the phenomenal achievement of Charismatic Christianity in the 20th century, and there is every reason to suppose that it will make a major contribution to Christian formation in the 21st. In the past 20 years, a number of academic studies have been positively smitten by Charismatic Christianity and its potential prospects (Cox, 1994; Hummel, 1975; Martin and Mullen, 1984; Tugwell *et al.*, 1976). However, charismatic Christianity is, for many people, also becoming a *less* intense form of religion, a resource 'pool' to dip into, if you will, rather than a river that carries one in a particular direction. In a pluralist and post-modern world, believers increasingly behave like consumers; they *relate* to practices and doctrines, without necessarily believing in them entirely, or pursuing them wholesale. The initial experience of the 'rush' of the rivers of revival, so apparent in the post-war years, appears to have given way to a markedly calmer flow.

There may be many reasons for this. Cognitive dissonance – the psychological disassociation that occurs amongst believers when prophecies are not fulfilled (Festinger, 1956) – tends to make successive generations of believers more cautious and circumspect about extravagant claims. Put simply, Charismatic Christianity has significantly influenced the churches, and, to an extent, the world, but the early visions of Charismatic Christianity coming to dominate denominations have not come to be; the prophecies of worldwide revival have not yet come to pass. Equally, charisma itself, over time, becomes routinized. What begins as fresh, authentic, groundbreaking and novel – all legitimate descriptions of Charismatic phenomena – can soon become ritualized, replicated, domesticated and fossilized (Smith, 2000; Percy, 1998). The evidence for this can be seen in the leadership of Charismatic churches. To a large extent, churches and movements are being led by the same people who were leading 30 years ago. Potential younger leaders are either still waiting in the wings (but lack the actual charisma of the founder leaders) or have left to join other churches. For some within Charismatic Christianity, the recognition that charisma becomes routinized over time has driven them out of the movement and back to the mainstream denominational churches. For others, it has driven them out of Charismatic Christianity and into other movements, including those that are communitarian (such as The Nine O'clock Community in Sheffield), spiritually diverse and novel (such as the 'Toronto Blessing') or the post-institutional (for example, Post-Evangelicalism). (See Tomlinson, 1995.) As one leading figure within British Charismatic Christianity said to me recently,

> ... the sea is all rather flat at the moment ... I sense that people are rather bored with charismatic phenomenon, and a bit nervous of just jumping on to the next bandwagon, in case they get their fingers burned again. They've had Signs and Wonders, the Kansas City prophets, power evangelism, power healing, deliverance, the 'Toronto Blessing', and more besides ... But where has it taken us? I think that people are just tired. (Percy, private correspondence, July 2000)

Understanding the complexity of the situation in which Charismatic Christianity now finds itself is vital if some predictions are to be made about its future. What follows, then, are some remarks about the present that are suggestive of impending directions. In offering these reflections, I am largely confining my comments to Charismatic Renewal in Britain (rather than Restorationism or Pentecostalism), which represents an interesting case study of the way Charismatic Christianity has sought to distance itself from, yet also to embed itself within, existing ecclesial traditions, accommodating them and resisting them by turns: to be distinct, yet related (see Bridge and Phypers, 1982). (Much of what I have to say does not necessarily apply to the Americas, Africa or to East Asia.) In saying this, I acknowledge that there can be no doubt that the 'new wine' of Charismatic Christianity has had a powerful effect on the Church of England in recent decades (Gunstone, 1982). A once marginal movement has become mainstream. Charismatic Renewal now has its own seat at the 'High Table' of Anglican ecclesiological expression. To the terms 'high', 'low', 'middle', 'evangelical' and 'catholic', 'charismatic' can also now be added as a prefix.

Bearing these preliminary remarks in mind, the discussion in this chapter will proceed as follows. First, some general cautions will be noted, which give further shape both to the parameters of the discussion and to the conclusion. Second, the theological coherence of charismatic Christianity is discussed. Third, we note some sociological considerations, which lead, fourth, to some remarks on ecclesiology. A conclusion then follows.

A General Note of Caution

As we have already noted, statistics appear to show that Charismatic Christianity, as an ecclesiological expression, is the only 'growth' area in the firmament of Christian expression, and is therefore, somehow, 'the future' (see Brierley, 1994/5; 1998/9). Furthermore, the type of religion offered – tactile and immediate – is particularly and perfectly suited to a post-modern world, with its emphasis on fulfilment, healing, the individual and celebration. In contrast, some cautionary notes should be expressed on a number of fronts. These comments are based on general observations made about Britain. Again, it should be stressed that it is the future of Charismatic/Renewal Christianity that we shall be exploring, rather than Pentecostalism as such.

First, some commentators claim that the apparent growth rate of Charismatic Christianity is highly questionable. Peter Brierley's statistical work, which is largely sympathetic to Charismatic Christianity, cannot decide if there were 20 000 people in 'New Churches' in 1980 or more than 50 000; or 95 000 in the year 2000 – or as many as 198 000 (compare his *UK Christian Handbook* of 1994/5 (p.258) with that of 1998/9 (p.212)). Brierley's national estimates for members of the New Churches seem to grow with each new survey, even though most major national independent

Charismatic groups – such as Ichthus or Pioneer – report static or even declining numbers. Furthermore, the burgeoning Post-evangelical movement (which includes many 'ex-Charismatics') suggests that, whilst many have been influenced by Charismatic Christianity, just as many have left it. It may still be true that many continue to enter through the front door of revivalism (Tomlinson, 1995); but the rate of attrition *via* the back door is not being properly attended to. There is, in fact, a vast army of ex-Charismatics waiting to be interviewed (Walker, 1998, p.303).

Second, Charismatic Renewal remains a *movement* within the Church: it is rarely a viable type of ecclesiology in its own right. Evidence to support this thesis comes from the sharp decline in numbers attending independent 'house churches'. Charismatic renewal must be a 'renewal' not just of the individual, but also of tradition, liturgy, sacramental worship and the like. The 'movement' drives people either out of the Church and into 'Restorationism', or deeper into the Church itself (Walker, 1998, pp.348–67).

Third, charismatic renewal is subject to the normative Weberian constraints that apparently govern charisma, namely eventual routinization. New Wine, rather like New Labour, can only be 'new' for a while. Eventually it becomes part of the establishment; subversion gives way to maturity and participation (Walker, 1998, pp.310–15).

There are also other reasons to be cautious about the future of Charismatic Christianity. Instances of schism in charismatically influenced churches are often high. David Martin (1990), for example, has noted that Neo-Pentecostal churches in South America have mushroomed partly because they operate and franchise in the high streets like any other shop, competing for the 'commerce' of belief. This looks impressive and engaging, but as Lesslie Newbigin (1988) warns, we should not judge quality of belief through quantity of adherents: 'the multiplication of cells unrelated to the body is what we call cancer' (p.35). This may seem a harsh judgment, but the divisiveness of charismatic phenomena should not go unremarked. The cancerous analogy is also helpful in suggesting that, whatever growth is produced, it has frequently seemed to lack any purpose other than further growth and enthusiastic intensity.

One of the keys to understanding the past, present and future of Charismatic Christianity is to perceive its 'revivalist' identity. Revivals, of course, are no stranger to Christian history. Since the Reformation, there have been revivals of piety (17th century, Puritan), of holiness and its sociality (early 18th century, Methodist), of catholic ritualism (19th century, the Oxford Movement), of 'speaking in tongues' (20th century, *glossolalia* in Pentecostalism), of enthusiastic religion (late 19th century, Cane Ridge, Kentucky) and of Creation Spirituality (late 20th century, and allegedly resonant with Celtic Christianity). There is almost no time in Christian history which cannot lay claim to its own revival. Each of these revivals, although different phenomenologically, shares a common 'genetic code'. So what are revivals, why are they so often found breaking out in apparently ordinary, established churches, and how does this help us in assessing the future of charismatic Christianity?

First, they are all attempting to reach back to the past, to restore 'something' that is deemed to have been 'lost' by the church. Revivals seldom offer something that is entirely new: their credibility depends on it being shown that their practices and teachings are somehow part of the *original* Christian message. Second, revivals arise out of their own distinctive social and cultural genres. They are partly produced by, while also being reactions against, their own society, and are therefore necessarily relative; in effect, they are parasitic upon the culture they purport to reject. Third, revivals often occur during times of social upheaval. The end of an age, the passing of an era, or a particular calamity often produces religious fervour. In times of peace and security, a form of liberalism often thrives. But when, say, society moves *en masse* from an agrarian way of life to an urban one, revivalism can flourish (see Butler, 1990). Social uncertainty can make people flock to a rekindling of religious certainty, and the recovery of *communitas* for a church that is becoming lost in the world. And last, they stress the experience of revival as a key to self-knowledge. Revivalism is not taught but 'caught': in conferences and churches, the necessity of personal experience is brought home to believers in worship, teaching and ministry.

Modern Charismatic Christianity has been gestating within mainstream churches for almost 50 years. The main tributaries lie in Pentecostalism and Fundamentalism and, like all revivals, it seeks to exchange the perceived absence of God for a new sense of presence. Pentecostalism was an experiential response to modernity, in a similar way that fundamentalism was a sort of rational (or cognitive) response to the same. The movements began within a decade of each other, and were reactions against theological and moral liberalism, together with being drives towards embodying a form of religious clarity that could provide an alternative to the muddied waters of increasing pluralism and relativism. Both movements sired their own denominations, seminaries and schisms, as well as developing their own distinctive cultures.

After World War II, the skeleton of the Smith Wigglesworth prophecy started to take on some flesh of its own. Charismatic Christianity began to emerge as a movement that was deeply syncretic, born out of a peculiar alliance. Lapsed Fundamentalists were waking up to discover themselves as evangelicals, and those still in Pentecostalism were searching for new emphases on the immanent power of the Holy Spirit. The result was a new conflation that stressed revival. Rational religion and the certainty it brought was valuable: but many people wanted more than this – they wanted to *experience* something as well (Hopewell, 1987, pp.75–9). Faith was not just thinking about God, but feeling him too. This became the *sui generis* of modern Charismatic Christianity. Even those sympathetic to the movement agree that the drive for experience is a key to understanding its identity.

Theological Coherence

Here is an irony. In spite of the millions involved in modern Charismatic Christianity, there is very little that could be classed as 'charismatic theology'. Like Fundamentalism and Pentecostalism, the movement has spawned its own seminaries, notable preachers and exponents; but a theologian of national or global significance has yet to emerge. Charismatics tend to appeal to the work of theologians to feed their 'theological' outlook, without they themselves necessarily being paid-up revivalists. For example, just one work of James Dunn (1979) is widely read in almost all the Charismatic churches and fellowships that I know of, although Dunn himself remains a sanguine Scottish Presbyterian. The works of George Eldon Ladd, James Kallas and Walter Wink are also highly esteemed within the movement.

They are, nonetheless, scholars associated with the movement. Historians, such as Walter Hollenweger (1972) or Peter Hocken (1986) have written about charismatic thinking and praxis, but neither has constructed a 'charismatic theology'. Gifted scholars such as Simon Tugwell (1976) or David Watson (1965), who clearly can be identified as charismatic, have tended to produce popular 'testimony-teaching' type books, rather than serious works of scholarship that outline a theology. Similarly, Edward O'Connor (1975) and Heribert Muhlen (1978) have produced accessible theological appraisals that have attempted to mediate the Charismatic or Pentecostal tradition *to* denominations. Cardinal Suenens (1978; Suenens and Camara, 1979) has also attempted to show how Charismatic reflections can shape pastoral encounters or social action.

Such contributions, already slight in number, must be balanced by the obvious lack of theology in the mainstream of the Charismatic tradition. Indeed, in the moderately recent *A Dictionary of Pentecostal and Charismatic Movements*, there is no entry for 'Theology' at all (Burgess *et al.*, 1988). Naturally, this does not mean there are no 'doctrines' in Charismatic Christianity: ideas about the person and work of the Holy Spirit are critical to its identity. However, beyond this, there is unlikely to be a developed Christology, soteriology, doctrine of the church and the like.

This observation is important in addressing several questions. Why is it that there can be so much schism in Charismatic Christianity? Answer: there is no doctrine of the church, and no theological template for tolerating plurality. (All that can be said to exist is a notion of gathered homogeneity, which emphasizes size.) Why is evangelism so poor at recruitment, numerical growth usually coming from converting people who are already Christians? Answer: Charismatic Christianity has no soteriology of its own. Why does Charismatic Christianity apparently succeed so quickly where others have failed for so long before? Answer: there is no real Christology, creeds, sacramental or Trinitarian theology and praxis to burden believers with. Adherents are offered an immediate form of spiritual experience – a kind of bathetic sentience through which one encounters quasi-numinous phenomena. Faith is nurtured not through knowledge, but through a community of feeling in which one learns to appreciate power, charisma and non-order – yet often within an authoritative structure. The opposite of movement is stability; the latter is the enemy of Charismatic Christianity.

The observation that modern Charismatic Christianity has no real systematic theology, as such, is not meant to be patronizing. There are actually good reasons why this is the case. But let me say something about how the movement attempts to compensate for the void. First and foremost, it has a strong background in biblical fundamentalism. Whilst not everyone who would identify themselves as charismatic is a fundamentalist, most will be 'fundamentalistic' (Coleman, 2000, p.27). That is to say, they will use the Bible in a literalistic, pre-critical fashion, hold their beliefs in a similar way to classic fundamentalists (that is, intolerant of plurality and liberalism, prone to schism, monologue, and so on), and yet be looking for spiritual power that is linked to, but beyond, a tightly defined biblical authority. As one author puts it, revivalism offers 'an eschatologically justified, power-added experiential enhancement' (Hopewell, 1987, p.76; c.f., Poewe, 1994, pp.103ff).

Second, Charismatic Christianity purports to be, at least in part, a movement that has *distanced* itself from theology. Harvey Cox (1994) sees Charismatic Christianity as the major component in an 'experientialist' movement, that is tired of the arid, overrational religion of modernity that was split between liberals and conservatives. Charismatic renewal is often a self-conscious religion of experience and feeling, that deliberately pitches itself against too much 'thinking' about God. Cox is at least partly right in his observation: whenever and wherever I have attended a revivalist gathering, believers are often encouraged to desist from rationalizing, to abandon critical faculties, and are instead to 'let God touch their heart'.

Third, the absence of a theological, doctrinal or ecclesiological basis makes Charismatic Christianity incredibly free in its reactions to and inculcation of contemporary culture. Indeed, social relevance is a trademark. Card-carrying Charismatics are not bogged down by centuries of tradition, nor do they have much of a past to justify or carry. Thus they tend to use any theologians or aspect of Christian history selectively, to resource their beliefs (Percy, 1996, pp.172ff), but at the same time eschew a depth of participation in theological, ecclesiological, historical or sociological processes for fear it will weigh them down. Charismatic Christianity is essentially a matter of the heart, and works best when it travels lightly.

A Sociological Comment

With these theological considerations in mind, it must be acknowledged that the best appraisals of charismatic Christianity are sociological. Here I think especially of Andrew Walker (1985; 1998), Meredith McGuire (1988), David Martin (1990) and Simon Coleman (2000), to name but a few. And another voice must be added to these, namely that of Danièle Hervieu-Léger. Hervieu-Léger shows how movements like Charismatic Christianity appeal to social elements for whom self-realization and personal accomplishment have particular resonance. In her *Religion as a Chain of Memory* (2000), she suggests that charismatic movements may be seen as a sign of protest against the establishment, and therefore parasitic upon it. Thus

> One could ask whether the search within these communities for non-verbal forms of emotive communication does not also express a protest against the stereotyped nature of approved religious language, something about the diminished quality of (articulate) religious language in modern culture. The place taken in these groups by the gift of tongues raises the question directly … tongues, defined by scholars as 'a phonologically structured human expression without meaning, which the speaker takes to be a real language but which in fact bears no resemblance to any language living or dead', is not a vehicle for communication but for expression. The content is of little importance: glossolalia finds its meanings not in what is said but in the very fact of speaking and responding, in this form, to an immediate experience of great emotional intensity. In the emotive response there is a general sensation of the presence of the divine, profound joy, and inward well-being which finds the means of expressing itself. (Hervieu-Léger, 2000, p.59)

This is undoubtedly an interesting observation, but it raises a more intriguing question. If these forms of emotive and spiritual expression were originally protests against the establishment and the status quo – as they were in Pentecostalism and its 19th century predecessors, such as the Irvingites – what happens to the identity of the movement that produces them when it too becomes part of the establishment? If the label 'Charismatic' now has a place at High Table with other respectable ecclesiastical prefixes, and can be part of a mainstream rather than a marginal spiritual diet, how will the movement fare? Certainly, much can be said about the capacity of the Charismatic Movement to influence the wider church. But surely, if the wider church has comparatively little difficulty in accepting that same movement, we are only a few steps away from taming and domesticating a body of belief that was once at odds with the mainstream. In other words, in the very act of influencing the wider church, Charismatic Christianity has run the (necessary) risk of self-expenditure. (Such a position is, of course, entirely consonant with the parables of Jesus, and indeed, his own self-understanding.) For this reason, Hervieu-Léger comments:

> At the same time it has been seen that the absorption of Utopia into religion in the form of dogmatic glaciation or of innovative routinization secretes its own antibodies, paradoxically by allowing the possibility of an alternative reading of the foundational stories retriggering the utopian dynamic of protest from within religion itself. From the radical movements of the Reformation to the efflorescence of leftism, there is no shortage of examples to illustrate the resurgence of Utopia, even when and to the extent that it loses strength by becoming institutionalized in a new religion. Such resurgence presents a religious character (or a religious feature) whenever it takes the form of radicalizing demands based on devotion to an inspirational source for which the religion it is opposed to claims to provide the only legitimate reading. In these dialectics of religious conflict, Utopia constitutes the third term, as essential as it is destined for annihilation. (Hervieu-Léger, 2000, p.148)

Destined for annihilation? Is that the fate awaiting Charismatic Christianity, as it finally sits down at High Table? In one sense, yes. It does begin to lose its cutting edge and its *raison d'être* if it moves from being a marginal counter-cultural movement to something more mainstream. And yet it has little alternative. Apart from the Church, and as a movement, it cannot survive as a complete culture without becoming a kind of spiritual ghetto. And as Tomlinson's (1995) study of post-evangelicals has already shown, Charismatic consumers will not be bound by doctrinal or ecclesial frontiers. The options appear to be, first, communion and participation within mainstream denominations, which risks dilution and annihilation, but at least guarantees a kind of extensive influence; or second, separatism, which might guarantee purity and power, but risks alienation, marginalization and ghettoization. Sociologically, we can say that Charismatic Christianity has largely chosen the former path; Restorationists in the more purist House Church Movement tradition have chosen the latter. At the risk of inverting a well-worn phrase of Jesus, it may be that the broad road leads to salvation, and the narrow path to annihilation.

Ecclesiological Issues

There are some problems that arise directly from these observations relating to the charismatic theology, together with the sociological observations we have been making. First, although some people claim Charismatic Christianity is an ecumenical, uniting movement, it tends to be anything but this. History shows that Charismatics tend to be highly divisive: each new revival within the movement brings fresh division and more schism. Modern Charismatic Revivalism has no history of uniting denominations, although it sometimes brings together federations of like-minded people. The reason that ecumenism and unity is difficult to achieve in revivalism lies in the subjective, individualistic nature of the religion.

Second, and linked to this point, the worship of modern Charismatic Christianity compounds the problem of persistent ecclesial fracture. Classic revival worship, under Wesley, Moody or Edwards, for example, had a tendency to use hymns as didactic material. In the case of Wesley, his theology was both taught in his hymns and sung by converts. The creeds, sacraments and traditions of the Church were caught up in 18th and 19th century rhythm: people were bound together by shared doctrines. Modern Charismatic Christianity, in contrast, attempts no such thing. It does not supplement sacraments, but replaces them: it is in worship that you meet God, not bread, wine, word or creeds. Furthermore, the function of worship is not didactic but emotive: it is a vehicle to move people closer to God, to 'release' them, to stir the heart. Consequently, most songs in modern revivalism are devoid of serious doctrinal content: they express feelings about or to God. This, of course, is no basis for theological or ecclesial unity – it just creates a 'community of feeling' which is always open to the ravages of subjective individualism (Percy, 1999).

Third, the fundamentalistic roots of Charismatic Christianity almost guarantee ecclesial problems. In such communities, it is never the Bible that rules, but always the interpreter (Boone, 1989). Consequently, some Charismatic churches can look quite totalitarian. Even here, though, there is a theological account for the lack of ecclesial breadth. Although Charismatics have done much to promote the Holy Spirit in recent years, there has been no move towards developing a Trinitarian doctrine that might offer an ecclesial basis for openness, mutuality and plural forms of sociality. Ironically, the stress on experience in Charismatic Christianity means that there is no 'coping stone' to keep orthodox views together. Schism occurs in the movement precisely because one person of the Godhead is invariably promoted or ignored over another. There is never any agreement over the basis for ecclesial authority. It is nearly always driven by charisma, authority, power and emotion, and therefore always open to a charismatic counter-coup.

Conclusion

The future for an enthusiastic Christian movement without a real theology is potentially troublesome. It has no way of preventing schism, lacks depth in discernment, colludes in social abrogation, and may well become a spent force in the new millennium. But a movement that stresses personal empowerment, intimacy and love, yet is 'doctrine-lite' (but still with all the fizz of New Wine), innovative and novel, may in the end turn out to be a highly popular credo for the third millennium. Many mainstream denominations, for the moment at least, seem content to supplement their diets with the spice of enthusiastic, paranormal and esoteric religion. As one Anglican charismatic vicar explained to me recently, they have not 'sold out' to the consuming fire of total revivalism, they have just been 'warmed in a gentle way' (Percy, private correspondence, May 1996, influenced, but not possessed. Passion and enthusiasm may be dish of the day, but it is not the only item on the menu.

For a Western world that is increasingly privatized and individualistic, a post-modern, enthusiastically driven religion may be the one that proves to be the most popular at the dawn of a new millennium: yet that is no guarantee of ultimate longevity. Charismatic Christianity is often a fashion-led, consumerist religion; full of fads – a populist, culturally relative and relevant phenomenon. We should learn to read the signs: the charismatic crazes of today are often destined to become tomorrow's footnote in the history of revivalism. In my view, the bright and beautiful plumage that once made up Charismatic Christianity is fading fast. A healthy and vibrant body of 'belief' with a once lustrous skin is now showing signs of age: wrinkles, worry-lines and some middle-age sagging have set-in. But perhaps growing up is not all bad? Ecclesial maturation and ultimately denominational inculcation may yet be the greatest achievement of British Charismatic Christianity. Yet some will resent this future, even though it was prophesied long ago:

On the train, I took an old *Restoration* magazine out of my briefcase. In it, he [Bryn Jones, a prominent House Church Movement 'Apostle'] sets out the yardstick to measure all new movements of the Spirit of God ... Let it determine its own future: 'The charismatic awakening that does not deal with the root of independence, individualism, sectarianism and denominationalism will be deficient as far as the heart of God and the need of our generation is concerned. It will inevitably follow the well-trodden path of decline back into the slough of spiritual paralysis and sectarian strife.' (Walker, 1985, p.296)

This, then, accords with my prophetic conclusion. So far as Charismatic Christianity is concerned, the party is largely over. The celebrations, the abundance and the optimism of the last quarter of the 20th century have reached their peak, and while people are still crowding in through the front door, plenty have already left through the back door too. The charisma that has driven the movement will be routinized, and the cognitive dissonance will ultimately settle on the corporate Charismatic psyche, ameliorating memories but also postponing (indefinitely) the realization of promises and prophecies for the future. Already 'fellowships' that boldly proclaimed in the 1970s that they were not a new denomination (Walker, 1985), but a restoration of God's kingdom, have quietly adopted the label 'new churches', and taken their small but significant place at the tables of ecumenical dialogue. The journey from being a *movement* (which was originally against structures, stability and settlement) to being a *church* (which knows its place, values its order and practices its rituals) is already well under way.

Yet this is not the end of the story. To indulge the 'High Table' metaphor, and extend the dietary analogy, the 'Charismatic Catering Corp.' will continue – it has earned its place alongside those other ecclesiastical prefixes, and will keep it. However, scholars and researchers will be watching the next 10 years with keen interest. In a post-modern climate, how will Charismatic Christianity maintain its market share within the ever-mutating Christian tradition? Is the growth that Charismatic Christianity has enjoyed in recent decades sustainable? Or has there been too much diversification and dissipation already? And what about identity – what exactly will keep Charismatic Christians together, once the tents of Spring Harvest and New Wine have been folded up and put away? In an increasingly post-institutional world, how will Charismatic Christianity, which once thought of itself as *the* future, cope with being just one option amongst many? Can you keep your customers without changing the menu? Will you lose clients if you do? Academics will be watching to see who and how many continue to be fed by Charismatic Christianity – individuals and denominations – and asking how else, if at all, those spiritual diets are supplemented. Perhaps most intriguingly of all, scholars will focus not only on what Charismatic Christianity delivers, but also on what it feeds to itself. *Caveat emptor*? Or suck it and see?

References

Boone, Kathleen 1989: *The Bible Tells Them So: The Discourse of Protestant Fundamentalism*. London: SCM.

Bridge, Donald and Phypers, David 1982: *More Than Tongues Can Tell: Reflections on Charismatic Renewal*. London: Hodder & Stoughton.

Brierley, Peter 1994/5; 1998/9: *The UK Christian Handbook*. London: Marc Europe.

Burgess, Stanley, McGee, Gary and Alexander, Patrick (eds) 1988: *A Dictionary of Pentecostal and Charismatic Movements*. Grand Rapids, Michigan: Zondervan.

Butler, John 1990: *Awash in a Sea of Faith: Christianizing the American People*. Cambridge, MA: Harvard University Press.

Coleman, Simon 2000: *The Globalisation of Charismatic Christianity*. Cambridge: Cambridge University Press.

Cox, Harvey 1994: *Fire From Heaven, Pentecostalism, Spirituality and the Reshaping of Religion in the Twenty-first Century*. New York: Addison-Wesley.

Dunn, James 1979: *Baptism in the Spirit: A Study of the Religious and Charismatic Experience of Jesus and the First Christians*. London: SCM.

Festinger, Leon 1956: *When Prophecy Fails*. New York: Harper & Row.

Gunstone, John 1982: *Pentecostal Anglicans*. London: Hodder & Stoughton.

Hervieu-Léger, Danièle 2000: *Religion as a Chain of Memory*. Oxford: Polity.

Hocken, Peter 1986: *Streams of Renewal: The Origins and Development of the Charismatic Movement in Britain*. Exeter: Paternoster.

Hollenweger, Walter 1972: *The Pentecostals*. London: SCM.

Hopewell, James 1987: *Congregation: Stories and Structures*. London: SCM.

Hummel, Charles 1975: *Fire in the Fireplace: Contemporary Charismatic Renewal*. London: Mowbray.

Martin, David 1990: *Tongues of Fire*. Oxford: Blackwell.

Martin, David and Mullen, Peter 1984: *Strange Gifts? A Guide to Charismatic Renewal*. Oxford: Blackwell.

McGuire, Meredith 1988: *Ritual Healing in Suburban America*. New Brunswick: Rutgers University Press.

Muhlen, Heribert 1978: *A Charismatic Theology*. London: Burns & Oates.

Newbigin, Lesslie 1988: On Being the Church for the World. In Giles Ecclestone (ed.), *The Parish Church?* London: Mowbray.

O'Connor, Edward 1975: *Perspectives on Charismatic Renewal*. Indianapolis, IN: University of Notre Dame Press.

Percy, Martyn 1996: *Words, Wonders and Power*. London: SPCK.

Percy, Martyn 1998: *Power and the Church: Ecclesiology in an Age of Transition*. London: Cassell.

Percy, Martyn 1999: Sweet Rapture: Sublimated Eroticism in Contemporary Charismatic Worship. In Jan Jobling (ed.), *Theology and the Body: Gender Text and Ideology*. Leominster: Gracewing/Fowler Wright.

Poewe, Karla (ed.) 1994: *Charismatic Christianity as a Global Culture*. New York: Columbia University Press.

Smith, Craig 2000: *The Quest for Charisma: Christianity and Persuasion*. Westport, CT: Praeger.

Suenens, Cardinal 1978: *Ecumenism and Charismatic Renewal: Theological and Pastoral Orientations*. London: Darton, Longman & Todd.

Suenens, Cardinal and Camara, Dom Helder 1979: *Charismatic Renewal and Social Action: A Dialogue*. London: Darton, Longman & Todd.

Tomlinson, David 1995: *The Post-Evangelical*. London: SPCK.

Tugwell, Simon, Hocken, Peter, Every, George and Mills, John 1976: *New Heaven? New Earth?* London: Darton, Longman & Todd.

Walker, Andrew 1985: *Restoring the Kingdom: The Radical Christianity of the House Church Movement.* London: Hodder & Stoughton.
Walker, Andrew 1998: *Restoring the Kingdom: The Radical Christianity of the House Church Movement.* Revised and Expanded edition. Guildford: Eagle Press.
Watson, David 1965: *Towards Tomorrow's Church.* London: Faber.

CHAPTER 9

The Decline of the Church in England as a Local Membership Organization: Predicting the Nature of Civil Society in 2050

Helen Cameron

Introduction

The number of people who are members of a local church in England is declining (Brierley, 2000). Much of the academic discussion of this fact has focused either on disputing the way in which the figures are calculated or on looking at what is happening to the role of religion in society. This chapter takes a different approach by focusing on membership as one way in which people voluntarily engage with society. It asks about the ways in which membership organizations in general are changing and looks at a theory of civil society that can be applied to them, including implications for local churches.

What is Happening to Church Membership?

My interest in this topic developed from my doctoral research into the social action of the local church. In that research, case studies were undertaken of five congregations in an English city that were providing small-scale welfare services to their neighbourhood. These included activities such as day centres, a supplementary school and an after-school club. Whilst some of these activities were led by paid staff, they mostly depended upon the unpaid efforts of church members for their operation.

Looking at the way the work of these churches was organized made me aware of gradual changes in the activism of church members and changes in the expectations associated with belonging to a local church (Cameron, 1998). Not only were the churches studied experiencing static or declining membership numbers, they were also finding it increasingly difficult to get the work of the church done. Local churches typically have clergy as their only full-time paid staff, so the unpaid time of their members is crucial (Harris, 1998). In one church which was studied, with 300 members, there were nearly 100 different roles and responsibilities that needed to be covered if all the activities of the church were to run smoothly.

My research uncovered a number of problems. Church officer posts were going unfilled when they became vacant. Some people were taking on several responsibilities just to make sure tasks were completed. Rotas were replacing regular postholders for some tasks; for example, people would take it in turns to teach in the Sunday School rather than do it every week. Older members were finding themselves unable to hand over responsibilities to a younger generation because younger people said they were too busy at work or with family life. Clergy reported spending increasing amounts of their time coaxing involvement from members and then stretching that involvement to cover the work that needed to be done. Members were more willing to undertake highly specific tasks on an occasional basis (such as making coffee after a service) rather than open-ended 'jobs' such as secretary or treasurer. These changes had been happening over two to three decades, but on reflection members could see significant differences. The expectations placed on members had also shifted subtly over the same period. The most obvious were expectations about attending worship, with older members recalling the time when attendance twice on a Sunday was the norm. Some felt that the expectation of weekly attendance was now breaking down. Younger members felt it was acceptable to attend church when it was convenient rather than as part of a weekly routine.

The Purpose and Structure of this Chapter

Exploring the literature on civil society, it became apparent that other traditional membership organizations are experiencing a decline in member activism (Knight and Stokes, 1996; Nichols and King, 1998). This increased my curiosity as to what was happening to membership as a social phenomenon. This chapter does not report empirical data but attempts to develop a framework for examining changes in membership by discussing Adalbert Evers' (1995) model of civil society. It is also an attempt to speculate about the future of the Church in England as a membership organization. In much of the discussion about the decline of the Church, there is an assumption that local churches and denominations will continue to describe and measure themselves primarily as membership organizations. While not challenging the view that church membership will continue to decline, I want to suggest some alternative scenarios. The disciplinary base of this chapter is primarily voluntary sector studies with a particular interest in associational organizations. The chapter seeks to contribute to the debate on Church decline by drawing on the wider debate about civil society.

Before outlining the structure of the chapter, a definition of membership organization is necessary. A local membership organization is a face-to-face group of people engaging in common activities in an unpaid, voluntary and public capacity. Members are likely to contribute money, time and participation in decision making but will decide for themselves the level of their involvement (Perrow, 1970). The term 'association' is widely used in the sociological literature (Knoke, 1990), although this term often includes the connotation that decisions are made democratically, and this is not true of all membership organizations. Some membership organizations have paid staff, but they are usually few in number and facilitate rather than substitute for the work of the members.

The purpose of this chapter then, is to explore the pressures on the institution of church membership and suggest possible future scenarios. It starts by looking at the evidence for decline in church membership and the explanations that have been offered. It then moves on to describe Evers' model of civil society and develop its implications for membership as a social phenomenon. On the basis of this discussion of the model some predictions are offered and conclusions drawn.

Explanations for Decline

Statistics on church membership and attendance are difficult to collect and compare. Different denominations use different definitions of membership and attendance and different methods of collecting data from local churches. However, there can be little doubt that church membership is in decline in the mainstream denominations. The most dramatic statistics issued in recent years were those from the Methodist Church who reported a 6.8 per cent decline in membership between 1992 and 1995 (reported in Richter and Francis, 1998). The prediction made is that, within 41 years, at the current annual rate of loss (2.47 per cent), the Methodist Church would have no members.

The latest overview of church attendance comes from the 1998 English Church Attendance Survey reported in Peter Brierley (2000). This reveals that Sunday church attendance has dropped by one million in the nine years from 1989 to 1998. As a proportion of the population in England, Sunday church attendance was 7.5 per cent in 1998.

Substantial empirical work on reasons why people leave the local church was undertaken by Philip Richter and Leslie Francis in 1997. They report (Richter and Francis, 1998) that the three most common reasons for leaving a local church are unfulfilled expectations, changes in life circumstances and loss of faith. Other authors have used historical statistics to analyse the reasons for decline. Steve Bruce (1995) sees decline as the outcome of a more pluralist society in which Christianity has moved from being a dominant influence in the public realm to being a matter of private choice. Robin Gill (1993) undertook a historical analysis of the provision of church buildings and concluded that the church building programmes of the 19th century resulted in over-provision of church buildings, creating the impression of half-empty and therefore failing churches. Grace Davie (1994) agrees that participation in organized Christianity has declined since 1945, but argues that a high proportion of the public still believe in God and express their spirituality in ways other than church attendance. Robert Putnam (2000), looking at US church attendance, sees decline as part of a wider decline in sociability and social engagement. There are some voices suggesting that church attendance has fragmented rather than declined, that is, similar numbers of people are attending, albeit less frequently. Brierley's (2000) figures do not bear this out, suggesting that only one-third of the decline in Sunday attendance is due to people attending less frequently.

My reading of the evidence is that church membership is in steady decline and that that decline will continue. However, alongside this we need to consider at what might happen to 'membership of' and 'attendance at' the local church as the key measures of church affiliation. Will the concept of membership itself fragment and how might denominations respond to this?

Evers' Model and its Implications

Having assessed the evidence for declining numbers of church members, this chapter now moves on to discuss Evers' model of civil society and develop its implications for the church as a local membership organization. Examples of the implications will be offered in order to develop predictions.

The purpose of Evers' (1995) article is to analyse the increasing delegation of welfare provision from the state to the voluntary sector during the 1980s and 1990s. In doing this, he proposes a four-sector model of society comprising the market, the state, the informal or family sector and the voluntary sector. He envisages the first three sectors being arranged like a triangle with the voluntary sector as a field lying between them (see Figure 9.1).

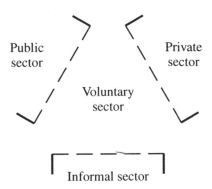

Figure 9.1

The voluntary sector experiences tensions and constraints depending upon the dominant ideologies in the other three sectors in any particular society. The voluntary sector is also capable of resisting these ideologies and undertaking innovation in a way that will have an impact on the mainstream of society. Evers sees the boundaries between the sectors as being permeable, with hybrid organizations that have the characteristics of more than one sector being possible. Voluntary sector organizations are seen as being able to combine economic, political and social rationales in ways that shape civil society.

This model bears resemblance to the work of David Billis (1993) whose own model of the voluntary sector is more concerned with organizational forms. He argues that the association is the typical organizational form of the voluntary sector, the bureaucracy the organizational form for the private and public sectors, and that the informal sector lies outside the world of formal organizations. Like Evers, he sees blurring between the sectors, with many voluntary organizations having both bureaucratic and associational characteristics. These he terms agencies (Figure 9.2). Billis' work is helpful in locating membership organizations in the voluntary sector and seeing them as subject to pressures and influences from other sectors.

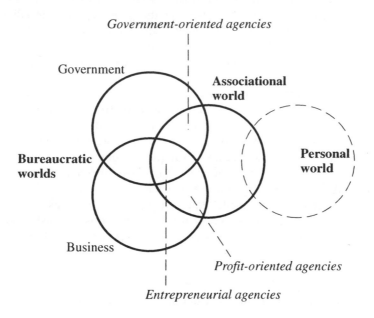

Figure 9.2

Evers sees the public space inhabited by voluntary organizations as subject to tensions from the market, the state and the informal sector. He gives examples of these tensions.

From the market, he sees tensions in those societies where the market is sufficiently dominant to be able to commodify activities previously undertaken on a voluntary basis. An example of this is the sport of football, which had its origins in the voluntary sector; indeed many clubs were started by churches (for example, Aston Villa). Now there is a highly commodified dimension to the game, which is seen as 'big business' and influences culture through the media and merchandise. Nevertheless, the popularity of the game rests on a mountain of voluntary effort.

From the state, Evers sees tensions in societies where the state is able to coopt some of the effort and legitimacy of the voluntary sector for its own ends. Evers points to the way in which in democratic Western countries the state has captured the energies of the sector to deliver state-funded welfare services. Given the universalistic and standardizing tendencies of the state, there are tensions with the more particularistic tendencies of voluntary organizations. The National Lottery could be seen as another example of the coopting tendencies of the state. Some voluntary organizations' incomes have declined, and money for 'good causes' is now being used to augment public services.

From the informal sector, Evers (1995) detects tensions around privatizing activities that would formerly have been in the public sphere. He talks of 'the defensive privatization of modern small-scale households suspicious of any intervention from outside' (p.169). As an example of this tension he talks of the development of self-help groups 'intermeshing anonymity with the need for personal exchange' (p.169).

To summarize, Evers sees the voluntary sector as a tension field vulnerable to the forces of commodification, cooption and privatization from the other three sectors. However, the tensions are not just one way. In a democratic society, Evers sees the voluntary sector as being capable of resisting dominant ideologies and upsetting the settlement between the other sectors. Examples of this could include the green movement and the animal rights movement: movements that have been able to move from the margins of society to influence mainstream thinking.

Having presented Evers' model, this chapter now proceeds to develop its implications for church membership. If the local church is seen as inhabiting the same public space as the voluntary sector, what impact might the tensions Evers detects have on it?

First Implication: the Commodification of Church Membership

Are there any signs that church membership and the voluntary effort that it represents is being commodified? What might be the implications of further commodification for the future of church membership? Two areas of activity related to church membership will be examined namely, leisure and heritage.

From the 19th century, the local church can be seen to have taken an interest in the way in which people spent their leisure time (Yeo, 1976). Much of this effort was organized on an informal local basis. Accompanying the growing commodification of leisure activities in England since the 1960s, cross-denominational groups have formed to provide leisure opportunities for Christians.

In the late 1960s, the Caravaners and Campers Christian Fellowship was formed. This organization promotes caravan rallies for its members on Bank Holiday weekends, including Easter, which take them away from local church attendance. More recently, Christian holiday weeks such as Spring Harvest and Soul Survivor have attracted cross-denominational followings amongst Evangelicals. At present, these activities are seen as adjuncts to local church membership. But it is possible to envisage affiliation to these leisure activities with a Christian content strengthening, and with affiliation to the local church weakening.

Heritage is an area that already supports large voluntary organizations such as the National Trust and English Heritage. Although these organizations have members, they are not member-controlled and the participation of members is largely as consumers of the service provided rather than engaging in face-to-face relationships with each other (Lansley, 1996). Many churches are faced with the challenge of maintaining a historic building, and being by extension part of the tourist industry. Some of these churches have formed 'friends', groups of people who, while not wishing to belong to the church, are willing to contribute to the upkeep of the building. It is not difficult to imagine a National Trust for Churches, indeed the Open Churches Trust might be seen as the beginnings of such an enterprise. Might someone choose to volunteer for such an organization in preference to membership of their local church?

Commodification turns the member into a user who pays a fee in order to receive a product or service that they chose in a manner convenient to them. Trust in commodities is engendered by clear branding that has legitimacy in the relevant societal sub-culture. Highly valued brands are usually national or global rather than local. The development of the Alpha course can be seen as an attempt to offer national branding and marketing for an activity portrayed as leisure learning. Within the evangelical sub-culture, Spring Harvest and Soul Survivor are brands with clear identities drawing people from across the country rather than building local face-to-face affiliations.

Second Implication: the Cooption of Church Membership

Turning now to cooption, it is possible to ask whether membership is being affected by this tension. So we now look at the existence of distinctively Christian campaigning organizations and the increased inclusion of denominations in statutory consultation systems. (The next chapter, by Jenny Taylor, develops this last point in more detail.)

The church has spawned many campaigning organizations that have built upon pre-existing networks of local church membership. Campaigning organizations now tend to be a mix of local activism and 'national members' who support financially and by letter writing. In the era of the e-mail, mail shot and direct debit, participation in a campaign may involve no face-to-face interaction. Drop the Debt (formerly Jubilee 2000) and Church Action on Poverty can be offered as examples of Christian campaigns offering different levels of involvement.

Is it possible to envisage a process whereby for some people their affiliation to a campaigning organization grows stronger and their affiliation to the local church weaker? Malcolm Brown (2000), reflecting on the work of the William Temple Foundation, writes,

> We have to get real about the decline in institutional religion whilst pursuing the potentials of an enduring faith, rooted in alliances for social justice. Organisations like the William Temple Foundation may do good work but they remain marginal if they do not contribute to wider movements for change. Impact is going to mean everything in the coming decades. (Brown, 2000, p.19)

If organizations like this succeed in making an impact, they may fit more comfortably the life styles of some people than does local church membership.

The focus of campaign organizations is usually to change the behaviour of the state, whether directly or in its role as regulator of the private and informal sectors. The trust of face-to-face relations is replaced by trust in a well-regulated society, which can therefore provide security and justice for its citizens.

It is a similar impetus that brings many Christians to involvement in public governance. The devolution of governance in the 1990s has drawn many people into being school governors, NHS Trust board members or Regeneration Project committee members. With the advent of English regionalization, churches are included in regional voluntary sector networks that have a seat in the Regional Assemblies. In total, this type of activity must involve a substantial redirection of voluntary effort by church members to the purposes of the state. Many of these new governance roles are so demanding that they leave little room for other unpaid work, including the work of the local church. Again, it seems possible that, for some members, affiliation to campaigning or governance activities could strengthen at the expense of local church affiliation.

Third Implication: the Privatization of Church Membership

Turning to privatization, there seems to be support in the literature for the contention that this tension has had an impact on the church. Robert Wuthnow (1994) has demonstrated the importance of small groups to US religion. In the UK, David Edwards (1969) writing in the late 1960s was advocating the value of house groups, retreats and pilgrimages for the revitalization of the institutional church. Recent data suggests that as many as 64 per cent of English church attenders may be involved in small groups (CIM, 2001).

As belief has become a matter of private opinion rather than public conviction, small informal groups have been seen as a mechanism for socializing new believers and sustaining existing members. As well as house groups within the local church, there are affinity groups within denominations and cross-denominational groups meeting to explore particular spiritualities. The growth in retreats and pilgrimages suggests a growth in the value of the opportunity to explore spirituality privately or in intimate settings.

These groups build trust on the basis of shared experience. They often attract people of the same socioeconomic status. Putnam (2000) raises concerns that these groups generate binding social capital rather than bridging social capital. In other words they exclude those who do not share their experience rather than bringing together people from different perspectives. It seems possible that affiliation to these groups may strengthen at the expense of participation in the local church.

Is there Room for Resistance?

The final tension from Evers' model is that of resistance, whereby the voluntary sector generated new approaches and ideologies that were in conflict with mainstream thinking but which eventually made changes to the mainstream.

Resistance and dissent are part of church history. However, there are few present-day examples of English Christians taking direct action. Most prefer the campaigning route as a means to achieve change. Some Christians undoubtedly do engage in direct action, but it is through secular groups rather than being under the auspices of mainstream denominations.

Discussion and Predictions

If the tensions from the Evers model do have an impact on church membership, how will the mainstream churches react? One scenario would be for those engaged in alternative affiliations to that of local church membership to be regarded as falling outside the boundaries of the church. A second scenario would be for the denominations to legitimate one or all of the alternative types of affiliation discussed in this chapter, and for them to be seen as acceptable means of affiliation to the church.

It is possible to envisage that local church members might resent these alternative forms of affiliation much in the way that Labour Party activists are uncomfortable with the 'telephone members' recruited through party political broadcasts and not involved in local groups. However, it could be that membership becomes seen as an unreasonably onerous means of social engagement, and other forms of engagement become recognized as equally legitimate.

Crucial to this second scenario would be the ability to count these other forms of activity. There would be no difficulty in counting those who affiliate to para-church organizations providing leisure and heritage services. These organizations treat their affiliates like customers, and are able to contact them and take surveys of their views. Similarly, those affiliated to campaigning organizations, or engaged in governance on behalf of the church, will be recorded on a database somewhere. The more privatized small groups may be more difficult to count but these groups seem highly likely to spawn Internet discussion groups that again can be counted and surveyed. Measuring those engaged in resistance through direct action seems the most difficult as these groups are unlikely to want to affiliate to mainstream denominations. It may be that the Internet will generate further means of social engagement not envisaged in this chapter but which may eventually be seen as participation in the church. (See also Chapter 16, by Anastasia Karaflogka.)

What will become of local church membership? Because of the weight of tradition it seems likely that a proportion (if only a small proportion) of those who see themselves as affiliated to the Church will continue to do this through membership of a local church. These few will face the challenge of maintaining buildings and clergy with very limited resources. Those with other types of affiliation may well attend worship occasionally, but they will feel under no obligation to take part in the work of the local church.

To draw on my interpretation of the Evers model as it affects church membership, let us finish with five predictions.

1   The number of people affiliated to the Church will continue to decline but denominations will start to encourage and count other forms of affiliation.
2   Therefore, by 2050, of those describing themselves as actively involved in the church only about one-quarter will be members of a local church.
3   By 2050, some people will claim their affiliation to the Church through para-church organizations that have clear branding and provide their affiliates with products and services.
4   By 2050, some people will claim their affiliation to the Church through campaigning organizations or by engaging in civic governance on behalf of the Church.
5   By 2050, some people will claim affiliation to the Church through participation in an informal small group that may be networked to other groups with a similar shared experience.

Obviously, it is impossible to test the veracity of these predictions, and I doubt I will be available in 2050 to be held to account for them. However, the aim of this chapter has been to raise questions about the changing nature of activism in the local church on the basis that what we are unable to count may be changing in ways which are just as significant as the church attendance and membership figures that we are able to count.

References

Billis, David 1993: *Organising Public and Voluntary Agencies.* London: Routledge.

Brierley, Peter 2000: *The Tide Is Running Out: What the English Church Attendance Survey Reveals.* London: Christian Research Association.

Brown, Malcolm 2000: The William Temple Foundation: Making a Difference?, *Foundations,* 3 (1), p.19.

Bruce, Steve 1995: The Truth About Religion in Britain. *Journal for the Scientific Study of Religion,* 34 (4), pp.417–30.

Cameron, Helen 1998: The Social Action of the Local Church: Five Congregations in an English City. London School of Economics.

Churches Information for Mission (CIM) 2001: *Faith in Life.* London: Churches Information for Mission.

Davie, Grace 1994: *Religion in Britain since 1945.* Oxford: Blackwell.

Edwards, David L. 1969: *Religion and Change.* London: Hodder & Stoughton.

Evers, Adalbert 1995: Part of the Welfare Mix: The Third Sector as an Intermediate Area. *Voluntas,* 6(2), pp.159–82.

Gill, Robin 1993: *The Myth of the Empty Church.* London: SPCK.

Harris, Margaret 1998: *Organizing God's Work: Challenges for Churches and Synagogues.* Basingstoke: Macmillan Press.

Knight, Barry and Stokes, Peter 1996: *The Deficit in Civil Society in the United Kingdom.* Birmingham: Foundation for Civil Society.

Knoke, David 1990: *Organising for Collective Action: The Political Economies of Associations.* New York: Aldine de Gruyter.

Lansley, John 1996: Membership Participation and Ideology in Large Voluntary Organisations: The Case of the National Trust. *Voluntas,* 7 (3), pp.221–40.

Nichols, Geoff and King, Lindsay 1998: Volunteers in the Guide Association: Problems and Solutions. *Voluntary Action,* 1 (1), pp.21–32.

Perrow, Charles 1970: Members as Resources in Voluntary Organizations. In William R. Rosengren and Mark Lefton (eds), *Organizations and Clients: Essays in the Sociology of Service.* Columbus, OH: Merrill, pp.93–116.

Putnam, Robert D. 2000: *Bowling Alone: The Collapse and Revival of American Community.* New York: Simon & Schuster.

Richter, Philip and Francis, Leslie J. 1998: *Gone but Not Forgotten: Church Leaving and Returning.* London: Darton, Longman & Todd.

Wuthnow, Robert 1994: *Sharing the Journey: Support Groups and America's New Quest for Community.* New York: The Free Press.

Yeo, Stephen 1976: *Religion and Voluntary Organisations in Crisis.* London: Croom Helm.

CHAPTER 10

After Secularism: British Government and the Inner Cities

Jenny Taylor

Introduction

Bryan Wilson, arguably the most widely-quoted exponent and therefore popularizer of secularization theory, defined this theory in 1982 as a 'long-term process' by which religion 'ceases to be significant in the working of the social system' (p.150). There is ample literature demonstrating the tenacity of this view, though its handling, as Sharon Hanson's (1997) skilful survey for the *Journal of Contemporary Religion* has shown, is often imprecise: 'Most theorists just refer to "Wilson", yet often it is impossible to discern whether they are referring to those aspects of his definition that would constitute a Broad or a Narrow approach' (p.161).

Hanson describes the 'Broad approach' as those arguments relating to the secularization thesis at the level of social system. In contrast, the 'Narrow approach' considers whether religion has lost significance at the level of individual consciousness. This chapter argues that there is new evidence of individual consciousness affecting the social system which indicates a need to merge both approaches, the Narrow and the Broad, to get a truer picture of both religion and the system, and how the system works.

Wilson's (1982, p.155) understanding of 'the system' should first be elucidated. He lists four categories of social organization:

1 the processes of production and consumption (the economy);
2 the coordination of activities (government);
3 the agencies of control (the law);
4 the methods of transmission of knowledge (education).

These 'secular' entities exist, he states, within their own increasingly self-defined boundaries; autonomous, constrained only by the boundaries of adjacent and interpenetrating spheres, without reference to anything 'transcendent'. Says Wilson (1982): 'The assumptions on which modern social organization proceeds are secular assumptions' (p.155). Whereas before the Protestant Reformation the polity and its economy were shot through with a sense of higher purpose, of ultimacy or superstition in *raison d'état*, informed by religious meaning and intent, after it, and by dint of secularizing forces, they became ends in themselves.

José Casanova's herculean 1994 survey of 'public religion' in Poland, Brazil, Spain and the USA uses the same secular/sacred differentiation, dividing the secular into 'primary and sub-spheres': 'Religious traditions are now confronting the differentiated secular spheres, challenging them to face their own obscurantist, ideological and inauthentic claims. In many of these confrontations, it is religion which, as often as not, appears to be on the side of human enlightenment (p.234). He thus overturns Wilson's thesis, concluding that religion *is* relevant to the system – but *because* it is outside it. Casonova still accepts the differentiation aspect of the secularization thesis as its core, but does so in order to argue the opposite case from Wilson.

It is curious to find that Casanova still feels the need to reassert the false, Hellenistic 'sacred/secular dichotomy' that gave us secularization theory in the first place. His suggestive analysis obscures the fact that the spheres employ human beings, whose religious motivation may be more or less coherent, susceptible or consistent at any one time – and whose influence may or may not be tacit. The 'spheres' interpenetrate according to the data, and more so than has been taken into account. This penetration happens as a disciplined opportunism and, as Casanova suggests, need offer no threat to the system – quite the contrary, it can act as a life-enhancing leaven within it. To repeat, the Broad approach needs to be merged with the Narrow version to see what is truly going on.

This chapter essentially summarizes my doctoral thesis, namely that individual religion is having a significant impact on that bit of the system which 'coordinates activities', to use Wilson's language. And it is doing so for good religious reasons such as 'God wills it', or out of a concern for the poor. The chapter is based on a study of a British government phenomenon, the Inner Cities Religious Council, administered by the Department of the Environment (as it then was), and a short narrative sketch of the work thus far is offered below. Some definitional work is also attempted, before going into the background of the ICRC. A short analysis of the signs of 'dedifferentiation' that are discernible is attempted, before some concluding remarks.

Beginnings

The research has been designed to address a general question about the impact, if any, made on secularization by immigration, taking a lead from Grace Davie (1994), who has written of a lack of attention to patterns of minority religious practice and how it might fit into the bigger picture: 'how we accommodate the religious aspirations of diverse communities within a continent dominated for centuries by one religious tradition rather than another is not immediately apparent' (p.26). Migrants tend to seek their identity continuum and social reconstruction in religion and religious markers. Thus Callum Brown (1995) has shown this to be the case during the second quarter of the 19th century in Britain, when agricultural and other workers flooded out of the countryside into the cities, and it persisted for some decades: 'For as long as replenishing migration of any group, ethnic or "non-ethnic", was maintained, urban religion was attached to and revitalized by its rural roots' (p.254).

Pnina Werbner (1991), Tariq Modood (1992), Roger Ballard (1994) and Werner Menski (1996) have all written about 20th-century migration into Britain in the same terms, though with different emphases. Their work perceives community organization, self-perception, self-advocacy and communal legal reconstruction, respectively, all along religious lines. There has been a clear need to situate the work of these scholars within the secularization discourse. Religion has been having a major impact on ethnic micro systems: but what about the macro system? The new Inner Cities Religious Council, which began work in 1992, seemed to offer a suitable project for the burgeoning questions on the position of religion in the post-Thatcher era – an era that saw the Ayatollah Khomeini, Bishop Desmond Tutu and the report published as *Faith in the City* (1985). I was kindly given free access to all the records and the archives, and the 30-year embargo on government and ecclesiastical records was waived.

The ICRC is a forum of 'leaders' of the five major faiths, chaired by a government minister, which during the survey period (1992–8) met three times a year, organized two annual regional conferences and initiated a wide range of events and policies that affected 'the system'. It is served by a small secretariat (the Faiths Branch) in the Department of the Environment's (subsequently Environment, Transport and the Regions) Regeneration Directorate. The secretaries have so far all been Anglican clerics. It was announced on 12 November 1991 by a government minister (the son of an Anglican bishop) to a fringe meeting of urban bishops at synod in Westminster (to which all the mainstream press were invited). It concerns itself with those areas of ethnic settlement (and for 'ethnic' read, following Modood *et al.* (1997), 'religious'), known by the shorthand expression 'inner cities'. Its remit is ostensibly practical: to 'seek to create opportunities for action in the inner cities' by contributing to policy making. After five years, to quote its Five-Year Review (Review of the Inner Cities Religious Council; RICRC, 1998), the ICRC's influence had succeeded in 'permeating the culture of government' (para. 2.7). Simon Green's confident assertion (1996), that 'the state does not construct economic or even social policy with reference to ecclesiastical sentiment' (p.301), can no longer be regarded as correct.

Definitions

There is not the space here to characterize adequately the 'inner cities' and the problem they presented to government by the end of the 1980s. John Rex's (1981) still useful work on Sparkbrook defined the 'inner cities' as the 'improvement areas' that grew out of the 'twilight zones' – areas of multi-occupancy lodging houses which became targets of 'improvement initiatives' in 1967 and 1973 (pp.31ff). Migrants entered Britain from the former colonies with rights to citizenship but evidently no realizable rights to adequate housing, through either mortgages or tenancies. The situation it created resulted in the 'inner cities' of which Rex comments:

> This term is ambiguous in its reference. Of course it refers to a particular physical fact (not actually, it should be noted, the literal inner city, but rather the secondary ring containing the worst housing, after the slum-clearance programme was complete) but it also refers to a *social* fact of the coexistence of white and black and of two quite disparate immigrant communities, the Asian and the West Indian. (Rex, 1981, p.31)

Thus he uses the expression 'inner city' to cover both problems of physical fabric and 'the coexistence of incompatible populations'. By 1981, following 15 years of what Gareth Rees and John Lambert (1985) called 'truly phenomenal research and policy innovation, directed at the eradication of [these] problems' (p.4), the Toxteth and Brixton riots erupted, described by the *Guardian* (7 July 1981) as 'the most frightening civil disorder ever seen in England' (p.1). In 1985, there was an even worse headache for the government, namely the publication of *Faith in the City* (1985), the church's somewhat belated but politically spectacular response to the same problems which merely advocated more of what had exacerbated the problems: big-spend government intervention.

It is against this background that in 1988, a civil servant – Douglas Hollis – who was also a non-stipendiary Anglican minister, formerly at the Department of Trade and Industry, was one of two people drafted in from other departments to oversee the new Inner City Task Forces. He had, as part of his previous remit, convened and then chaired the Churches' Liaison Group at the Department of Trade and Industry. This Liaison Group was an innovatory government sounding board on the inner cities, concerned particularly with black unemployment. It consisted of representatives of groups already active in inner-city relief including the Evangelical Enterprise (set up and run by black evangelical Mike Hastings at the Evangelical Alliance), the ecumencial Church Action with the Unemployed (CAWTU), and Linking Up, run by Chris Beales, chairman of the Industrial and Economic Affairs Committee of the Church of England Board for Social Responsibility. Hollis met an officer of the Archbishop's Commission on Urban Priority Areas at Church House, literally just down the same road in London. He wanted not just to improve relations between the third Thatcher government and the Church in light of what Jonathan Raban (1989) has described as 'open acrimony' (p.21), but also to seek a more constructive way forward. Hollis describes a situation of 'awful angst' over the inner cities, and unemployment and mutual hostility between many sectors of the system, especially between the churches and the government:

> I looked 150 yards down Great Smith Street to Church House, the entrance, and I can assure you the only thing going backwards and forwards between Church House and

the DTI was brickbats. There was no dialogue. And that seemed to me to be generally unsatisfactory. So, after a little while, it seemed to me that the churches were doing a great deal in the inner cities, and it would be more productive if church and government were to work together than to shout at each other. (Interview conducted at informant's home, Haywards Heath, Sussex, 6th August 1998)

Secularization processes of differentiation and rationalization resulting in social fragmentation, alienation and religious privatization – processes already well under way before immigration began at the end of the 1940s – had resulted not just in divorce (how can it be called just 'separation' at this juncture?) between government and Church, but, much more importantly, between government and the poor. The Church was in the inner cities, the state was not. And the churches on their own were only able to scratch the surface of the immense problems. Playgroups and holiday clubs were not going to change the world. The way forward was in fact the way back: to a quasi-19th-century partnership of government and governed by a retrieval of the old state/Church synthesis.

Douglas Hollis was intending to offer strategic financial support to the Church's charitable work in the inner cities. He was, as he said in a letter, 'interested in what they could do'. He was also concerned to gain access to the ethnic minorities:

> I had also come to realise that communication with the ethnic communities living in the inner cities was seriously impeded by language, social and structural difficulties. A large proportion of those ethnic residents practised their faith, however, and it seemed probable that the religious axis could provide a potential channel for communication with these people. (Letter to author dated 6 April 2000)

Hollis believed that God had put him in a position to contribute to regeneration, and knew both that the churches had at least a useful presence in the target areas and that religion was a means of access to people. He uses specifically religious language in describing both the sequence of events that led to his appointment and what he believed he had to do:

> I had come in *providentially*. It wasn't entirely accidental. For the diocese here, I had been asked to write a paper on the diocesan response to the FITC which found some favour. I received a letter one morning from the diocese saying thank you, and in the afternoon was called over by the Home Office personnel officer to see him. And amongst other things, I was told I was due for a move from the job I had been doing. He said, 'Douglas, you can have anything you like; you can go to the Police Department, the Immigration and Nationality Department' – he read out a whole list of vacancies – 'I've got something on inner cities if that's of any interest.' I said, 'I'll have that.' It turned out to be to go into this Inner Cities Unit, to be seconded to it and take charge of half this task force. *The coincidence was too great to be ignored. So I don't know what that says.* (Interview, 6 August 1998, my italics)

In a letter to the author he later wrote:

> We despaired of the churches. I had three thoughts in mind which I think [the minister], given his background, understood though we did not discuss them. The first was that by offering the Christian denominations a place at a government table I hoped they would be forced out of their carping triviality and into constructive dialogue. The second was to make the religious dimension explicit in the formation of policy and the development of strategies. The third was that the ethnic religions should be given an equal opportunity alongside the Christians. (Letter dated 6 April 2000)

Yet the Church *qua* institution balked. The Church officer whom Hollis saw at Church House, to discuss his financial proposition, barely recalls his overture, and the meeting they had was certainly unproductive. A letter from the officer concerned explains the problems: 'it would undoubtedly have been the case that many Church people would have been worried about the Church accepting direct financial assistance from the State (irrespective of the complexion at the time of the governing party) as the (so-called) 'establishment' of the C. of E. has never been of the same nature as the state Church in some Continental countries' (letter to the author, 20 January 2000).

The 'church' in its institutional guise at that moment saw itself as literally outside 'the system', and for whatever reason did not seize the opportunity to change this. This suggests that establishment in Britain, during the middle decades of the last century, was a secularizing force, in the sense that the Church *qua* institution construed separation as rigidly as did the social scientists. The money was not being offered to promote religion, but to promote social work where none was being done.

However, Hollis still had his money to give away – and he had his sense of calling. He was in touch with a maverick Anglican with a background in Industrial Mission, Chris Beales, already working in Manchester with a broad spectrum of private, public and government agencies. Work associated with his project became the eventual recipient of a £2.5 million package of aid announced by a government minister at the first meeting of the Inner Cities Religious Council held on 20 July 1992. (The announcement also included a £25 000 grant towards a review of the Church Urban Fund.) As a result of this contact, Beales became the Council's first secretary in 1992.

The ICRC was set up by Robert Key, the Parliamentary Under Secretary of State at the Department of the Environment. This man, the son of an Anglican bishop, had been invited to address synod urban bishops, following riots in Newcastle and further political fall-out over deprivation, skilfully amplified by the Archbishop of Canterbury. The minister consulted his ecclesiastical colleague (Douglas Hollis) on what he should say. The invitation offered a golden opportunity to Hollis to suggest the minister present as a *fait accompli* a new government initiative which could guarantee closer cooperation between the Church and government in the inner cities, and consolidate his earlier work. Beales confirmed this to be the case: '[The ICRC] was set up not to solve the problem of riots but to mobilize the faith communities in order to enable government to have better dialogue with people on the ground because in so many inner city areas the faiths were actually the only structures which existed for organizing people' (interview conducted at the Charing Cross Hotel, London, 4 July 1998).

It emerges from this that the coordination of activities in a religiously plural society – the second component of Bryan Wilson's definition of 'the system' – is not possible without 'religious' participation: not merely as an agency of bureaucracy, but also, as becomes clear below, as integral to decision making.

Dedifferentiation: governance and the 'faiths'

Dedifferentiation – the blurring of the rationalized spheres of religion and state – cannot be attributed to the promotion of minority religious agendas and the need to change the mechanisms of response to them. Indeed, in many respects the arrival of religious minorities in Britain was but a further *symptom* of secularization itself. More specifically, the furore surrounding immigration was always regarded as racial, not religiostructural. Indeed, the religion of the minorities, as Philip Lewis (1994) points out in an important essay, largely evaded the notice of sociologists until the mid-1980s and beyond.

It would be true to say, however, from the following evidence, that the articulation of minority religious issues at ICRC meetings and conferences has largely driven the agendas, so that government ministries are having to apply religion to a whole new range of areas, not least the constitution itself.

Paradoxically, the internal logic of secularization in a context of pluralism, liberalism and human rights has put other religions in the driving seat. The voluntary religion question on the 1991 Census, the first since 1851, was largely pushed through as a result of Muslim demand to be recognized as a *religious* minority:[1] they are too divided to have an effective voice as a racial group, the usual criterion. The question of religious discrimination was driven from the start by Muslim lobbies, particularly Iqbal Sacranie's UK Action Committee on Islamic Affairs. The churches, however, began jumping on this bandwagon. On 9 February 2001, the evangelical Faithworks Campaign was launched with cross-denominational support (including the Bishop of London, Richard Chartres, and the Chief Rabbi Jonathan Sacks) with a high-profile protest about religious discrimination against church project funding by some local authorities: a news item which was carried, among others, by the Radio 4 *Today* programme.

Findings as to the new state–faith dynamic are manifold. The ICRC's Five-Year Review (Review of the Inner Cities Religious Council; RICRC, 1998), carried out in 1997 by the Bishop of Aston (John Austin) and the former Chief Inspector of Probation at the Home Office (Roy Taylor), shows the following:

● Advice and draft briefings on the faiths dimension of specific policy issues were supplied by the secretariat not only to a number of DETR ministers but also to other departments such as the Home and the Cabinet Office, government offices for the regions and non-departmental public bodies including the Commission for Racial Equality and the National Lottery Charities Board. It was able, for example, to input into general policy on asylum law, the census and housing. In more general terms, it was able, for instance, to increase awareness of the Islamic calendar when arranging public events. Specific changes for which the Council was responsible included ensuring that single sex wards were retained in national health trust hospitals. The secretary also drafted speeches for ministers addressing meetings and events with a religious dimension, such as the Shaftesbury Annual Lecture, given by Hilary Armstrong MP, then Minister for Regeneration (see Review, paras 2.5b and 7.6). The Review also recommended 'assisting RDAs [Regional Development Agencies] in their strategic thinking on and involvement of the faith communities' (see Review, para. 8.12).

- Regional conferences encouraged faith communities to apply for funding and to persuade government that faith communities were legitimate users of funds for regeneration (see Review, para. 8.6).
- New local inter-faith structures emerged as a result of ICRC regional conferences (see Review, para. 7.23).
- The ICRC recommended that government should 'integrate the faith communities into the processes of developing guidelines for SRB [Single Regeneration Budget] ... and support their inclusion in regeneration partnerships to form and manage bids' (Review, para. 8.18).
- It had secured a formal agreement between the Church authorities and the Department of the Environment as to the nature and extent of the secretary's dealings with Church committees and other structures (see Review, para. 7.26).
- The Review recommended collaboration between the Secretariat and officers in Church House involved in regeneration and inter-faith issues (see Review, para. 7.27) and noted the input by the secretary into Church of England issues 'including the Millennium, racial justice and religious discrimination, and the Archbishop's paper on Partnership with government' (see Review, para. 7.27).
- The Review recommended that government should assist faith communities financially, 'looking for example at the allowances paid for jury service', where demands were made of them to participate in state processes, yet where they apparently lacked the infrastructure or resources to do so on an equal footing (see Review, paras 10.1–4).

Outcomes not mentioned in the Review, but nonetheless crucial, were as follows:

- Input into the Social Exclusion Unit, based in the Cabinet Office – at the very heart of government. The ICRC was charged by the Minister for Regeneration, Hilary Armstrong, to 'help in getting the message across. All faith communities should also do all they could to support the work of the Unit' (Minutes of 15th ICRC Meeting, 28 October 1997, Item 6, p.6).

● Co-publication with the Central Council for Education and Training in Social
  Work of the report *Visions of Reality: Religion and Ethnicity in Social Work*
  (1998) launched by the Parliamentary Under Secretary of State, Department of
  Health (Paul Boateng) in 1997, to look at the religious dimension of health and
  social welfare. In the minister's own words: 'In our multi-cultural multi-faith
  society, it is important to the strategic planning, care management and service
  delivery processes for social care managers and practitioners to appreciate the
  importance of religion and faith to people's lives and values' (cited in Patel *et al.*,
  1998, p.1).

There is further interesting evidence to show how 'the inter-faith process' itself
begins to function as a new form of 'civic religion'. Religious affiliation (as opposed
to 'no religion') is being harnessed to government objectives, such as social
inclusion, integration and regeneration. Funding bids under the Single Regeneration
Budget are required to show evidence of cooperation by the faiths acting *together*.
Bids from any one religion are discouraged. The Council sometimes has the force
of a constituency in the name of 'religion-in-general' in any representations the
secretary or ministers might make.

On the 'secular' side, conference reports testify to ministers confessing their
religious enthusiasm when addressing the conferences. And civil servants, local
mayors and dignitaries feel able to draw on latent and overt religious sentiment to
galvanize often anomic areas of cities into moral and social activity. Christian civil
servants revel in being able to use the word 'theological' to mean more than the
abstruse or irrelevant.[2]

It is possible to see the nature, force and effects of the different political self-
understandings of the different religious groups. The remit was focused on practical
issues of environmental 'life quality', yet Muslims for example have been very
vocal from the beginning on issues of religious discrimination: not in terms of jobs,
housing, and the *hijab*, but rather in terms of status – and the status of religion –
within the constitution. They achieved through the ICRC platform, during the
survey period, a notable re-education of government in this regard. Religious
discrimination was at or near the top of every ICRC agenda from the fifth meeting
onwards, rarely dropping below the fourth item (after welcome, minutes of the last
meeting, and matters arising) throughout the period. It usually emerges as the first
and principal 'matter arising' (Minutes 6, 7, 8 where it is Item 2, after Welcome; 14;
15 where it is joined by Islamophobia and the 2001 Census question). Alternatively,
it appears as Item 4, as the first substantive item on the agenda, above youth
unemployment, social exclusion or crime (Minutes 11,12,13,16).[3] For the purposes
of the research, it was pursued as a key to what was emerging as a new religious
discourse.

Hindus address their minority status by using the ICRC to further their demands
for government funds for 'capacity building'. If the government wishes to consult
'the faiths', runs the argument, it will have to resource them for it, for they cannot

participate on a level playing field with the established Church and other Christian denominations which have historic resources and infrastructures. The government could find itself, by the logic of egalitarianism, in the fateful position of paying religious groups to serve it. The Church, presumably, will have to refuse any such offer. The ICRC, wrote the Review writers, 'has opened up Establishment in a new way' (RICRC, 1998, p.1).

Conclusion

This research corroborates Casanova's findings that religious marginalization is not the inevitable precursor to extinction even where there is an established Church which, according to him, is an expression of resistance to differentiation while paradoxically becoming a force for deep secularization. He writes that America's early acceptance of differentiation permitted the modern denominational principle of voluntarism, helping it to survive differentiation and even lead to revival (1994, p.214). Yet Establishment in Britain, perhaps being the very product of compromise over differentiation, has allowed possibilities for religious initiative to meet both the crisis caused by secularization in the cities and the new pluralism resulting from it. Casanova did not study Britain, but it seems clear that the British government turned to the Church at the end of the 1980s, following the futile and almost catastrophically expensive post-war period of inner-city secular social policy.

As Casanova says, utilitarian secularization explanations reduce the phenomenon of such deprivatization to the 'instrumental mobilization of available religious resources for non-religious purposes or to an instrumental adaptation of religious institutions to the new secular environment' (p.215). The data studied here indicate, with Casanova, that this is a reductionist position that does not do justice to the facts as enacted by religious people within the British government of the 1990s. Against Casanova, the evidence shows that such people have acted with and on behalf of other faiths to limit the rationalist hubris of the differentiated state sphere – *from within*. Such individuals worked to break down the purported divides that were stifling initiative and causing immense frustration, inertia and exclusion. The Church's own resistance to religious initiatives demonstrated that secularization begins as a state of mind. It is a state which infects both so-called 'religious' and 'non-religious' minds. It is an intellectual resistance with problematic social and spiritual outcomes.

The Church seeking to recoup its power on a wave of revivalism is not the explanation for the ICRC. The Church 'sphere' was particularly hostile to the government 'sphere' in the 1980s and early 1990s, and despite the former's 'weakness' refused an offer that would have given it more 'power'. It did not even seek an imaginative way around the supposed constitutional obstacles. Further, the presence of minorities with a religious agenda did not catapult the government into a 'religious' response either. They still had no particular visibility in *religious* terms.

Religion was merely a signifier for the people who lived in the target areas in organizational terms. However, large numbers of people of pronounced religion were able to settle in the cities without any particular note being made on *religious grounds* to this phenomenon. This alone is indicative of the correctness of the Wilson hypothesis that, fundamentally, and in systemic terms, religion *had*, for a while, ceased to 'matter' in Britain. But this was a temporary phenomenon. My own evidence suggests that this was due simply to a homogenous society taking its religiously unchallenged mores for granted. A prediction one might make in this regard is of a significant religious reaction in Britain as people increasingly become aware that *religious* proximity has more far-reaching social and political implications than a discourse based purely on race might suggest.[4]

The data also show that *theory* about religion needs to be constantly examined in the light of everyday reality. The coming into being of the ICRC shows that individual religion has the potential for creative renewal of the system. More work needs to be done to indicate how the 'Narrow approach' – religious consciousness – must be merged with the 'Broad approach' – significance of religion in the system, the better to understand what we mean by 'religion', and, indeed, 'government'. Oliver O'Donovan's (1996) critique of the loss and recovery of a religiously derived political consciousness in *The Desire of the Nations*, though a work of theology and not sociology, very helpfully shows how the two disciplines might draw from each other in this regard.

Prophecies and Predictions

Religious personnel are already acting as social entrepreneurs, in projects funded and sometimes staffed by government. They are contracted to deliver regeneration initiatives that can demonstrate inter-faith cooperation, without which funding bids are invalid. There are regeneration conferences and projects (Victoria Mills in Manchester is one example, the nationwide Employment Forums another) levering in sizeable public funds for social ends for good religious reasons. On 22 June 2000, Britain's first political multi-party conference on religion and welfare began, with speakers invited from George Bush's 'faith-based welfare' campaign joining the Chief Rabbi and Frank Field MP at Westminster. Prime Minister Tony Blair himself addressed a Christian Socialist-organized event at Westminster on 29 March 2001, entitled 'Faith in Politics'.

Archbishop Robert Runcie warned against 'Salvation by Project'. Might the religions themselves therefore increasingly demand a *quid pro quo* in terms of their own religious values and trajectories, as the Hindu Council is doing in terms of capacity building? On the other hand, when framed within the discourse of religious 'discrimination', should any such religious privilege not carry a price tag in terms of social welfare? In other words, by their fruits shall ye not only know them, but accord them status?[5] In the debate about regeneration, can we, at the very least, anticipate a re-emergence of a more informed focus on religious particulars, since it is those that are so relevant to status, health and social welfare: to the system in fact?

Notes

1   The first Census Religion Question 'would represent a monumental step in the campaign to be recognised as a religious group' (*Q News*, 1995).
2   An example of this is found in the report of the third regional Multi-faith Conference held in the West Midlands on 21 June 1993. The regional Director at the Department of the Environment states: 'It is a privilege to be addressing such a distinguished gathering. I have had a long standing interest in religion including two years studying Theology at University. Usually I keep quiet about that, but for the first time in my career I can declare it to a sympathetic audience! Quite frequently in Government – and no doubt in many other areas of life – if someone says something that is technical, complicated and of little obvious relevance, people accuse them of making a "theological" point. I have grown tired of challenging them; however to this audience I can say that if someone makes a genuinely theological point, it might or might not be complicated, it should not be technical, but it most certainly should be of the utmost importance' (RRM-FC, 1993, p.3).
3   Only in two sets of Minutes did it not appear at all, those of the first and last meetings.
4   A prediction already being realised in the post 9/11 world.
5   The Turkish scholar Mahmut Aydin (2002), following Hans Kung, has argued along these lines: 'in a globalized world, the duty of adherents of different religious traditions should not be to claim the superiority of their own religious tradition as an *a priori* entity but should be to show in practice how much their faith brings liberation to the poor and how much it contributes to the development of the common good' (p.180).

References

Aydin, Mahmut (2002): Globalization and the Gospel: A Muslim View. In Tom Foust, Andrew Kirk and Werner Ustdorf (eds), *A Scandalous Prophet: The Way of Mission After Newbigin*. Grand Rapids, Michigan and Cambridge: Wm.B. Eerdmans Publishing Co., pp.174–81.
Ballard, Roger 1994: *Desh Pardesh: The South Asian Presence in Britain*. London: Hurst.
Ballard, Roger 1996: Racial Inequality, Ethnic Diversity and Social Policy: Prerequisites for the Professional Delivery of Public Services. Unpublished paper for symposium entitled 'A Comparative Study of the South Asian Diaspora Religious Experience in Britain, Canada and the USA', SOAS, London.
Brown, Callum 1995: The Mechanisms of Religious Growth in Urban Societies. In Hugh McLeod (ed.), *European Religion in the Age of Great Cities 1830–1930*. London: Routledge, pp.239–88.
Casanova, José 1994: *Public Religions in the Modern World*. Chicago and London: University of Chicago Press.
Davie, Grace 1994: *Religion in Britain Since 1945: Believing Without Belonging* Oxford: Blackwell.
Green, Simon J.D. 1996: Survival and Autonomy: On the Strange Fortunes and Peculiar Legacy of Ecclesiastical Establishment in the Modern British State *c*1920 to the Present Day. In Simon J.D. Green and Richard C. Whiting (eds), *The Boundaries of the State in Modern Britain*. Cambridge: Cambridge University Press, pp.299–324.
Hanson, Sharon 1997: The Secularization Thesis: Talking at Cross Purposes. *Journal of Contemporary Religion*, 12 (2), pp.159–79.

Lewis, Philip 1994: Being Muslim and Being British: The Dynamics of Islamic Reconstruction in Bradford. In Roger Ballard (ed.), *Desh Pardesh: The South Asian Presence in Britain*. London: Hurst, pp.58–88.

Menski, Werner 1996: Law, religion and South Asians. Unpublished paper for symposium 'A Comparative Study of the South Asian Diaspora Religious Experience in Britain, Canada and the USA', SOAS, London, 4–6 November 1996.

Modood, Tariq 1992: *Not Easy Being British*. London: Trentham Books.

Modood, Tariq *et al.* 1997: *Ethnic Minorities in Britain: Diversity and Disadvantage*. London: Policy Studies Institute.

O'Donovan, Oliver 1996: *The Desire of the Nations: Rediscovering the Roots of Political Theology*. Cambridge: Cambridge University Press.

Patel, Naina, Naik, Don and Humphries, Beth 1998: *Visions of Reality. Religion and Ethnicity in Social Work*. London: Central Council for Education and Training in Social Work.

Q News 1995: Census Office set to Announce Religion U-turn. 8–13 November, p.1.

Raban, Jonathan 1989: *God, Man and Mrs Thatcher: A Critique of Mrs Thatcher's Address to the General Assembly of the Church of Scotland*. London: Chatto & Windus.

Rees, Gareth and Lambert, John 1985: *Cities in Crisis: the Political Economy of Urban Development in Post-War Britain*. London: Arnold.

Rex, John 1981: Urban Segregation in Great Britain. In Ceri Peach, Vaughan Robinson and Susan Smith (eds), *Ethnic Segregation in Cities*. London: Croom Helm, pp.25–42.

Werbner, Pnina 1991: The Fiction of Unity in Ethnic Politics. In Pnina Werbner and Muhammad Anwar (eds), *Black and Ethnic Leaderships in Britain: The Cultural Dimensions of Political Action*. London: Routledge, pp.113–45.

Wilson, Bryan 1982: *Religion in Sociological Perspective*. Oxford: Oxford University Press.

Reports

1993: *Faith and the Inner Cities. West Midlands Multi-Faith Conference on Inner Cities*. London: Inner Cities Religious Council. 21 June (RRM-FC).

1985: *Faith in the City: a Call for Action by Church and Nation*. The Report of the Archbishop of Canterbury's Commission on Urban Priority Areas. London: Church House Publishing.

1998: *Review of the Inner Cities Religious Council: A Report of the Review Team*. (RICRC). A Report of the Review Team appointed by Hilary Armstrong, MP, Minister for Local Government and Housing. London: Department of Environment, Transport and the Regions.

1998: *Visions of Reality: Religion and Ethnicity in Social Work*. London: Central Council for Education and Training in Social Work.

III
PREDICTING ALTERNATIVES

The Self as the Basis of Religious Faith: Spirituality of Gay, Lesbian and Bisexual Christians

Andrew K.T. Yip

Introduction

Sociologists of religion do not speak with one voice regarding the social position of religion (specifically Christianity) in late modern society. Some (for example, Bruce, 2001; 2002), using official statistics which indicate dwindling church attendance, argue that religious beliefs and practice are in decline. Others (such as Davie, 1994; 2000a) argue that the decline of religious affiliation need not imply the decline of religious beliefs in the population at large. Religious beliefs, Davie argues, could be independent of religious practice, defined, say, in terms of church attendance (for a detailed discussion of this, see Davie, 2000b; 2002). I am inclined to support Davie's view: non-affiliation to institutionalized churches and the decline of religious practice within this context should not be equated with 'despiritualization'. Some believers might not define themselves as 'religious' in the traditional sense, but this does not mean that a 'spiritual' dimension is absent from their lives. Even for those who consider themselves 'religious', the construction of their religious faith and identity takes on a more personal dimension. And this characteristic of individual religious orientation reflects the construction of personal identities in late modern society in general, on which this chapter focuses.

Giddens has argued that late modern society is a world of traditions, but not a traditional world. This denotes that, while traditions and institutions still exist in their transformed form, their scope and extent of influence in the lives of individuals are decreasing. In turn, life in late modernity has become increasingly internally referential and reflexively organised. While traditions are still in existence and continue to provide the overarching but fragmented framework for social behaviour, the individual increasingly relies on the assessment of the self for life choices and decisions. In other words, the self, rather than traditions, has become the ultimate point of reference in the individual's life course (for example, Giddens, 1991; 1999; Giddens and Pierson, 1998). This process of 'detraditionalization', as Heelas (1996) has argued, 'involves a shift of authority: from "without" to "within"... "Voice" is displaced from established sources, coming to rest with the self' (p.2). Accordingly, traditions are increasingly losing their scope and influence on the individual's life, and in turn, the individual's self becomes increasingly dominant in the fashioning of her/his life. The self, with its assessment of and reflection on increasing options and risks, functions as the primary basis for the construction of identities.

The process of detraditionalization, it should be emphasized, by no means necessarily involves the total disappearance of traditions (if that were possible) and the complete reign of the self in the construction and management of individual and social life (if that were possible). I subscribe to the 'coexistence thesis', espoused by Heelas (1996), which argues that the self (that is, agency) and traditions (that is, structures) coexist and intermingle inextricably, albeit with varying emphases, in the construction and operation of social life. (For a good discussion of 'detraditionalization' and the 'coexistence thesis', see Heelas 1996.) What is salient for this chapter, though, is that within the late modern context, the self (agency) seems to have the upper hand in this complex process of construction. In the case of individual religious orientation in late modern society, there is no doubt that the individual is more inclined 'to locate God within, where spiritual agency can enhance true "human" authority' (Heelas, 1994, p.105).

Within this conceptual framework, this chapter specifically examines the religious orientations of gay, lesbian and bisexual Christians in the UK. In the past two decades, this sexual and religious minority has been much embroiled in ideological and theological debates, some of which were widely publicized (for more details, see, for instance, Yip, 1997a; 1997b; 1999a; 1999b). The chapter will present research evidence which suggests that the self plays a far greater role than church authority as the basis of the respondents' Christian faith. This is heightened by the fact that their sexuality is 'problematic' to the churches, thus facilitating a process of reflexivity and self-evaluation. This leads to their learning to trust their personal experiences in positioning themselves in relation to a potentially stigmatizing institution. In fact, their continued affiliation to the churches much rest on their ability to distance themselves psychologically, or even to challenge the churches, on the basis of positive personal lived experiences. This is particularly true in relation to their sexualities (for example, being in a committed and long-standing relationship that upholds perceived Christian values such as love and faithfulness).

The Research Project

The data are drawn from a national survey of 565 self-defined non-heterosexual Christians, which was designed to examine a host of issues in relation to sexuality and spirituality. The project consisted of two stages. Stage 1 involved the collection of primarily quantitative data through the use of postal questionnaires (14 pages each) across the UK, between May and October 1997. Stage 2 involved semi-structured interviewing, between October 1997 and January 1998, of 61 respondents living in Scotland, Wales and every region of England. The majority of respondents were recruited through non-heterosexual groups/organizations whose members were either exclusively or predominantly Christian, such as the *Lesbian and Gay Christian Movement*.

The sample consisted of 389 gay men (68.8 per cent), 131 lesbians (23.2 per cent), 24 bisexual women, and 21 bisexual men (total 8.0 per cent). Their ages ranged from 18 to 76, with 297 (52.6 per cent) within the 31–50 category. Not surprisingly, the majority of respondents were affiliated to the Church of England (271, 48.0 per cent) and the Roman Catholic Church (149, 26.4 per cent). Other denominations included the Methodist (29, 5.1 per cent) and the Baptist (16, 2.8 per cent). As mentioned, this almost all-white (95.4 per cent) sample was scattered across the UK, with the majority living in Greater London (164, 29.0 per cent), the south east (74, 13.1 per cent) and the north west (64, 11.3 per cent) of England. In terms of occupation, the top three were clergy/chaplains (96, 23.9 per cent), teachers/lecturers (54, 13.5 per cent) and medical professionals (47, 11.7 per cent).

Religiosity and Spirituality

Table 11.1 shows that a vast majority of respondents (an overall 91 per cent) considered 'religiosity' different from 'spirituality'. Regardless of sexuality, over 88 per cent of respondents held this view. In terms of gender, a higher proportion of women (96.8 per cent) drew this line of demarcation, compared to their male counterparts (88.8 per cent). Qualitative data show that those in the 'No' category were inclined to view these terms as distinctive yet related, but not different.

Table 11.1   'Religiosity' is different from 'spirituality', by sexuality and gender

		By sexuality			By gender	
	All (N=565)	Gay men (N=389)	Lesbians (N=131)	Bisexuals (N=45)	Men (N=410)	Women (N=155)
Yes	514 (91.0%)	345 (88.7%)	126 (96.2%)	43 (95.6%)	364 (88.8%)	150 (96.8%)
No	51 (9.0%)	44 (11.3%)	5 (3.8%)	2 (4.4%)	46 (11.2%)	5 (3.2%)

The 514 respondents in the 'Yes' category were asked to select from a list, of up to three statements, that best described their understanding of the terms. The results are presented in Tables 11.2 and 11.3.

Table 11.2   Top five statements that describe being 'spiritual', by sexuality and gender

	All (N=514)	By sexuality			By gender	
		Gay men (N=345)	Lesbians (N=126)	Bisexuals (N=43)	Men (N=364)	Women (N=150)
(A) Exploring the inner self	324 (63.0%)	218 (63.2%)	81 (64.3%)	25 (58.1%)	230 (56.1%)	94 (60.6%)
(B) Meditating	304 (59.1%)	209 (60.1%)	66 (52.4%)	29 (67.4%)	222 (54.1%)	82 (52.9%)
(C) Searching for the meaning of life	272 (52.9%)	180 (52.2%)	68 (54.0%)	24 (55.8%)	189 (46.1%)	83 (53.5%)
(D) Praying privately at home	157 (30.5%)	104 (30.1%)	39 (30.9%)	14 (32.5%)	112 (30.8%)	45 (30.0%)
(E) Upholding humanistic values (e.g. justice, equality)	151 (29.4%)	93 (26.9%)	40 (31.7%)	18 (41.9%)	96 (26.4%)	55 (36.7%)

Table 11.3   Top five statements that describe being 'religious', by sexuality and gender

	All (N=514)	By sexuality			By gender	
		Gay men (N=345)	Lesbians (N=126)	Bisexuals (N=43)	Men (N=364)	Women (N=150)
(A) Participating in rituals at church (e.g. Eucharist, holy communion)	398 (77.4%)	262 (75.9%)	100 (79.4%)	36 (83.7%)	278 (67.8%)	120 (77.4%)
(B) Subscribing to religious doctrines	366 (71.2%)	230 (66.7%)	104 (82.5%)	32 (74.4%)	243 (59.3%)	123 (79.4%)
(C) Sharing in worship at church	352 (68.5%)	249 (72.2%)	78 (61.9%)	25 (58.1%)	260 (63.4%)	92 (59.4%)
(D) Studying the bible at home	118 (22.9%)	84 (24.3%)	24 (19.0%)	10 (23.2%)	90 (21.9%)	28 (18.1%)
(E) Respecting nature	91 (17.7%)	65 (18.8%)	17 (13.5%)	9 (20.9%)	69 (16.8%)	22 (14.2%)

The quotations below, extracted from questionnaires, further illustrate the distinction between the terms 'spiritual' and 'religious'.

> Being spiritual is a way of being in the world, constantly asking the question 'Who am I?' in relation to myself, the world, and god. It is about journeying through life searching for myself and god. Being religious is about adhering to a rigid set of doctrines and participating in specific rituals. (Michelle, an Anglican lesbian from the East Midlands)

> I understand being religious as attending church, observing and receiving sacraments and participating in the life of the parish. As a spiritual person I do none of these things, but participate more in a personal journey or exploration around faith and the meaning of life. (Michael, Catholic gay man from Northern Ireland)

The typical narratives below, drawn from interviews, further elaborate the differences they drew:

> Spirituality is about being filled with the pureness, grandeur and earthiness of everything. You become in tune with absolutely everything, to the tiniest molecule. You are flooded with a sense of god's presence and energy. It is a fusion of both matter and spirit, creating a sense of oneness. It is deep within your soul. Being religious, that's like somebody going along with a set of rosary beads, going to a mass because it is an obligation, going to confession because the rule book says so. That's being religious: a set of obligations. Religion is a structured entity. You have got X, Y, Z, and if you don't follow this, you are out. There is a big chasm between the two. (Jim, a Pentecostal gay man, late 40s)

> Religion is safe, spirituality is dangerous. Religion offers a clear view of how life should be lived. You could tick the boxes, and you are sound. That's what matters: in being sound. … Spirituality is a journey, and it's not being scared of asking the questions and not receiving the answers, but actually it's part of it. The journey is in asking the questions, and there will be times when you have some understanding, but there is no guarantee. (Janet, a Baptist bisexual woman, late 30s)

On the whole, 'religiosity' seems to embrace two significant components: the adherence to doctrines and beliefs, propagated by the religious institution; and the observance of rituals and practices, within a communal religious context. 'Spirituality', on the other hand, denotes a self-based internal journey of experience with the divine. It is about the relationship between the individual and her/his faith, not necessarily mediated through the church. It is personal and experiential.

Quantitative data show that the majority of respondents argued that 'religiosity' and 'spirituality' are distinct. Qualitative data from questionnaires and interviews, on the other hand, suggest that the respondents, if asked to choose, would consider 'spirituality' rather than 'religiosity' as a more accurate description of their Christian faith. However, they also acknowledged that, in an ideal situation, the two should feed each other for a more wholesome and comprehensive Christian faith. Therefore these two terms are not completely independent of each other, as found in the study by Zinnbauer *et al.* (1997) and Marler and Hadaway (2002). The typical account below illustrates this:

> Religion without spirituality is dead. Spirituality without religion tends to drift loose from its moorings as it were. I think it is too easily led astray. I think one needs not only the help and support, but also the structure of Christianity as a whole. This is where I think religion can be a helpful aspect of one's overall Christianity. But, I would say, if you have to choose between the two, then the inner reality is more important than the outward form. If religion proves to be a hindrance rather than a help to one's relationship with god, then I think it has to be questioned and, if necessary, jettisoned. I know some people who leave the church, temporarily or permanently. It is a barrier, rather than an aid, to their relationship with god. (Simon, an Anglican bisexual man in his 50s)

The primacy given to spirituality is telling. Most respondents appeared to place greater emphasis on the self rather than religious institutions and their perceived trappings. This is demonstrated even more clearly in the following section, where the basis of their Christian faith is examined specifically.

Basis of Christian Faith

In the questionnaire, the respondents were asked to rank, in order of importance, four items as the core components of their Christian faith. The results are presented in Tables 11.4 and 11.5. These tables demonstrate that there is a consistency in the ranking of the items: regardless of sexuality and gender, the majority of respondents ranked 'personal experience' the highest, and 'church authority' the lowest. 'Human reason' and 'the Bible' interchange for the second and third positions, depending on the categories. Once again, the data signify the primacy given to the self: the use of *their* own human reason in *their* interpretation of the Bible, within the framework of *their* personal experience, in the fashioning of *their own* Christian faith and living. The respondents seemed to have no qualms in relegating church authority to the sidelines, when it clashes with personal experiences, as in the area of their sexualities. The following narratives highlight the justification for this relegation:

> I certainly know why I put church authority at the bottom. That's because of my attitude towards the church. The reason I put personal experience on the top is that any Christian will tell you that their relationship is about their personal experience of god. That's the same with me. When people talk to me about Christianity, the only way I can relate it to them is to talk about my own personal experience of god, and how my life has changed as a result of coming into contact with god. That would never have happened by the church authority telling me god existed. Having encountered god, my own reasoning told me that there was god. The Bible, in a sense also backs up what I have experienced. So yes, it is my reasoning and my reading of the Bible, in relation to my experience, not what the church has to say. (Sandra, a Catholic lesbian from Greater London)

Table 11.4   The basis of Christian faith: ranking of items, by sexuality

		Number and percentage of respondents who gave the items *top two* rankings	Number and percentage of respondents who gave the items *bottom two* rankings
Personal experiences	All (N=565)	463 (81.9)	102 (18.1)
	Gay men (N=389)	314 (80.7)	75 (9.3)
	Lesbians (N=131)	111 (84.7)	20 (15.3)
	Bisexuals (N=45)	38 (84.4)	7 (15.6)
The bible	All (N=565)	333 (58.9)	232 (41.1)
	Gay men (N=389)	224 (57.6)	165 (42.4)
	Lesbians (N=131)	82 (62.6)	49 (37.4)
	Bisexuals (N=45)	27 (60.0)	18 (40.0)
Human reason	All (N=565)	303 (53.6)	262 (46.4)
	Gay men (N=389)	206 (52.9)	183 (47.1)
	Lesbians (N=131)	71 (54.2)	60 (45.8)
	Bisexuals (N=45)	26 (57.8)	19 (42.2)
Church authority	All (N=565)	95 (16.8)	470 (83.2)
	Gay men (N=389)	69 (17.7)	320 (82.3)
	Lesbians (N=131)	14 (10.7)	117 (89.3)
	Bisexuals (N=45)	12 (26.7)	33 (73.3)

The Bible is a good source, but it can say different things to different people. It has been used to oppress gay people, women, blacks and so on. You therefore have to use your reason to think and evaluate the situation. You read the Bible, and you ought to ask yourself, 'Why was it written, and in what context was it written?' If you just practise the Bible literally without using your brain, there is something very wrong ... You then tie this to your personal experience, which itself needs to be governed by objectivity. As for church authority, well, take it with a bucket of salt. You are an autonomous human being. You are real and your freedom is valuable. You don't jump just because the church authority tells you to. God gives you these gifts. Use them and not be submissive to any church authority. Exercise responsibility, and take into account the fact that you are a person in your own right, who is loved by god and who is responsible to god. (James, an Anglican gay man in his early 30s)

Many of the respondents had had negative experiences with the churches on the ground of their sexuality, and some were disheartened by the churches' lack of affirmation and support. As a result, some had ceased attending church altogether (for more detail, see Yip, 2000), while the majority continued their participation by maintaining some kind of social and psychological distance. In their journey to

Table 11.5   The basis of Christian faith: ranking of items, by gender

		Number and percentage of respondents who gave the items *top two* rankings	Number and percentage of respondents who gave the items *bottom two* rankings
Personal experiences	All (N=565)	463 (81.9)	102 (18.1)
	Men (N=410)	331 (80.7)	79 (9.3)
	Women (N=155)	132 (85.2)	23 (14.8)
The bible	All (N=565)	333 (58.9)	232 (41.1)
	Men (N=410)	237 (57.8)	173 (42.2)
	Women (N=155)	96 (61.9)	59 (38.1)
Human reason	All (N=565)	303 (53.6)	262 (46.4)
	Men (N=410)	217 (52.9)	193 (47.1)
	Women (N=155)	86 (55.5)	69 (44.5)
Church authority	All (N=565)	95 (16.8)	470 (83.2)
	Men (N=410)	77 (18.8)	333 (81.2)
	Women (N=155)	18 (11.6)	137 [88.4)

construct a negotiated personal identity that incorporates both their sexuality and spirituality, they have learned to rely on their personal experiences, rather than church authority that in general does not affirm their sexuality. In other words, their reliance on the self in the fashioning of their Christian living has been intensified by church authority, in which they have lost confidence. A vast majority of respondents (538 or 95.2 per cent) argued that their journey of exploration had 'made me challenge and examine my Christian faith' and 'strengthened my Christian faith'. The following accounts demonstrate this argument:

> I think personal experience is significant. But, obviously, the Bible and our reason are important too. But I often feel that the church has lost touch with Jesus Christ. The church says things that are in direct opposition to what I think Jesus would say, like the whole thing about it being a sin to be gay. I don't believe it at all. I think the church restricts people. Their attitude towards gay people should be about what Jesus himself said about it, not about all those old rules. (Julia, a Methodist lesbian from the West Midlands)

> I think it is important to use the Bible, to historically look back and see what various people are saying about what has happened at the time. I just don't think you should look at the Bible as the be all and end all. I think it is [in] relation of experiences that you can [do this]. It's like a reference text. It should be interpreted based on our reasoning and experiences. As for the church authority, my experience [having had to

leave the church due to the lack of acceptance] informs me that it cannot be relied on. (Paul, an Anglican gay man in his late 40s)

The Ethic of Authenticity: Lived Experiences as the Ultimate Referential Framework

On the whole, the data presented in this chapter lend credence to the argument that, in late modern society, the organization of religious faith and spiritual identity are characterized, increasingly, by privatization and individuation (for example, Luckmann, 1999; Roof, 1996; 1999; Houtman and Mascini, 2002). The self, not religious authority structures, emerges as the primary determining factor in shaping the expression of the individual's spirituality, whose authenticity rests, not on doctrines, but on personal experiences. This involves 'the decline of the institutional determination of life choices and instead the reflexive reconstruction of identity. What the traditional used to demand has transformed into lifestyle options' (Heelas, 1998, p.5). The 'temple', as Casanova (1994) has argued, 'has moved inside' (p.53).

This is a reflection of late modern society at large, in which the construction of personal identities is guided primarily by an 'ethic of self-fulfilment', whose authenticity rests on personal biographies (Taylor, 1991), promoted by capitalist consumerism. Thus the self as a basis of Christian faith occurs against a backdrop of the consumerization of religion, which emphasizes free choice, self-authentication, self-affirmation and self-gratification (Roof *et al.*, 1995; Lyon, 2000). This is evidenced by case studies from both sides of the Atlantic (for example, Hammond, 1992; McNamara, 1992; Osmond, 1993).

In the same vein, Grace Davie (2000b), with reference to institutional religion in western Europe, has argued that 'religion diminished in public significance; religious aspirations continued to exist, but were increasingly relegated to the private sphere' (p.126). These 'religious aspirations' are what the vast majority of respondents in this study called 'spirituality', which could germinate and mature independently of the religious institution. It is more a 'spirituality of seeking' than 'dwelling' (Wuthnow, 1998) and a process of 'journeying' that sacralizes the self and inner space (Inoue, 2000). This is a journeying out of religious institution and authority, and into the self, remembering, however, that the vast majority of our sample have still remained in the churches (Shallenberger, 1998).

The respondents' personal experiences of possessing 'problematic' sexualities significantly inform the construction and expression of their Christian identities. In the face of lack of acceptance and affirmation, their reliance on the self is heightened as they embark on a journey towards integration, whose course is steered by the self. Ironically, this often facilitates their continued presence in the churches, instead of leaving a potentially stigmatizing and exclusive community.

It must be emphasized that the internal religious pluralism that could result from the working of the self does not mean that the respondents do not draw upon a broader Christian framework in constructing their Christian living. I do not agree with some queer theorists who tend to overemphasize the role of the self (agency) in the construction of social life, as if traditions (structure) are no longer present or relevant. Undoubtedly, detraditionalization has empowered the self, but 'it is seen as competing, interpenetrating or interplaying with processes to do with tradition-maintenance, rejuvenation and tradition-construction' (Heelas, 1996, p.3). This 'coexistence thesis' espoused by Heelas cautions us about the intricate and complex interconnectedness of agency and structure in the construction of social life.

What is salient in the case of the respondents is that, although they still draw upon broad Christian principles and values, this process is now increasingly guided and filtered by the self. The reliance on the self, while drawing upon a broad Christian framework, has led to much diversity within the gay, lesbian and bisexual Christian community in terms of, for instance, theological orientations, involvement in political activism and lifestyles, as well as sexual values and practices (for example, Yip, 1997c).

As the religious landscape in the West shifts its focus from the institution to the individual, and institutional meta-narratives give way to the more expressive, experiential and personal, such transformation will lead to the decline of churches' moral and spiritual authority and influence. This does not denote the decline of religion (specifically Christianity in this context). In fact, as the lived experiences of the respondents reported here testify, this process could lead to the empowerment of the self, and the growth of self-based spirituality which selectively draws upon broad religious themes and values, and adapts them in accordance with the individual's salient personal circumstances. I predict that this transformation, coupled with the secularization of sex and the increasing tolerance of sexual diversity in the society at large, means that gay, lesbian and bisexual Christians will find an increasingly conducive spiritual environment to practise their spirituality in corporation with their sexuality. While interacting with structures and institutions, they, as many other individuals, are now more likely to look within themselves for the voice of the self that authenticates and validates their experiences and identities, serving as that which gives meaning to their religious faith and identities.

References

Bruce, Steve 2001: Christianity in Britain, R.I.P., *Sociology of Religion* 62 (2), pp.191–203.

Bruce, Steve 2002: *God is Dead*. Oxford: Oxford University Press.

Casanova, José 1994: *Public Religions in the Modern World*. Chicago: University of Chicago Press.

Davie, Grace 1994: *Religion in Britain Since 1945: Believing without Belonging*. Oxford: Blackwell.

Davie, Grace 2000a: *Religion in Modern Europe: A Memory Mutates*. Oxford: Oxford University Press.

Davie, Grace 2000b: Religion in Modern Britain: Changing Sociological Assumptions. *Sociology*, 34(1), pp.113–28.

Davie, Grace 2002: *Europe an Exceptional Case*. London: Darton, Longman and Todd.

Giddens, Anthony 1991: *Modernity and Self-Identity: Self and Society in the Late Modern Age.* Cambridge: Polity Press.

Giddens, Anthony 1999: *Runaway World: How Globalisation is Shaping Our Lives.* London: Profile Books.

Giddens, Anthony and Pierson, Christopher 1998: *Conversations with Anthony Giddens: Making Sense of Modernity.* Cambridge: Polity Press.

Hammond, Phillip E. 1992: *Religion and Personal Autonomy: The Third Disestablishment in America.* Columbia, SC: University of South Carolina Press.

Heelas, Paul 1994: The Limits of Consumption and the Post-modern 'Religion' of the New Age. In Russell Keat, Nigel Whiteley and Nicholas Abercrombie (eds), *The Authority of the Consumer.* London: Sage, pp.102–15.

Heelas, Paul 1996: Introduction: Detraditionalization and Its Rivals. In Paul Heelas, Scott Lash and Paul Morris (eds), *Detraditionalization. Critical Reflections on Authority and Identity.* Oxford: Blackwell, pp.1–20.

Heelas, Paul 1998: Introduction: On Differentiation and Dedifferentiation. In Paul Heelas (ed.), *Religion, Modernity and Postmodernity.* Oxford: Blackwell, pp.1–18.

Houtman, Dick and Mascini, Peter 2002: Why Do Churches Become Empty, While New Age Grows? Secularization and Religious Change in the Netherlands. *Journal for the Scientific Study of Religion,* 41 (3), pp.455–73.

Inoue, Nobutaka 2000: From Religious Conformity to Innovation: New Ideas of Religious Journey and Holy Places. *Social Compass,* 47 (1), pp.21–32.

Luckmann, Thomas 1999: The Religious Situation in Europe: The Background to Contemporary Conversations. *Social Compass,* 46 (3), pp.251–8.

Lyon, David 2000: *Jesus in Disneyland: Religion in Postmodern Times.* Cambridge: Polity Press.

McNamara, Patrick H. 1992: *Conscience First, Tradition Second: A Study of Young American Catholics.* New York: State University of New York Press.

Marler, Penny L. and Hadaway, C. Kirk 2002: 'Being religious' or 'Being spiritual' in America: A Zero-sum Proposition?, *Journal for the Scientific Study of Religion,* 41 (2), pp.289–300.

Osmond, Roselie 1993: *Changing Perspectives: Christian Culture and Morals in England Today.* London: Darton, Longman & Todd.

Roof, Wade C. 1996: God Is in the Details: Reflections on Religion's Public Presence in the United States in the mid-1990s. *Sociology of Religion,* 57 (2), pp.149–62.

Roof, Wade C. 1999: *Spiritual Marketplace: Baby Boomers and the Remaking of American Religion.* Princeton: Princeton University Press.

Roof, Wade C., Carroll, Jackson W. and Roozen, David A. 1995: *The Post-War Generation and Establishment Religion.* Oxford: Westview Press.

Shallenberger, David 1998: *Reclaiming the Spirit: Gay Men and Lesbians Come to Terms with Religion.* New Brunswick: Rutgers University Press.

Taylor, Charles 1991: *The Ethics of Authenticity.* Cambridge, MA: Harvard University Press.

Wuthnow, Robert 1998: *After Heaven: Spirituality in America Since the 1950s.* Berkeley: University of California Press.

Yip, Andrew K.T. 1997a: Attacking the Attacker: Gay Christians Talk Back. *British Journal of Sociology,* 48 (1), pp.113–27.

Yip, Andrew K.T. 1997b: Dare to Differ: Lesbian and Gay Catholics' Assessment of Official Catholic Positions on Sexuality. *Sociology of Religion,* 58 (2), pp.165–80.

Yip, Andrew K.T. 1997c: *Gay Male Christian Couples: Life Stories.* Westport: Praeger.

Yip, Andrew K.T. 1999a: The Politics of Counter-rejection: Gay Christians and the Church. *Journal of Homosexuality,* 37 (2), pp.47–63.

Yip, Andrew K.T. 1999b: Listening to Lived Experiences: The Way Forward in the Debate on Homosexuality. In Leslie J. Francis (ed.), *Sociology, Theology and the Curriculum.* London: Cassell, pp.187–96.

Yip, Andrew K.T. 2000: Leaving the Church to Keep My Faith: The Lived Experiences of Non-heterosexual Christians. In Leslie J. Francis and Yaacov J. Katz (eds), *Joining and Leaving Religion*. Leominster, UK: Gracewing, pp.129–45.

Zinnbauer, Brian J., Pargament, Kenneth I., Cole, Brenda, Rye, Mark S., Butter, Eric M., Belavich, Timothy G., Hipp, Kathleen M., Scott, Allie B. and Kadar, Jill L. 1997: Religion and Spirituality: Unfuzzying the Fuzzy. *Journal for the Scientific Study of Religion*, 36 (4), pp.549–64.

CHAPTER 12

The Quakers: towards an Alternate Ordering

Gay Pilgrim

This chapter will suggest that Foucault's concept of 'heterotopia', as defined by Kevin Hetherington (1996), names a continuing thread which links the first Quakers (who emerged in the mid-17th century) with those in Britain today. The diversity of belief amongst Friends today no longer supports the original religious basis for their utopian vision which resulted in their heterotopic stance, and which provided early Friends with their identity and unity. The chapter will go on to argue that, instead of an overarching belief, it is the sense of being 'other' and living out an 'alternate ordering' that is one of the key ways in which 21st-century Friends obtain a sense of identity and unity. Finally, given the implications of this theory, we will look at the possible shape (or shapes) that the Religious Society of Friends in Britain might take in the future.[1]

Heterotopia

This term was originally used by anatomists and referred to those parts of the body which were out of place, missing altogether, extra or alien; something incongruous and unsettling. Michel Foucault appropriated the term 'heterotopia' and used it to describe spaces which disturb, shock or unsettle. The two main works in which he writes about his concept of heterotopia are *The Order of Things* (1977) and *Of Other Spaces* (1986). In the former he uses the example of Borges' *Chinese Encyclopaedia* to illustrate how incongruous juxtapositions challenge preconceived assumptions; in this case through a text whose different ordering confuses as it is not in accordance with Western expectations of logical sequencing or relationship (1977, p.xv). In *Of Other Spaces*, he is concerned with spaces, physical and mythical, and how spaces can be used to subvert or invert normal relationships. Foucault (1986) states that sites or spaces which contradict or invert relationships are of two main types, utopias and heterotopias. He regards utopias as 'fundamentally unreal spaces', whereas a heterotopia is a 'kind of effectively enacted utopia', a counter-site which highlights issues of order and power through the confusion it creates through its unexpected and incongruous use (p.24): for example, holding a fun fair in a prison.

Kevin Hetherington (1996) is interested in Foucault's suggestion that the concept of heterotopia might further an understanding of the 'spatiality of the social ordering of modernity' (p.40).[2] Hetherington (1998) himself uses the term to denote 'sites of alternate order (which are) constituted through their incongruous character and (their) relationship to other less incongruous sites' (p.131). He defines heterotopia as

> Spaces of alternate ordering [which] organise a bit of the social world in a way different to that which surrounds them. That alternate ordering marks them out as Other and allows them to be seen as an example of an alternative way of doing things. (1996, p.2)

It is this definition which, I argue, provides a link between mid-17th century Friends and modern Quakers. My understanding of this concept has been illuminated and broadened by its use in other disciplines, in particular cultural studies and geography where the discourse about space, conceptual or actual, marginal or central, illustrates power relations and therefore social ordering (Shields, 1991; Rose, 1993; Keith and Pile, 1993; Cresswell, 1996). The discourse on marginality, and on the opportunities that being marginal provide to rehearse an alternative social ordering, is relevant to Friends, both in the past and in the present.

The margins, whether geographical or social, have come to be seen as offering opportunities for empowerment, through practices of resistance, protest and transgression (Shields, 1991; Rose, 1993). They are spaces where alternate ways of living and ordering can be played with and practised, demonstrated and witnessed to. Louis Marin (1984; 1992) in particular explores the concept of spaces which can be experimented in and where ideas can be played with. He points out that Thomas More's word *utopia* was coined by bringing two Greek words together, namely *eu*-topia and *ou*-topia, one meaning a 'good place', the other 'no place or nowhere'. Marin is interested in what happens in the gap that exists between the 'nowhere place' and the 'good place', what he terms the 'neutral'. He posits that it is in this gap that it is possible to imagine and attempt to create utopias within the confines of the modern world. He created the word 'utopics' to describe what occurs in this gap. What Marin calls the neutral is where Hetherington (1996) believes heterotopias exist. He states: 'Heterotopia are not quite spaces of transition ... but they are spaces of deferral, spaces where ideas and practices that represent the good life can come into being' (p.3). Hetherington also points out, however, that

> Difference, while being different to the accepted norm within a culture, while it is indeed a source of marginality and resistance to marginalization, is always also implicated in social ordering, even if at the most fundamental level, it is opposed to everything that society, seen as a social order, stands for. (Hetherington, 1996, p.7)

I suggest that to provide a significant alternate ordering, the heterotopic would have to be *simultaneously* marginal and embedded in the prevailing social order. Heterotopias, or sites of Otherness, express their alternate ordering of society directly through the society which they seek to be different from. They must be juxtaposed to something in order to be heterotopic.

Quakers as 'Other'

Quakerism emerged during a time of enormous upheaval, political, religious and social. There were a plethora of other, equally bizarre and peculiar religious and quasi-religious groups around in the 1650s with whom Friends were anxious not to be confused. Moreover, since they were contesting the theological claims of the more established reformation churches whom they believed to be apostate (and whose apostasy was visible in the manner of their living) it was necessary that Quakers' alternate ordering should be distinctive, *visible* and clearly offering something 'Other'.

Their behaviour, even when not extravagant, such as 'going naked for a sign' or publicly rending their clothes and covering themselves in ashes (Fox, 1975), clearly differentiated them from 'the world'. They refused to engage with customary social manners at even the most trivial level. Thus they would not say 'good day' to anyone unless they had reason to converse with them, lest they should be tempted to speak frivolously and be led 'out of the Light' (Bauman, 1998). They did not bow, doff their hats or acknowledge the presence of another whomsoever they were; and this at a time when social nuances were finely tuned and adherence to social conventions regarded as central to the stability and order of society (Punshon, 1984). Furthermore, their plain speaking and assumption of equality between all people, including men and women, was widely taken to be deeply shocking and transgressive. In this way Quakers continuously highlighted power relations and social ordering.

Their court trials serve to illustrate the way Friends created heterotopic sites. Far from feeling intimidated, marginalized and properly subordinated (let alone silenced) as the judicial system intended, Friends used this arena as a space in which to evangelize and inspire; as a platform from which they could preach. They treated a courtroom as a 'church', which was incongruous, unexpected *and* confusing. Their refusal to pay customary respect by removing their hats, to swear oaths or to respect civil law above God's law, and their use of 'thee' and 'thou', rather than 'you' to their superiors, further confused, shocked and outraged (Bauman, 1998). A space designed to impose a proper social order was used instead to challenge the prevailing power relations, encourage resistance to the prevailing culture and witness to an alternate ordering. It became a heterotopic site.

Over time the alternate ordering and otherness of Friends changed, but up to the mid-to-late 19th century they were still visibly different, distinctively 'other' in dress, speech, life style and worship practices. They continued to challenge and highlight power relations and social ordering through their engagement with issues such as the treatment of criminals and capital punishment, the mentally ill and the abolition of slavery (Punshon, 1984; Isichei, 1970).

This was also the period when the evangelical movement and methodism were sweeping the country, and Quakers were not immune. From about 1830 to 1885, the influence of evangelical Quakers, with their insistence on the centrality of the Bible, made inroads on the theological distinctiveness of Friends (Isichei, 1970). Some commentators argue that the rise of liberal Quakerism in the 1890s (Punshon, 1984, Isichei, 1970) was the result of a reaction to the extreme rigidity and strictly applied rules and regulations of Quakerism at that time. It may have been a reaction to a diminution in their distinctiveness and alternate ordering, which was in danger of being lost under the domination of evangelical Friends.

The anti-evangelical reaction was broadly twofold. The traditional, so-called 'Quietist' Friends revered the early Friends' writings and theology and were cautious about how they involved themselves with 'the world'. They were dismayed not only by the evangelicals' theology, but by their vigorous proselytizing. And the radical, liberal, outward looking Friends who, whilst seeking to engage with the wider world and society around them, also held to 'traditional' teachings of Quakerism, such as the universality of the Light Within, the universal offer of salvation and a refutation of the centrality of the Bible, opposed the evangelicals' rejection of the Inward Light and insistence on biblical authority.

The differences between the quietists and the liberals, although less differentiated than those between themselves and the evangelicals, were nevertheless considerable, and the conflict generated by these three opposing views reverberated throughout the Society. In 1895, a conference was held in Manchester to consider and discuss late 19th-century Quakerism, and was significant for its 'call for Quakerism to return to some of the teachings of early Friends and the abandonment of the Bible as a source of religious authority' (Dandelion, 1996, p.xix). Ultimately, liberal Quakerism prevailed, returning Friends to their distinctive theology of the centrality of the Inward Light, but as Friends' engagement with the intellectual ferment in science, philosophy and religious thinking led to a questioning of religion and religious certainties, this was reinterpreted to mean individual personal experience (Isichei, 1970, p.5). Doubt was acceptable, even laudable. Henry Hipsley (1881) sourly wrote in a weekly journal of the Religious Society of Friends, *The Friend* (XXI, 248), 'Young men who have doubts are made so much of, invited about and patted on the back as intellectually superior' (p.144). By the mid-20th century, Friends' uncertainty about their theological underpinning had become an orthodoxy. In 1940, Elizabeth Cadbury wrote: 'Friends are so inclined to pride themselves on the nebulousness of their faith. There is a danger of our becoming something like the balloons that are at present swaying backwards and forwards around every big city.'[3] By the latter half of the 20th century, Quakers had ceased to be easily distinguishable, or noticeably different from society at large. Indeed the Religious Society of Friends reflected the pluralism, individualism and crisis of meaning common in the West (Dandelion, 2001).

Moving Margins

The first Quakers saw themselves as a prophetic people, and their alternative ordering and otherness arose out of this conviction. They did not have a vision of the world as it *ought* to be because of an ideology about social justice, peace and equality. It was *God's* vision for the world, and humanity's role, place and purpose within it, that was the inspiration and foundation for their otherness and alternate ordering (Gwyn, 1995). Their experience of being convicted by Christ was a liminal rite of passage that took them 'out of the world', returning them transformed, to a new place where their lives were visibly altered. Victor Turner (1969) writes that the liminal rite of passage is one which forms strong bonds, strengthening relationships and obligations within the group, and there is little doubt that the inward spiritual experience, combined as it was with the outward persecution, was an effective liminal rite of passage for Quakers.

Today the experience of a Meeting for Worship is largely liminoid, as opposed to liminal. That is, a person can choose whether or not they wish to participate this week, this month, or this year.[4] With the collapse of Quaker certainty about Christianity as the only true and proper faith, the experience of being convicted by Christ has diminished in power, if not gone altogether, and it is certainly no longer regarded as an obligatory point of passage. Liminoid rites of passage are much weaker (Turner, 1982). They do not carry the same weight of obligation, and consequently do not strengthen the integration of the group as effectively as the liminal. Nor do they produce such a strong sense of identity. I would argue that they also allow a much greater degree of diversity, since it is no longer necessary for everyone to have been seen to have participated in a similar experience to be part of the group.

It is generally accepted amongst British Quakers that Christians no longer have a critical mass amongst Friends (Dandelion, 1996; Heron, 1992, 1999). The Quaker culture of openness makes taboo any certainty about Christ, God, divine will or the sacred. But, as Gordon Lynch writes in an unpublished paper, 'the death of conviction' also leads to an openness to a range of beliefs which become evaluated not so much with regard to the truth claims involved in them as with regard to the kind of life they make possible. Throughout their history, Quakers have maintained that it *is* possible to live an alternate ordering: to witness and be an example to something 'Other'. For early Friends, this heterotopic stance was a consequence of their belief that they were called by God to live in a particular way in order to create the conditions for the coming of God's Kingdom on earth. Their utopian vision quest was rooted in a common religious experience. Today, while many Friends remain committed to working towards peace and social justice, it cannot be claimed that this is a consequence of a commonly shared religious experience. It owes more to the concept of 'elect moral status' (Hetherington, 1998): a concept which describes those who believe they have access to a heightened sense of experience, resulting in the expression of moral values to do with better ways of living and interacting with one another.

Despite the diversity of faith belief amongst Friends, their sense of themselves as being Other and offering an alternate ordering to the rest of society is undiminished (Wildwood, 1999; Dale, 1996; Britain Yearly Meeting Minutes). It offers them both

a sense of identity and a sense of unity. This heterotopic stance was demonstrated at
the Britain Yearly Meeting of 1999, when the topic of peace and reconciliation work
in Kosova arose. Time and again Friends spoke of the unique contribution of
Quakers and the importance of this. Their drive was to create a space of peace in the
midst of a war zone; a space on the margins in a marginal space; a space of alternate
ordering that is clearly 'other': a heterotopic site. Friends present at the Yearly
Meeting were passionately united in this, a unity subsequently upheld.

Today, Friends' concerns are no longer exclusively, or even mainly, Quaker issues.
'The world' has caught up with them, or they have been caught up with 'the world',
and as the distinctiveness of their otherness and alternate ordering comes under
threat, the quest for a new heterotopic site, or sites, becomes urgent. One of the
heterotopic aspects of modern Friends is their determination to be open to everyone
and anything.[5] Ironically, while this certainly marks them out as 'other' to most
religions, and possibly even secular groups, it also contributes to their current
uncertainty about what they are about and who they are. This was expressed by Keith
Redfern in the autumn of 1999, in the national Quaker publication, *Quaker News* (no.
33): 'We live in a time which could be described as Quaker uncertainty or confusion;
in a Yearly Meeting of many differences, particularly differently expressed beliefs,
but also varied perceptions of what we should be about as Friends' (p.7).

It can no longer be assumed that those attending Meeting for Worship, or
applying for membership of the Religious Society of Friends, are necessarily
'Christian', even in the very loose Quaker interpretation of that label. This
breakdown of an overarching religious paradigm has meant that modern Friends'
sense of unity and identity no longer rests on a commonly shared religious belief; a
belief out of which their heterotopic stance emerged. Rather, Friends' unity and
identity have come to rest on their heterotopic stance itself: their sense of difference,
of Otherness and alternate ordering.

As even the latter has become increasingly threatened, so has Friends' unity. The
wide differences between them with regard to what, in the words of *Quaker News*,
'we should be about as Friends', have resulted in conflict and challenges to the
mainstream of Quakerism. The loss of a religiously based utopian vision, the loss of
a corporate discipline and authority and the loss of visible distinctiveness as they
became increasingly assimilated into the 'world', have led to Quakers' heterotopic
stance becoming increasingly internally contested.

Current British Quakerism

With the above in mind, modern Friends can be seen as falling into three groups,
namely the exclusivists, the inclusivists and the syncretists. All consider themselves
'true' Quakers, though not necessarily extending this judgment to each other.

The exclusivists are a discrete, but extremely small, group who call themselves
Friends in Christ. They regard themselves as a separate Yearly Meeting from the

Britain Yearly Meeting, although they are not acknowledged by the latter.[6] They are emphatically Christocentric, seeking a return to 'primitive' Christianity and a Quaker theology emphasizing the Christ within, a 'gospel order', and meetings for worship which are not timed or constrained to one hour. They consider the Britain Yearly Meeting as being irremediably 'out of the Light' and apostate (*The Call*, 1996, no. 1). Their vision quest is religiously inspired. And they seek to make visible their heterotopic stance by the use of 'plain' speech (the use of 'thee' and 'thou') and 'plain' dress (*The Call*, 2000, no. 1). Friends in Christ have no doubts that there is 'one true church'. The continual questioning of the concept of the 'one true church' by those within the Britain Yearly Meeting, and their conviction that the only certainty is being absolutely *un*certain (what Dandelion, 1999, has termed the 'absolute perhaps') has no warrant for the Friends in Christ. There is some 'crossover' with members of the larger, mainstream, Yearly Meeting who are concerned about the loss of explicit Christianity within the Britain Yearly Meeting, but Friends in Christ are too certain, and their clearly defined faith position too 'exclusive', to attract a widespread following amongst modern Quakers.

The inclusivists, the bulk of the Britain Yearly Meeting, consist of those who hold to the mainstream traditions and adhere to a 'behavioural creed' (Dandelion, 1996), which permits enormous flexibility of belief while constraining the performance of Quaker identity. They are still corporatist in their outlook and very often their 'Quakerism' is a given: a way of life which they take for granted and cannot imagine being without. They are loosely Christian, though Jesus may not be considered divine, his value lying more in his teachings and example than in his divinity. The concept of his atoning sacrifice is unlikely to be accepted, or acceptable (Pilgrim, 2000). Nevertheless, there is a belief in God and the possibility of discernment. And over the last five years or so there has been an upsurge of interest in learning about practices of discernment, both for individuals and for Meetings as a whole.[7] Members of this group may express understanding of and sympathy with the syncretists' pluralism, but continue to value the discipline and authority of the corporate body over and above the individualized spirituality of the syncretists. Inclusivists do not view the adoption of Quaker values by society at large with disapprobation, since they see themselves as leading the way. Their heterotopic stance rests on continuing to live at the radical edge, but not so far out of mainstream society as to lose their influence and voice.

The syncretists are much more amorphous, and appear to be concerned about their personal spiritual quest rather than theological certainties. Many of them have a sense of disconnection from traditional sources of meaning and are sceptical about fixed systems of belief which obscure more than they reveal. They seek and value comfort, healing and hope, wherever it might be found, and often pursue other non-Quaker religious and quasi-religious activities as well as attending Quaker meetings for worship (Pilgrim, 2000). They place emphasis on freedom, authenticity, the recovery of rejected knowledge and a synthesis of spiritualities. One such Friend describes herself as a Daoist Quaker with Pagan leanings (Pilgrim, 2001). They include those who are drawn by a *life style*, but *not* a religion; who in fact will often explicitly reject religion. Then there are those who are interested in *religion*, but *not* in a belief system, and those who *have* a religion of some kind, but who seem to need to appropriate a belief system with which they have some familiarity. (Current fieldwork substantiates this.) They wish to locate themselves in a group providing a powerful sense of social solidarity within which it is acceptable to construct a highly personalized spiritual belief system. They are attracted by the alternate ordering and otherness of Friends, but wish to remould it, seeing traditional Quakerism as anachronistic and acting as a brake on developing a newly distinctive alternate ordering and otherness. The heterotopic stance sought by this group is not so much about an alternate ordering, as about alternate *orderings*, thereby reflecting the spiritual market-place attitude of the wider society.

Implications and Predictions

The Religious Society of Friends is not alone in offering a heterotopic site, but few are so substantially embedded in society, or provide such a robust environment within which expressive identities may be constituted and utopic play engaged with. Friends today speak of being 'seekers'. They see themselves as on a pilgrimage towards a more spiritual, meaningful, integrated and life-revivifying existence where they can freely express all that they are. It could also be described as an attempt at escape (Cohen and Taylor, 1992; Cohen *et al.*, 1987) on the part of those who find the routines of everyday life oppressive, soulless, and ethically and morally unsatisfying. Both pilgrimage and escape attempts are transitional processes, occurring in a space in which new identities can be constructed. The spaces best suited to this transitional process are marginal, although they will always have a social centrality for those inhabiting them. They are likely to include spaces of occasion where the re-forming of identity can be rehearsed (Hetherington, 1998; Shields, 1991; 1992).

The Quaker Meeting for Worship is such a space, an occasion which allows identity performance through the expression of the values and principles of the group. This is what Friends term 'ministry'. The Meeting for Worship is the primary space where Friends come to recognize and know one another, where they develop a sense of belonging and communitas (Turner, 1969). The acceptance into membership of Friends bringing the mores and ethos of a culture committed to a personal, rather than a shared spiritual path (Heelas, 1996), is having a profound effect, not only on the understanding of what it is to be Quaker, but on the way in which identity and belonging are experienced and learned. The diminution of corporate authority no longer requires identity performance to be expressed in terms of Quaker theology. This, combined with uncertainty about what Quakerism is or should be, has created an unboundaried space which may be colonized by anyone espousing an alternate ordering. As a consequence this is an ideal utopic site, enabling the development of an expressive identity while simultaneously developing ideas about how to create a better world, the practical progressing of which 'fits' Quaker 'ideology' and the modern Quaker vision quest.

As the Religious Society of Friends is steadily penetrated by those seeking a place to express their personal spirituality rather than to follow a religion, sustaining unity and a shared identity is becoming increasingly problematic. The exclusivists have already seceded from the main Yearly Meeting, deeply disturbed by what they perceive as the apostasy of the many and the disappearance of an explicitly Christian 'ministry' in the Meeting for Worship rooted in an understanding that God's call and guidance can be given to all through any one of those present. They have reconstituted clear boundaries and offer a very specific identity. The heterotopic space they provide is unlikely to appeal to many, but it will probably continue as a small group consisting of those who are passionate about God, but who cannot tolerate the formalism and hierarchy of other Christian groups.

To date, the inclusivists have been willing to tolerate with goodwill those who are seeking to discover their own spirituality, but this goodwill is seeping away as the voices of those more recent members who wish to incorporate other traditions into Friends practice gain in volume and influence. Inclusivists place great value on the behavioural creed's ability to provide their meetings for worship with structure and order without unduly constraining the individual's 'ministry'. However, with increasing numbers of people coming to Quakerism because of its perceived lack of boundaries ('you don't have to believe anything' – Pilgrim, 2000) and provision of a space in which to rehearse their personal spirituality, the behavioural creed is coming under pressure. There is some evidence that inclusivists are concerned that a willingness to be 'open to new Light from whatever source it may come' [Quaker Faith and Practice, 1995, 1.02.7] is being misconstrued to mean that 'anything goes' (Pilgrim, fieldwork, 2000–2001). Their ironically humorous comment – 'Ask four Friends what Quakerism is about, and you'll get five different answers!' – illustrates this (Pilgrim, current fieldwork). Whether inclusivist Friends, in order to retain their identity, will ultimately be driven to establish clearer boundaries and separate themselves from their more post-modern, post-Christian element remains to be seen.

The syncretists are drawn by Friends' heterotopic stance and the utopic space it offers, rather than to an explicit religious enterprise. They are drawn to a space in which differing ideas, alternative forms of expression, alternate orderings and emerging theological concepts can be expressed without hindrance. The space allows transgressive voices a considerable audience, and it is this, together with a recognition of one another's spiritual explorations, that provides unity amongst syncretists. Their identity as a Quaker is merely one among many, and signifies an alternate ordering rather than a particular religious belief. They push at the limits of what is acceptable within the mainstream, and there are indications that syncretists are becoming increasingly exasperated with the stolidity of the inclusivists. (Pilgrim, 2000–2001). Should inclusivists feel compelled to clarify their boundaries and provide a vigorous exposition of their Quakerism, they will alienate many syncretists.

So this is my prediction. There will certainly be two Yearly Meetings in Britain, and it is likely that there will be three, by the year 2050. Friends in Christ already consider themselves a second Yearly Meeting, making for two Yearly Meetings as I write. I believe they will continue to exist, although they are unlikely to grow in size significantly, or to acquire the status that the main Britain Yearly Meeting currently holds.

My research indicates that inclusivist Friends are becoming concerned about the extremes of openness which mainstream Quakerism permits. They are caught in a double bind. Firstly, many of them are reluctant to term themselves Christian because of all that word has come to imply over the last 30 years, in particular its exclusivity; and secondly, their theological uncertainty, combined with their desire to be non-prescriptive about belief, makes it hard for them to be confident about teaching 'Quakerism'. Friends speak of Quakerism as 'being caught, not taught' and have relied on the behavioural creed to convey what Quakerism is about. Its failure in this respect is now becoming clear, and there is the beginning of a determination not to suppress expression of different understandings of spirituality but to exercise a more explicit Quaker understanding and authority (Pilgrim, 2001). If, as seems likely, this curbs the utopic space syncretists have become accustomed to, and curtails the heterotopic stance available to them, they will probably seek to form their own Yearly Meeting.

It is at present not clear whether inclusivist Friends, as a whole, feel sufficiently strongly or are sufficiently confident about their Quakerism to overcome their reluctance to lay claim to it. If they are not, syncretist Friends will not need to form their own Yearly Meeting. They will simply subsume what now constitutes Britain Yearly Meeting. Outwardly, since it would be important for the belief system to remain relatively intact, Britain Yearly Meeting might look much the same, but in fact it would be a very different kind of Quakerism, possibly signified through being renamed the Spiritual Society of Friends, as opposed to the Religious Society of Friends. If this should happen, some inclusivists may choose to leave and join Friends in Christ. It is more likely, however, that they will choose to leave and re-form a separate Yearly Meeting more in keeping with their understanding of what it is to be a Quaker and a member of the Religious Society of Friends.

Notes

1   I shall be using the terms 'Friends' and 'Quakers' interchangeably. It should be noted that this chapter is solely focused on the Quaker group in Britain.
2   Although Hetherington (1996, p.1) points out that, in fact, it has largely been applied to ideas about *post*modernity and has been used in a variety of ways. (See also Connor, 1989; Soja, 1990, 1996; Delaney, 1992; Bennet, 1995; Gennocchio, 1995.)
3   Ms in Bournville Cocoa Works Archives – letter to Carl Heath, 13 September 1940.

4   In my field work I have come across people who regard themselves as Quakers even though they
     have not attended Meeting for Worship for 10 to 20 years.
5   Examples abound in the letter pages of *The Friend*; see, for example, p.16, 'All Inclusive', 26 May
     2000.
6   This was made clear to me in conversations which took place earlier in 2001, when I queried their
     status with Britain Yearly Meeting.
7   Note the frequent requests and the long waiting lists for courses on discernment run by Woodbrooke
     Quaker Studies College (although these are attended by only 5 per cent of the Yearly Meeting).

References

Bauman, Richard 1998: *Let Your Words Be Few.* London: Quaker Home Service.

Bennett, Tony 1995: *The Birth of the Museum.* London: Routledge.

Cohen, Eric, Nachman, Ben-Yehuda and Aviad, Janet 1987: Re-centering the World: the Quest for
    'Elective' Centres in a Secularised Universe. *The Sociological Review*, 35 (2), pp.320–46.

Cohen, Stanley and Taylor, Laurie 1992: *Escape Attempts: the Theory and Practice of Resistance to
    Everyday Life.* London: Routledge.

Connor, Stephen 1989: *Postmodernist Culture.* Oxford: Blackwell.

Cresswell, Tim 1996: *In Place/Out of Place.* Minneapolis: University of Minnesota Press.

Dale, Jonathon 1996: *Beyond the Spirit of the Age.* London: Quaker Home Service Press

Dandelion, Pink 1996: *A Sociological Analysis of the Theology of Quakers.* Lampeter, Wales: The Edwin
    Mellen Press.

Dandelion, Pink 1999: The 'Absolute Perhaps'. Quakers an an Uncertain Sect. BSA Sociology of
    Religion Conference 'Religion and Identity', Durham.

Delaney, Jill 1992: Ritual Space in the Canadian Museum of Civilization: Consuming Canadian Identity.
    In Robert Shields (ed.), *Lifestyle Shopping.* London: Routledge, pp.136–48.

Flanagan, Kieran and Jupp, Peter C. (eds) 2001: *Virtue Ethics and Sociology: Issues of Modernity and
    Religion.* Basingstoke: Palgrave Publishers.

Foucault, Michel 1977: The Order of Things. An Archaeology of the Human Sciences. London:
    Tavistock Publications.

Foucault, Michel 1986: Of Other Spaces. *Diacritics. A Review of Contemporary Criticism*, Spring, 16 (1),
    pp.22–7.

Fox, George 1975: *The Journal of George Fox.* John L. Nickalls (ed.). London: London Yearly Meeting.

Gennocchio, Benjamin 1995: Discourse, Discontinuity, Difference: The Question of 'Other' Spaces. In
    Sophie Watson and Katherine Gibson (eds), *Postmodern Cities and Spaces.* Oxford: Basil Blackwell,
    pp.35–46.

Gwyn, Douglas 1995: *The Covenant Crucified.* Wallingford, PA: Pendle Hill Publications.

Heelas, Paul 1996: *The New Age Movement.* Oxford: Blackwell Publishers.

Heron, Alastair 1992: *Caring Conviction Commitment.* London: Quaker Home Service.

Heron, Alastair 1999: *Quaker Identity: Religious Society – or Friendly Society.* Kelso: Curlew
    Productions.

Hetherington, Kevin 1996: *The Badlands of Modernity: Heterotopia and Social Ordering.* London:
    Routledge.

Hetherington, Kevin 1998: *Expressions of Identity.* London: Sage Publications.

Isichei, Elizabeth 1970: *Victorian Quakers.* London: Open University Press.

Keith, Michael and Pile, Steven (eds) 1993: *Place and Politics of Identity.* London: Routledge.

Lynch, Gordon (unpublished manuscript): The Crisis of Meaning in Western Culture. Personal Response
    to the Novels of Douglas Coupland.

Marin, Louis 1984: *Utopics: Spatial Play.* London: Macmillan.

Marin, Louis 1992: Frontiers of Utopia: Past and Present. *Critical Enquiry*, 19 (3), pp.397–420.

Pilgrim, Gay 2000–present: unpublished fieldwork.

Punshon, John 1984: *Portrait in Grey*. London: Quaker Home Service.

Quaker Faith and Practice: the Book of Christian Discipline of the Yearly Meeting of the Religious Society of Friends (Quakers) in Britain 1995. UK: The Yearly Meeting of the Religious Society of Friends (Quakers) in Britain.

Rose, Gillian 1993: *Feminism and Geography*. Oxford: Polity.

Shields, Robert 1991: *Places on the Margin*. London: Routledge.

Shields, Robert (ed.) 1992: *Lifestyle Shopping: the Subject of Consumption*. London: Routledge.

Soja, Edward 1990: Heterotopologies: A Remembrance of Other Spaces in the Citadel-LA. *Strategies*, 3, pp.6–39.

Soja, Edward 1996: *Thirdspace*. Oxford: Blackwell.

Turner, Victor 1969: *The Ritual Process*. London: Routledge & Kegan Paul.

Turner, Victor 1982: *From Ritual to Theatre: the Human Seriousness of Play*. New York: Performing Arts Journal Publication.

Wildwood, Alex 1999: *A Faith to Call Our Own*. London: Quaker Home Service.

CHAPTER 13

Understanding the Spirituality of People who Do Not Go to Church

Kate Hunt

'And then I felt I gave up religion, but the God bit didn't leave me.'[1] What happens to 'the God bit' in people when the common opinion is that institutional religion is outdated? As we begin the new millennium, the influence of traditional religion is in seemingly terminal decline in Britain (Brierley, 2000). But does this mean the end of spiritual awareness amongst ordinary people? Not for Mary: 'God's important to me, I talk to Him every day. And I wouldn't have said I'm a religious person.'

This chapter introduces a research project, based at the University of Nottingham, that looked at this very issue. David Hay and I wanted to take seriously the experience of people such as Mary; people for whom the spiritual realm is a reality, but who feel alienated from the religious tradition of this country: 'And nobody wants to feel a fool anymore. ... I mean, religious is now associated with being slightly cranky, slightly nutty really.'

The aim of the project was to listen to people who generally distrust the idea of religious orthodoxy, but who consider themselves to have a spiritual aspect to their lives. These are the people who feel that the Christian religion is too much to take on board completely, but who find that they are left with 'the God bit' that will not go away. We were interested in finding out how they construct their own faith journeys without the support of a formal religion or structured set of beliefs. As Christianity is still the traditional religion of Europe, we were also keen to see how far people's individual spiritualities either connect or are in conflict with Christian spirituality.

Perspectives

Every research project has a perspective, and it often helps to know something about the people involved in order to appreciate the particular flavour of that research. David Hay and I come from quite different backgrounds, but have a similar understanding of the role of spirituality in people's daily lives. David, himself a biologist, has been influenced by the work of the Oxford zoologist Alister Hardy. From his childhood, Hardy was aware of a spiritual or religious dimension to his experience, while also being conscious of the tension between his scientific education and his religious beliefs. This was particularly so in the case of his studies in evolutionary theory. For Hardy (1966), spiritual awareness is an inbuilt predisposition in all people; it is biological. David Hay (1994) has continued Hardy's work investigating people's spiritual experiences. Through his work with Rebecca Nye (1998) researching children's spirituality, he has developed the concept of 'relational consciousness' as the predisposition underlying spiritual awareness.

My own background is in theology, and so my language is often very different to David's. I may speak of how all people are made in the image of God, and he may speak of spiritual awareness being hard-wired in people; but we are actually meaning the same thing. The ability to be spiritually aware is part of what it means to be human.

Nuts and Bolts

What is the best way to find a sample for such a research project? Our target sample was anyone who did not go to church or to any other religious activity, which amounts to the majority of the British population. It was obvious that we would need some way of refining our sample. After much debate, we decided to speak with people who had no involvement with formal religion, but who felt that they were either spiritual or religious. We designed a recruitment questionnaire and stopped people outside a local supermarket in a suburb of Nottingham. Those who said they did not attend church, but who identified themselves as either spiritual or religious, were asked to attend a focus group to discuss these issues further. Four focus groups met, one made up of people over the age of 40, another of those under 40, a third made up entirely of women, the fourth of men. From these groups, 31 people were interviewed in their own homes.

We were interested in finding out what people think about their own spirituality and so the research conversations were semi-structured, giving individuals the freedom to speak about their own experiences or beliefs. The project has yielded a wealth of data, in this chapter there is only room to discuss three specific themes. Here we focus on what it means to be spiritual, the need for sacred space, and the taboo on speaking about religion and spirituality.

What it Means to be Spiritual

Over the past 30 years, the word 'spiritual' has gone from being a technical word within Christianity to being part of everyday parlance. Spirituality is now used as a concept in education circles, in health care, even in the commercial world. As its usage has grown, so have its possible meanings. For this reason, we were careful not to define the word 'spiritual' at any time in the recruitment process or the research conversations. We felt it was important to give individuals the opportunity to interpret the word for themselves. The way people use the word illustrates the myriad of meanings and the confusion over what is actually meant when people say something is 'spiritual'.

Spirituality and Morality

As we read the conversations, it becomes clear that there is a link between people's understanding of spirituality and morality:

> I think spiritual means do you feel there is something out there? Do you believe? Do you have an open mind about things? Do you believe in goodness, and in friendship, and in helping others? And yes, I do.

For Lucy, a young woman in her twenties, being spiritual is about the way she relates to those around her. The content of her belief in 'something out there' may be vague, but her actions are concrete. Lucy understands her own spirituality in terms of the depth of her friendships and her desire to care for others in society.

Jenny, who is in her thirties, continues this theme of spirituality being about relationships. For her, being spiritual is about having a deep sense of connectedness with other people:

> I think for me it's more to do with the human spirit, the connection that we have with other people and how incredibly strong that can be, even sometimes with people you don't know. ... On the surface we might have those human connections, but without that kind of deeper connection with somebody it would be very shallow, and life would be sort of quite meaningless if we didn't have that with people.

But there is another strand to Jenny's spirituality, and that is her sense of connectedness with herself:

> It's how you feel within yourself as well, it's not just that connection with other people. It's like your own spirituality, your own feelings about yourself. And this is why I do actually sort of sit and I do spend quite a lot of time on my own now. But I'm quite happy to do that, I'm quite happy to sort of sit, and think, and contemplate, and work things out in my head.

Spirituality has depth. It is a serious aspect of life, and those who are not spiritual are often considered to be shallow and superficial by the people we spoke with.

Spirituality and Religion

For the people in our study, the difference between spirituality and religion tends to be that religion is linked with specific beliefs and actions, whereas spirituality is more about a frame of mind, or a way of looking at the world. Sharon, a woman in

her thirties who has had hardly any contact with institutional religion, describes it
in this way:

> Religious means that you go to church very regularly, you know, and you do all the things.
> And spiritual ... I just think that it's an awareness of knowing that there's something and
> you don't really know what, you know, without going to church all the time.

Without the structure and framework of a traditional (in our case Christian)
religion, credal and doctrinal beliefs become either incomprehensible or irrelevant.
Again, this is illustrated by Sharon, who describes her acute embarrassment at
finding herself at a Communion Service and having little understanding of the
meaning of the ritual. Her belief is in 'something', and not in Christian doctrine:

> So that was quite off-putting, I must admit, because I thought if my husband went, he'd
> never go again, never ever go again, because he felt a fool, you know. And to tell you the
> truth, I wasn't a hundred percent sure what it was meant to be symbolising, because I've
> never had anything like that at a church before. ... That was quite embarrassing really, yes.

Traditional religion is an alien world for Sharon, and yet she is happy to describe
herself as being spiritual.

Spiritual people are seen as open-minded, something that is highly prized in our
society. By contrast, religious people are often considered narrow-minded; allegedly
they only believe what they are taught to believe. In a society where children are
encouraged to question from an early age, the idea of believing in a rigid set of
doctrines is seen as immature.

> I think people that are spiritual are people that think a lot about lots of things. Whereas
> religious people just base their thoughts and stuff on God and traditional religious type
> things.

Joanne, who is also in her thirties, echoes this:

> I think some people who are just religious, are just fanatical, aren't they? But I think if
> you're more spiritual, that's not, you're not fanatical, you're just, does that make sense?
> [Yes] You know, it's more within yourself, but you can reach out to other people
> without ramming things down their throat, if you know what I mean, going constantly
> on about God, and things like that.

There is a strong value judgment being made here; religious people do not think
deeply about life, but are spoon-fed on an old-fashioned diet of dogma. Matthew,
who is in his forties, picks up this theme when he describes his reasons for disliking
religious people:

> It's this certainty of belief very often [by religious people], it's monomania, you know,
> it's just totally irrational, it's not allowing any light in. It's, this is right and it'll be right
> for ever, it's a rail track to the horizon. And it's not like that, you know.

This version of spirituality does not resonate with Matthew's own experience of life. No wonder he is not alone in being adamant that he is spiritual and not religious.

Belief in 'Something'

However, belief itself *is* important. 'I definitely believe in something' is a phrase that occurs in nearly every conversation. This belief appears to have little, if any, substance. Yet it is important to people and they often become quite vehement in their affirmation of this simple creed, when challenged about it. Sharon describes her own belief in this way:

> I still do believe there's something, um, because I can't prove there isn't. I mean I can't prove there is, but you know, I do, yes I do definitely believe there is something, more to heaven and earth as they say, definitely.

The problem seems to be that people have no language with which to describe their experiences of the sacred or their beliefs. The Church itself has struggled to find an adequate language to speak of the divine, so it is hardly surprising that those who have had little or no contact with a religious tradition find themselves literally lost for words. The apophatic strand of Christianity suggests that the only way to describe God is negatively; what God is not. These matters are very difficult to put into words, even by professional theologians. Consequently people's conversations are filled with contradiction, incoherence and frustration, as they attempt to describe the indescribable. Sean, a man in his thirties who left the Church at the age of 13, says:

> I just find it hard to believe that there is nothing. That's where, yeh, where I sort of come from. I just, I can't accept that there is just a line in the sand, and once you reach that mark, then that's it, the shutter kind of drops. There just has to be something more.

When trying to speak about their belief in God, many people describe childhood pictures of God as a bearded old man, sitting on a cloud, or of Jesus as the baby, meek and mild. These are images that they have obtained almost by osmosis, either through attendance at Sunday School or simply through growing up in this culture. They instinctively know that these images are inadequate; they do not reflect their own experience of God. But the problem is that they do not have any other language to use to speak of the divine. Some are able to borrow words from other traditions, religious and secular, such as 'universal consciousness', 'driving force' or 'divine energy', but more often than not, they are left with believing in 'something'.

John, who is in his forties, describes his own spiritual awareness like this:

> So I developed my own connection with God, my own picture of what God is to me. And it isn't the same as I feel the Church portrays God, if you like. I feel that the Church, the formal Church as such, has a sort of propagandist view of what God should

be to you, and it's been more helpful to have my own view on what God is. I don't have a visual idea of a sort of a being if you like, a sort of a character, sort of a form or a shape, just a force, an energy if you like, uh, a driving force. *But I do feel there's perhaps more than that to what God is, but I can't visualise or see what that is.* Maybe in the future, it'll become more clear, but right now it's just this energy if you like, this force. (My emphasis)

John sees his journey into old age as being a journey into spiritual enlightenment. At the moment, it is as if he is walking on a foggy day. But one day he hopes that the sun will break through the clouds and he will finally understand the mystery of life. There are echoes here of St Paul's words: 'For now we see in a mirror dimly, but then face to face. Now I know in part; then I shall understand fully, even as I have been fully understood' (1 Corinthians 13:12 RSV).[2] And this from a man who has not had a religious upbringing at all.

So there is belief, but it is not 'believing without belonging', to use Grace Davie's (1994) phrase. Believing without belonging implies that the belief has some Christian content, but, as we have seen, many people have little actual knowledge of the Christian faith. It is belief, yes, but not belief in an orthodox Christian God, rather a belief in 'something'.

The Need for Sacred Space

Another theme that comes through in the conversations is the continued need for what may be called 'sacred space', both physical and metaphorical. People feel the need to withdraw from the busyness and turmoil of daily life and find space to reflect and simply 'be'.

Sacred space can be found in traditionally religious places, even for people who are generally dismissive of organized religion. Throughout the conversations the popular view of the Church is that it is an institution full of hypocrites. And yet some people still speak of the importance of attending church services at Christmas-time (in spite of asserting that they are not churchgoers). There seems to be a desire to rediscover a mythical golden age when people lived in harmony and the world was a safer place. Belinda describes the feeling of being with her family in church at Christmas:

> [On Christmas Eve] we have the candles and everything and it's lovely when everybody's all together and everybody's ... it just seems as though it's peaceful and everything's all right even if it's only for that one night or that one day, you know.

People see the church building as a sacred space that is open to them. In much the same way that Philip Larkin (1988) speaks of going into an empty church in his poem, *Church Going*, written in 1954, and not quite knowing why he is there, some people find church buildings to be full of resonance. Matthew says:

> I like going into churches, from an aesthetic, you know. I think they're great places, and they have weight and silence and tranquillity and beauty and you can find, you know, solace.

There seems to be an atmosphere in church buildings that people cannot account for in any rational way. Graham, a policeman in his thirties, describes with some surprise his own reaction to a trip to a cathedral:

> Something that I do find strange is that last year we went up to North Yorkshire, we went to Ripon and we visited Ripon Cathedral. Now, as I've said, I'm not particularly religious. I don't go to church. But the feeling of calmness inside there and the feeling of humbleness if you like, you know, it was amazing. And I mean, I was obviously with my wife and she sort of agreed with me, but I don't think she really had the feeling that I had. It was just one of complete humbleness if you like. It was a strange, strange feeling, strange feeling.

For Graham, the experience was alien and yet compelling. His ambivalence towards the experience comes through in his repetition of the phrase, 'a strange, strange feeling'. Perhaps there are echoes of Otto's (1950) *'mysterium tremendum et fascinans'* here.

There is something about the actual building that appeals to people, particularly men, as these quotations illustrate. Tom describes it in this way: 'Rock, brick – it's like a tape recorder, it echoes things from the past.'

Simon describes at length how he had found himself going into his local parish church after learning of the tragic death of his young nephew. He says:

> they've got a stained glass window straight in front of the altar. And I don't know what it was, but when I walked out of there I felt a hundred per cent better. Just being there. I don't know if … I don't know, I can't explain it. I haven't got the words to explain it, but I can definitely say I felt a hundred per cent better as I walked out after that about the events.

So the traditional sacred space of our culture retains some hold over people, even when they have no desire to attend for formal worship.

Sacred space is not limited to traditionally religious buildings. During the conversations, people shared ways in which they create their own sacred space, either physical or metaphorical. Joanne looks back to her childhood and remembers how her mother took her to church for the Brownie Parade Service each month. But she then goes on to describe how it was actually her proudly atheistic father who encouraged her to reflect on her place in the universe. Every Sunday morning they swam up and down the local pool, discussing infinity and the meaning of the universe under the vaulted roof of their own secular cathedral.

Jenny has been through a painful divorce and describes how she began to sit on her back-door step each night, after she had put her children to bed. To begin with she listened to music, drank a few glasses of wine and smoked a cigarette. But gradually the music was turned off, the wine was kept in the fridge and she began to discover her own style of meditation. As she describes it:

> And it is quite, um, spiritual is such a funny word, it encompasses so many things, but it is quite a spiritual feeling, that sort of peace that you get, that sort of peace with the world.

This has now become a daily ritual for Jenny.

Belinda is a busy woman who sees her life as a frantic juggling act of her roles as worker, mother and wife. Her garden has become a refuge where she is able to spend time away from the demands of family life, but it is during her annual holiday by the sea that truly she finds her own sacred space:

> I think it goes back to the pace of life that I lead and the fact that when I do get away from my everyday life I'm almost absorbing the serenity that you get when you can get away from this frenetic pace of life. That's the only way I can describe it really. And as I say, it happens so rarely that it's blissful when I get the opportunity. ... There's just something about the sea. I love going to the seaside. It just brings ... I don't know. Brings everything closer somehow and slows everything down. Crazy!

Listening to people's stories, it seems as if it is vitally important to create these moments in the busyness of life, or else life becomes empty and meaningless.

The Taboo on Speaking about Religion or Spirituality

As people talk, they share how difficult it is to discuss their own beliefs or spiritual experiences with anyone else. Even raising the issue of religion in general is considered risky. People use strong language to describe the penalties for this kind of talk; you would be considered strange, weird, or even crazy. Every conversation alludes to this fear at some time.

Evelyn, who is in her thirties, describes her experience of being confirmed in an Anglican church a few years previously. She had begun to go to church after the birth of her children and had been persuaded to attended confirmation classes. As Evelyn herself admits, this was more a chance to meet other people than a definite religious conversion. However, she was amazed at how she had felt when the Bishop confirmed her:

> And I sort of went along with it because it was nice, everybody was friendly and everything. But when I knelt down and he put his hand on my head and I, I felt absolutely overjoyed. And it was so surprising because it, I hadn't gone there in a fervour of religion or anything and it wasn't my life's work. It was, you know, it was something that I'd gone along and done. ... It was absolutely overwhelming.

This was obviously a powerful religious experience for Evelyn. However, she is careful who she shares this experience with, as she is afraid that she will be mocked and the experience tarnished by other people's negative reactions.

> But I don't think any of them [her friends] would have understood it ... I wonder if any of them, if I would have cheapened it really by telling everybody about it ... Or perhaps, you know, if any of them had made a joke out of it and perhaps brought it up at a later date, you know, at parties and things. 'Oh well, she was confirmed, you know, she's seen the light, haven't you Evelyn?' You know like this sort of thing?

She prefers to keep it safe in her own memory.

The men are particularly vulnerable to this social taboo. They think about these issues, often a great deal, but they *never* speak to anyone about them. The only time that this kind of discourse is permitted is late at night when they are drunk. Presumably this is because no one will remember what has been said the next day. Matthew has been attempting to describe his own spirituality when he says: 'I play, these guys I play football with on Sunday, you know, they'd think I was a lunatic if they could hear me sort of talking, you know...'. Matthew's conversation is full of profound spiritual discourse, and yet he is deeply aware that there are places where this kind of talk is dangerous.

Sean is quite happy to talk about mysterious events that members of his family have experienced, but he is adamant that this is not part of his own life. He is aware of the spiritual dimension of life, but somehow feels that it does not apply to himself:

> I just think some people are mentally in tune that way, and some people aren't. I've probably deadened most of my brain cells that are to do with it by sort of vast quantities of alcohol or something [laughter].

Sean takes refuge in the traditional image of the 'lad' whose only concern is in drinking 10 pints every Saturday night. This behaviour is acceptable, even desirable, for a young man. Admitting to spiritual feelings is definitely not.

And yet Sean was prepared to attend a focus group and then be interviewed again in his own home about this taboo area. Why? This does seem to have become the society of the focus group, and so there may be something in people not wanting to be left out, wanting to have their opinions heard. But there is more to it than that. People seem to value the opportunity of being able to talk about what they believe or have experienced, because this very rarely, if ever, happens in their daily life.

But this sharing does not always happen easily. There is a distinct shift in the tone of many of the conversations. People begin somewhat superficially, or use humour as an avoidance tactic, and it is only towards the end of the conversation that they begin to open up and share something personal. They seem to be sounding me out. Am I safe? Will I respect them or think them mad? Sarah illustrates this well. In the midst of telling me about a powerful vision she had seen during labour, she breaks off to say: 'Are you laughing at me?' I like to think that my powers of empathy are rather better than that, but her fear comes across as genuine. This is a precious memory, and she is afraid that I will not take it seriously. I wonder whether this is a particularly British phenomenon? It is more than embarrassment, rather a fear of being ridiculed or even shamed by the dominant, rational culture.

Summary

The research conversations are rich in detail. In this chapter it has only been possible to concentrate on three particular themes that run through the narratives: what people mean when they say they are spiritual, the need to create sacred space in life, and the fear of admitting to spiritual experiences or awareness that is present in our culture.

Looking to the Future

In our project we have been focusing on spirituality outside institutional religion at the turn of the century. But what of the future? If this research were to be repeated in 30 years, would there be similarities in the findings? Although the people we spoke to have had little or no contact with traditional religion, the remnants of Christianity can still be found in their language and understanding of spirituality. Even those who have deliberately chosen to follow their own spiritual path, and have rejected Christianity, are still in dialogue with the Christian tradition. It cannot be otherwise in our culture which, even though it is secularized, is steeped in Christian assumptions. So will this remain true for the next generation?

This book is concerned with the future and so here I must be brave and make my own predictions for the course of spirituality in Britain. The traditional religion of this country appears to be in terminal decline and it seems highly unlikely that this trend will change. People will not suddenly return to the institution. However, spiritual awareness will continue. It has to, because it is part and parcel of being human. But the way that spirituality is expressed will continue to evolve. The language and symbols of Christianity will become increasingly remote to most people, but the 'nagging instinct' for a belief in 'something more', as Tom put it, will remain. The danger is that, without a shared language, spirituality will continue to be privatized. Individuals will create their own sacred space, but will not know how to share that with others. The challenge for those of us who believe in community will be to encourage people to look outwards and realize that they are not alone; there are many, many others who also value the spiritual aspect of life.

I'm not religious ... I definitely believe in something.

Acknowledgments

I would like to thank Dr David Hay for his comments on this chapter, and for all that he has taught me as we have worked together for the past four years. David has been a very generous teacher, and I have learnt a great deal about research and also about the spiritual life from his example.

Notes

1   All the quotations are taken from the transcripts of the research conversations; all names have been changed.
2   The Revised Standard version of The Bible.

References

Brierley, Peter 2000: *Religious Trends 1999/2000*. London: Christian Research.
Davie, Grace 1994: *Religion in Britain Since 1945 – Believing Without Belonging*. Oxford: Blackwell.
Hardy, Alister 1966: *The Divine Flame: An Essay Towards a Natural History of Religion*. London: Collins.
Hay, David 1994: 'The Biology of God': What is the Current Status of Hardy's Hypothesis?, *International Journal for the Psychology of Religion*, 4 (1), pp.1–23.
Hay, David with Nye, Rebecca 1998: *The Spirit of the Child*. London: HarperCollins.
Larkin, Philip 1988: *Collected Poems* (ed., Anthony Thwaite), London: Faber & Faber.
Otto, Rudolph 1950: *The Idea of the Holy*. Oxford: Oxford University Press.

CHAPTER 14

'Witchcraft will not soon Vanish from this Earth': Wicca in the 21st Century

Jo Pearson

Introduction

In the conclusion to his 1980 work *A History of Witchcraft: Sorcerers, Heretics and Pagans*, Jeffrey Russell stated, 'For good or ill, magic continues to appeal and witchcraft will not soon vanish from this earth'. Certainly, given the proliferation of various types of witchcraft at the beginning of the 21st century, one is inclined to agree. For those who identify themselves as witches, the claim might be extended to encompass the entirety of human history; witchcraft will not vanish, for it has always been, and always will be, a part of human experience of the world. Such claims are not so surprising when one takes into account the multivalent nature of 'the witch' as an image or symbol. The very lack of definitional precision which surrounds the witch and witchcraft lends an all-pervasive fluidity to the atemporality of a practice which exudes an aura of mystery, danger, fear and excitement across times and across cultures. But in 1940s England, a framework was established around witchcraft which allowed for the initial creation and subsequent development of a specific magical and initiatory mystery religion, Wicca.[1]

The focus of this chapter is, therefore, a religion which is approximately 60 years old.[2] It is 'the only religion which England has ever given the world' (Hutton, 1999, p.vii), and its global spread across northern Europe, the USA, Canada, Australia, New Zealand and South Africa indicates that it has evolved and, at times, mutated quite dramatically in the second half of the 20th century. Influences have come and gone, having a distinct impact in some countries and leaving little recognizable mark in others. In some areas, debates have raged as Wicca has acclimatized: in the southern hemisphere, for example, discussions continue as to how the seasonal rituals of the Wheel of the Year should be celebrated, given that Midwinter/Yule in the northern hemisphere is Midsummer in the southern. In the USA and Canada, practices borrowed from First Nations peoples have been adopted by Wiccans which mean little to some Europeans, who may instead opt for Celtic, Saxon or Germanic inspiration, making a link to the supposed indigenous traditions of northern European ancestry. Likewise, feminist witchcraft, which emerged from the feminist consciousness movement in the USA, has had a profound impact on Wicca in that country; whilst feminism has certainly influenced English Wicca, feminist witchcraft itself is far less pronounced, and has had a far greater impact on practices in, for example, New Zealand (Rountree, 2001).

This admittedly brief summation of Wicca in global perspective suggests something of its success and its development since its inception: the mere fact that we can trace the processes of transmission among the far-northern and far-southern hemispheres perhaps indicates its relevance to those of a Protestant background.[3] But Wicca has also been instrumental in the subsequent development of a variety of forms of Paganism.[4] Indeed, Hutton (1999, p.401) contends that Wicca is the classical form from which all other Pagan groups evolved – a moot point, for it may be that other forms of Paganism would have developed independently. Nevertheless, the subsequent developments to which I have alluded include the transformation of Paganism from the attitude or mind-set associated with various figures of the 18th and 19th centuries to a set of self-consciously religious practices splintered into myriad forms: modern Pagan Druidry, Goddess spirituality, shamanism, Heathenism/Northern Traditions, Isis worship, non-aligned Paganism, feminist witchcraft, and various other types of witchcraft, which heavily outnumber initiatory Wicca.[5] Some forms, such as Goddess spirituality and feminist witchcraft, overlap to a certain extent, share common histories and practices, and influence each other in stimulating and productive ways. Nevertheless, conflation is unhelpful; these myriad forms require disentangling and situating with reference to each other, a complex task which requires separate treatment.[6]

Thus, whilst present-day Paganism may have *originated* in 1940s Britain in the form of a 'relatively self-contained, England-based occultist religion' (Hanegraaff, 1998, p.85) known as Wicca, an increasing variety of forms of witchcraft and Paganism has developed, as a consequence of which Wicca has moved from being at the forefront of the development of modern Paganism to becoming one of many Pagan traditions.[7] This chapter sets out to explore the relationship between Wicca and Paganism as well as that between Wicca (and to a lesser extent Paganism) and Christianity. Based on this exploration, and on sociological data, the chapter assesses the significance of Wicca, and predicts its future in the religious milieu of the third millennium. What are we to expect of the future? Will Wicca be able to maintain its distinctive identity in the face of religious diffusion, and if so, how will this be achieved? And how will the relationship between Wicca and Christianity develop, particularly in light of the catastrophic event of 11 September 2001 and its religious implications?

Wicca and Paganism

In 1996, of the estimated 110 000–120 000 Pagans in Britain, only 10 000 were initiated Wiccans.[8] Initiatory Wicca quite clearly remains small, despite the growth of Paganism, and despite Wicca's position as the core group around which Paganism has emerged.[9] In addition, as Paganism has increased in popularity and alternative traditions to Wicca have become established, the distinctiveness of Wicca in relation to the wider, non-aligned Pagan community has become, somewhat paradoxically, both more *and* less pronounced. Within Wicca, a distinctive identity is pronounced: practitioners increasingly feel that the growing popularity of Pagan spiritualities is 'eroding the previously closely guarded secrecy of Wicca' (Harrington, 2000, p.7), and that the specific nature of Wicca needs to be re-established.[10] As a consequence of the appropriation of 'Wicca' by uninitiated people, annoyance has grown among initiates, who see themselves as practitioners of a serious religion which demands a great deal of commitment and dedication.[11] The terminology of identification seems to have become confused, so that the distinctiveness of Wicca is no longer recognized by those identifying with the current cultural trendiness for identifying oneself as Pagan, and in particular Wiccan.[12] Thus, whereas even 10 years ago one could assume that those who identified themselves as 'Wiccan' were initiates of the Alexandrian and/or Gardnerian traditions of Wicca, there is no longer any guarantee that someone who describes themselves as 'Wiccan' is initiated as such.

Instead, the last decade of the 20th century saw the commodification of witchcraft which 'facilitates an ideology of consumption by attempting to manipulate people's decisions about their spiritual practices for the purpose of selling commodities such as books of spells and bottles of lotion' (Ezzy, 2001, p.31). Commodified witchcraft thus exists at the point of overlap between Paganism and the commercial side of the New Age, often regarded as the epitome of religious consumerism.[13] At the opposite end of the spectrum, Wiccans regard the commercial market as antagonistic to their teaching, for which one should not make a charge: commodification 'reduces esoteric knowledge about the sacred to a thing to be used . . . Simply, the commodification of Wicca reduces the sacred to the profane' (ibid., p.35).

Practitioners thus feel that Wicca has suffered, from both *dilution* through the development of Paganism and *trivialization* through the commodification of witchcraft, both of which Steve Bruce (2002) notes as signs of vulnerability in his discussion of 'diffuse religion' (in which he includes Wicca and Paganism) (p.109). Yet it is also likely that at least some of the people who seek out initiatory Wicca have done so as a result of the increased awareness facilitated by this dissemination of information. If so, perhaps Wicca has been the victim of its own success: the popularity of witchcraft, Wicca and Paganism at present shows no signs of abating, but it is this very popularity which has led to the proliferation of 'how-to' books which claim to equip anyone of any age or level of experience with the tools of Wicca, be it histories (often myths), rituals of initiation, forming one's own coven or working magic.[14] One cannot help but agree with Bruce's (2002) claim that such triviality 'allows novices to become adepts without the difficult bits in between' (p.113).

So how is Wicca responding to the growth of Paganism (of which it is ambiguously a part) on the one hand, and the proliferation of the 'do-it-yourself', commodified witchcraft market on the other? In terms of its relationship with

Paganism, there are signs of a desire for increased differentiation on both sides. Greater levels of diffusion may, in fact, strengthen Paganism since, as Ramsay MacMullen (1997) has pointed out with regard to ancient paganism, 'This religion had no single center, spokesman, director, or definition of itself; therefore no one point of vulnerability ... A very resistant thing then, this paganism – to anyone who wanted to do away with it' (pp.32–3).

Wicca, since its inception, has used initiation, secrecy and intimate community to maintain strong, concrete boundaries which demarcate who is an 'insider' and who is an 'outsider'. In doing so, it keeps its structure and practice distinct from the general mêlée of Paganism in which 'inside' and 'outside' status is not an issue. 'All Wiccans are Pagans, but not all Pagans are Wiccans' used to be a popular saying among Wiccans. But this statement, indicating a pervasive Wicca which influences Pagans but allows entry only to a few, now seems to require revision. Paganism has found its own identity/identities, and these tend to be at the opposite end of the scale from occultism; as Justin Woodman (2000) has pointed out, stellar-based occultism seems far removed from earth-based Paganism. Wicca, in fact, remains precariously balanced between the two, for as Wouter Hanegraaff (1998) has noted, Wicca is 'a neo-pagan development of traditional occultist ritual magic, but ... the latter movement is not itself pagan. In other words [Wicca] gradually and almost imperceptibly shades into a non-pagan domain' (p.86).

Nevertheless, it is likely that Wicca will continue to play an important role within Paganism and to a large extent ignore the cultural trend to identify as Wiccan, treating commodified witchcraft as a passing phase. Whether this trend will continue is debatable. If it does, we may see Wicca withdrawing from the public eye, leaving it to the non-initiated Wiccan 'gurus' to fight it out among themselves. Given this, one can hardly avoid speculating on what has happened and what it might indicate for the future. As Catherine Bell (1997) has pointed out, 'the histories of Christianity, Islam and Judaism are full of times when the tendency to be a highly prescriptive religion for the few and thereby maintain tradition and a clear identity has come into conflict with a tendency towards flexibility that could allow the religion to be embraced and appropriated by increasingly different communities' (p.195), and these tendencies seem to be already a part of Wiccan and Pagan history. But it is almost impossible to say how the core of initiatory Wicca will respond if the growth and popularity continues, and it is unlikely that there will be any unified response: since all covens are autonomous, responses will differ according to context and perspective. In general terms, we might expect a continuation – of initiation, training, ritual and magic – without reference to what is going on in the simulacrum of a perceived fad. What we can be certain of, and what we must be aware of, is that esoteric, initiatory Wicca is at present veiled by a plethora of peripheral Wiccan-derived groups, and it is therefore imperative that scholars take care to establish as fully as possible the nature of the groups they study.

Some Sociological Data: do Numbers Matter?

Contrary to my point above (which admittedly relates to ancient paganism, though I think that in no way lessens its implications!), Bruce (2002) claims that 'diffuse religion has little social impact. . . . It does not drive its believers to evangelise' (p.109), and indeed, we are concerned in this chapter with a religion, numbering at most 10 000 adherents, which claims not to seek converts.[15] Undoubtedly, in terms of numbers, it has very little social impact. Yet the implicit assumption in Bruce's statement is that all religions *want* to have a social impact. Likewise, Rodney Stark and William Sims Bainbridge's (1985) assertion that new religions 'rarely amount to much because modern societies are so large [and] must grow at astonishing rates in order to reach significant size in a generation or two' (p.365) assumes that *all* 'new religions' have a desire to bring large numbers of people under their control and significantly affect society as a whole. In fact, slow organic growth is the preferred norm in Wicca, and indeed is the most realistic means of increase given that entry into Wicca is through covens containing on average only five to eight people. Wicca neither grows rapidly nor fails, and its structure in autonomous covens, although making it unlikely that Wicca will become a mainstream religion, also ensures that it does not fail.[16] Wicca regards itself as marginal and esoteric, as a religion which is inappropriate for the majority of people, and thus it does not seek to become mainstream. Nevertheless, its effect on society has come about through the heightened awareness bought through the dissemination of carefully chosen information about Wicca in popular publications, and through media publicity, which has fed into the development of Paganism and of the trendy fads mentioned above. And although the idea that 'unless one constantly works to preserve a body of doctrine, the ideas will gradually accommodate to the cultural norms' (Bruce 2002, p. 116) seems highly unlikely when those ideas – witchcraft, magic, ritual nudity and so on – have always been seen as antagonistic to the cultural norms (and, indeed, this is part of their continuing appeal), Wiccans themselves do correspond to cultural norms in every respect but their religion.

Religious Background

It may be an obvious point to make that, since most people involved in British Wicca were initiated over the age of 25, they have had different religious backgrounds before initiation. Wicca is not what we could call 'generational' in that its numbers do not grow with either the birth of babies or with the acceptance of children into membership. There are very few people who have grown up as Pagans, but a new generation of children is now being brought up by Wiccan or Pagan parents, which is not so surprising given that Wicca is predominantly made up of people in their twenties, thirties and forties – what might be called the usual age range for child-bearing.[17] Pagan parents claim that they are careful not to indoctrinate their children, deeming it important that their children be left to make their own choices when they are old enough. Thus, whilst children are clearly influenced by their parents' beliefs and practices, they are not under any pressure to 'convert'. They are not deemed to be Wiccan because they were born to Wiccan parents, and they are required to seek initiation in the same manner as anyone else, as and when they are old enough to decide their spiritual path for themselves. Thus, although the birth of children to Pagan parents may indicate a change in the religious upbringing of potential future members of Wicca, it remains to be seen how many children raised by Wiccan/Pagan parents will choose to become Wiccans/Pagans themselves as they mature to adulthood.

In the future, therefore, we may see many more Wiccans stating that they were brought up with a Pagan religious background. For the present, however, we might note that Wiccans in Britain are overwhelmingly of Protestant religious background (62 per cent), with only 14 per cent having a Catholic background, and 21 per cent stating no religious background at all.[18] This can be compared with Jone Salomonsen's (1996) portrait of the religious background of Reclaiming witches in the USA, where Catholic and Protestant were roughly equal in representation (35 per cent and 32 per cent respectively) and 21 per cent were of Jewish background. Stark and Bainbridge (1985, p.401) also note the proportion of witches in North America who have had a Jewish upbringing. Jewish Pagans and witches are becoming more noticeable, particularly in North America and amongst women who are comfortable with an identity incorporating both Judaism in Paganism and Paganism (usually in the form of Goddess worship) within Judaism. Starhawk is perhaps the most notable example of a Jewish witch (or 'Jewitch') who is 'increasingly happy to retain Jewish traditions within her Paganism, claiming that as she grows older both her Jewish and her Pagan identities have strengthened' (Raphael, 1998, p.202). In contrast, only one of the respondents to my 1996 survey of Wiccans in the UK indicated that she had a Jewish cultural background, but added that she was brought up with no religion.

That Protestantism is the religious background of the majority of initiated Wiccans in Britain is consistent with the religious background of the general populace at large. Figures from the *UK Christian Handbook* indicate that there are some 32 million Protestants in England and Wales, compared to only five and a half million Roman Catholics and three hundred thousand Jews. Vivianne Crowley (1998, p.171) puts forward the idea that Wicca is more popular in northern European, Protestant countries where people lack any focus for the divine feminine (that is, the Goddess), rites of passage and a sense of ritual, factors which remain popular in the Catholicism of Eire, southern Europe and the Mediterranean. Certainly, the very small number of respondents of Catholic background in my 1996 survey, together with the fact that responses from Europe outside Britain were from Scandinavia, Germany, Austria and the Netherlands, rather than Spain, Portugal and Italy, suggests that Crowley's assertion may have some truth in it (an interesting area for future study).

In my UK study, then, 76 per cent of Wiccans claimed a Christian background, possibly nominal, but certainly at times practising. Almost a quarter (21 per cent) had no religious background. However, no research has to my knowledge been published to suggest that Wiccans move straight from Christianity to Wicca, and fieldwork suggests that there is usually a gap of some years between people feeling that Christianity is no longer relevant to their lives and finding Wicca. A straightforward disaffection or disillusionment with Christianity is therefore unlikely to be the main cause of Wiccan membership; otherwise we might be tempted, like Baudelaire ([1930], 1990), to claim that 'Paganism and Christianity confirm each other' (p.26)! In fact, rather than asserting any disaffection with Christianity, conversion motifs among Wiccans are predominantly mystical and concerned with recognition of oneself as a witch.[19]

Wicca and Christianity

What, then, is the relationship between Wicca and Christianity, with which – to say the least – it has a mythically intensified chequered history? Undoubtedly, many Wiccans and Pagans today see themselves as opposing Christianity, identifying with the persecution of witches in early modern Europe by the Church, and reacting against the patriarchal, monotheistic religion of Western culture. This may be particularly true among people who have recently decided to identify themselves as witches or Pagans, and who are perhaps rebelling against their upbringing, education, society and culture. Hutton ([1991] 1993) points out that the writings of modern British Pagans exhibit

> an intense and consistent hostility to the Christian Church. The follies and deficiencies of this institution are regularly held up to ridicule and abuse. Such bitterness may be therapeutic for those who have recently rejected Christianity, and is natural in view of the conviction of modern pagans that the Church was directly responsible for the Great Witch Hunt with whose victims they identify. (Hutton [1991] 1993, p.336)

Such an attitude of 'being Pagan' in opposition to 'being Christian' is, in my experience, becoming more rare. Much has changed during the 1990s, with more accurate research into Wiccan and Pagan history pervading practitioner understanding of their own roots and challenging traditionally held views.[20] In the majority of my conversations with Wiccans I have found toleration and respect for other religions and practices to be extremely high. Wicca has, for example, been instrumental in the development of inter-faith meetings with members of other religions and, as Paganism has grown in popularity and public awareness of it has increased, it has adopted a less reactive posture which no longer requires legitimization through false histories or hatred of the Christian Church.[21]

It is clear, however, that hatred of Christianity is still in evidence among a minority of Pagans. Discussions of inter-faith activities often centre upon an unwillingness to 'get together with Christians to explain [Paganism]' (Macintyre, 1998, p.21) and a failure to understand that inter-faith work consists of many religions rather than just Christianity. Protests against inter-faith work occasionally take the form of accusations that inter-faith Pagans are engaging in 'a dangerous activity . . . completely ignoring the fact that it goes against *all* Xtian teaching to accept *any* form of alternative religion' (Ruthven, 1998, p.20, emphases in original). Much of the anti-inter-faith, anti-Christian feeling appears to stem from fears of persecution aroused by the ritual child abuse cases of the late 1980s/early 1990s, 'which attempted to embroil everyone of an alternative belief in the tendrils of "Satanic child abuse"' (ibid., p.19), as well as from the continuing and general Pagan affinity with the witchcraft reputedly persecuted in the Great Witch Hunt.

If we leave behind the mythic associations with the Great Witch Hunt, however, and instead focus on tracing Wicca's lineage through occult/magical history, then, despite reactionary hostility to Christianity for the persecutions of the past, it may in fact be the case that Christianity and Wicca are not quite so mutually exclusive as they first appear. Such a mixture of Wicca and Christianity would, in fact, be in keeping with Wicca's heritage from esotericism. The Renaissance magicians Marsilio Ficino (1433–99) and Giovanni Pico della Mirandola (1463–94), so important to the development of the Western Esoteric Tradition, were both devout Christians; even Giordano Bruno (1548–1600), who sought the re-establishment of the Egyptian 'religion of the world', believed this should be brought about through a reformed Catholicism (for which he was burned at the stake). As Salomonsen (2002) has pointed out, 'because of the obvious connection between Witchcraft and western esoteric traditions, correlations must also be assumed with the religious heritage [Gerald] Gardner insisted to have rejected: Jewish and Christian religions' (p.5).

In terms of more recent history, membership of the Hermetic Order of the Golden Dawn did not necessitate a revolt against Christianity, and many members – A.E. Waite being perhaps the most famous – remained Christian mystics as well as magicians. As an example, I offer the following record of an astral vision experienced by Florence Farr (1860–1917) in November 1882. In the vision, the Egyptian goddess Isis explains the symbolism of a cup emblazoned with a heart and filled with a ruby-coloured liquid:

> This is love, I have plucked out my heart and given it to the world; that is my strength. Love is the mother of the Man-God, giving the Quintessence of her life to save mankind from destruction, and to show forth the path to life eternal. Love is the mother of Christ.
> Spirit, and this Christ is the highest love – Christ, is the heart of love, the heart of the Great Mother Isis – the Isis of Nature. He is the expression of her power – she is the Holy Grail, and he is the life blood of spirit, that is found in this cup. (Cited by Greer, 1995, p.119)

Likewise, Maud Gonne (1866–1953) saw no conflict between her Catholicism and her involvement in Pagan rituals:

> To me it seems the spear of the soldier piercing the side of Christ & letting the essence
> of God flow into the Graal cup is the same symbolism as the spear of Lug piercing the
> night & letting the essence of God the spark of fire of the soul flow down into the
> Cauldron of regeneration and rebirth, & the font of baptism & the holy water seem to
> me the same as the purifying cauldron of Dana which begins initiation, or the deep well
> of the tree of knowledge. (Cited by Greer, 1995, p.280)

Similarly another, slightly later, influential figure, Dion Fortune (1890–1946), was as much an esoteric Christian as she was a proto-Pagan and ritual magician, bridging the dichotomy between 'the Gods and the one God; between the Mystery at Bethlehem and those of Karnak, Atlantis, and Avalon' (Richardson, 1991, p.42). In fact, of the figures influential on the development of Wicca, only Aleister Crowley (1875–1947) was vehemently anti-Christian and Helena Blavatsky (1831–91), co-founder of the Theosophical Society which had less of an impact on Wicca, also became increasingly anti-Christian as she turned to the East for inspiration.

I am not, of course, saying Wicca and Christianity are the same, or that Christianity will find Wicca acceptable. And given the (not always unwarranted) suspicion with which Wiccans and Pagans tend to view the Church, I would in turn suggest that any research on Christianity within modern Wicca would have to be undertaken with a great deal of sensitivity and care, to say the least![22] Present tensions and unresolved conflicts are important dynamics to consider when looking at the present in an effort to determine the future, and what is indicated here is more of a change in attitude – which may in future bring greater understanding and toleration.

Conclusion

Wicca is predominantly made up of educated, professional people who tend to engage with scholarly research in order to better understand themselves and their practices. Their reflexive attitude and willingness to exchange outmoded myths for greater historical accuracy has allowed Wiccans to reassess their relationship, not only with those persecuted during the period of the Great Witch Hunt, but also with the Christian Church which conducted the persecution. This is, of course, a continuing process, but it is one which will be worth taking note of over the next 50 years as Wicca comes to greater maturity.

In addition, the differentiation between Wicca, witchcraft and Paganism aids this process of re-evaluation. Wicca is beginning to be recognized as something different from witchcraft and as having a greater affinity with magic, esotericism and the occult than with early modern witchcraft. Although Wicca has been intricately bound up with the development of witchcraft and Paganism, the growing differentiation between them may mean that, although Wicca is most often classed as 'Pagan', by both practitioners and scholars, this may not necessarily be accurate, or may not be so in the future. We must question whether it is necessary to be Pagan in order to be Wiccan. But we must also question whether the diffusion encountered in this chapter is necessarily a 'bad thing' for 'alternative spiritualities', which in turn leads us to question the centrality of Christianity in the discourses utilized by Religious Studies. We need to look beyond Christianity to uncover modes of transmission, attitudes towards the desirability (or not) of societal impact, and a variety of reactions/responses to the modern world in which we live. Such thinking must take into account the nature of interreligious exchange and the contexts in which religions develop and transform: if 11 September 2001 showed religion to be a still powerful force which cannot be ignored, it also offered a timely reminder that religions do not exist in isolation, either from each other or from society in general. Thus, if Paganism is parasitic on Christianity, it may merely be a reflection of the past (and possible future) hosting of Christianity by Paganism. There never has been, and never will be, a cut-off point at which one religious tradition completely disappears and another appears; periods of overlap are contiguous with the development of humanity and the societies in which it perpetuates itself. They remain both necessary and desirable if we are to learn from each other.

Thus, whilst it is at present veiled by the ever-increasing commodification of witchcraft (which itself resembles Christianity in certain periods of its history), Wicca may in the future organize itself institutionally, or retreat to a position of secrecy, in order to maintain its identity. It is unlikely to allow itself to be smothered by the confusion of identities surrounding it, but which of the above options it will take is difficult to say. However, one thing we can say with some certainty is that Wicca, witchcraft, Paganism and magic are all increasingly popular, and will not soon vanish from the religious milieu. Neither, however, will Christianity. The claim outlined elsewhere in this volume – that liberal Christianity at least will collapse owing to its inability to articulate, police and transmit its beliefs with clarity and conviction – is, in my opinion, precisely why it *will* remain: the antithesis to institutional dogma is wholly in line with the *Zeitgeist* which has allowed Wicca and Paganism to proliferate. Thirty years from now, Christianity in Britain will not have 'largely disappeared' – it will have transformed. Likewise, Wicca, Paganism and their relationship with Christianity will also have transformed in the matrix of change which we call life.

Acknowledgments

I am grateful to Doug Ezzy for supplying a copy of his article from the *Australian Religious Studies Review*, and to Steve Bruce for providing me with a draft chapter of *God is Dead*.

Notes

1   Wicca is capitalized, as are all other references to religions and their practitioners.
2   Although it arose from the nexus of three often conflated and imprecise co-ordinates – esotericism, the occult and paganism (as an attitude or mindset) – which are obviously much older.
3   An idea explored later in this chapter.
4   Throughout this text, 'Pagan/Paganism' refer to modern religions, partly inspired by the ancient 'pagan' religions of Europe.
5   Regarding the 19th century, in the latter part of this century the 'pagan spirit' of Romanticism – exemplified by poets such as John Keats (1795–1821) and Percy Bysshe Shelley (1792–1822) – was developing into a Paganism as an attitude of mind: celebrated most obviously by poets such as Algernon Charles Swinburne (1837–1909) and writers such as Algernon Blackwood (1861–1951), Arthur Machen (1863–1947) and Saki (1870–1916) (see Freeman, 2002). Regarding the term 'Heathen', it equates with the Latin 'Pagan', was coined by the Goths and was used throughout the Germanic languages of the Middle Ages to indicate a follower of a non-Christian religion. Some present-day Heathens regard themselves and their traditions as something distinct from Paganism, whilst others are happy to see themselves as something distinct within Paganism. Finally, and now regarding the term 'Paganism', the term refers to those people who identify themselves as 'Pagan' but who do not belong to any specific Pagan tradition such as Wicca or Druidry. Hutton (1999, p.400) uses the term 'non-initiatory' to describe this group. However, since many Druids, shamans and followers of Asatru prefer not to use an initiatory structure either, 'non-aligned' is perhaps a more accurate description of Pagans who belong to no specific Pagan tradition.
6   See Pearson (2000) and (forthcoming).
7   Regarding Hanegraaff's observation, this specifically concerns Gardnerian Wicca, joined by Alexandrian Wicca in the early 1960s. It can also be noted that later in this chapter, and following Hanegraaff, I argue that Wicca is not necessarily wholly situated within Paganism.
8   See Hutton (1999, p.401) on figures.
9   In part this is due to the tendency among Pagans to regard Wicca as hierarchical in structure. The anti-hierarchical nature of Paganism leads the majority to remain outside the initiatory traditions such as Wicca, remaining committed to Paganism in general rather than to a specific spiritual tradition.
10   Rob Hardy, a Wiccan priest for over 20 years, expressed his opinion, saying he would 'hope to see the Craft keep its individuality and not be swallowed up by general Paganism' (*Pagan Dawn*, 122, Imbolc, 1977, p.21). Others refuse to call themselves 'Wiccan' because it has become associated too much with the portrayal of Wicca in films such as *The Craft* (1996) to any longer have real meaning. (Although one might argue that the alternative, 'witch', is equally vague!)
11   This is *contra* the claims of secularization theories – that spiritualities outside 'traditional' religion constitute shallow leisure activities, a distraction from 'real life', a mere entertainment. The characterization of spirituality as a leisure activity perhaps only holds true if leisure is defined as what one does outside work: a compartmentalization which is arbitrary, artificial and which does not lend itself to understanding 'alternative spiritualities'. Indeed, it is possible to argue that such a distinction in fact reveals a marked lack of understanding of such spiritualities, failing to take into account practitioner attitudes towards ritual and magic as 'work', or self development as 'life work'. For many, this work is prioritized, and can no more be construed as a 'leisure activity' than can the daily training of a competing athlete.
12   And indeed may not be recognized by scholars either, unless a stance of awareness of both Wicca and 'commodified' or 'culture' witchcraft is adopted – which insists on attention to particularities rather than on conflation in order to fit meta-theories.
13   Ezzy (2001) defines commodified witchcraft as 'a set of products inscribed with beliefs and practices broadly consistent with the religion of Witchcraft but for which the dominant institutional goal is profit' (p.33). He uses 'Wicca' to refer to the older, initiatory tradition and 'commodified

Witchcraft' to refer to the more recent popularized movement: a useful distinction employed in this chapter.

14   Although one is tempted to argue that, in the scramble to 'educate' the public and make Wicca more acceptable/palatable, Wiccan authors both have helped create the problem of uninitiated Wiccans and continue to feed the cultural trend of, for example, teen-witchcraft. Publications by Wiccans aimed at a general readership have continued in a steady stream since Gardner (1954), but became especially prevalent in the 1980s and 1990s.

15   I suspect that this estimate of Hutton is in fact far too high.

16   Although commodified witchcraft is arguably 'mainstream'.

17   No figures are available for the UK. Helen Berger (1999, p.83) estimates that there are 82 600 children currently being raised in US neo-pagan families. Pagan parenting is currently being researched by a PhD student at King's College, London.

18   The source for these figures is a survey of 120 Wiccans conducted by the author in 1996. Of the remaining Wiccans, 1.5 per cent gave 'Pagan' as their background, and a further 1.5 per cent did not answer the question.

19   See Harrington (2000).

20   The influence of Hutton (1991), for example, had a dramatic effect on the Pagan view of history. As he comments in the introduction of the 1993 edition, Wicca at least 'has proved capable of re-evaluating its own claims with some genuine scholarly rigour' (p.xiii).

21   *Pagan Dawn*, 128 (Lughnasadh, 1998) explains Pagan involvement with Interfaith, trying to allay fears that Interfaith is used by Christians as a means of converting people (pp.19–23).

22   Though, as we have already noted Jewitches and Judaeo-Pagans, we might also note the presence of Christo-Pagans (also in North America).

References

Baudelaire, Charles [1930] 1990: *Intimate Journals*, trans. Christopher Isherwood. London: Picador.

Bell, Catherine 1997: *Ritual: Perspectives and Dimensions*. Oxford: Oxford University Press.

Berger, Helen A. 1999: *A Community of Witches: Contemporary Neo-Paganism and Witchcraft in the United States*. Columbia, South Carolina: University of South Carolina Press.

Bruce, Steve 2002: *God is Dead: Secularization in the West*. Oxford: Blackwell.

Crowley, Vivianne 1998: Wicca as Nature Religion. In Joanne Pearson, Richard H. Roberts and Geoffrey Samuel (eds), *Nature Religion Today: Paganism in the Modern World*. Edinburgh: Edinburgh University Press, pp.170–79.

Ezzy, Doug 2001: The Commodification of Witchcraft. *Australian Religious Studies Review*, 14 (1), pp.31–44.

Freeman, Nick 2002: 'A Longing for the Wood World at Night': The Influence of the Literature of the Occult Revival on Modern Paganism. Paper presented at the conference 'The Development of Paganism: Histories, Influences and Contexts, c.1880–2002', The Open University, Milton Keynes.

Gardner, G.B. 1954: *Witchcraft Today*. London: Rider.

Greer, Mary K. 1995: *Women of the Golden Dawn: Rebels and Priestesses*. Vermont: Park Street Press.

Hanegraaff, Wouter J. 1998: *New Age Religion and Western Culture: Esotericism in the Mirror of Secular Thought*. New York: SUNY.

Harrington, Melissa 2000: Conversion to Wicca? In Marion Bowman and Graham Harvey (eds), *Pagan Identities*, special issue of DISKUS (*www.uni-marburg.de/religionswissenschaft/journal/diskus/harrington.html*).

Hutton, Ronald [1991] 1993: *The Pagan Religions of the Ancient British Isles: Their Nature and Legacy*. Oxford: Blackwell.

Hutton, Ronald 1999: *The Triumph of the Moon: A History of Modern Pagan Witchcraft*. Oxford: Oxford University Press.

Macintyre, John 1998: Climbing Into Bed With the Enemy?: Interfaith and Pagan Fundamentalism. *Pagan Dawn*, 128, pp.20–21.

MacMullen, R. 1997: *Christianity and Paganism in the Fourth to Eighth Centuries*. New Haven and London : Yale University Press.

Pearson, Joanne E. 1998: Assumed Affinities: Wicca and the New Age. In Joanne Pearson, Richard H. Roberts and Geoffrey Samuel (eds), *Nature Religion Today: Paganism in the Modern World*. Edinburgh: Edinburgh University Press, pp.45–56.

Pearson, J. 2000: Demarcating the Field: Paganism, Wicca and Witchcraft. In Marion Bowman and Graham Harvey (eds), *Pagan Identities*, special issue of DISKUS (*www.uni-marburg.de/ religionswissenschaft/journal/diskus/ pearson.html*).

Pearson, J. (forthcoming): *Wicca: Magic, Spirituality and the 'Mystic Other'*. London: Routledge.

Raphael, Melissa 1998: Goddess Religion, Postmodern Jewish Feminism, and the Complexity of Alternative Religious Identities. *Nova Religio*, (1) 2, pp.198–215.

Richardson, Alan [1987] 1991: *The Magical Life of Dion Fortune: Priestess of the 20th Century*. London: Aquarian Press.

Rountree, K. 2001: The Past is a Foreigner's Country: Goddess Feminists, Archaeologists, and the Appropriation of Prehistory. *Journal of Contemporary Religion*, 16 (1), pp.5–27.

Russell, Jeffrey B. [1980] 1991: *A History of Witchcraft: Sorcerers, Heretics and Pagans*. London: Thames & Hudson.

Ruthven, Suzanne 1998: Paganism Today and the Interfaith Debate. *Cauldron*, 88, May 1998, pp.19–20

Salomonsen, Jone 1996: 'I Am a Witch – A Healer and a Bender': An Expression of Women's Religiosity in the Contemporary USA. University of Oslo: PhD thesis.

Salomonsen, Jone 2002: *Enchanted Feminism: The Reclaiming Witches of San Francisco*. London: Routledge.

Stark, Rodney and William Sims Bainbridge 1985: *The Future of Religion: Secularization, Revival and Cult Formation*. London: University of California Press.

Woodman, Justin 2000: Lovecrafting the Art of Magick: Secularism, Modernity, and Emergent Stellar Spiritualities within Contemporary Occult Discourses. Paper delivered to the British Sociological Association, Sociology of Religion Study Group Conference, 'Prophets and Predictions: Religion in the 21st Century', University of Exeter, April.

CHAPTER 15

Alexis de Tocqueville, Pantheism and the Religion of Democracy

S.J.D. Green

The Sociology of Religion, Secularization and Sacralization

It is of the essence of the sociology of religion that it seeks to relate the significance of religious phenomena to broader aspects of society and, by implication, changes in religion to wider changes in society. This is true in general. It is particularly true of the theory of secularization. In Weberian and neo-Weberian theory, the declining social significance of religion was characteristically traced to the developing rationalization of social institutions and norms in the advanced societies (Weber, 1978, pp.24–6, 85–6, 476–80, 576–83). In Durkheimian and neo-Durkheimian analysis, it was generally related to the gradual substitution of increasingly transparent, and distributionally normative, social relations under the complex division of labour for the mystical, collective, whole conceived in traditional communities (Durkheim, 1984, pp.118–20). Variations on these themes abound. The insights of the so-called 'British School', exemplified in the writings of David Martin and Bryan Wilson, represent only some of the most important developments within the theory (Wallis and Bruce, 1989, pp.493–520). All, however, emphasize the growing importance of those aspects of modern society increasingly hostile to the continuing social significance of religion. More: all point to a quantity and quality of social change, historic but untranscended, indeed untranscendable, which has diminished and will continue to marginalize any place for the sacred in the organization, self-perception and legitimation of the advanced societies (Martin, 1978, pp.1–11; Wilson, 1982, pp.153–9).

So much so – put another way, so effective has this line of argument generally proved – that most contemporary opponents of secularization theory have either resorted to a strict subordination of the sociological perspective to a prior, existential imperative or they have simply rejected the sociological dimension to religion altogether and insisted upon religious life itself as the independent variable in historical change. For the former, the religious needs of humanity remain constant. They argue that, whilst the characteristic forms and typical loci of the sacred in society may change, the amount of the sacred circulating around the religious economy at any given time will never vary significantly (Stark and Bainbridge, 1985, pp.1–3, 425–35). For the latter, the intensity of collective religious existence may indeed decrease (or increase) over time. But, they insist, no theory of social change will ever be sufficient to account for this (Brown, 1992, pp.31–50). Yet the most intriguing of recent anti-secularization arguments have been avowedly sociological; that is, sociological in the sense of emphasizing the significance of social change in the genesis of religious change. It is simply that their conclusions about the direction of that change have been different. Here the suggestion has been that, whilst the theory of secularization once provided the best description of the fate of religion in industrial societies, a hitherto unimagined historical shift beyond industrial society – into post-industrial society – will create, in the words of Grace Davie (1994), 'a space for the sacred – and, by implication, a new space for the sacred – albeit often in forms different from those which have gone before' (p.192).

In this scheme of things, secularization will turn out (perhaps, already, has turned out) to have been a phase in the history of society, an historical era lethal for the 'institutional churches', more specifically the Christian churches. But it will only have been a phase. Post-industrialization, through its characteristic forms of social organization – altogether looser and less compartmentalized; by its characteristic promotion of previously marginalized social groups – especially women and the elderly; and finally, in its characteristic commitment to more self-consciously subjective forms of self-perception, will prove to be more of a friend to a different kind of religion: varied, fragmented, almost amorphous. For better or worse? The question simply does not arise. To quote Davie again: 'Change does not imply that things are ... getting better or worse. They are simply changing' (p.193). This is an intriguing argument. If true, its historical and sociological ramifications can scarcely be overstated. But is it true?

Most of us concede that modern society is changing in significant ways. Even those sceptical about the very coherence of notions such as post-industrialism or post-modernity commonly accept that our inherited understandings about so-called 'industrial society' do not adequately describe a great deal of what is actually going on in Europe and North America today (Davies, 1999, pp.345–53). So let us also acknowledge that recent religious change in the West is not wholly captured by the simple presumption that the institutional decline of religious organizations reflects a concomitant diminution in the social significance of sacred beliefs. In that way, we can also agree that 'believing without belonging' now represents one of the most important dimensions in the sociology of religion of the advanced societies. But believing what? In residual forms of older faiths? Or in something quite new? Davie, properly tentative, tends to the first explanation (Davie, 1994, p.193). Others, either more daring or foolhardy, opt for the latter (Stark and Bainbridge, 1985, pp.478-80). Even to speak of *The Elementary Forms of the New Religious Life* is to suggest at least something in this respect (Wallis, 1984).

Let us, if only for the sake of argument, assume both. And let us, for now at least, ignore the question of respective quantities. What of the quality? Must our understanding of these phenomena be so neutral as to insist that 'change' can never mean more than change itself? Is it not possible for religion not merely to decline but actually to degenerate? After all, Weber looked into the secular future with profound misgivings (and he was scarcely alone in this). Might we not conceive of a theory of religious change, that is, of the continuing social significance of religion which might disturb us just as much? One man, once, did.

Alexis de Tocqueville, Democracy and Pantheism

Consider the following observations, drawn from chapter 7 of volume 2 of Alexis de Tocqueville's *Democracy in America* (Tocqueville, 2000). The book was published in 1840, completing Tocqueville's account of the state of American society as he found it during his nine-month journey of 1831 and 1832. The relevant chapter is entitled 'What Makes the Mind of Democratic Peoples Lean Towards Pantheism'. And this is what Tocqueville observes:

> As conditions become more equal, each man in particular becomes more like the others, weaker and smaller, one gets used to no longer viewing citizens so as to consider only the people; one forgets individuals so as to think only of the species.
>
> In these times, the human mind loves to embrace a host of diverse objects at once; it constantly aspires to be able to link a multitude of consequences to a single cause. The idea of unity obsesses [the mind]; it seeks it on all sides and when it believes it has found it, it willingly wraps it in its bosom and rests with it. Not only does it come to discover only one creation and one Creator in the world; this first division of things still bothers it, and it willingly seeks to enlarge and simplify its thought by enclosing God and the universe within a single whole. [Things] material and immaterial, visible and invisible . . . are considered as no more than diverse parts of an immense being which alone remains eternal in the midst of continual change. [Such] a system, although it destroys human individuality, or rather because it destroys it, will have secret charms for men who live in democracy: all their intellectual habits prepare them to conceive it and set them on the way to adopting it. It naturally attracts their imagination and fixes it; it nourishes the haughtiness and flatters the laziness of their minds.
>
> Among the different systems with whose aid philosophy seeks to explain the universe, pantheism seems to me one of the most appropriate to seduce the human mind in democratic centuries; all who remain enamoured of the genuine greatness of men should unite and do combat against it. (Tocqueville, 2000, p.426)

What did he mean? Of one thing we can be sure. He did not mean to confine the phenomenon of democratic pantheism to America. The text clearly mentions both France and Germany (p.425). Indeed, he expressly believed that the USA, despite being 'the most democratic country in the world' in the 1830s was, on account of its historic, continuing and vital Christianity, unusually well-equipped to resist this particular modern pathology, at least in the short term (ibid.). Similarly, he did not mean to limit the chronological scope of these remarks to his own era. Indeed, he took it as given that 'time [had] not yet shaped [the] definite form of [the] new society' (Manent, 1997, p.98). Finally, for Tocqueville it was axiomatic that 'democracy' meant more than just the rule of the people, politically defined. It meant the ' sovereignty of the people' in every area of life, religion included. And that meant an 'equality of conditions' in every area of life which such sovereignty implied, religion included, once again (ibid., p.101).

This last point is important, for it identifies how Tocqueville had established an essential connection between the emergence of political and of civic equality; similarly, between civic equality and moral equality. Moreover, he insisted that the first inevitably led to the second; and the second to the third. Put another way, popular government dissolved social hierarchy, and social equality led to a plurality of values amongst men (and women). The history of the last 150 years of political and social change in the West has surely proved that prognosis correct. Indeed, one might reasonably argue that, notwithstanding the historic and continuing importance of Weberian rationalization and Durkheimian distribution, the principal preoccupation of the advanced societies during the 21st century will be the pursuit of the egalitarian project broadly conceived (and resistance to it). Consider our most pressing current concerns: minority rights, the empowerment of the oppressed, the pursuit of universal self-love; then think of those egalitarian impulses which go beyond the merely humanitarian: animal rights, ecological balance and radical environmentalism. Tocqueville would have understood them all.

The significance of all of this from our point of view is that Tocqueville also believed that the concomitant revolution in social mores would have a profound impact on democratic religious life. The presumed transformation can be summarized as (a) a decline in the social significance of Christianity, (b) a rise in the popularity and pervasiveness of pantheistic doctrine and morality, and (c) a concomitant diminution in human dignity, individuality and freedom. None of these propositions is self-evident. The development of democracy may have coincided with a decline in the social significance of Christianity in the advanced societies, at least outside the USA, but few modern social theorists treat it as a cause. Most look to other forms of social change to explain this phenomenon, alternatively minimizing or simply ignoring the contribution of democracy, *per se*, to the process. Moreover, even to the extent that the correlation is significant, it does not follow that a decline in Christianity, under the influence of democracy, will lead necessarily to pantheism. It could conceivably encourage either religious individualism – the sovereignty of every soul – or religious charisma – the self-imposed subjugation of the many to the one. Finally, even to the degree to which Christianity is supplanted by pantheism in a democratic regime, it is by no means clear why pantheism, so construed, dominates human individuality. It could serve as the 'spirit' or the 'light' within each individual. So why was Tocqueville so certain of the force of his argument?

Tocqueville believed that Christianity was an inheritance of democracy. That, in a sense, was obvious. It came into the world before democracy; certainly before *egalitarian democracy* (Tocqueville, 2000, p.413). More contentiously, he insisted upon its continuing value for and in democracy, arguing that it furnished an essential moderator to democracy's otherwise unrestrained instincts; providing the one form of non-democratic authority which, in 19th-century America at least, democracy nevertheless acknowledged. In that way, it held democracy's ambitions within the limits of reason and prudence. Hence the American internalization of the doctrine of self-interest, well understood; that is, their almost universal capacity to combine 'their own well-being with that of their fellow citizens' (ibid., p.501). Hence too their capacity to uphold the natural rights of man; if necessary, even against the wishes of the majority (ibid., pp.227–9).

But, historically conceived, religions in general and Christianity in particular succeeded in tempering democracy only as democracy also tempered them, with this result: democracy, so constrained, stopped short of claiming that absolute human sovereignty which its fundamental principles otherwise presupposed; but religion in general and Christianity in particular, thus tolerated, increasingly turned itself into something like 'common opinion', or social convention superficially sacralized (ibid., p.409). And that, Tocqueville predicted, would prove fatal for Christianity in the long run. For Christianity is an inherently authoritative religion; minimally, in the authority of revelation. Reduced to convention, it will become vulnerable as convention. This is because democratic convention continually assumes the task of eroding authority – all authority – whether institutional or individual, until, as Pierre Manent has put it, 'nature alone makes its speech heard' (Manent, 1997, p.102). Revelation gives way to custom and then custom cedes to individual preference. Consequently, Christianity becomes the ultimate victim of the democratic spirit.

The result, however, will not be universal atheism; still less a thousand-year rule of reason. Rather, it will be a different kind of religion. To understand why this is so, it is necessary to appreciate that Tocqueville presumed the need for religion to be natural to humanity: at once 'depend[ent] upon one of the constituent principles of human nature' and part of the 'permanent state of humanity' (2000, p.284). This propensity, however, was he believed less the product of genetic inscription than the result of that disproportion between hope and reality in life that inevitably provoked thoughts of another world. Only philosophers could be expected to resist this imperative. (David Martin has made this same point in conversation, albeit less reverently: 'Atheism is the froth of the intelligentsia.') So democratic convention does not entail that 'intellectual aberration', coupled with 'moral violence', that detaches men from religion (ibid.). It merely pushes democratic man towards democratic religion. And in its *final* form, this is pantheism: the doctrine that God is in everything and everything is God. Why?

Tocqueville took the democratization of religion to be a process. He believed it to be perfectly compatible with Christianity in its early forms. America was proof of that (ibid., pp.282–8). But America was also proof of how Christianity thrived in early democracy only by changing: first by separating church from state; then by acknowledging the equal merits of the different forms of Christianity; finally, by denuding religion of its external forms (ibid., pp.275–82, 421–2). The problem was that external forms, which 'revolt[ed] the human mind in times of equality ... as ... nothing else', are also essential to 'the contemplation of abstract truths' (ibid., p.421). Thus the repudiation of form ultimately undermines the significance of content in religion, reducing doctrine to convention. The subjection of convention to democratic scrutiny will, in turn, dissolve democracy's greatest passion, 'the love of well-being', into a purely personal, or individual, sentiment: the desire to be at one with the world (ibid., p.422). And that desire will ultimately collapse the distinction between human beings and the world, reducing all the various forms of post-Christian, humanistic belief to the various branches of pantheism.

But what is the peculiar attraction of pantheism for democratic men? First, it is the ultimate general idea. Democracy, precisely because it presumes human equality, considers each human being subject to the same laws of general behaviour, 'equally and in the same manner'. Democratic man, 'having contracted the habit of general ideas in the one study with which he most occupies himself', then 'carries over this same habit to . . . discover common rules for all things', seeking to explain any set of facts, and ultimately all facts, by a 'single cause'. This becomes an 'ardent and blind passion' (ibid., p.413). In these circumstances, pantheism furnishes him with the 'single, unitary and rational metaphysic' which he craves (Kessler, 1994, p.149). Secondly, it is the ultimate egalitarian idea. Democracy enables democratic men to arrive at an insight previously denied to even the 'most profound and vast geniuses of Rome and Greece'. This is the 'similarity of men' (Tocqueville, 2000, p.413). Democratic man, motivated by an overwhelming desire to reduce the diversity of the world to the power of interpretative uniformity, discovers in pantheism the simplest idea of all: the equality of everything. In that way too, human beings cease to be meaningfully different not only from each other but from everything else. The very idea of individuality disappears. Finally, it is the ultimate idea of repose. That 'feverish ardour' which drives individuals to bring everything under their control, initially provoking their unhappy quest for happiness, at last finds contentment in a world of subjective experience placed comfortably beyond the will. This, in the words of Peter Lawler (1993), is the 'lullaby ... that ... soothes the [democratic mind] to sleep' (p.35).

And, for Tocqueville, that is why it is a pathology, not just a change. More: that is why it is a pathological religion appropriate to a pathological social state. For pantheism becomes credible and attractive to human beings only when they experience their individuality too extremely; when, in effect, social relations and social aspirations have degenerated to the point where men see themselves in radical detachment from each other, as wholly separated individuals (Tocqueville, 2000, pp.482–4). In that deracinated state, men and women experience their individuality not as strength but as weakness. Their freedom feels contingent, their existence seemingly provisional. Everything appears in doubt, including their very humanity. And into that doubt comes pantheism, the perfect common antidote to scepticism.

Tocqueville (2000) did not believe this process to be wholly inevitable. Indeed, so appalled was he at its possibility that he implored 'all those who remain enamoured of the genuine greatness of man [to] unite and do combat against it' (p.426). Nor did he presume that it would ever account for all the beliefs of all men under democracy. France, anyway, would go on having its non-believers, and its believing zealots, for the foreseeable future (Manent, 1997, p.89). What Tocqueville was concerned about was what might be called the current of common ideas in democratic societies more generally. What he anticipated for these was a widespread drift from conventional Christianity to atomized pantheism. What he feared as a consequence was the degeneration of a Christian citizenry into an apathetic people: unconnected, unwilled, ignoble (Tocqueville, 1998, p.88).

Democracy and Pantheism: Today and in the Future

Tocqueville offers less a testable prediction than a melancholic prophecy. But he should not necessarily be condemned for that. It remains to this day scarcely easier to plot than to predict the course of popular pantheism. As its most learned modern proponent tells us: 'In terms of practice, one of the most striking things about pantheism is that it has not produced a church or any kind of organisation in overseeing its practice.' And this not as a matter of accident or misfortune either. For 'Pantheists tend to regard churches and religious leaders with suspicion' (Levine, 1994, pp.354–8). Yet the historical broadening of pantheism's once strictly esoteric appeal is unmistakeable. What was once almost entirely confined to an elite had, by the early 20th century, acquired a commonness of touch which alone explains the extraordinary contemporary success of Richard Jeffries' *The Story of My Heart*, the mushiest of pantheistic prose poems which was reprinted 14 times between its publication in 1883 and the end of World War I (Bullock, 2000, pp.7–8).

Today, the literature of so-called 'New Age' religions, to the degree that it can be accorded any philosophical coherence at all, is regularly infused by the various forms of natural mysticism. And much of that amorphous doctrine displays a vague repudiation, or at least a diminution, of ontological transcendence together with the rejection, or anyway marginalization, of human distinctiveness and that curious celebration of subjectivity tempered by the absence of will that defines vulgar pantheism (Barker, 1989, pp.25–33). Modern survey material allows us to go a little further still, for, whilst it reveals an avowedly unsecular people, it also demonstrates that decentring of common religious narratives which Davie (1994), amongst others, has observed; specifically, a characteristic modern interpretation of the sacred which places increasing emphasis on the Holy Spirit rather than the flesh of God. Certainly, a larger proportion of the population (in Britain anyway) now claims to believe in a life force than in a personal deity; and the numbers are seemingly increasing (Davie, 1994, p.78).

Need any of this matter? What if we all became pantheists? Would religion be better or worse? Let us quote the expert, Michael Levine: 'The pantheist tries to achieve the kind of accord with unity, the integration of the cosmos, that will result in well-being and happiness. *Any activity that leads to this goal can legitimately be practised*' (1994, p.352; emphasis added).

Perhaps Tocqueville was right. One final thought: Tocquevillian sociology identified the essence of modernity neither in a novel form of production (capitalism or industrialism) nor in the relocation of social life (urbanization or privatization) but rather in a political regime: democracy. As such, it also projected an historical sociology of religion almost entirely detached from most contemporary debates about 'European exceptionalism' or even the East/West divide in matters of the future social significance of religion. This might suggest that it is, at least in this respect, rather vacuous: a generalization beyond scientific verification or falsification. But it could also make it altogether more pointed; a real portent for the future and an explanation of why Europe – exceptional today – may eventually cease to be so.

References

Barker, Eileen 1989: *New Religious Movements: A Practical Introduction*. London: HMSO.

Brown, Callum 1992: A Revisionist Approach to Religious Change. In Steve Bruce (ed.), *Religion and Modernisation*. Oxford: Oxford University Press, pp.43–70.

Bullock, Alan 2000: *Building Jerusalem: A Portrait of My Father*. London: Allen Lane.

Davie, Grace 1994: *Religion in Britain Since 1945: Believing Without Belonging*. Oxford: Blackwell.

Davies, Christie 1999: The Fragmentation of the Religious Tradition of the Creation, After-Life and Morality: Modernity not Post-Modernity. *Journal of Contemporary Religion*, 14 (3), pp.339–60.

Durkheim, Emile 1984: *The Division of Labour in Society*. London: Macmillan.

Kessler, Sanford 1994: *Tocqueville's Civil Religion: American Christianity and the Prospects for Freedom*. Albany: State University of New York Press.

Lawler, Peter Augustine 1993: *The Restless Mind: Alexis de Tocqueville on the Origins and Perpetuation of Human Liberty*. Lanham: Rowman and Littlefield.

Levine, Michael P. 1994: *Pantheism: A Non-Theistic Concept of Deity*. London: Routledge.

Manent, Pierre 1997: *Tocqueville and the Nature of Democracy*. Lanham: Rowman and Littlefield.

Martin, David 1978: *A General Theory of Secularization*. Oxford: Blackwell.

Stark, Rodney and Bainbridge, William 1985: *The Future of Religion: Secularization, Revival and Cult Formation*. Berkeley and Los Angeles: University of California Press.

Tocqueville, Alexis de 1998: *The Old Régime and the Revolution*. Chicago: University of Chicago Press.

Tocqueville, Alexis de 2000: *Democracy in America*. Chicago: University of Chicago Press.

Wallis, Roy 1984: *The Elementary Forms of the New Religious Life*. London: Routledge & Kegan Paul.

Wallis, Roy and Bruce, Steve 1989: Religion: The British Contribution. *British Journal of Sociology*, 40, pp.493–520.

Weber, Max 1978: *Economy and Society*, 1. Gunder Roth and Claus Wittich (eds). Berkeley and Los Angeles: University of California Press.

Wilson, Bryan 1982: *Religion in Sociological Perspective*. Oxford: Oxford University Press.

CHAPTER 16

Religion on – Religion in Cyberspace

Anastasia Karaflogka

Introduction

Manifestations of religion in cyberspace raise significant issues not only about the status and nature of religion and spirituality on computer networks but, more generally, about the evolution and development of religion in what some chose to call a 'postmodern' age (O'Leary, 1996). Only in the last few years have a number of scholars begun to address the topic: for example, Zaleski (1997) explores the relationship between religion and cyberspace; Wertheim (1999) suggests an understanding of cyberspace as a sacred space; Cobb (1998) considers the question of spiritual life in cyberspace; and Davis (1998) addresses the mystical aspect of the medium of information technology.

For some years now, institutionalized religions, churches, temples and new religious movements have been rushing to put up pages on the Web. Online services have large areas devoted to religion, from traditional Christian Bible study groups to neopagan rituals conducted in virtual 'chat rooms'. Believers and practitioners can choose from a wide variety of options: socializing at the First Church of Cyberspace, touring the Holy Land or Durham cathedral, e-mailing prayers to Jerusalem's Western Wall, performing cyber-pilgrimages, cyber-meditating on BuddhaNet, or debating the fine points of Mormon, Catholic or Scientology doctrine.

This chapter draws attention to the polymorphic identity of cyberspace, and distinguishes two different kinds of religious cyberspatial utterances – *religion on* and *religion in* cyberspace – which are then classified and analysed. It predicts the development of the already existing cyberreligions and the creation of New Cyberreligious Movements (NCRMs).

Cyberspace as a Polymorphic Conception

The Internet,[1] since its creation and until the beginning of the 1990s, was a territory occupied solely by computer specialists. Today, its widespread usage suggests that the 'computer world now supports a new and real social space' (Cybernauts Awake, 1999) where people can 'meet' to interact; to exchange ideas, knowledge, information and experience; to give substance to creative, imaginative and innovative new concepts and ideas; and to relocate, re-evaluate and deconstruct old concepts and ideas in a new setting. This is possible because, unlike any other media, 'cyberspace is something that cannot be demarcated in geographical terms at all. It is a reality that can be localized 'nowhere' and yet its presence is felt 'everywhere' (Benschop, 1997), and also because the Internet belongs to no one, and at the same time belongs to everyone. These unique qualities of CMC (Computer Mediated Communication) are enriched by two more aspects which revolutionize not only the Net but the *medium* itself.

A key differentiating factor between CMC and other media is the interactivity between the medium and its users. In contrast to television or radio, which broadcast their messages to an inactive and isolated audience, the Internet depends entirely upon its users not only for content contribution, but also for playing an active and communal part in its distribution. Its second major advantage is that, as technology becomes more accessible to more people, so the possibilities for liberating public discourse from the control of governmental and/or private publishers and broadcasters progress from potentialities to actualities.

These possibilities, and the fact that CMC is a global communication network, mean that the medium embodies a dual identity; that is, it can be perceived either as a tool or, as Lorne Dawson and Jenna Hennebry (1999) suggest, as a new 'environment in which things happen' (p.30). Cyberspace can be viewed more as a social space than as a technology (Poster, 1995) because virtual technologies 'are themselves contexts which bring about new corporealities and new politics corresponding to space-worlds and time-worlds that have never before existed in human history' (Holmes, 1997, p.3).

There is always the danger of idealization. Although some argue that human computer interaction, especially via the NET, offers a vision of freedom and a shared humanity, others claim that it may become the means of global surveillance and personal alienation (Aycock, 1995). Yet the fact remains that CMC and everything in it, imagined or real, is its users' product; they made it as it is, in order perhaps to fulfil their longing for unconditional freedom of expression and communication. The 'magic' of the Internet, to cite Poster (1995) is that it is a

> technology that puts cultural acts, symbolizations in all forms, in the hands of all participants; it radically decentralizes the positions of speech, publishing, filmmaking, radio and television broadcasting, in short the apparatuses of cultural production.

Poster's point reinforces Pauly's (1991) proposal that studying CMC as 'practice' (p.15) might involve emphasis on 'cultural process rather than products' (p.4).

As a rapidly evolving global technology, the Internet has now become a part of the lives of 'netizens' all over the world and it has created a fascinating new environment for the development of religious imagination. The vast quantity of religious information and the innumerable forms of religious interaction published on the NET call for the creation of a methodology which will enable us to observe and investigate the creation and the development of cyberspatial religious productions. Thus, as users become more adjusted to the idea that cyberspace can be a 'metaphysical laboratory for examining [their] very sense of reality' (Heim, 1993, p.82), and as technological advances become more easily and widely accessible, so the tools for researching CMC phenomena need refinement and readjustment. Pointing out the inadequacy of the already existing theories and methods to the study of cyberspatial phenomena, Steve Jones (1999) suggests a 'conscious shift of focus' in order to build our knowledge of the NET as a social medium (pp.x, xi).

Having in mind the present status of cyberspace and its possible future developments and functions, and pointing out its dual capacity – as something which can be perceived either as merely a communicative tool and/or as a sociocultural environment – there is clearly a need to develop a fresh methodological approach to religion in cyberspace. As a starting point it may be useful to develop a typology of religious hyper-discourse which distinguishes between religion *on* and religion *in* cyberspace.

Religion on – Religion in

Almost all religions, large- and small-scale, old and new, known and unknown, are present, and they occupy different amounts of space on the NET. There are sites for the Mormons, the Church of England,[2] the Holy Mountain,[3] Jehovah's Witnesses,[4] the Vatican,[5] the Atheists, the Christadelphians,[6] Shinto shrines,[7] the Church of Scientology[8] and other Japanese, African and American Indian religions – to mention but a few.

Research on the different forms of religious cyberspatial space and discourse suggests an initial typology which distinguishes three main categories of site: confessional, personal and academic (Karaflogka, 1998). Apart from the official web sites of the institutionalized or non-institutionalized religions, which form the *confessional* type (Karaflogka, 1998), there are the personal pages and the scholarly sites, which constitute the *subjective* and *academic* types, respectively (Karaflogka, 1998).

Having in mind this initial differentiation between the various sites, a critical investigation of cyberspatial religious discourse suggests a further distinction between *religion on* cyberspace and *religion in* cyberspace. The two are dissimilar in that *religion on* cyberspace refers to the information uploaded by any institutionalized or non-institutionalized religion, church, individual or organization, which (information and the uploader) also exist in the off-line world. In this sense the Internet is used merely as a communicative tool. On the other hand, *religion in* cyberspace, which could be called cyberreligion, is a religious, spiritual, and/or metaphysical expression, which is created and exists exclusively in cyberspace, where it enjoys a notable degree of 'virtual reality'. The Internet in this case is used as an environment which supports and nurtures the 'rise of a new conceptual framework and language for religious experience suited to the changed environmental conditions of postmodern society' (Dawson and Hennebry, 1999, p.36).

The distinction is important not only because the two phenomena are completely different from one another, but because (a) it facilitates the research process and the analysis of cyberspatial religious discourse, and (b) it provides the necessary tools for observing and monitoring the creation, evolution and development of new cyberreligious movements (NCRMs).

Religion on

Official Sites

Each web site is like a fingerprint: unique in design and content. The official pages *on* religion project how a religion or a religious institution is perceived by its leaders and how they convey this perception. The site reflects the identity and mentality of the religion, and clearly illustrates what the leader/s think the essential message of the page should be. This is achieved by the morphology of the idiosyncratic language employed in electronic discourse which is far richer than its linguistic content alone, for a new activity – human–computer interaction – is involved. This new field of visualized information, the product of an imaginative approach in designing, can transmit the doctrinal, social, ritual, mythological, ethical and material dimensions of a religion.

Personal Sites

Apart from the official sites of different religions, the Web includes personal pages uploaded by individuals who want to share their beliefs, to communicate with other fellow believers, to exchange ideas and experiences, and sometimes to debate about the doctrinal dimension of either their own or another religion. Personal pages project the personal perception and understanding of a particular system of belief; they may explore and communicate a unique religious experience or praxis; they may project the views of a person or a group about a socioreligious situation; they may criticize a current event, a television programme and so on. The pages of individuals, as well as those of groups, comprise the *subjective* type (Karaflogka, 1998).

Scholarly Sites

The final component of the *religion on* discourse is the scholarly sites. In a similar way to personal pages, the scholarly sites can be found in a great variety of different forms, including essays, journals, forums, discussion groups and books. Although the focus here is more on content and less on elaborate design, visual attractiveness can be a component.

At a conference in 1998, in my final remarks, I posed the question: can the idea of cyberchurch become a reality or will it remain cyberfiction? The answer came just a year and a half later, when I discovered that there were indeed cyber-churches,[9] cyber-sanghas,[10] cyber-synagogues,[11] and cyber-mosques,[12] each one of them giving the opportunity to their followers to participate in and be part of the 'community' when physical contact, for whatever reason, is not possible or desirable. Cyberspatial religious discourse would not be complete if there were no virtual religious practice. A wide range of forms and an array of diverse approaches to and perceptions of prayer, ritual and pilgrimage exist online.

With the development of online communication and the explosive growth of the Internet, the shape of ministry in the future is likely to be transformed. It could be suggested that changes are already occurring in ministry, because of changes in our culture brought about by the new ways people interact, communicate and exchange information, thus deconstructing the world and restructuring their views of reality. Pope John Paul II, in his statement in connection with World Communications Day, 27 May 1990,[13] said,

> With the advent of computer telecommunications, the Church is offered further means for fulfilling her mission ... She can hear more clearly the voice of public opinion and enter into continuous discussion with the world around her, thus involving herself more immediately in the common search for solutions to humanity's many pressing problems.

The impact and the role of the Internet in the future of the Church were also the subject of reflection at Newtech 1998 and ECIC 1999. At Newtech 1998, an international conference[14] on 'The New Technologies and the Human Person: Communicating the Faith in the New Millennium' hosted and co-chaired by Denver's Archbishop Charles Chaput, papers presented referred to the impact of CMC on social and religious life, the position of the Church and new justice issues, and so on. The European Christian Internet Conference 1999 (ECIC)[15] addressed different issues, such as being a church on the Internet, supporting mourners on the Internet, and pastoral care on the NET. The participants, mostly clergymen, expressed their enthusiasm about integrating the NET into their pastoral activities, one of their most striking ideas being the possibility of a 'cyberfuneral'.

Religion in

Cyberreligions

'Religion *in*' cyberspace constitutes a novel form of religious phenomenon within the milieu of the global, innovative medium of CMC. As with religion *on* the NET, so religion *in* encompasses two different expressions. The first, 'cyberreligion', constitutes a form of post-modern religiosity, and immediately raises issues about cyberspace as a sacred space, and the metaphysics of virtual reality, immortality and disembodiment. Typically, cyberreligions have a living founder or founders (who is also their author or initiator). A search using 'cyberreligion' or 'virtual religion' as keywords provides a list of sites which exhibit some of the features of 'conventional' religions, but may seem more or less unusual by normal standards. Several are intended to be satirical, if not cynical, while others are quite serious. They illustrate a wide range of human motivations and attitudes concerning religious thinking, emotions, beliefs, impulses, practices and responses to the religious reality such as the creators of these sites perceive it to be.

A characteristic cyberreligion is the 'Church Ov MOO'.[16] In their detailed analysis of the Church, Dawson and Hennebry (1999) point out that the site reveals 'an elaborated development of alternative sets of scriptures, commandments, chronicles, mythologies, rituals and ceremonies' (p.35). The size of the web site is enormous (around 800 pages) and the discourse shows an acute appreciation of religious history, comparative beliefs and practices, and significant knowledge of philosophy, anthropology, and sociology of religion (ibid.). The founders of MOOism, according to Dawson and Hennebry, are attempting to devise a 'self-consciously post-modern, socially constructed, relativist, and self-referential system of religious ideas' (ibid.). In MOOism's discourse there are elements that suggest a connection to neopaganism, and the 'religion' could be characterized as representative of what is coming to be called Technopaganism (p.36). MOOism, along with other cyberreligions, challenges the status quo of institutionalized and hierarchical religions. Along with its equivalents, it uses the NET as an environment where human imagination and creativity can deconstruct established sociocultural concepts and reconstruct religious, spiritual and philosophical ideas and practices.

New Cyberreligious Movements (NCRMs)

By virtue of the way in which it was created, the Internet is organized horizontally rather than vertically; there is neither central authority, nor hierarchy. Precisely because of this quality and because 'the medium influences the message', Zaleski (1997) argues that 'in the long run the Internet will favour those religions and spiritual teachings that tend toward anarchy and that lack a complex hierarchy. ... Authority loses its trappings and force on the Net' (pp.111–12). In the anarchy of the Internet, cybercommunities and movements have evolved, having their own rules, agendas and codes of practice. These have been regulated by the members themselves rather than by any outside authority. It is within these parameters that my second type of cyberreligion is placed, what I call 'New Cyberreligious Movements'. 'New' because they address issues using a new medium and introducing new possibilities; 'cyberreligious' because they use the NET both as environment and tool; 'movements' because they can, potentially, mobilize and activate some part of – or even the entire – human population. NCRMs may take the form of a response to, or a reaction towards, or a call for action, or even a rebellion against a religious establishment of the offline world.

Two characteristic examples of NCRMs are Falun Gong and Partenia[17] (Karaflogka, 2000a). Partenia came into being through the following set of circumstances. In the early 1990s, Bishop Gailot of Evreux in Normandy expressed his views on controversial issues including priestly celibacy, homosexuality, women's ordination and homelessness. What the bishop said was not in accordance with the Church's teachings as proclaimed by the Vatican. By January 1995, the Vatican had heard enough, but for constitutional reasons the Church had to give Bishop Gailot a place where he could still be bishop. So Bishop Gailot was taken from Evreux and transferred to the diocese of Partenia. Where is Partenia? In fact it is nowhere. The diocese of Partenia is in Algeria, on the slopes of the Atlas Mountains, covered by the Sahara desert and home for lizards and scorpions; in effect it is a virtual diocese (Zaleski, 1997, p.3). Leo Sheer, a French media philosopher and the bishop's friend, thought that Gailot should embrace that virtuality: why not put Partenia online? His argument was: 'Instead of a metaphysical idea of a bishop, attached to a real place, we would have a metaphysical idea of a place attached to a real bishop (Cobb, 1998, p.75). Partenia.org was born.

Although Partenia is a Catholic diocese, its web pages reflect the particular understanding of Jacques Gailot (Zaleski, 1997, p.4). The site does not publish papal encyclicals but letters and bulletins from both the bishop and Partenia's virtual congregation. Through cyberspace the bishop can move horizontally, communicating in a wholly new way religious as well as social and political issues he believes to be important. In addition, Partenia's congregation is offered a place where it can express its views about both religious and sociopolitical issues. Partenia is a response to the concreteness of the Catholic Church and proves, as Cobb (1998) indicates, that cyberspace provides opportunities for 'evolutionary social function, enabling spiritual and political work to unfold in new ways' (p.76).

The second example of an NCRM is Falun Gong. On 25 April 1999, 10 000 followers of Falun Gong gathered in Tiananmen Square, in an astonishing demonstration – coordinated and organized mainly by e-mail – which stunned the Chinese government and the rest of the world. They were protesting against the decision of the Chinese regime to outlaw the Falun Dafa meditation movement. Since then, several demonstrations have taken place (the latest in December 2000)[18] with the same demands: freedom of speech, expression and association. However, perhaps the most striking result of the 1999 demonstration is that, while there were 8.9 million Chinese Internet users at the end of 1999, the number leapt to 16.9 million in the first half of 2000, as the survey by the China National Network Information Center (CNNIC) showed.[19]

Although Falun Dafa does not exist purely on cyberspace (its followers do meet in the offline world), it qualifies as an NCRM because of its proficient utilization of cyberspace (supplied mainly from Internet providers in the West) as a communicative space and tool for followers and sympathizers, as well as an information and 'action taking' place where people can learn about and act for Falun Dafa.[20] Consequently, whilst it projects the movement as a spiritual path into the international arena, thus recruiting new followers, it also produces a counter-authoritarian resistance which not only demands more respect for human rights, but also challenges the Chinese regime's methods and places the totalitarian tactics of the Chinese government under international scrutiny.

Predicting the Future

Religious discourse in cyberspace takes many different forms. Each web page is a 'self-governing discourse' (Karaflogka, 1998). The nature of computer networks tends to bring people closer together, people who would otherwise never meet. It is an open space for anyone who wants to participate, and as such it provides the freedom for propaganda, debate, criticism, humour and exchange of information – as well as misinformation, hostility, rudeness and vulgarity. On newsgroups' bulletin boards individuals post all kind of messages, from religious jokes to theological, spiritual and metaphysical analyses.

In today's electronic age, information is astonishingly easy to access. The NET embodies two fundamental features: a unique form of interactive communication that no other medium can offer, and free access in both downloading and uploading information. This freedom is partly responsible for the existence of this parallel universe, which is expanding faster and faster and becoming more independent from its physical counterpart, thus creating the need to study it and understand it in its own terms. In this respect this chapter has argued that the distinction between religion *on* and religion *in* is important, facilitating exploration of technoreligious constructions; enabling us to follow the creation of new and the development of existing cyberreligions; offering a 'map' for identifying (a) NCRMs and (b) their relationship with and utilization of cyberspatial technology; making it possible to distinguish people's understanding of and responses to cyberreligious formations; providing the necessary tools for observing the probable future shift of religions *on* into religions *in* – that is, the extent to which religions which use cyberspace as a tool will accept and adopt it as an environment (Karaflogka, 2000a).

Religion is thus changed by the medium it adopts. Every expression of human devoutness, according to Chris Arthur (1993), is inevitably a 'mediated expression' that comes through a selection of instruments of communication: words, symbols, music, architecture, art and so on (p.1). Moreover, as William Fore (1993) states, 'the primary common function of religious activities is communication' (p.55). For this reason, the NET potentially provides unexpected and dramatic new possibilities for religion. Charles Henderson (1999) puts it like this:

In the prologue of St. John's Gospel we read: 'In the beginning was the Word and the Word was with God.' The Word really is, refers to the wisdom. It is the structure of truth that ties the whole cosmos together. And we, we say that that is part of God or it is God. Now, the whole idea of the World Wide Web is that ultimately all of human knowledge could be tied together through the links of hypertext. Now if you achieve that and you had all human wisdom tied together in an interconnecting web, or a structure, this would be analogous to the Biblical concept of the Word. So couldn't you say, in the beginning was the Web?

The point is echoed by the Foreign Liaison Group of Falun Dafa Research Society's Bulletin Board (15 June 1997):

Since 1995, Internet has been used to spread Falun Dafa. With the joint participation of the cultivators around the world, a new aspect in the multilingual transmission of Falun Dafa has been formed by the communication of E-mail and the carrier of Internet. Some of the predestined persons are able to gain the Great Law on Internet from different regions. With the development of human informationalized course, Falun Dafa's expansion and extension through Internet to every cultivator will come true. The open Internet can provide service to the development of human society.

Such statements demonstrate how cyberspace already has the capacity to be perceived as a sacred space, a spiritual space and a sociopolitical space. As such, it does not only carry institutionalized religions but, as Zaleski (1997) points out, it allows 'a world-wide hearing of every voice within these religions' (p.4), as well as the creation of new religions.

Will the spread of cyberreligions have a corrosive or an invigorating effect on religion in modern society? Richard Thieme (1997) suggests that religious structures are bound to change, and he identifies three defining realities that will determine the religious structures of the future:

Religious structures will be shaped by the 'space' created by a singular global economy.
Religious structures will be determined by the shape of the virtual world.
Religious structures will be determined by the dynamics of interplanetary culture.

Presumably such effects will be both corrosive and creative. As we have seen, cyberspace offers a fascinating new setting for the development of religious imagination, which manifests itself in ways beyond the conventional channels. This may prove challenging for ordered, traditional, regulated, hierarchical forms of religion. It is apparent, as the examples of Partenia and Falun Gong show, that,

[as] public sources multiply through the Internet, it's [sic] likely that the number of sites claiming to belong to any particular religion but in fact disseminating information that the central authority of that religion deems heretical also will multiply. (Zaleski, 1997, p.108)

Cyberspace, as a 'blessed'[21] space, influences religious practice with unprecedented results. Empirical evidence (Karaflogka, 2000b) shows that already significant developments have taken place in the realm of cyberreligious praxis, in the shape of cybermarriages, cybermemorials and Pagan cyberrituals, to mention but a few. At the extreme of speculation, it is even held that cyberreligion may reshape the structure of the religious economy and imagination. For, as David Tomas (1991) suggests, cyberspace

> has the potential to not only change the economic structure of human societies but to also overthrow the sensorial and organic architecture of the human body, this by disembodying and reformatting its sensorium in powerful, computer-generated, digitalised spaces. (Tomas, 1991, p.32)

The more computer science and technology advance, that is, as they move from atoms to bits and from desktops to Things That Think (TTT) and wearable computers, the more the shape of the virtual world may be expected to change dramatically, and the more what now seem 'far-fetched' predictions may come true. The cheaper technological advances become (as in 3-D software available now free on the NET), the more widely available, and so the more the structure of religion may be expected to evolve (Karaflogka, 2000b) because these technologies might constitute, to quote Tomas (1991), the 'central phase in a post-industrial "rite of passage" between organically human and cyber-psychically digital life forms as reconfigured through computer software systems' (p.33).

Turning to the academy, it thus becomes clear that it is not only the field of humanities that will be affected by its contact with progressive information systems (ibid.); a new theoretical and methodological field is needed which will address religious, cultural, social and anthropological issues as they arise within the field of 'cyberstudies' (Karaflogka, 2000b). One cannot but agree with Tomas who imagines a 'postorganic' form of humanities which will exclusively focus on undertaking the questions of constructing 'cyberspatial forms of intelligence as opposed to the more conventional humanistic, more or less reflexive, study of premodernist, modernist, or postmodernist humankind' (p.33). In one way or another it seems, then, that the future will bring remarkable transformations not only of religion, but of the study of religion.

Notes

1   Although the term 'Internet' refers to the hardware (computers, wires and so on), scholars tend to use it as synonymous with CMC and cyberspace. Here all three terms are both used to refer to the 'same set of phenomena [which is to say], they are generic terms which refer to clusters of different technologies, some familiar, some only recently available, some being developed and still fictional, all of which have in common the ability to simulate environments within which humans can interact' (Featherstone and Burrows, 1995, p.5). For more details on the different definitions, see Sterling (1990), Featherstone and Burrows (1995), Herring (1996).

2   *http://www.church-of-england.org/*, accessed 10/11/98.
3   *www.medialab.ntua.gr/athos.html*, accessed 19/11/00.
4   *http://www.watchtower.org/html*, accessed 20/12/97.
5   *http://www.vatican.va/*, accessed 23/6/98.
6   *http://www.christadelphian.com/*, accessed 23/6/98.
7   *www.asahi-net.or.jp/~LM2O-ARKW/shrine.html*, accessed 10/11/00.
8   *www.scientology.org*, accessed 10/6/98.
9   *http://www.vIrtualchurch.org/vcwelc.htm*, accessed 25/11/00.
10 *http://clint.aldigital.algroup.co.uk/wpb/oshocs.htm*, accessed 25/11/00.
11 *http://www.syn2000.org/*, accessed 25/11/00.
12 *http://www.premamusic.com/CyberTemple/islam.html*, accessed 25/11/00.
13 *http://www.cs.cmu.edu/afs/cs.cmu.edu/user/spok/www/catholic/computer-culture.html#note5*, accessed 17/8/99.
14 *www.sni.net/archden/dcr/1998100101.html*, accessed 21/9/99.
15 *www.ecic.org/ecic4/workshop-develop.html*, accessed 20/9/99.
16 *http://members.xoom.com/gecko23/moo*, accessed 20/9/99.
17 The site of Partenia can be found in *<www.partenia.org>*. Falun Gong's official site is *<www.falundafa.org>*.
18 *http://www.clearwisdom.net/eng/2001/Jan/11/EWA011101_3.html*, accessed 15/04/01.
19 'China Internet Users Double to 17 Million', CNN report on technology and computing in China. Web posted 27 July 2000 by Reuters. Available online: *http://www.cnn.com/2000/TECH/computing/07/27/china.internet.reut/*, accessed 14/04/01.
20 Falun Dafa InfoCenter *http://www.faluninfo.net/activity_center_frame.asp*, accessed 15/04/01.
21 The blessing of cyberspace was performed by the monks of the Namgyal Monastery, the personal monastery of the Dalai Lama, who thought that the Kalachakra Tantra, believed to have been first taught by the Buddha, would be highly appropriate as a blessing vehicle because it especially emphasizes space, itself (along with consciousness), as one of the six constituent elements of the universe, in addition to the more familiar elements of earth, air, fire and water. The blessing was performed on 8 February 1996. It can be accessed in *http://www.namgyal.org/blessing.html*.

References

Arthur, Chris (ed.) 1993: Introduction. In *Religion and the Media: An Introductory Reader*. Cardiff: University of Wales Press, pp.1–23.

Aycock, Alan 1995: Technologies of the Self: Michel Foucault Online. *Journal of Computer Mediated Communication*, 1 (2). Retrieved 10 June 1997 *<http://www.ascusc.org/jcmc/vol1/issue2/aycock.html>*.

Benschop, Albert 1997: Building Blocks for an Internet Sociology. *The Cyber Studies Resources*, October 1997. Retrieved 22 February 1998 *<http://www.pscw.uva.nl/sociosite/websoc/indexE.html>*.

Cobb, Jennifer 1998: *Cybergrace: The Search for God in the Digital World*. New York: Crown Publishers.

Cybernauts Awake 1999. Retrieved 6 October 1999: *<http://starcourse.org/sciteb2/starcourse/cyber/>*.

Davis, Eric 1998: *Techgnosis: Myth, Magic, and Mysticism in the Age of Information*. New York: Harmony Books

Dawson, Lorne L. and Hennebry, Jenna 1999: New Religions and the Internet: Recruiting in a New Public Space, *Journal of Contemporary Religion*, 14 (1), pp.17–39.

Featherstone, Mike and Burrows, Roger 1995: *Cyberspace/Cyberbodies/Cyberpunk: Cultures of Technological Embodiment*. London: Sage Publications.

Fore, William 1993: The Religious Relevance of Television. In Chris Arthur (ed.), *Religion and the Media: An Introductory Reader*. Cardiff: University of Wales Press, pp.55–65.

The Foreign Liaison Group of Falun Dafa Research Society, 15 June 1997, Falun Dafa Bulletin Board. *http://falundafa.ca/FLDFBB*. Retrieved 10 July 1998.

Heim, Michael 1993: *The Metaphysics of Virtual Reality*. New York and Oxford: Oxford University Press.

Henderson, Charles 1999: *Does God Surf the Net?* Interview. Retrieved 30 January 2000. *<http://christianity.about.com/religion/christianity/library/weekly/aa012699.htm>*.

Herring, Susan 1996: *Computer Mediated Communication: Linguistic, Social and Cross Cultural Perspectives*. Philadelphia: John Benjamin Publishing.

Holmes, David 1997: *Virtual Politics: Identity and Community in Cyberspace*. London: SAGE.

Jones, Steve 1999: Preface. In Steve Jones (ed.), *Doing Internet Research*. Thousand Oaks, London and New Delhi: Sage Publications, pp.xi–xiv.

Karaflogka, Anastasia 1998: Religious Discourse in Cyberspace. Paper presented at the 1998 BASR Annual Conference University of Wales, Lampeter.

Karaflogka, Anastasia 2000a: Religious Discourse and Cyberspace. Paper presented at the 18th Quinquennial Congress of the IAHR, August 2000, Holiday Inn Durban Elangeni, South Africa.

Karaflogka, Anastasia 2000b: Cyberritual: Multivocal Evolution and Development of Religious Practice. Paper presented at the Annual Study Day 2000 of the British Sociological Association (BSA), Sociology of Religion Study Group, Birkbeck College, University of London.

O'Leary, Stephen D. 1996: Cyberspace as Sacred Space: Communicating Religion on Computer Networks. *Journal of the American Academy of Religion*, LIX (4), pp.781–807.

Pauly, John, J. 1991: A Beginner's Guide to Qualitative Research in Mass Communication. *Journalism and Mass Communication Monographs*, No 125.

Poster, Mark 1995: *CyberDemocracy: Internet and the Public Sphere*, University of California, Irvine. Retrieved 5 April 1999. *<http://www.hnet.uci.edu/mposter/writings/democ.html>*.

Sterling, Bruce 1990: Cyberspace (TM). *Interzone*, November. Retrieved 25 January 1991 *<http://www.locusmag.com/index/t154.html#A18379>*.

Thieme, Richard 1997: The Future Shape of Religious Structures. *Computer Mediated Communication Magazine*, March 1997. Retrieved 30 March 1998 *<www.december.com/cmc/mag/1997/mar/last.html>*.

Tomas, David 1991: Old Rituals for New Space: Rites of Passage and William Gibson's Cultural Model of Cyberspace. In Michael Benedikt (ed.), *Cyberspace The First Steps*, Cambridge, MA: The MIT Press, pp.31–47.

Wertheim, Margaret 1999, *The Pearly Gates of Cyberspace*, London: Virago.

Zaleski, Jeff 1997: *The Soul of Cyberspace*, San Francisco: HarperEdge.

CHAPTER 17

The Paranormal in Swedish Religiosity

Ulf Sjödin

Along with Denmark, Sweden is regarded as the most secularized country in Europe (Halman, 1994). On a societal level this means that the Church as an institution has lost its impact on other institutions in society. At the individual level too, secularization is evident in a steadily decreasing level of belief in Christian dogma, and decreasing attendance at religious services (Gustafsson, 1997). On the other hand, the membership rate of the Church of Sweden, although also decreasing slowly, is still about 85 per cent. The Swedes may thus be labelled a people who 'belong without believing'.

So these facts do not necessarily imply that Swedes are not religious. A change in the way religiosity is expressed may have taken place. One indication of this may be that empirical studies show beliefs in the paranormal to be widespread among Swedes. Although these beliefs turn out be somewhat more common among the young, they are common among the population as a whole (Sjödin, 1994; 1995). In the media this is now treated as an established truth, with headlines like 'Swedes believe in Aliens but not in God' being common. Of course, this is a simplified way of looking at the facts. A government investigation found that there are about 60 000 core members of New Religious Movements (Mormons, Scientology and Faith-movement included) in Sweden out of a total population of 8.8 million people.

Even if beliefs in the paranormal are not new, it may still be said that such beliefs are much more tolerated and accepted today than 20 or 30 years ago. The *Zeitgeist* seems to have changed. An earlier minor study also indicates that these beliefs were less frequent among the Swedes in the 1970s. Stark and Bainbridge (1985) have presented the hypothesis that, where traditional religion declines, alternative religious beliefs – rather than atheism – emerge. This hypothesis has been confirmed both by their study and by independent research in Sweden (Sjödin, 1994). In the Swedish case, paranormal beliefs turned out to be strongest where traditional religion was weakest. In the secularized urban areas in Sweden, where we find a particularly high incidence of paranormal beliefs, one can assume that these beliefs have taken the place of traditional religion. Thus there seems to have been a change in preferences concerning religious outlook. Nowadays it is a widespread and established 'truth' that Swedes to a great extent believe in ghosts and similar phenomena. One could say that such paranormal belief has become a component of 'our generally accepted "storehouse" of truths' (Truzzi, 1974). Thus the para-normal no longer is para-normal, but rather normal.

Even if belief in the paranormal is widespread, however, is it central and salient? An often neglected but essential aspect of values and value change is their importance to the holder in question. Is a certain value in the periphery of the individual's outlook on life, or is it regarded as a central aspect of the individual, and the individual's identity? A person can hold a number of values – and normally does so – but only an individual's central, or important, values will have a real impact on the person's thinking and acting. According to Ronald Inglehart's (1977, 1997) theory of value change, the question of centrality is crucial. According to this theory, central values do not change during an individual's adult lifetime. Thus, if paranormal beliefs were central to young people today, this, according to Inglehart, would create a major value change as these young people grew up, compared to the values upheld by today's adults. On the other hand, if they turn out not to be central but peripheral, one will have to look for other ways of understanding the emergence of paranormal values. One such perspective could be that the paranormal values are mainly chosen because of the lack of other adequate alternatives in the field of ideologies. Deprived of trustworthy alternatives, the young are attracted (indulged) by the 'new' set of values provided by the paranormal.

Beliefs which at first sight appear central may thus turn out under further investigation to be more peripheral. Belief in reincarnation in Sweden illustrates the point well. In several major studies (Sjödin, 1994; 1995; 1999) it has been found that 20 per cent of Swedes believe in reincarnation. It is an easily drawn conclusion that every fifth Swede believes in reincarnation. However, in these surveys the concept of reincarnation was standing isolated from other alternative understandings of afterlife. What would happen if one let the 'market forces' free and had reincarnation compete with other possible options for what happens after death? This was done in a later study, where four alternatives could be chosen. The result was that the alternative of reincarnation only attracted 6 per cent of Swedes. Thus the believers in reincarnation were reduced by two-thirds when the reincarnation option was challenged by other options. This result clearly indicates that belief in reincarnation is not as important, or central, as it may at first appear. It also strengthens the hypothesis that the same may go for other forms of belief in the paranormal.

The crucial question is therefore whether these obviously widespread beliefs in the paranormal are really important to those who believe in them. On the basis of a research project devised to answer this question (and unique in Sweden), this chapter argues that this is not the case. Our finding is that, while belief in the paranormal is common amongst young people, its salience and centrality is low.

Testing Belief in the Paranormal

At the outset, it is important to clarify the concept of centrality, for it is far from self-evident how to interpret this concept. One can consider, for example, a value's intensity, stability, strength, importance, visibility, external or internal saliency and degree of ego-involvement. High intensity of a value often means high stability, strength, external and internal saliency and ego-involvement. In the research on which this study is based, we decided to look at the strength, the degree of ego-involvement and the internal saliency of the values in question. We wanted to find out how certain, or positive, the respondents are about their beliefs, how important certain values are for their outlook on life and if these values are regarded as holy or not. The concept of the holy is understood as the remote, untouchable and unquestionable. What a person considers holy also has a high degree of internal saliency.

The research selected 622 representative high school students from different kinds of urban areas in Sweden. Of these, 296 students came from two minor towns with about 30 000 inhabitants, 171 students from one major city with about 300 000 inhabitants, and 155 students lived in another small city very significant in the Swedish 'Bible Belt'. From earlier studies in Sweden we could predict that the degree of belief in the paranormal would be significantly lower in the Bible Belt town than in the three others. Young people in an ideologically strong surrounding seem to be far more 'immune' to influences from alternative outlooks on life, as Rodney Stark and William Bainbridge (1985) predicted.

The first element of the research involved asking respondents whether or not they believed in nine paranormal phenomena. The results were congruent with earlier youth studies in Sweden (Sjödin, 1994; 1995; 1999), that is, young people in general believe to a high degree in the paranormal, and young women believe more than young men (p>0.001). Belief in extraterrestrial beings, however, is an exception, since boys believe far more often in their existence than do girls. Again, this result echoes the findings of previous studies (Clarke, 1991; Boy and Michelat, 1993; Sjödin, 1994).

In the second stage of the research, respondents were asked to indicate how certain they were concerning each of these nine beliefs, that is, how convinced they were that their beliefs were correct. On the basis of previous studies, we knew that 'health' and 'peace' are highly important values among young Swedes. We also knew that traditional Christian values (such as 'Jesus Christ' and 'Salvation') are not at all important to most young Swedes (Skolöverstyrelsen, 1971; Sjödin, 1995). By using this knowledge we easily constructed two extremes on a spectrum of 'value centrality'. By asking about the importance of paranormal values alongside these other values we would be able to see where on the spectrum the paranormal values would end up – close to one or the other extremes, or scattered between the two.

The phrasing of the initial question was 'Are your beliefs about the following features important or unimportant for your way of looking at existence?' The respondents could choose from five alternatives: 'Very important', 'Rather important', 'Neither important, nor unimportant', 'Rather unimportant' and 'Very unimportant'. See Table 17.1.

Results confirmed that health and peace were regarded by respondents as the most important values, while Jesus and salvation were regarded as least important. The results concerning the importance of paranormal beliefs can be interpreted in two ways. One argument would be that some paranormal values are regarded as more important than Jesus, and that most paranormal values are seen as more important than salvation, which could be seen as an indication that the paranormal is more important than traditional Christian values. On the other hand, the difference in salience between the paranormal and Christian values is marginal, and both appear to be relatively unimportant to most young people. These findings therefore suggest not only that traditional Christian beliefs are unimportant, but that the 'replacement' of these by paranormal values could be seen as a protest against the lack of trustworthy alternatives. That is, neither church-related values nor paranormal values are important to young Swedes today.

Table 17.1   'Are your beliefs about the following features important or unimportant for your way of looking at existence?' N=621

	Very important	Rather important	Neither – Nor	Rather unimportant	Very unimportant	Total
Peace	75	20	3	2	0	100
Jesus	11	11	25	27	26	100
Health	85	13	1	1	1	101
Salvation	8	5	24	25	37	99
Telepathy	3	8	35	25	29	100
Premonitions	6	20	41	16	17	100
Reincarnation	7	13	25	22	33	100
Astrology	5	16	27	20	32	100
Extraterrestrials	7	18	24	18	32	99
Seers	4	15	31	23	27	100
True dreams	7	25	34	19	15	100
Ghosts	6	12	22	21	39	100
Healing	3	10	28	22	37	100

Note: 'N' indicates the number of persons interviewed.

A factor analysis reveals three dimensions, health and peace making up the central dimension, Jesus and salvation the Christian dimension, and the rest of the items the paranormal dimension. As expected, the Bible Belt students assign significantly more importance to the Christian dimension than do students from the other towns ($p > 0.001$), but also to health ($p > 0.05$) and to peace ($p > 0.001$). Concerning the paranormal dimension, there is only a significant difference between the Bible belt students and the others on two of the items. Bible Belt students thus find reincarnation ($p > 0.001$) and ghosts ($p > 0.01$) significantly less important than do the other students; since neither reincarnation nor ghosts are compatible with Christian dogma, this may well explain this difference.

It is also interesting to note that there are specific gender differences. Health seems to be of equal importance to both girls and boys, but with one exception girls estimate all the other values as far more important than boys do (p>0.001). This outcome is not very surprising, since the values in question could all be labeled 'soft' or feminine values. The same goes for the only exception, extraterrestrials, which boys find far more important than do girls (p>0.001). These results reflect traditional gender roles and correlate with findings from some previous studies in the field (Clarke, 1991; Boy and Michelat, 1993; Sjödin, 1995). It is worth noting that while both girls and boys find health to be a very important value, girls significantly find Jesus and salvation more important than do boys (p>0.001), and girls find peace significantly more important than do boys (p>0.01). Yet all the paranormal values are found clustered in the range of salvation and Jesus, that is, they are all gathered round the most insignificant end of the spectrum.

A further question concerned religious self-identity. When respondents were asked to choose from the alternatives 'I am a Christian', 'I am a Christian in my personal way' and 'I am not a Christian', 20 per cent called themselves Christian, 44 per cent Christian in a personal way and 36 per cent non-Christian. One could expect the Christians to score high, and the non-Christians to score low, on the values Jesus and salvation, yet, when it comes to paranormal beliefs, using the dimensions found in the factor analysis and comparing the three types of religiosity, one finds no significant difference between the self-identity groups. Comparing Christians with non-Christians, the former value the central dimension significantly higher (p>0.01), a difference also found when comparing Christians with 'personal Christians' (p>0.01). Not very surprisingly, the Christians differ from the two other groups on the Christian dimension (p>0.001) by assigning greater importance to this dimension. Finally, comparing personal Christians with non-Christians on the Christian dimension, the personal Christians finds this dimension significantly more important than do the non-Christians (p>0.001). This brings us to the conclusion that the paranormal dimension is equally unimportant independent of type of religious self-identification. The most important difference is found on the Christian dimension, which includes the traditional values Jesus and salvation, which is more important to Christians than to personal Christians or non-Christians, and also more important to personal Christians than to non-Christians. Once again we see that paranormal items do not have a big impact on the respondents.

Turning to another way of measuring the centrality of paranormal beliefs, we used the concept of the holy. On a scale from 1 to 10, the respondents were asked to indicate the degree of holiness (or unholiness) they assigned to certain features. These were selected from pilot studies carried out in different settings, where people were asked to write what they regarded as holy. Paranormal items were added to this list, as were items that we know from experience to play an important role in the

daily life of young people. No definition of the holy was presented, since it was left
to the respondent to define the concept.

Table 17.2 shows the percentage assigning holiness to the various items listed.
On the scale from 1 to 10, where 1 is the most holy, only responses in the range 1
and 2 are included in the table. Thereby, we only measure what is regarded by the
respondents as very holy. Including more responses (3–5) does not change the
outcome greatly.

As shown in the table, we find a range of holiness from 80 to 7. For some reason,
health was not included. However, close ones, life, joy and peace form the top four,
standing out as especially holy and thereby central values. Low ratings are given to
paranormal items like UFOs, ghosts and telepathy, as well as school! (From another
part of the study we learn that school is very important to the students, but obviously
not holy.) Generally, features regarded as important do not have to be regarded as
holy. However, conversely, the respondents always regard what is regarded as holy
as important. Thus the paranormal clearly does not appear to be regarded as holy,
not even when presented under the overall concept of 'the supernatural', thus
suggesting once more that paranormal values are peripheral rather than central to
most young people in Sweden.

Table 17.2   The degree of holiness assigned to various items. Per cent N=621

Item	Per cent	Item	Per cent
Close ones	80	Hospital	35
Life	79	Prayer	26
Joy	79	Sports	24
Peace	73	Ancient remains	21
Nature	61	Supernatural	18
Churchyard	51	Petroglyph	16
Death	51	Runes	15
Baptism	50	Ghosts	11
Music	45	School	9
Jesus	38	UFO	7
Church	36	Telepathy	6

A factor analysis reveals five dimensions. Life, close ones, nature, peace, death,
joy and music form the dimension we call 'existential'. There is a strong correlation
between joy and music, which means that music is associated with the joyous. A
second, religious dimension, consists of prayer, churchyard, funeral, baptism,
church and Jesus. The historical dimension includes ancient remains, the
supernatural, petroglyph and runes. The paranormal dimension contains items like

ghosts, telepathy, UFOs and the supernatural. Finally, in an institutional dimension, we find sports, school and hospital. In relation to gender, there is no significant difference between girls and boys for the historical and the paranormal dimensions. Girls score higher than boys on the existential and religious dimensions ($p>0.001$), which is what one could expect, since the values included in these dimensions refer to traditional gender role values. Boys, on the other hand, dominate the institutional dimension ($p>0.05$). Of the three items, school, sports and hospital, making up the institutional dimension, boys and girls score equally on school, but, typically, boys find sports more holy than girls do ($p>0.001$) and girls find hospital more holy than the boys do ($p>0.05$). It has to be admitted, however, that these items are seldom uppermost when thinking of the holy, a circumstance which may have confused the respondents.

The picture is more complicated when we cross-refer with religious self-identity. As one would expect, Christians ascribe greater holiness to the religious dimension than do the other two religious groups ($p>0.001$). Also the personal Christians regard the religious dimension as more holy than do the non-Christians ($p>0.001$). Of course, this is a normal outcome, which confirms the different types of religious preferences. While there is no significant difference between the Christians and the non-Christians on the existential dimension, however, the personal Christians assign more holiness to that dimension than do the Christians ($p>0.05$) and the non-Christians ($p>0.001$). This seems to imply that one reason for these respondents to choose the alternative 'Christian in my own personal way' is their religious quest, driven on the one hand by a distrust of traditional Christianity and on the other by a yearning for an adequate answer to existential questions.

It also turns out that there is no significant difference between the three types of religiosity on the historical and paranormal dimensions. Concerning the institutional dimension, there is no significant difference between personal Christians and non-Christians, or between Christians and non-Christians. However, between the Christians and the personal Christians there is a significant difference, since the personal Christians regard the institutional dimension as more holy than do the Christians ($p>0.001$). This may be interpreted as an expression of dissatisfaction with established religious institutions, such that the quest for answers (holiness) has to be located outside such domains.

Conclusion

It appears that the widespread belief in the paranormal among Swedish youth – and probably among the Swedish population as a whole – plays only a peripheral role in shaping people's self-identity and outlook on life. That, however, leaves open the question why people actually hold such beliefs and why these seem to have become more popular during recent decades. To answer such questions fully, of course, is a very complicated task, and here we can only suggest one possible explanation.

As argued above, one can expect deviant beliefs to enter the scene to the same degree that traditional beliefs leave it. The loss of tradition is likely to create a vacuum in the field of beliefs, leaving the individual alone to choose from whatever is to be found in the market place of beliefs. In countries like Sweden, the secularization process – as it affects traditional religion – may actually have the effect of enriching the variety of offerings in the market-place, to the degree that it takes place in an open society where there is a rich exchange of ideas with other cultures. If human beings are meaning-seeking creatures, they will continue to need adequate alternatives to believe in, even as the traditional beliefs no longer meet their needs. Thus paranormal beliefs may help them to find a meaning and purpose in life, even in the face of secularization. Though peripheral in the minds of most young people, such beliefs can be regarded as a substitute for other, perhaps more adequate, beliefs and world-views.

If the above line of reasoning has some validity, one should expect young people to dwell upon the question of the purpose of life to a high degree. The results summarized in Table 17.3 suggest that this is indeed the case. As is shown, the vast majority of young people do think about the purpose of life fairly frequently. There is not even a great gender difference; this appears to be a vital issue for all young people in Sweden. Such findings are echoed in other recent studies (Bäckström, 1997; Sjödin, 1995) which show that existential questions have become ever more important in people's lives. Thus one could say that the decline in traditional beliefs has been accompanied by an increased commitment to existential questions in general.

It is, however, a different thing to raise a question about purpose and the meaning of life than to find answers. And a lack of clear answers, articulations and formulations in relation to the divine is exactly what we do find when we measure young people's attitudes towards the question of the existence of a 'higher power'. What is particularly revealing is what happens when, in one sample, an imprecise alternative formulation is included, as shown in Table 17.4.

Table 17.3 How often do you think of the purpose of life? N=622

	All	Girls	Boys
Often	35	41	25
Sometimes	45	46	43
Seldom	17	11	26
Never	4	1	7
Total	101	99	101

Looking at the total outcome in the two samples, the higher range of belief in a personal God in the 1999 sample seems to be explained by the fact that Bible Belt students made up a good portion of this sample and, to a larger degree than the others, chose this alternative. In the other towns, 14 per cent of the students chose the theism alternative. In the 1999 sample, the deism 2 alternative is the highest rated of all alternatives. However, the deism 1, agnosticism and atheism alternatives all show lower ratings as the deism 2 alternative is included as an option. This could be interpreted as a demonstration of the attractiveness of the deism 2 alternative. It seems, in other words, that the number of atheists is reduced by including such an option. This is congruent with the fact that an earlier study (Sjödin, 1994, pp.45ff) found that a considerable number of students labelling themselves absolutely non-religious still believed in a higher power or an afterlife. So it could well be that a latent religiosity is manifested in the attractiveness of the deism 2 alternative. The same might be said, of course, for the agnosticism alternative. Thus the fact that a majority of the students have chosen the two deism alternatives clearly shows that thoughts about the transcendent today are mainly expressed in a vague and, probably, individual way. It also is likely that the quest for meaning is one factor underlying this outcome, since students choosing the two deism alternatives occupy themselves with thoughts about the purpose of life to a far higher extent than the others. Thus, from a methodological point of view, it seems that blurred alternatives actually best capture young people's attitudes towards the transcendent.

Table 17.4   Two ways[1] of measuring belief in a higher power among Swedish youth. Question: 'Which of the following statements come closest to your conviction?' Per cent

	1999 N=622			1994 N=1488		
	All	Girls	Boys	All	Girls	Boys
Theism	20	22	17	15	17	12
Deism 1	25	31	15	33	39	27
Deism 2	29	29	29	—	—	—
Agnosticism	17	14	22	34	34	35
Atheism	9	5	17	18	10	27
Total	100	101	100	100	100	101

Notes: The 1994 survey did not include the alternative Deism 2, 'There is something, but I don't know what', and thus was not as inclusive as the 1999 survey.

Alternatives are shortened in the table. Full phrasing in the questionnaire: 'Theism' = There is a personal God; 'Deism 1' = There is some kind of spirit or life force; 'Deism 2' = There is something, but I don't know what; 'Agnosticism' = I don't know what to believe; 'Atheism' = There is no God, spirit or life force.

Returning to our point of departure, this chapter has demonstrated that students' beliefs in the paranormal are not very important to their outlook on life. Rather, it could be stated that, deprived of trustworthy alternatives for understanding life, they turn to these beliefs as something of a last resort. Since the majority of those most involved in New Age activities appear to be middle-aged – constituting 'an aging New Age' (see Heelas and Seel in this volume) – there does not seem to be much support for either Christian or New Age values amongst the younger generation. Young Swedes today appear to be most attracted by those articulations relating to the transcendent that are imprecise or open to individual interpretation. Exactly how this is to be understood, however, still demands further exploration. On the whole the results provide reason to characterize Swedish youth as a group who are 'seeking without really finding'. In relation to their quest, we seem to find both a shrinking and an expanding transcendence.

In the light of such findings, we may expect the younger generation to create new public arenas for their search. An interesting example is furnished by increasingly popular 'philosophy cafés', where, in a relaxed atmosphere, people can use the tools of 'rational philosophy' to discuss existential questions. What becomes of organized religion in such a context? One possibility, though rarely entertained, is that the lack of a stabilizing authority in an era of individualism and relativism, combined with a growing lack of knowledge about such religions, will in the long run make them attractive once more to the younger, seeking, 'non-atheistic' generations.

References

Bäckström, Anders 1997: *Livsåskådning och Kyrkobyggnad. En Studie av Attityder i Göteborg och Malmö, Tro & Tanke*. Stockholm: Svenska Kyrkans Forskningsråd.

Boy, Daniel and Michelat, Guy 1993: Premiers Résultats de l'enquête sur les Croyances aux Parasciences. In *La Pensée Scientifique et les Parasciences*. Paris: Albin Michel. Cité des Sciences et de L'industrie, pp.201–17.

Clarke, Dave 1991: Belief in the Paranormal: A New Zealand Survey. *Journal of the Society for Psychical Research*, 57 (823), pp.412–25.

Gustafsson, Göran 1997: *Tro, Samfund och Samhälle. Sociologiska Perspektiv*. Örebro: Bokförlaget Libris.

Halman, Loek 1994: Scandinavian Values: How Special are They? In Thorleif Pettersson and Ole Riis (eds), *Scandinavian Values. Religion and Morality in the Nordic Countries*. Uppsala: Acta Universitatis Upsaliensis, Psychologia et Sociologia Religionum, pp.59–85.

Heelas, Paul 1996: *The New Age Movement. The Celebration of the Self and the Sacralization of Modernity*. Oxford: Blackwell.

Inglehart, Ronald 1977: *The Silent Revolution. Changing Values and Political Styles Among Western Publics*. Princeton, NJ: Princeton University Press.

Inglehart, Ronald 1997: *Modernization and Postmodernization. Cultural, Economic, and Political Change in 43 Societies*. Princeton, NJ: Princeton University Press.

Sjödin, Ulf 1994: *Flygande Tefat, Spöken och Sanndrömmar. Ungdomars Syn på Paranormala Företeelser*. Religionssociologiska Skrifter nr 8, Teologiska Institutionen, Uppsala Universitet.

Sjodin, Ulf 1995: *En Skola – Flera Världar. Värderingar hos elever och lärare i Religionskunskap i Gymnasieskolan*. Stockholm: Bokförlaget Plus Ultra.

Sjödin, Ulf 1999: Ungdomars Religiösa Värderingar. In Antoon Geels and Owe Wikström (eds), *Den Religiösa Människan. En Introduktion till Religionspsykologin*, Falkenberg: Natur & Kultur, pp.343–61.

Skolöverstyrelsen 1971: Gymnasieeleven och Livsfrågorna: Studiematerial för lärare i so-ämnen, i första hand Religionskunskap, på Gymnasieskolan, utarbetat på uppdrag av Skolöverstyrelsen. Utbildningsförlaget, Stockholm.

Stark, Rodney and Bainbridge, William Sims 1985: *The Future of Religion. Secularization, Revival and Cult Formation*. Berkeley:University of California Press.

Truzzi, Marcello 1974: Definition and Dimensions of the Occult: Towards a Sociological Perspective. In Edward A. Tiryakian (ed.), *On the Margin of the Visible. Sociology, the Esoteric, and the Occult*. New York: John Wiley and Sons, pp.243–57.

CHAPTER 18

Are the Stars Coming out?
Secularization and the Future of
Astrology in the West

Wayne Spencer

Introduction

Opinion polls and other surveys routinely find that substantial proportions of the general public of western Europe and North America express belief in various 'paranormal' phenomena (Zusne and Jones, 1989; Vyse, 1997). Indeed, a Gallup poll of American adults conducted in June 1990 found that 93 per cent of respondents said they believed in at least one of a list of 18 paranormal claims, and almost one-half accepted the reality of five or more (Gallup and Newport, 1991). Similarly, in a poll of a representative sample of the residents of Reading, England, 88 per cent of respondents said they thought at least one of a series of paranormal propositions was definitely true, and 68 per cent definitely assented to at least three (Brown, 1987, cited in Humphrey, 1995, p.4).

The social consequences of widespread belief in the paranormal in Western societies have been the subject of speculation by both scholarly and lay analysts. William Sims Bainbridge (1997), for example, said of the range of ideas to be found in the New Age section of contemporary bookshops:

> At one level, all this seems quite trivial. But when we find these topics showing up frequently in movies and television dramas, and when a president of the United States is revealed to have regularly consulted an astrologer, the possibility arises that we are witnessing a gradual but significant cultural change that might result in repaganization of Judeo-Christian civilization. (Bainbridge, 1997, p.363)

More recently, Erich Goode (2000) has stated, 'It is inconceivable that, given the worldwide acceptance of paranormal thinking, it also does not have an impact on a range of social institutions (p.4).

But is it really the case that the type of paranormal belief typical in Western societies today has profound social consequences? This chapter considers whether the belief in the paranormal revealed by opinion polls has indeed operated to retard or reverse the processes of secularization in western Europe and North America or will do so in the future. It approaches these questions by looking at just a single paranormal belief, namely astrology, and also offers some predictions as to what the future of astrology may be in the light of the analysis below.

Secularization

In view of the considerable talking at cross-purposes that has occurred within the debate over the secularization thesis (Hanson, 1997; Yamane, 1997), it would seem advisable to state at the outset the sense in which the term 'secularization' is used here. For the purposes of this chapter, a definition of 'secularization' given by Bryan Wilson in 1988 will be adopted. That is, 'secularization' means 'a process occurring within the social system ... that process by which religious thinking, practice and institutions lose social significance and become marginal to the operation of the social system (p.196). It should be stressed that such a conception of secularization does not necessarily postulate a decline in religious belief and practice at the level of the *individual*; rather, its focus is on the *social system*. Thus, to quote Bryan Wilson (1985) again:

> Basically, the inherited model of secularization is concerned with the operation of the social *system*. It is the system that becomes secularized. Conceptions of the supernatural may not disappear, either as rhetorical public expressions or as private predilections, but they cease to be determinants of social action. (Wilson, 1985, p.19)

Given this conception of secularization, it follows that, before evidence of current belief in astrology can properly be accepted as an indication that secularization has not occurred or is now in reverse, two things must be shown. The first is that belief in astrology has a substantive effect on the basic operations of the social system. The second is that astrology is religious in nature. This chapter will focus on the first of these matters.

Extent and Depth of Belief in Astrology

At first glance, it would appear that astrological belief permeates society. The astrology or horoscope column is nearly ubiquitous in newspapers, appearing for example in 84 per cent of American daily newspapers and 86 per cent of American Sunday newspapers in 1987 (Bogart, 1989). Astrology is also well represented in other print media (Dean *et al.*, 1996, p.60), and on popular television and the World Wide Web (Ashmun, 1996/7). As regards public belief in astrology, numerous surveys of various populations indicate that a substantial proportion of the general population accept the truth of astrology. For example, a 1990 Gallup poll found that 25 per cent of American adults believe in astrology (Gallup and Newport, 1991).

This evidence may appear to suggest that astrological belief is a broad-based social phenomenon such as may give rise to the widespread use of astrological information and considerations in the conduct of important social institutions. A rather different picture emerges if we examine the depth and not the breadth of contemporary astrological belief. Thus a survey of representative national samples conducted in Britain in 1988 (Durant and Bauer, 1992; Bauer and Durant, 1997) and Sweden in 1994 (Fjaestad, 1994) found respectively that 44 per cent and 49 per cent of respondents read a horoscope often or fairly often. However, only 6 per cent of the British sample and 11 per cent of the Swedish sample said they took such material very seriously or fairly seriously. Perhaps more revealingly, only 1 per cent of the Swedish sample took horoscopes very seriously. The percentage of the British sample that admitted to taking horoscopes very seriously is only given in graph form, but it appears to be around 1–2 per cent (Durant and Bauer, 1992, 2nd table, p.12). An earlier survey of residents of the San Francisco area also found that firm belief was relatively rare (Wuthnow, 1976).

A 1977 survey that asked respondents how much space they would dedicate to various subjects in 'a paper tailor-made to your own interests' found that only 22 per cent would dedicate at least some space to astrology or horoscopes (Bogart, 1989). Respondents indicated that, for them, 1.6 per cent of newspaper space would ideally be given to astrology and horoscopes, which would amount to a reduction to one-half of current levels (Bogart, 1989). Astrology was also included in the top four items respondents would be willing to eliminate from newspapers altogether (Bogart, 1989).

A series of polls has investigated the extent to which Americans report basing decisions in daily life on astrological considerations (see Table 18.1). The reading of horoscopes is far more common than the use of astrology to guide decisions. The latter is fairly infrequent. Similar results were found in a 1998 British survey (MORI, 1998), where 38 per cent of this nationally representative sample professed belief in astrology, but only 16 per cent of these believers (or 6 per cent of the total sample) said that they had ever based a decision on their belief in astrology. In all of these surveys, the nature of the decisions influenced by astrology is unknown. The decisions may have been trivial.

Table 18.1   American adults who read a horoscope often or fairly often and who sometimes base decisions in daily life on astrology

Year	1979	1983	1985	1988	1990
Horoscope readers	22%	24%	15%	17%	16%
Base decisions on astrology	5%	9%	8%	6%	4%

Source: Miller (1992).

Further relevant evidence comes from a 1985 *New Scientist* poll of British adults' attitudes to government research priorities (*New Scientist*, 1985). Astrology was assigned last place in the list of funding priorities and first place in the list of research areas meriting reductions in government funding.

Personnel Selection

More directly relevant to the secularization thesis is the nature and extent of the use of astrology within social institutions. Organizations and personnel consulting firms use personnel selection methods such as references and tests in order, amongst other things, to identify potential problems and weakness and to determine applicants' traits, aptitudes and abilities (Taylor *et al.*, 1993). This is the kind of information that astrology purports to provide. If, therefore, astrology has substantively permeated social institutions, it seems reasonable to expect to find it widely utilized in the field of personnel selection.

Table 18.2 shows the proportion of employers or recruiters in various countries of Europe that use astrology in the selection of personnel. This suggests that astrology is very rarely used. The highest incidence reported is 8.5 per cent for France. It should be noted that this survey distinguished between (a) occasional use either in the latter stages of personnel selection or for particular positions, and (b) systematic use. The figure of 8.5 per cent is for occasional use amongst external recruitment consultants. As the table also shows, surveys of the methods used to select top managers in leading French companies (Shackleton and Newell, 1991) and graduates by French employers (Hodgkinson and Payne, 1998) revealed no use of astrology at all. In view of this, it would not seem appropriate to generalize from the data on French consultants to French recruitment practices as a whole. Furthermore, the remaining surveys point to minimal or no reliance on astrology in other countries, and even occasional use by 8.5 per cent of recruiters in France would appear to be a relatively marginal phenomenon. Certainly, other recruitment methods are used far more frequently (see references cited in Table 18.2 and Cook, 1998, for a review).

Table 18.2   **Percentage of recruiters or organizations using astrology in personnel selection**

1986	1990	1990	1991	1991	1991	1998	1998
Britain	Britain	Norway	Britain	France	France	Netherlands	France
0%	0%	1%	1%	0%	8.5%	0%	0%

Sources: Robertson and Makin (1986), Abrahamsen (1990) as given in Smith (1991), Shackleton and Newell (1991), Bruchon-Schweitzer and Ferrieux (1991), Hodgkinson and Payne (1998).

State Decision Making

Another important part of the social system is the state. Astrological information could in principle be utilized in legislatures and government bodies, perhaps in the form of astrological predictions as to the most propitious time to carry out or begin an act, initiative or decision (known as 'electional' astrology). After all, it is said that Nancy Reagan allowed astrological indications to influence the scheduling of her husband's actions as President of the United States (see *Skeptical Inquirer*, 1988; Quigley, 1990).

To obtain at least a sense of the extent to which astrological considerations influence state decision making, I first conducted a search using the online search engine for the *UK Parliamentary Pages* (*http://www.parliament.the-stationery-office.co.uk/cgi-bin/tso_fx?DB=tso*) using the keywords 'astrology', 'astrologer', 'astrological' and 'horoscope'. At the time the search was conducted, this engine covered the complete texts of *Hansard* (the official record of proceedings in the House of Commons and the House of Lords) for the period 21 November 1989 to 16 March 2000, plus a wide range of other parliamentary documents.

After eliminating repetitions, this search produced a total of eight hits: one historical reference, one etymological reference, three references to astrology as an exemplar of irrationality, and three references to a legal pilot project in which subjects were allocated to the study or control groups on the basis of whether or not they were born in the first two months of the year (this had been described locally as 'trial by astrology'). In short, no evidence at all was found of astrological considerations influencing parliamentary affairs or decisions.

I next turned to the United Kingdom's *Open Government* World Wide Web facility (*http://www.open.gov.uk*), a site linking together the homepages of around 1500 national and local government departments and other official bodies and initiatives. Employing the same keywords as before, a search was conducted using the site's search engine. This produced seven non-redundant hits. The items located were a list of Oxfordshire community groups, two trademark decisions on astrology-related services, a report of a consumer survey that included questions on horoscope telephone services, a report on the August 1999 solar eclipse that mentioned the historical role of astrology in eclipse prediction, and descriptions of two courses run by a division of the Army Training and Recruitment Agency. In both of the Army pages, the word 'astrological' was used in connection with geographical survey techniques and it appeared that the word 'astronomical' was meant instead. Major David Cooke of the Army Training and Recruitment Agency, contacted for clarification, confirmed that my supposition was correct (personal correspondence).

In short, the above research found no evidence of the use of astrology in state decision making or the operation of official bodies in the UK.

The Law

Although it appears that astrology has no role in government, it may perhaps feature in judicial proceedings or decision making. For example, under English law, a person accused of a criminal offence is at liberty to present evidence of her good character during her trial, and, where such evidence is submitted, the prosecution can produce evidence that she has a bad character in rebuttal (James, 1989, p.86). Also evidence of character may be a relevant factor when a court is deliberating on the sentence to be handed down to a person convicted of a crime (ibid.). In a legal system that recognized astrology, evidence from astrologers could in principle be admitted for these purposes. Other legal applications of astrology can also be imagined, for instance in the timing of trials.

If astrology were regarded as a valid technique in the legal system, it would seem reasonable to expect that approval or other evidence of its use would appear in legal judgments. I therefore conducted a search using *Casetrack* (*http://www.casetrack.com*), a commercial database of the full texts of English judicial decisions, using the same keywords as previously. At the time the search was conducted, the database contained Court of Appeal and Crown Office judgments from April 1996 to 19 March 2000, High Court Cases from July 1998 to 19 March 2000, and Employment Appeals Tribunal judgments from July 1998 to 19 March 2000. My search located two High Court decisions. One of these concerned the *Horoscope Chinese Restaurant* but was otherwise unrelated to astrology. The second contained a quotation from the judgment of Lord Justice Diplock in the case *R* v. *Deputy Industrial Injuries Commissioner ex parte Moore* [1965] 2 W.L.R. 89. This passage is about evidence and may help explain why no further references to astrology were found by my search:

> The requirement that a person exercising quasi-judicial functions must base his decision on evidence means no more than it must be based upon material which tends logically to show the existence or non-existence of facts relevant to the issue to be determined, or to show the likelihood or unlikelihood of the occurrence of some future event the occurrence of which would be relevant. It means that he must not spin a coin or consult an astrologer, but he may take into account any material which, as a matter of reason, has some probative value in the sense mentioned above.

Given the results of my search and the terms of Lord Justice Diplock's judgment, it would appear that astrological considerations play no part in the deliberations of the English judicial system.

The Future

Although astrology currently seems to exert a minimal influence over important social institutions, what are its prospects for the future? One important consideration to take into account is the attitude of science towards astrology. Astrological propositions have been extensively tested by social scientists. In the case of astrology as it is practised by professional or amateur astrologers and in the mass media, the results have been strongly unsupportive of the claims of astrology (Dean *et al.*, 1996). This scientific falsification poses obstacles for astrology. What is relevant here is not the truth of the matter, or the evidence and arguments circulating within the scientific community, but rather the ability of the scientific community to appropriate to itself the social authority to determine matters of objective fact about the natural world. This authority does not arise as an automatic or natural consequence of the work that scientists do or the theories and evidence they produce, but is constructed in separate processes in which the scientific community defines for others the nature and content of science and its claims to epistemological superiority over actual or potential competitors (Gieryn, 1999, pp.1–28).

Although science has been subjected to some criticism in recent years, it retains considerable epistemic authority in society. The amount spent in the major industrialized nations on science and engineering research and development is huge (see, for example, Schiele, 1994), exceeding $200 billion in the USA alone in 1997 (National Science Board, 1998); even the sums spent on the social sciences are considerable (Oba, 1999). This seems inconsistent with the proposition that scientific perspectives are regarded with contempt by governments and important social institutions. The same could be said of such indicators as the number of science graduates (see National Science Board, 1998; Oba, 1999), the support by the state of public understanding of science initiatives (Schiele, 1994; OECD, 1997), and even the far from perfect reliance of social and other policy makers on scientific data (Jasanoff, 1990; Oh, 1996; May, 1997; Office of Science and Technology, 1998; Padilla and Gibson, 1999; Weiss, 1999). Indeed, the UK's Secretary of State for Education – David Blunkett – recently concluded a speech with the following words:

> We need to be able to rely on social science and social scientists to tell us what works and why and what types of policy initiatives are likely to be most effective. And we need better ways of ensuring that those who want this information can get it easily and quickly. (Secretary of State for Education, 2000, p.25)

Social scientific research influences legal decision making, education, policy making, professional training and other relevant fields through a variety of means, and social scientists deliberately seek to exercise influence over official and other bodies (see, for example, Fiske *et al.*, 1991; Lorion *et al.*, 1996). As a result, there is a flow of information into social institutions that, on the strength of the authority of science, either actively discourages the use of astrology or merely encourages the adoption of alternatives validated by scientific methods. In the event that astrology came by some means to be increasingly widely adopted in important social institutions, this would represent a challenge to the epistemic authority of the social sciences that have tested astrology as well as those branches of the natural sciences, such as astronomy, that equally reject it. Such a challenge can reasonably be expected to stimulate strong 'boundary work' (Gieryn, 1999) by scientists concerned to re-establish their authority and assign to astrology the status of pseudo-science or mysticism.

Given current levels of scientific epistemic authority, it seems difficult to imagine political or organizational policy makers choosing to disregard the opposition of scientists to astrology for an extended period of time, particularly as the representations of the differences between sciences and astrology advanced by the scientific community would be likely to stigmatize the adoption of astrology in the face of evidence from scientific testing as an embracing of irrationality, mysticism and archaic magic. In the case of areas such as personnel management that have, or are seeking to secure, professional status (see, for example, Roberts, 1997), such a repudiation of science in favour of popular occultism seems little calculated to advance their interests (on professionalization in general, see Abbott, 1988; Neal and Morgan, 1999). The same seems to hold for image-conscious politicians and corporations in general too. It should also be noted that, in sectors where institutional review or advisory boards of scientists exist, there is likely to be strong internal opposition and adverse in-house advice from scientists seeking to retain positions of influence and prestige for themselves and their disciplines. This may be significant in that empirical research suggests that policy makers are particularly influenced by social science information that comes from sources within their own organizations (Oh, 1996, pp.131–2). It is noteworthy that, when appraisals of the usefulness of 'New Age' training techniques and extrasensory perception were recently commissioned by the American Army and the CIA, the commissions were given to behavioural scientists and were conducted scientifically (Druckman and Swets, 1988; Mumford *et al.*, 1995).

More generally, the basing of decisions on astrology may attract adverse legal consequences. In many legal jurisdictions, it seems that astrological evidence would be excluded under the rules governing expert and scientific testimony. In the USA, the criteria that are likely to be applied are those given in the case of *Daubert* v. *Merrell Dow Pharmaceuticals, Inc* 113 S.Ct. 2786 (1993). These are not exhaustive but include (1) the testability of the theory or technique, (2) the extent of support in peer review publications, (3) the error rate, (4) the standards controlling the technique, and (5) the degree of acceptance amongst scientists. Popular astrology is testable and so meets the first of the *Daubert* criteria; but it does very badly on the remaining four elements of the basic *Daubert* test. In other jurisdictions, the relevant criteria and the degree of controversy surrounding the admissibility of scientific evidence vary (see, for example, Raitt, 1998; Roberts, 1998).

However, there is little or no indication of a move to establish standards such as would admit astrology; rather (at least over the medium to long term), the trend is towards stricter standards that conform more closely with those endorsed by scientists (Bernstein, 1996). That being so, we may anticipate that astrological evidence will eventually be excluded from the courts. As the example of anti-cult brainwashing testimony shows (Ginsburg and Richardson, 1998), this process is likely to be slow and uneven but it seems plausible to expect that legal opinion will eventually accumulate decisively against astrology. The result would be that organizations would find themselves devoid of legally admissible justifications for their use of astrology and potentially exposed to a range of legal penalties (cf. Reagh, 1992; Carswell, 1992, on graphology; see also Cook, 1998, on equal opportunities legislation and the legal burdens placed on employers in proceedings under such legislation). It would also mean that official decisions with an astrological basis would be vulnerable to challenge by way of appeal or judicial review.

There would seem to be a considerable number of additional factors militating against the acceptance of astrology in major social institutions. For example, in the workplace, it seems difficult to see how a technique that is as difficult to justify scientifically or intersubjectively as astrology is can be made consistent with the objectivity, transparency and rational decision making apparently advocated by the influential ideologies of equal opportunities and 'human resource management' (on the latter, see Armstrong, 1999). Also relevant are the responses of astrologers to the scientific case against astrology. It seems that many astrologers are not aware of that case or choose to ignore it. When there are express reactions, these generally take the form of attempts at scientific defences of astrology or critiques of the extant evidence that bear little resemblance to orthodox scientific methodologies (Dean, 1993; 1997; 1998/9; Kelly, 1998), repudiations of the epistemic authority of science, or denials that astrology is within the ambit of experimental science (see Perry, 1994; Irving *et al.*, 1995/6 for examples). The latter response appears to offer astrology a means of escaping the conflict with science by defining itself as a tool for the exploration and discovery of essentially subjective and personal meanings (see Kochunas, 1999/2000 for an example; also Kelly, 1997). Moreover, given the limited interest in (Dean *et al.*, 1996) and resources for orthodox scientific theory justification available to astrology, it may become increasingly preponderant in public statements by astrologers. However, such a strategy would seem to make it difficult for astrology to penetrate social institutions, for if astrology does not offer clear statements about objective events or discernible personality traits or abilities, it will cease to be a source of the information that would in principle be of value to managers, personnel officers, government ministers, officials and so on.

It would seem that, if astrology is to secure a position of influence in the social system, a widespread change of public attitudes is required. This change would have to reduce radically the prestige and influence of science and correspondingly enhance the standing of astrology. It seems highly unlikely that any such social revolution will occur in the foreseeable future.

Popular astrology itself seems to confine its focus almost exclusively to the individual level and the private sphere. For example, content analyses of astrology columns in the print media suggest that these columns advocate an individualistic adherence to conventional aspirations (Svenson and White, 1995; Evans, 1996; see also Nederman and Goulding, 1981), while other astrological material in popular magazines, newspapers and television programmes seems to be no more than entertainment or a rendering into astrological terminology of material, perspectives and aspirations absorbed from the wider secular culture (for an example, see the astrological fashion advice in Snowden, 2000). The more serious chart-based astrological services seem to be akin to individual counselling (Lester, 1982; Tyson, 1982; Dean, 1986/7). There seems to be little impetus amongst astrologers to go beyond individual client services and obtain positions of institutional influence.

With regard to public attitudes, there is no obvious trend towards beliefs that are more than superficial (see Table 18.1). Also, even as a technique for exploring or healing the self, astrology seems to be far less popular than various alternatives widely available in advanced and pluralistic Western capitalist societies such as 'self-help' books and movements and psychotherapy (Dean *et al.*, 1998/9; on 'self-help', see also Starker, 1989; 1990; 1992; Marx *et al.*, 1992; Simonds, 1992; 1996; Katz, 1993; Delin and Delin, 1994; Greenberg, 1994; Borkman, 1999). There seems to be no obvious reason to anticipate a change in the relative fortunes of astrology and its competitors in the coming decades.

As for science, data from representative samples from various national populations generally indicate that public attitudes towards science and scientists are quite favourable (for relevant data on this and the points following, see INRA (Europe) and Report International, 1993, pp.65–86; Fjaestad, 1994; National Science Board, 1998; 2000, pp.7.1–7.22; Office of Science and Technology and the Wellcome Trust, 2000). According to these surveys, fairly stable majorities of the public tend to regard science and technology as generally beneficial in its impact on everyday life and holding out promise for the future. Majorities also approve the carrying out of basic research that advances scientific knowledge but brings no immediate benefits. This is not to say that the public view science with unreserved favour and trust. Within advanced industrial countries, there is widespread reservation or opposition to particular areas of applied science or technology (such as nuclear power and genetic engineering). There is also, amongst other things, scepticism about the ability of science to deliver such utopian goals as inexhaustible natural resources, and concern that science possesses a power that is dangerous and is changing life too fast. Furthermore, substantial minorities (a majority in Japan) consider that we depend too much on science and not enough on faith.

However, just what is meant by this preference for faith, and in what domains faith is considered to be an appropriate guide, is unclear. For this reason, we should be slow to conclude from this or other reservations about science that the public will in the future be prepared to reverse the current restriction of astrology to private consumption and have employment prospects, government programmes, legal disputes and other important matters decided by a technique that scientists strenuously maintain is no better than simply tossing a coin. In addition, it should be noted that thoroughgoing anti-science is evidently rare. For example, a recent

British survey that sought to identify attitudinal groups within the nationally representative sample of respondents found nothing that would obviously seem to correspond to a fundamental repudiation of science and scientific epistemology, and even the most sceptical group detected ('The Concerned') constituted only 13 per cent of the sample (Office of Science and Technology and the Wellcome Trust, 2000).

Conclusion

The data reviewed and presented in this chapter suggest that astrological belief is broad but shallow, a finding consistent with the analyses and typologies offered by Truzzi (1972, pp.20–22) and Dean *et al.* (1996, p.62). These data also suggest that astrology is of little consequence for the functioning of major social institutions in particular and the social system in general. Astrology is mostly produced and consumed as mass entertainment or individualized and often conventional advice and predictions for personal clients or media audiences. The possibility that this state of affairs may be reversed in the future seems slight. Astrologers and their audiences appear to be taking no substantial steps in that direction. Also any attempt seriously to introduce astrology into important sectors of the state or economy would probably provoke a strong reaction from influential scientific organizations and collectivities. There is no evidence of a trend towards the rejection of science by policy makers or the general public such as would motivate long-term resistance to scientists' educational and lobbying initiatives against astrology. Science retains its epistemic authority, and over time its rejection of astrology is likely to influence policy makers and the legal domain in ways adverse to the interests of institutional users of astrology.

Although it is my prediction that astrology will not, in the next 50 to 100 years, influence the social system in a substantive way, it by no means follows that popular belief will decline. Provided that astrological belief remains confined to the private sphere, it seems unlikely that the community of scientists will make widespread or systematic attempts to bring the current scientific case against astrology to the notice of the wider public. In the absence of major propaganda and educational initiatives against astrology, it seems likely that personal experience (Dean *et al.*, 1996) and media coverage (Weimann, 1985; Bryant and Zillmann, 1994; Sparks, 1998; Sparks *et al.*, 1998) will continue to help foster weak but widespread public suspicion that there is something in astrology. Indeed, even if scientists seek publicly to repudiate astrology, the persistence in modern society of a substantial level of ignorance of even the most elementary propositions of scientific theory (see, for example, INRA (Europe) and Report International, 1993) would seem to indicate that the osmosis of ideas from the scientific community to the general public is sufficiently imperfect as to leave space for a scientifically incredible astrology to flourish amongst at least a substantive minority of non-scientists.

Astrology also seems likely to serve as at least part of the private spiritual explorations of relatively small numbers of serious adherents (see, for example, Luhrmann, 1994, pp.157–62, 267–8; Feher, 1994).

Acknowledgments

For their critical comments on earlier drafts, I should like to thank Mark O'Leary, Jo Pearson, Michael Stanwick and, especially, Nick Campion and Geoffrey Dean.

References

Abbott, Andrew 1988: *The System of Professions*. Chicago: University of Chicago Press.
Abrahamsen, Morton 1990: Personnel Selection in England and Norway. A Comparative Study of Current Practice. Unpublished BSc dissertation. Manchester School of Management.
Armstrong, Michael 1999: *A Handbook of Human Resource Management Practice*. London: Kogan Page.
Ashmun, Joanna 1996/7: Astrology on the Internet. *Correlation*, 15 (2), pp.35–51.
Bainbridge, William Sims 1997: *The Sociology of Religious Movements*. New York: Routledge.
Bauer, Martin and Durant, John 1997: Belief in Astrology: A Social–Psychological Analysis. *Culture and Cosmos*, 1 (1), pp.55–71.
Bernstein, David 1996: Junk Science in the United States and the Commonwealth. *Yale Journal of International Law*, 21 (1), pp.123–82.
Bogart, Leo 1989: *Press and Public: Who Reads What, When, Where, and Why in American Newspapers*. 2nd edn, Hillsdale, NJ: Lawrence Erlbaum.
Borkman, Thomasina 1999: *Understanding Self-Help/Mutual Aid: Experiential Learning in the Commons*. New Brunswick, NJ: Rutgers University Press.
Brown, Jennifer 1987: A Survey of the Public's Belief in and Experience of Paranormal Phenomena. Unpublished Report, No. 101.
Bruchon-Schweitzer, M. and Ferrieux, D. 1991: Une Enquête sur le Recrutement en France. *European Review of Applied Psychology*, 41 (1), pp.9–16.
Bryant, Jennings and Zillmann, Dolf 1994: *Media Effects: Advances in Theory and Research*. Hillsdale, NJ: Lawrence Erlbaum.
Carswell, Robert 1992: Graphology: Canadian Legal Implications. In Barry Beyerstein and Dale Beyerstein (eds), *The Write Stuff: Evaluations of Graphology – The Study of Handwriting Analysis*. Buffalo: Prometheus Books, pp.477–87.
Cook, Mark 1998: *Personnel Selection: Adding Value through People*. Chichester: John Wiley.
Dean, Geoffrey 1986/7: Does Astrology Need to be True? Part 1: A Look at the Real Thing. *Skeptical Inquirer*, 11 (2), pp.166–84.
Dean, Geoffrey 1993: Astrology Strikes Back – But to What Effect?, *Skeptical Inquirer*, 18 (1), pp.42–9.
Dean, Geoffrey 1997: Crooked Thinking is Alive and Well. *Skeptical Inquirer*, 21 (2), pp.46–8.
Dean, Geoffrey 1997/8: The Truth of Astrology: A Summary of Each Entry, and Some Implications for Researchers. *Correlation*, 16 (2), pp.40–56.
Dean, Geoffrey, Kelly, Ivan and Mather, Arthur 1998/9: Astrology and Human Judgement. *Correlation*, 17 (2), pp.24–71.
Dean, Geoffrey, Mather, Arthur and Kelly, Ivan 1996: Astrology. In Gordon Stein (ed.), *The Encyclopedia of the Paranormal*. Buffalo: Prometheus Books, pp.47–99.
Delin, Catherine and Delin, Peter 1994: Self-Selection of Self-Help Reading: Readers and Reasons. *Australian Psychologist*, 29 (3), pp.201–6.

Druckman, Daniel and Swets, John 1988: *Enhancing Human Performance: Issues, Theories and Techniques*. Washington: National Academy Press.

Durant, John and Bauer, Martin 1992: British Public Perceptions of Astrology: An Approach from the Sociology of Knowledge. Paper presented at the Annual Meeting of the American Association for the Advancement of Science, Chicago.

Evans, William 1996: Divining the Social Order: Class, Gender and Magazine Astrology Columns. *Journalism and Mass Communication Quarterly*, 73 (2), pp.389–400.

Feher, Shoshanah 1994: The Hidden Truth: Astrology as Worldview. In Arthur L. Greil and Thomas Robbins (eds), *Between Sacred and Secular. Research and Theory on Quasi-Religion. Religion and the Social Order*. vol 4, Greenwich, CN: JAI Press, pp.165–7.

Fiske, Susan, Bersoff, Donald, Bordiga, Eugene, Deaux, Kay and Heilman, Madeline 1991: Social Science Research on Trial: Use of Sex Stereotyping Research in *Price Waterhouse* v. *Hopkins*. *American Psychologist*, 46, pp.1049–60.

Fjaestad, Björn 1994: The 1994 Swedish Survey on Public Understanding of Science. Paper presented at the 1994 International Conference on the Public Understanding of Science and Technology, Science Museum, London.

Gallup, George and Newport, Frank 1991: Belief in Paranormal Phenomena Among Adult Americans. *Skeptical Inquirer*, 15 (2), pp.137–46.

Gieryn, Thomas F. 1999: *Cultural Boundaries of Science: Credibility on the Line*. Chicago: University of Chicago Press.

Ginsburg, Gerald and Richardson, James 1998: 'Brainwashing' Evidence in Light of Daubert: Science and Unpopular Religions. In Helen Reece (ed.), *Law and Science*. Oxford: Oxford University Press, pp.265–88.

Goode, Erich 2000: *Paranormal Beliefs: A Sociological Introduction*. Prospect Heights, IL: Waveland Press.

Greenberg, Gary 1994: *The Self on the Shelf: Recovery Books and the Good Life*. Albany, NY: State University of New York Press.

Hanson, Sharon 1997: The Secularization Thesis: Talking at Cross Purposes. *Journal of Contemporary Religion*, 12 (2), pp.159–79.

Hodgkinson, Gerard and Payne, Roy 1998: Graduate Selection in Three European Countries. *Journal of Occupational and Organizational Psychology*, 71, pp.359–65.

Humphrey, Nicholas 1995: *Soul Searching: Human Nature and Supernatural Belief*. London: Chatto & Windus.

INRA (Europe) and Report International 1993: *Europeans, Science and Technology – Public Understanding and Attitudes*. Brussels: European Commission.

Irving, Kenneth, McPherson, Maggie, Pierce, Douglas Kyle and Urban-Lurain, Mark 1995/6: Astrology and Science. *Correlation*, 14 (2), pp.45–58.

James, Philip 1989: *Introduction to English Law*. London: Butterworths.

Jasanoff, Sheila 1990: *The Fifth Branch: Science Advisors as Policymakers*. Cambridge, MA: Harvard University Press.

Katz, Alfred 1993: *Self-Help in America: A Social Movement Perspective*. New York: Twayne Publishers/Macmillan.

Kelly, Ivan 1997: Modern Astrology: A Critique. *Psychological Reports*, 81, pp.1035–66.

Kelly, Ivan. W. 1998: Why Astrology Doesn't Work. *Psychological Reports*, 82, pp.527–46.

Kochunas, Brad 1999/2000: Why Astrology Works. *The Mountain Astrologer*, 88, pp.35–40.

Lester, David 1982: Astrologers and Psychics as Therapists. *American Journal of Psychotherapy*, 36 (1), pp.56–66.

Lorion, Raymond P. Iscoe, Ira, DeLeon, Partick H. and VandenBos, Gary R. (eds) 1996: *Psychology and Public Policy: Balancing Public Service and Professional Need*. Washington, DC: American Psychological Association.

Luhrmann, Tanya 1994: *Persuasions of the Witch's Craft: Ritual Magic in Contemporary England*. London: Picador.

Marx, Judith, Gyorky, Zsuzsanna, Royalty, Georgia and Stern, Tina 1992: Use of Self Help Books in Psychotherapy. *Professional Psychology: Research and Practice*, 23 (4), pp.300–305.

May, Robert 1997: *The Use of Scientific Advice in Policy Making: A Note by the Chief Scientific Adviser*. London: Office of Science and Technology.

Miller, Jon 1992: The Public Acceptance of Astrology and Other Pseudo-Science in the United States. Paper presented at the Annual Meeting of the American Association for the Advancement of Science, Chicago.

MORI, 1998: *Paranormal Poll. <http://www.mori.com>*.

Mumford, Michael, Rose, Andrew and Goslin, David A. 1995: *An Evaluation of Remote Viewing: Research and Applications*. Washington: American Institutes for Research.

National Science Board 1998: *Science and Engineering Indicators 1998*. Arlington, VA: National Science Foundation.

National Science Board 2000: *Science and Engineering Indicators 2000*. Arlington, VA: National Science Foundation.

Neal, Mark and Morgan, John 1999: The Professionalization of Everyone? A Comparative Study of the Development of the Professions in the United Kingdom and Germany. *European Sociological Review*, 16 (1), pp.9–26.

Nederman, Cary and Goulding, James Wray 1981: Popular Occultism and Critical Social Theory: Exploring Some Themes in Adorno's Critique of Astrology and the Occult. *Sociological Analysis*, 42, pp.323–32.

New Scientist 1985: Questions of Priorities. *New Scientist*, 21 February, p.14.

Oba, Jun 1999: The Social Sciences in OECD Countries: Key Data. In OECD (ed.), *The Social Sciences at a Turning Point?* Paris: OECD, pp.11–27.

OECD 1997: *Promoting Public Understanding of Science and Technology Organisation for Economic Co-Operation and Development*. Paris: OECD.

Office of Science and Technology 1998: *The Use of Scientific Advice in Policy Making: Implementation of the Guidelines*. London: Office of Science and Technology.

Office of Science and Technology and the Wellcome Trust 2000: *Science and the Public: A Review of Science Communication and Public Attitudes to Science in Britain*. London: Office of Science and Technology and the Wellcome Trust.

Oh, Cheol 1996: *Linking Social Science Information to Policy-Making*. Greenwich, CN: JAI Press.

Padilla, Ana and Gibson, Ian 1999: Science Moves to Centre Stage. *Nature*, 403, pp.357–9.

Perry, Glen 1994. (Untitled). *Correlation*, 13 (1), pp.32–6.

Quigley, Joan 1990: *'What Does Joan Say?': My Seven Years as White House Astrologer to Nancy and Ronald Reagan*. New York: Carol Publishing Co.

Raitt, Fiona 1998: A New Criterion for the Admissibility of Scientific Evidence: The Metamorphosis of Helpfulness. In Helen Reece (ed.), *Law and Science*. Oxford: Oxford University Press, pp.153–73.

Reagh, John 1992: Legal Implications of Graphology in the United States. In Barry Beyerstein and Dale Beyerstein (eds), *The Write Stuff: Evaluations of Graphology – The Study of Handwriting Analysis*. Buffalo: Prometheus Books, pp.465–76.

Roberts, Gareth 1997: *Recruitment and Selection*. London: Institute of Personnel and Development.

Roberts, Paul 1998: Expert Evidence in Canadian Criminal Proceedings: More Lessons from North America. In Helen Reece (ed.), *Law and Science*. Oxford: Oxford University Press, pp.175–219.

Robertson, Ivan and Makin, Peter 1986: Management Selection in Britain: A Survey and Critique. *Journal of Occupational Psychology*, 59, pp.45–57.

Schiele, Bernard (ed.) 1994: *When Science Becomes Culture: World Survey of Scientific Culture (Proceedings I)*. Boucherville, Quebec: University of Ottowa Press.

Secretary of State for Education 2000: *ESRC Lecture Speech*. London: Economic and Social Research Council/Department of Education and Employment.

Shackleton, Viv and Newell, Sue 1991: Management Selection: A Comparative Survey of Methods Used in Top British and French Companies. *Journal of Occupational Psychology*, 64, pp.23–36.

Simonds, Wendy 1992: *Women and Self-Help Culture: Reading Between the Lines*. New Brunswick, NJ: Rutgers University Press.

Simonds, Wendy 1996: *All Consuming Selves: Self-Help Literature and Women's Identities*. Thousand Oaks, CA: Sage Publications.

Skeptical Inquirer 1988: Special Report: Astrology and the Presidency. *Skeptical Inquirer*, 13 (1), pp.3–16.

Smith, Mike 1991: Recruitment and Selection in the UK with some Data on Norway. *European Review of Applied Psychology*, 41 (1), pp.27–34.

Snowden, Rachel 2000: Star Sign Style. *Daily Mail*, 21 February, pp.40–41.

Sparks, Gary 1998. Paranormal Depictions in the Media: How Do They Effect What People Believe?, *Skeptical Inquirer*, 22 (4), pp.35–9.

Sparks, Gary, Pellechia, Marianne. and Irvine, Chris 1998: Does Television News about UFOs affect Viewers' UFO Beliefs? An Experimental Investigation. *Communication Quarterly*, 46, pp.284–94.

Starker, Steven 1989: *Oracle at the Supermarket: The American Preoccupation With Self-Help Books*. New Brunswick, NJ: Transaction Publishers.

Starker, Steven 1990: Self-help books: Ubiquitous Agents of Health Care. *Medical Psychotherapy: An International Journal*, 3, pp.187–94.

Starker, Steven 1992: Characteristics of Self-Help Book Readers among VA Medical Outpatients. *Medical Psychotherapy: An International Journal*, 5, pp.89–93.

Svenson, Stuart and White, Ken 1995: A Content Analysis of Horoscopes. *Genetic, Social and General Psychology Monographs*, 121 (1), pp.7–38.

Taylor, Paul, Mills, Aaron and O'Driscoll, Michael 1993: Personnel Selection Methods Used by New Zealand Organisations and Personnel Consulting Firms. *New Zealand Journal of Psychology*, 22, pp.19–31.

Truzzi, Marcello 1972: The Occult Revival as Popular Culture: Some Random Observations on the Old and New Nouveau Witch. *Sociological Quarterly*, 13, pp.16–36.

Tyson, Graham A. 1982: People Who Consult Astrologers: A Profile. *Personality and Individual Differences*, 3, pp.119–26.

Vyse, Stuart 1997: *Believing in Magic: The Psychology of Superstition*. New York: Oxford University Press.

Weimann, Gerald 1985: Mass-Mediated Occultisms: The Role of the Media in the Occult Revival. *Journal of Popular Culture*, 18 (4), pp.81–8.

Weiss, Carol Hirschon 1999: The Interface between Evaluation and Public Policy. *Evaluation*, 5 (4), pp.468–86.

Wilson, Bryan 1985: Secularization: The Inherited Model. In Phillip Hammond (ed.), *The Sacred in a Secular Age*. Berkeley, CA: University of California Press, pp.9–20.

Wilson, Bryan 1988: Religion in the Modern World. In Stewart Sutherland and Peter Clarke (eds), *The Study of Religions: Traditional and New Religion*. London: Routledge, pp. 195-208.

Wuthnow, Robert 1976: Astrology and Marginality. *Journal for the Scientific Study of Religion*, 15 (2), pp.157–68.

Yamane, David 1997: Secularization on Trial: In Defense of a Neosecularization Paradigm. *Journal for the Scientific Study of Religion*, 36 (1), pp.109–22.

Zusne, Leonard and Jones, Warren 1989: *Anomalistic Psychology: A Study of Magical Belief*. Hillsdale, NJ: Lawrence Erlbaum.

CHAPTER 19

An Ageing New Age?

Paul Heelas and Benjamin Seel

Kendal was not touched by the 1960s. But a lot of people who have since come here were influenced by the 60s. Alternative spirituality and therapy is definitely an over 40s phenomenon. It is the hippies/university people of the late 60s, who have either stayed in the alternative scene, or got into the commercial sector, then had a mid-life crisis and got out. (Celia Hunter-Wetenhall, Kendal yoga teacher)

Mid-Life is Worth Living. (Radio programme series, Monterry area)

I just think it's important, particularly as I get older, to think about the journey that's coming next. (Prince Charles, cited by Andrew Roberts, 2001)

Introduction

Few would dispute that New Age spiritualities of life – all about experiencing what belongs to the depths of life itself – are of growing significance. Whether it be by way of indicators such as book sales or the numbers attending festivals (Bruce, 1996, pp.198–9), the number of spiritual activities advertised in New Age listings (Heelas, 2002a, p.364), in the *Yellow Pages*, or by way of oral histories, the picture is one of expansion.[1] But what of the future?

This question is addressed by concentrating on the future of what is surely the core of New Age activities: not the more commercial territory of book sales and the like (which could well involve relatively superficial engagement) but the territory of spiritual practitioners. For spiritual practitioners, providing the face-to-face activities (groups for their group members and one-to-one encounters for their clients), provide the most significant way of pursuing what New Age spiritualities of life are ultimately all about: transformative experience by way of shared practice (with experience validating practice).

The question is more specifically addressed by way of two scenarios. The first – the 'die out and not be replaced', 'self-limiting', 'ageing cohort' or 'pessimistic' scenario – is driven by the fact that an *ageing* cohort of spiritual practitioners, drawn from baby boomers who came of age during the 1960s and 1970s, has played, and very much continues to play, the key role in sustaining, 'carrying' and developing New Age spiritualities of life. On the basis of the fact that much of this cohort came of age during the '60s' – namely the counter-cultural period which ran from the mid-1960s to the mid-1970s – it looks as though current (securely middle-aged) practitioners are (one of) the legacies of that period. Given that they are set to die out in the near(ish) future, the 'living legacy' will of course disappear. Yet relatively few younger people, who came of age after the 60s, have been attracted to the realm of practice. Accordingly, the longer term future appears to be bleak.

As for the (less obvious) 'die out and will be replaced', 'self-perpetuating', 'cultural transmission' or 'optimistic' scenario, which will be argued for later in this chapter, the basic argument is that spiritual practitioners will be replenished by virtue of the fact that New Age spiritualities of life have come to be widely transmitted within the culture. Accordingly, even if the '60s' experience is an important factor in explaining the involvement of current spiritual practitioners, people will become involved in the future (if not now) without having had this experience.

The Ageing Cohort Scenario

On the face of it, a considerable amount of evidence supports the ageing cohort scenario. We can begin with findings from a study ('The Kendal Project: Patterns of the Sacred in Contemporary Society'[2]) which, among other things, provides the first systematic locality research into those involved in the face-to-face practices (specifically groups and one-to-one encounters) of New Age spiritualities of life.

As of June 2001, 95 spiritual practitioners worked in Kendal (population 27 610 as of 1999, located just to the east of the Lake District in north-west England) and within five miles of the town (total population being approximately 37 000, also as of 1999). Of these, 41 are group practitioners (serving 63 different groups), while 63 are one-to-one practitioners serving individual clients (with an estimated average of four clients per practitioner per week). (Nine practitioners, it will be noted, serve both groups and individual clients.)

As for findings concerning the age profile of spiritual practitioners, they indicate that a very specific category of the population is involved, with few signs of younger people. The average age (mean) is 48.4, (median) 47.5 and (mode) 50; the mathematic average is thus 48.4; and although there are more spiritual practitioners who are younger than this than older, there are more 50-year-olds than any other age. Of the 94 spiritual practitioners, 48 per cent were aged between 45 and 54 as of mid-2001; 23 per cent are older; 30 per cent younger; with 17 per cent of the younger being aged between 40 and 44, just 11 per cent being in their thirties, and with only 1 per cent being under 30.

Thinking of the 48 per cent practitioners aged between 45 and 54, they were, of course, born between 1945 and 1954, and were 20 years old at some point between 1965 and 1974. Bearing in mind that the counter-cultural and (in measure) spiritually-informed '60s' did not die overnight with the end of 1969, spilling over well into the 1970s, such practitioners thus belong to those baby boomers who came of age during the '60s'. Thinking now of the most common age (mode) of practitioners, namely 50 as of mid-2001, this average takes us back to a (mode) birthdate of 1951. The 'average' (mode) one-to-one practitioner was thus 20 in 1971: again corresponding with the timing of the '60s'. Furthermore, there are certainly spiritual practitioners in Kendal, such as the yoga teacher cited at the beginning of this chapter, who emphasize the importance of the '60s' experience and transmission in their accounts of why spiritual practitioners are predominantly middle aged.

Given these findings, what can be predicted of the future of inner spirituality within Kendal and immediate environs? In the shorter term, account needs to be taken of the fact that spiritual practitioners – today – are predominantly focused on working with people to handle dis-ease, treating somatic or psychosomatic issues as symptoms or signals which call for holistic (body, mind and spirit) attention. Also in the shorter term, this focus is likely to bear further fruit. With more and more of their group members and clients – as well as other baby boomers who came of age during the 1960s and 1970s – encountering the stresses and strains of older age, it is virtually certain that demand will continue to increase. However, most of the spiritual practitioners will (quite naturally) die out in the not so distant future. And it therefore appears that key New Age provisions will suffer accordingly. But to what extent?

Much depends, in this regard, on the extent to which younger people are taking over the job of serving as practitioners (or will start doing so soon). Looking more closely at this crucial issue, 30 per cent of practitioners are younger that those born between 1945 and 1954; that is to say, are younger than those who came of age during the key '60s' decade running from 1965 to 1975 (and who are now all older than 44). However, of this 30 per cent (aged between 44 and 26), only 11 per cent are aged below 40, with only 1 per cent, as we have seen, being in their twenties. It thus very much looks as though the greater the age distance from those born between 1945 and 1954 (who came of age between the mid-1960s and the mid-1970s) the less the likelihood of people having become practitioners. In short, Kendal findings appear to confirm the importance of the role played by the baby-boom cohort of practitioners who came of age during the '60s'. And it looks as though that key cohort of practitioners has not been replenishing itself with enough younger people for their ranks not to be eroded in the future.[3]

Turning away from Kendal, a considerable amount of research serves to support key aspects of the 'pessimistic' scenario. Pioneering research carried out by Stuart Rose for a doctorate supervised by Heelas, involving a survey of readers of a New Age magazine (virtually all of whom also engaged in practice), shows that 'about half' had 'grown up during the 1960s counter-culture' (Rose, 1998, p.8). Turning abroad, recently completed research in Sweden (Lena Lowendahl, 2002) and Poland (Anna Kubiak, unpublished), for example, shows much the same age profile, albeit with somewhat more younger people. So does research from the USA which shows a close link between interest in, or involvement with, New Age spiritualities of life and the baby boom cohort which came of age during the '60s'.[4]

And it is not simply that few post-cohort people who came of age after the 1960s have become spiritual practitioners. For a fair amount of evidence suggests that younger people, coming of age since the mid-1970s, are nowhere nearly as interested in (involved with or knowledgeable about) New Age spiritualities of life as the '60s' cohort (which means that offspring will typically be significantly more secular than their parents were, or perhaps are). George Gallup and Robert Bezilla (1992), for example, found that only 2 per cent of a sample of college students in the USA cited 'New Age' as their major religious preference or philosophy (p.54). Regarding widespread clubbing, Gordon Lynch (unpublished) writes that 'it was striking how negatively the participants tended to react to the word "spiritual"' (p.15). More generally, survey findings show that fewer younger people buy New Age literature (James Meek, 1999, p.10; see also Stuart Rose and his finding that 71 per cent of his sample of readers of *Kindred Spirit* are aged between 35 and 64 (cited in Heelas, 1996, p.125)).[5] And this apparent lack of interest might be read as meaning few younger people have become 'primed' to become involved in the more 'serious' (time-consuming and dedicated) work of providing face-to-face practices when they get older. There might appear to be few 'waiting in the wings' to replenish the existing cohort as it dies out. And, to compound matters, it could be the case that few of the children of spiritual practitioners are 'on the road within'. Having been brought up in terms of the liberal, ontological individualism of their parents, with spiritual (or religious) choices being seen as a private affair, as dependent on the unique experience of the child, it might be expected that transmission has been weak. Accordingly, the cohort could be read as not having done much, by way of its close kinship links, to ensure New Age spiritualities' self-perpetuation.[6]

In sum, it looks as though the provision of the key face-to-face transmission agencies of New Age spiritualities of life is closely linked to a particular cohort. They and their peers are ageing and time will increasingly take its inevitable toll upon their bodies. In the short to medium term, this may mean that New Age spiritualities of life will continue to flourish, as so many of them cater for bodily disease. But as baby-boomers' ageing turns into their demise this short-term growth could turn out to be something of a final flourish.[7] From the perspective of the 'ageing cohort' scenario the longer-term future of New Age spiritualities of life looks bleak.[8]

The Cultural Transmission Scenario

Could it be the case, that rather than the future of the key realm of face-to-face spiritual practice *depending* on the destiny of the current cohort, many coming of age since the '60s' are in fact (relatively) predisposed towards 'inner spirituality' and so might be prompted to take over from the ageing cohort of practitioners (or come to serve as clients or group participants)? We now argue that the key face-to-face practices will indeed increasingly shift out of the hands of the current cohort of practitioners and into the hands of people who have come of age since the '60s'.

At the heart of the argument lies the claim that the current cohort of spiritual practitioners, apparently linked with those coming of age during the '60s', will increasingly be replaced by younger people who have grown up in *a post-'60s', but widely '60s'-inspired, cultural milieu.* For, since the '60s', New Age spiritualities of life have increasingly come to be carried or transmitted by relatively widespread cultural provisions rather than by what is left (even in memory) of the spiritual aspect of the '60s' counter-culture. And this means that many of those coming of age after the '60s' are encountering inner spirituality in mainstream culture, with the counter-culture no longer playing the role which it did for the older baby boomers. And then, the argument continues, with this cultural contact having 'primed' them (encouraged interest; generated favourable opinions or curiosity about what is promised; resulted in familiarization or acclimatization) for possible face-to-face involvement, actual face-to-face engagement is likely to happen (for some) during the mid-life period.

We turn first to the wide variety of cultural contexts in which people encounter spiritualities of life. Children today are quite likely to go to primary schools where the 'spiritual revolution' has taken place, such schools having completed the shift from learning 'about' religion to learning 'from' religion to learning from experience (when what is experienced is immanentist spirituality of a spirituality of life variety). In Britain, at least, it is certainly the case that many teenagers will encounter immanentist, holistic, universalistic spirituality during religious studies lessons (as well, if current plans work out, as in other lessons). (On educational matters, both primary and secondary, see Martin Ashley, 2000; Heelas' own collection of syllabuses, drawn from around the country, shows that 'spirituality', associated with experience and life, is now widely favoured over 'religion'.)

Nor should we forget the significance of the impact of fantasy worlds, in the form of *Harry Potter* (Rowling is expected to become the first billionaire writer), *Star Wars* and *The Lord of the Rings* (predicted to be the first film to make a profit of a billion); or, for that matter, *Buffy the Vampire Slayer.* Immensely appealing to younger people, as well as some older, productions such as these are clearly not New Age (there is too much emphasis on black and white morality, among other things). But they surely serve to fertilize the ground (for some) for future face-to-face involvement by opening up the boundaries of possibility (if only in fantasy) by providing a taste of re-enchantment. Youthful memories do not just disappear.

Turning to somewhat older people, despite what was said earlier about apparent lack of involvement, interest or knowledge, it is nevertheless possible to argue that New Age themes are far from absent among cultures of youth. Indeed, one survey carried out in Holland finds that 15 per cent have actually engaged in New Age practices (Janssen, 1999, p.62); Gallup and Bezilla (1992) report that 44 per cent of a sample of US college students are aware of the New Age Movement, with 14 per cent having a favourable opinion; Rosalind Coward (1990) reports a survey of medical students in Britain which shows that 80 per cent wanted to know more about alternative medicine and would contemplate referring patients to alternative practitioners (p.12); and Stuart Rose finds that 18.5 per cent of his *Kindred Spirit* sample are under 35 (cited in Heelas, 1966, p.125). Contrary to the argument that owing to the liberal ethos of New Age practices, they do not transmit well from parents to children, in Kendal the surprisingly high figure of 32 per cent of the practitioners, participants and clients who have children reported that those children share their own interest in spiritual activities or therapies. Or we can think of Sylvia Collins' (1997) study of three secondary schools in the south of England: she came across few 'New Agers', but 19 per cent believe in a higher power or life force (p.62); and, more significantly, the very great importance she found attached to what she calls 'immanent faith' – namely 'the organization of trust around a basic structure of the reflexive self, family and close friends' (p.vi) – involves exactly those 'life values' which are proto-New Age and which could thus prompt involvement in the future.

Then there is the consideration that teenagers and those in their twenties encounter spirituality of life themes while clubbing (an activity which attracts some one million people during a typical weekend in Britain). Thus Lynch (unpublished) writes of 'the power of clubbing experiences which transcend "normal" social experiences, and which may be interpreted by clubbers as having a transformative effect on their lives' (p.5). The term 'spirituality' might not be used (quite possibly because it has the wrong, 'religious' associations (p.15)), but clubbing themes, to do with 'transformative experiences', the 'new life' (p.10), 'unlocking things inside you' (p.9) or simply being 'luvved up', are implicitly or 'proto'-New Age, so to speak 'on the way towards' that which is more explicitly elaborated by New Age spiritualities themselves.[9] Also significant for younger age groups is that a survey carried out in Texas found that people in their twenties, not baby-boomers, are 'much more likely to be New Age consumers' (Mears and Ellison, 2000, p.302), suggesting younger people are interested enough to buy books and other products. In the process, they could well absorb ideas that prime them for future face-to-face involvement.

As younger people age, they are quite likely to encounter spiritualities of life in a number of cultural domains. First and foremost, inner spiritualities are increasingly in evidence within the domain of health provision. Judy Harrison and Philip Burnard (1993) have shown this with regard to nursing and Tony Walter (1996) and Wilfred McSherry (1998) with regard to hospices; there was also a boom in counselling training in the 1990s, which clearly encourages a culture of personal growth.[10] GPs in Britain also seem increasingly willing to refer or direct people to complementary therapies and alternative spiritual practices such as yoga and tai chi, while their surgeries provide magazines like *The Waiting Room*, replete with articles on yoga and suchlike. Furthermore, such developments seem well established: Sarah Boseley (2000), for example, describes how a recent House of Lords select committee report urged integration of complementary and alternative medicine into the NHS.

In Kendal, we have found considerable evidence of the rise of complementary health therapies. The number of complementary therapists working in the area has increased exponentially over the past 20 years, and the majority of these say that there is a spiritual dimension to their practice. CancerCare in Kendal receives referrals from Macmillan nurses and employs several complementary practitioners on part- and full-time bases, and the Lakeland College of Homeopathy, which was founded in 1993, has enjoyed rapid growth. One of its founders, Ian Watson, said in interview:

> The spiritual side of homeopathy has waxed. I'm pretty sure about that. It now attracts more students than ever that want that level … It reflects a larger change in consciousness. There has been an upsurge in interest in all things to do with spiritual and personal growth. It is to do with the level of openness there is to those things now. Twenty years ago you would say 'homeopathy' and people's eyes would glaze over. But now they know that the Royal Family, or someone they know, has had homeopathy. There has been an opening to and acceptance of the broader dimension.

Kendal also illustrates the kind of changes that are abroad in the NHS. The Helm Chase maternity unit is now run by midwives themselves, indicating a shift of trust in the medical world. Ian Watson again:

> If someone goes there now and wants to use homeopathy for giving birth, the midwives know about it and encourage them. Ten to fifteen years ago that would have been discouraged. There has been foot-dragging, but changes like these have been consumer-led by demand. That is a powerful force. And it applies in the regular hospital too. It's not OK anymore for the consultant to say, 'No, you can't do it', because people know they can. Doctors and nursing staff are now at least accepting, if not approving.

People are increasingly demanding a participative role in their healthcare and this is a trend that complementary therapies are both driving and well-suited to. (We will deal further with the question of how this introduces people to inner spirituality below.)

Spirituality has also become strongly embedded within commercial and mediated cultures. Spiritualities are increasingly abroad within the world of business, being the sacralized version of that increasingly powerful cultural current, the development of soft capitalism (Heelas, 2002b). In contrast to 40 or so years ago, New Age spiritualities of life have become acceptable, indeed fashionable. Think of the length of shelving now devoted to 'Mind, Body and Spirit' and cognates in Waterstone's; the popularity of music revolving around inner spirituality; adverts which touch upon the spiritual; or the number of articles in newspapers and magazines to do with the spiritually informed 'life' and health (virtually all the major papers in Britain run sections with titles like 'Life on Wednesday: mindbodyspirit' (*Express*), 'life&soul' (*Observer Magazine*), 'Self/how to get the most out of life' (*Daily Mail*), 'Spirit' (*Guardian Weekend*), 'What's the Alternative?' (*The Sunday Times Style*) which touch upon the spiritual). Or think of shopping, with the 'well-being' zones of Sainsburys and Boots providing a taste of spirituality, with spirituality also increasingly entering the beauty salon, leisure or 'total fitness' centres or gyms. Ursula Sharma and Paula Black (undated) report that the 'holistic' is now 'crucial for beauty therapy' (p.27). And to return to Kendal again, 35 per cent of shops on the high street contain one or more products that could be used in a spiritually significant way.[11] Indeed, we also have to think of holidays and restorative spells ('stress-busters' says a *The Sunday Times*, 25 November 2001, article on 'holistic resorts') away from the daily grind: the revitalization of the traditional spa by way of New Age practices. And then there is Hollywood, that 'church' (for those stars who are Scientologists) which serves to transmit – and legitimate – spirituality by virtue of the fact that so many celebrities are involved. Or we can think of the role played by stars in Britain: first Princess Diana, now Cherie Blair, and the perennial Prince Charles.

Whether it be by way of primary school experiential practices, clubbing, management training, the armchair (where 'mediated' spirituality provided by newspapers, books, films or cyberspace can be absorbed), advertising, the high street, healthcare or college courses,[12] it is clear that since the 60s counter-culture transmission has spread through domains which are not counter-cultural.[13] There is plenty of spiritual currency abroad in the culture at large, and this means that people living in the mainstream come across and become familiar with spiritual themes, acclimatized with regard to them, knowledgable about them; come to wonder about their plausibility or feasibility; might even become 'primed' enough to actually explore involvement with face-to-face practices. It can be concluded that many are more likely to encounter New Age provisions in the culture than they are to encounter Christianity: for in domain after domain (health provision, education, business life) Christianity is in decline (or dead) whereas spiritualities of life are expanding.[14]

Furthermore, and to return to younger spiritual practitioners in Kendal, a considerable proportion, 27 per cent, are aged between 35 and 44 and presumably 'missed' the '60s'. This group is likely to have been influenced by a 'mediated', culturalized legacy rather than the 'direct' legacy of the '60s' in the sense of the past experiences of that particular cohort. But what of the tiny numbers of spiritual practitioners under 35? Despite the fact that few are currently practising, there is evidence that significant numbers are being trained in the skills of complementary therapies. In 1994, Kendal College set up a one-year 'Holistic Therapy' diploma. Roughly half the intake of this course is under 30, and over eight years this certainly represents more than a hundred younger people who have done basic training with older therapists – enough waiting in the wings, in theory, to replace the ranks of current practitioners. Kendal College was part of a wave of Further Education colleges across the country launching these kinds of courses in the mid-1990s, so it appears direct transmission is occurring, yet at present there are few younger practitioners in active practice.

According to active practitioners in Kendal (including Celia Hunter-Wetenhall, one of the convenors of the Holistic Therapy diploma at Kendal College), this is probably best explained by a combination of circumstantial factors. First, clients tend to expect more mature practitioners and the nature of the work often requires life experience with which to counsel and sympathize with what clients are going through. This means that younger practitioners who do set up may either find some aspects of the practice beyond them or find it difficult to build up a client base. (They are more likely, it seems, to practise on friends and family.) People in their twenties and thirties are also more likely to be preoccupied with finding a partner, setting up home, having and raising children, financial security and building a career (most practitioners only have enough clients to practise part-time so this may not suit the needs of younger potential practitioners). In contrast, practitioners in their late forties or fifties are often filling time provided by their grown-up children having left home, from downsizing their work commitments or from a divorce. But since around the country from the mid-1990s there have been considerable numbers of younger people training as practitioners at Further Education Colleges, it seems safe to presume that in later life some of them may find a specialized course to rehone their skills and begin to fill the professional shoes of the '60s' cohort.

Turning from practitioners to the results of a questionnaire survey of group participants, clients and practitioners in Kendal gives further clues about participation. While the 45–54, '60s' cohort still make up a hefty 30.6 per cent of the sample, this is considerably lower than the 48 per cent in this age group for practitioners alone. Slightly fewer participants (than just practitioners) are younger, whereas far more – 42.1 per cent compared to 23 per cent – are 55 and over. Furthermore, only 33 per cent of all those involved in spiritual activities in Kendal and environs think of themselves as a 'child of the "60s"'. These figures suggest two things. First, considerable cultural transmission, especially to older age groups, has clearly already occurred, whether because they came of age before the '60s' and thus missed the experience, or because they came of age at that time but were not influenced by counter-cultural spirituality.[15] Second, while the 1960s may have been important in launching the cultural changes upon which New Age spiritualities of life have ridden, actual participation must also be explained in relation to life cycle factors; the formative role played by direct '60s' experience should not be overestimated. This is given further credence by the fact that 93 per cent of one-to-one practitioners have been practising for less than 15 years and 39 per cent less than five years, which does not suggest much reliance on the past.

If Kendal is anything to go by, current involvement with face-to-face spiritual practices is very much bound up with mid- and older-life 'issues': the 'is this all there is?' syndrome of (relative) success, the realization that 'my life is running out', middle-aged angst or 'homelessness', the empty home (after the divorce and with the children having gone to university or college), the divorce itself, the stresses and strains of increased responsibility at work, the challenging prospect of early retirement, and last – but by no means least – the waning of the body, the back pains, arthritis and so forth. So when younger people, especially those who are familiar with, or predisposed towards inner spirituality through the various kinds of cultural transmission we have explored, reach their later forties or fifties and encounter mid-life issues (especially those to do with the body and stress), it is only to be expected that some of them will get involved with face-to-face practices and have the mid-life resources of time and money to do so.

Finally, and more generally, the likelihood of the optimistic scenario being true is greatly enhanced by the way in which New Age spiritualities of life have (largely) come to operate in Kendal and elsewhere. As James Meek (1999) writes,

> New market research shows that people who venture into alternative healing, dissatisfied with the ability of the NHS to deal with niggling ailments, often end up moving away from mainstream religion as well, towards the spiritual buffet of alternative beliefs. 'People generally enter the market for health books, but once they buy a book like that, they're very open to purchasing across the mind, body and spirit range,' said Yvette Cowles, senior advertising and promotions manager with new age publishers Thorsons, which commissioned the research. (Meek, 1999, p.10)

With ageing comes an increase of 'niggling ailments' and, as people get older, *life-itself* becomes increasingly threatened. And in contrast with New Age spiritualities of life of the '60s', when *counter-cultural* concerns with 'breaking on through to the other side' or 'having the ultimate high' were well in evidence, we have seen that spiritualities of life have very much become part of the *everyday*, entering mainstream culture and, in their practical dimension, facilitating healing or the restoration/enhancement of well-being by (in particular) addressing dis-eases of a bodily kind. Counter-cultural practices of excess and celebration have given way to the more remedial, beneficial, pragmatic, 'measured' if not instrumentalized practices of the 'mainstreamed alternative'. Things have shifted from the 'oppositional' to the 'integrative' (Heelas, 2000b).

With these considerations in mind, it can now be emphasized that today's New Age spiritualities of life often introduce spirituality by way of relatively gradual, 'low threshold' and thus *'natural'* journeys or transitions. Spiritual practitioners in Kendal typically offer holistically unfolding paths 'within', gradually introducing clients to the mind, body and spirit interfusion. Newcomers do not run up against the high hurdle or challenge of immediately having to deal with fully-fledged New Age tenets ('You are a spiritual being responsible for your back pain'). Rather, their entry might look something like the following. Prompted by an everyday condition such as 'persistent back pain' (to recall Meek) or stress, one buys or borrows a health, self-esteem or de-stress book containing a combination of specialized health or stress advice and New Age messages about the need for personal and spiritual growth. Previous priming or acclimatization from encounters in the society at large – perhaps memories of spirituality at school or of a friend or family member's favourable account of visiting a complementary practitioner; or a visit to a holistic beauty salon, a well-being zone in a major store or leisure centre yoga class – comes to bear on one's bodily or bodily-cum-psychological complaint. The result? You go to see a complementary health practitioner, perhaps somewhere like 'Rainbow Cottage' in Kendal, one of a wave of new spiritual outlets springing up throughout the country especially since the early 1990s. Skilful instrumentalized practices of the practitioner (for if she was not skilful she would go out of business) might well initially attend to the back pain, perhaps without the practitioner even mentioning spirituality to begin with. The one thing that the majority of one-to-one practitioners have in common in Kendal, however, is that they see physical ailments as reflections of emotional, mental and spiritual habits; and in various different ways many clients are slowly, gently introduced to this experience.[16]

In comparison to the 1950s (when you more or less had to be a beatnik or upper class to turn to alternative spirituality), or the '60s' (when you more or less had to be counter-cultural), culturally primed, mid-life 'issued' people seeking answers to their (emotional, physical or well-being) problems can now become involved relatively easily. Whether '60s' cohort or not, people become increasingly engaged with New Age spiritualities of life by way of cultural transmission and ageing issues. By not being geared to '60s' counter-cultural, 'excessive', concerns ('break on through to the other side'), the spiritual path has opened up to include everyday 'issues' to do with the body, well-being, beauty, stress, eating and so on, new spiritualities of life thereby being in the position to operate through consumer culture to extend their appeal. Rather than aiming for life 'on the other side', quality of life is promised within the mainstream itself. In this way it can be seen that New Age spiritualities have become firmly embedded in our culture and are likely to continue to attract new participants, even as the influence of the '60s' cohort recedes.

Additional Support for the Optimistic Scenario

The optimistic scenario is also considerably enhanced by the fact that a fundamental shift is under way within the culture. Charles Taylor (1991) writes of 'the massive subjective turn of modern culture, a new form of inwardness, in which we come to think of ourselves as beings with inner depths' (p.26). Associated with the flight from deference and the celebration of the self, the shift is one of emphasis, from '*life-as*' or '*dictated life*' (life lived in terms of institutionalized or traditionalized formations *provided by* 'primary institutions') to '*subjective-life*' or '*expressed life*' (life lived in terms of personal, intimate, psychological, somatic, interior experiences *catered for* by 'secondary institutions') (see Heelas and Woodhead, 2001). Of particular note, this general 'cultural turn' includes a shift from 'religion' (involving 'life-as', which cannot deal with 'expressed life', and which is therefore declining) to 'spirituality' (associated with 'subjective-life', which can serve 'expressed life', and which is therefore expanding).[17]

What can be thought of as a 'spiritual revolution' is under way. The growing emphasis on subjective life, associated in increasing measure with inner spirituality, means that much of the culture (educational, business cultures, health provision, the high street, beliefs in 'spirit or life force', 'soul' and so on) is moving towards the position already staked out by (growing) New Age spiritualities of life. Themes which are richly elaborated in New Age circles (in particular those of a face-to-face nature) are thus also increasingly found – albeit in more inchoate or attenuated forms – amongst the population at large. And the fact that New Age spiritualities, which explicitly sacralize subjective life, provide more fully-fledged renderings of those more widespread, more attenuated or vague cultural developments means that the latter can serve to 'point' to what the former has to offer. There might be quite a difference between someone saying they believe in 'some sort of spirit or life force', then going silent, and the New Ager saying 'I am a Goddess' and engaging in regular practices to activate that in their life. But the fact remains that the former can lead at least some to the latter, especially given all those cultural provisions or 'pointers' that we have been discussing. Given the ever-increasing cultural emphasis on subjective life, if people *are* going to be spiritual or religious, they are much more likely to be the former (which directly caters for subjective-life) than the latter (where 'life as' dictated by deference to tradition remains well in evidence).[18]

Furthermore, whether or not widespread cultural developments continue to contribute to the appeal and maintenance of face-to-face spiritual practices, they will serve to ensure that something *akin* to fully-fledged New Age spiritualities of life – namely the tendency to equate inner, subjective-life (or, indeed, raw 'life-itself') with some sort of relatively ill-articulated, attenuated, diffuse or diluted spirituality – is set fair for the future. By virtue of being grounded in major sociocultural processes (with the ascription of 'ultimate' value to subjective-life almost certainly being at the heart of the matter) – processes which are much too general to owe much (if anything) to the impact of the New Age itself – *this* future is assured regardless of the fate of face-to-face practices.[19]

And this is not all. For developments within the orbit of traditional religion, also owing a very great deal to the cultural shift in emphasis towards subjective life, have to be taken into account. What can be thought of as the 'softening' of religious tradition is widespread: processes of immanentization (subjectivization, psychologization or interiorization) catering for concern with the 'growth' or 'healing' of the inner life, and resulting in a distinctly 'New Age' feel to the spiritual quest (the term 'spiritual' being favoured over 'religious'). In the USA, in particular, the Holy Spirit has come into prominence as the vehicle for interiorization, often serving in much the same fashion as the Higher Self of New Age circles. Taking place within religious 'tradition', subjectivization of religion might not result in the more radically detraditionalized spirituality found within the New Age, but this is not to say that immanentization will not serve to sustain the future of themes akin to those more radically (as de-theisized) articulated by New Age spiritualities of life. So the spiritual revolution is taking place within (much) religion, (often expanding) theistic spiritualities of life serving to carry themes which are strongly resonant with New Age themes, if not being, in functional regards, identical to them. (See Heelas, 2002a, for further discussion.)

In short, the strands of the widespread cultural turn to subjective-life, not least subjectivized, well-being consumer culture where spiritual signals and provisions are so often to be found, will provide a supportive environment for the continued flourishing of New Age spiritualities of life.

Summary and Prediction

According to Ken Wilber, 'the new age is a product of the baby-boom phenomenon, the "60s generation"' (cited by Rose, 1998, p.9). Or, as Daniel Mears and Christopher Ellison (2000) put it, 'It is widely believed that the baby-boom generation is the primary force driving the New Age movement' (p.293). Wade Clark Roof's book, *Spiritual Marketplace* (1999), which focuses on 1960s baby-boomers, was advertised with the point that Roof, 'returns to interview many of these same people, now in mid-life, to reveal a generation with a unique set of spiritual values'. Earlier in this chapter we showed that the age profile of spiritual practitioners in Kendal supports the contention that this '60s' cohort is of key significance in sustaining the New Age movement.

According to the 'ageing cohort' scenario, the immediate future of New Age spiritualities is promising. As those baby-boomers who came of age during the '60s' enter old age, it is likely that they will increasingly resource their decaying or threatened lives with spiritual provisions, perhaps seeking to combat the ravages of time with the 'spirit' of '60s' 'eternal youth'. It can be added, *contra* those such as Steve Bruce (2002) – who argue that New Age spiritualities are insignificant in that they lack salience – that it is highly likely that the 'ageing' issues which such spiritualities will increasingly be called upon to address will result, given their ever-increasing gravity, in enhancing the existential significance of what is facilitated by face-to-face activities at new spiritual outlets. But with so much apparently relying on a particular cohort, the longer-term prospects would appear to be poor.

However, we have suggested that our second 'cultural transmission' hypothesis overrides such a conclusion. The future of New Age spiritualities need not *depend*, at least so crucially, on that particular cohort of baby boomers, with its relatively distinctive life history, who came of age with the '60s'. The ranks of face-to-face groups and practices will be replenished by people who have come of age since the '60s' when they encounter mid-life (or older-life) 'issues'. This is by virtue of their growing up in a culture where the middle classes (at least) can hardly avoid encountering cultural carriers-cum-transmission agencies in the realms of healthcare, media, advertising and the high street, education, business and entertainment. Such cultural transmissions operating in the wider society mean that many become familiar with themes pertaining to New Age spiritualities of life, learn something about what they have to offer, and perhaps become 'primed' to adopt them when their 'stage of life' (resources and issues) is right. Cultural transmission paves the way for future face-to-face involvement in new spiritual outlets.

Furthermore, we have shown that, in Kendal, there are relatively large numbers of spiritual practitioners aged between 35 and 44. Moreover, transmission to the under-thirties is also occurring in the form of a wave of Further Education 'Holistic Therapy'-type diplomas and courses. True, very few under-35s are currently set up as practitioners, but this is due to their having other time-consuming commitments such as work and family, their not yet having mid-life issues to deal with, and the fact that setting up as a successful practitioner appears to require life experience. As this younger generation in turn comes to experience mid- and older life challenges, however, it seems likely that some (especially the more culturally primed) will become participants and practitioners of complementary health and inner spirituality.

It is surely of great significance that attitudes to New Age spirituality have shifted from the disapproval, if not alarm, of 'straight' society encountering the counter-culture of the '60s' to the (apparent) acclaim of so many receiving and propelling the cultural transmissions today, for this serves to demonstrate how deeply embedded this kind of spirituality has become. It is given that some of these transmissions instrumentalize and commodify New Age spiritualities of life in such a way that the existential significance of those transmissions themselves is radically watered down. But, below the surface, even the most commodified renderings such as a woman pictured in meditation posture to sell a black leather settee, or someone in a yoga posture illustrating 'peace of mind' to sell an ISA, carry significant encodings about well-being, happiness and the good life and reflect a powerful cultural current. That current will continue to fuel the more serious, existentially significant realm of face-to-face practices.

If our prediction is correct, although the '60s' have clearly played a highly significant role, and although face-to-face activities have remained closely associated with a particular (ageing) cohort (which, it can be noted, explains why the New Age has become so concerned with health cum – bodily well-being), the death of this cohort will only dent growth in the future. For the association with a particular cohort, including whatever formative or socializing role the '60s' may have played, will be replaced by the younger baby-boomers, who are greater in number than the older (Brierley, 2001, p.4.3).[20] It is reasonably well-established that people tend to get more concerned with ultimate matters as they move ever closer to death (Argyle and Beit-Hallahmi, 1975, ch. 4). Whereas until the '60s' it was 'natural' for people to turn to Christianity, it is becoming 'natural' for increasing numbers to turn to alternative spiritualities of life. So long as great value is attached to the development, cultivation and exploration of subjective-life, so long as we live in a subjectivized consumer culture propounding expectations of well-being, there is no reason to suppose that the future of New Age spiritualities is anything but promising. The wider cultural current of inner spirituality may very well become more important than declining traditional religion.

This chapter has raised a considerable number of issues which require further research (and which the Kendal Project is endeavouring to explore), but surely the most striking issue concerns the (relative) reversal which has taken place with regard to face-to-face practices since the '60s', from the youthful and counter-cultural locus of the '60s' to the mid-life and healing/well-being cultural locus of the mainstream today. Although, as should be apparent, we do not think that the future of New Age spiritualities of life depends – to any significant extent – on whether or not the youthful actually engage in face-to-face practices, it is still fascinating to ponder why so few of the youthful, relatively speaking, are involved with such practices today.

Notes

1   Evidence concerning *Yellow Pages* and oral history research is provided by the Kendal Project (introduced later in this chapter) and will be published in due course. See Heelas (1996) for more information on the numerical significance of New Age spiritualities, including book sale figures. Evidence is also provided by research into the numbers of people who have been attracted to alternative or complementary forms of healing, many of which have a New Age dimension. For example, an ICM survey, reported by Linus Gregoriadis (1999), found that the number of people using non-conventional treatments has doubled in the past six years, with one in five Britons having recently turned to complementary or alternative therapies.

2   Together with Paul Heelas (Principal Applicant) and Ben Seel (one of the two Research Associates), the team involves Bronislaw Szerszynski (co-applicant), Linda Woodhead (co-applicant) and Karin Tusting (Research Associate). The Leverhulme Trust is thanked for financing much of the Project, which ran from October 2000 to June 2002) . Much of Heelas' interest in Kendal results concerning ageing and baby boomers, it can be added, arise from the fact that he was born in 1946.

3   It should be added that Eileen Barker's (1998) claim that 'new religions have been disproportionately attractive to persons in their early twenties or thirties' (p.20) has virtually no bearing on our 'ageing' portrayal of Kendal, for there are virtually no new religious movements (NRMs) in the town. Neither are there signs of that (supposed) growth area among younger people – paganism – in that there is only one small Pagan group.

4   Thinking of the general connection between baby-boomers and those involved in New Age spiritualities, research indicates that baby-boomers are more likely to be involved than other sectors of the population. A key finding of research carried out by Wade Clark Roof and his team in the USA, for example, is that, by the end of the 1980s, 55 per cent of the 75 million or so baby-boomers born between 1946 and 1964 were 'family attenders' (basically involved with mainstream religion), the remaining 45 per cent being 'religious individualists', of whom half were New Age or New Age inclined (Roof and Gesch, 1995, p.64). Approaching a quarter of the baby-boomers, in other words, were then associated – to varying degrees – with New Age spiritualities. And there is no evidence – at least which I can find – which suggests that anything like a quarter of older people (born before 1946) were associated with New Age spiritualities at the close of the 1980s, or that anything like a quarter of younger people (born after 1964) have become involved. For more specific findings regarding the USA, the middle age profile is supported by Danny Jorgensen (1982, p.389), Meredith McGuire (1988, p.12), and Thomas Robbins (1988, pp.10, 45, 62). For other findings, see those reported by Heelas (1996, ch. 6), Rose (1998) and York (1995); see also

Ursula Sharma (1995), who reports that 'the majority of respondents [in her study of complementary medicine in Britain] were between forty and sixty years old' (p.35; see also pp.20–22). It should be borne in mind that in certain New Age quarters, such as communities, the age range is more diverse.

5 Regarding university students, the following comment (made by a Lancaster student interviewed by a student of Heelas', Amy Pickford) is probably pretty accurate: 'It [religion or spirituality) doesn't fit in with the whole uni thing. I don't know much about it to be quite honest. It's not what I see as religious – to go out drinking all the time.'

6 It is significant to note that the most liberal forms of Christianity in Kendal have very 'poor' transmission with regard to younger people, with only 2.8 per cent of such churches' attendance being younger people, as opposed to the 16.8 per cent average for all churches in Kendal.

7 Reflecting on this final flourish, the market is surely bound to expand for those of the baby-boom cohort who have come to offer life-enhancing or 'being' spirituality, in particular for those clients or group members who belong to the same cohort. Baby boomers will increasingly be seeking to make the *most* of their (for many well-financed) retirement. Habits acquired during the celebratory '60s' – not least smoking and drinking – will increasingly extract their toll and require attention (as we write this, George Harrison – that 'spirit of the age', as one newspaper puts it – dies of smoking-induced cancer). Bodies will get more and more worn out. And so New Age nursing homes or hospices, ways of 'being old with grace', groups on 'facing up to death' or providing 'spirituality to enhance life in the face of death', or events celebrating ageing as a journey of spiritual growth and discovery, will flourish. 'How to' volumes, such as Starhawk, Marcha Nightmare and the Reclaiming Collective's *The Pagan Book of Living and Dying: Practical Rituals, Prayers, Blessings, and Meditations on Crossing Over* (1997) or Deepak Chopra's *Ageless Body, Timeless Mind. A Practical Alternative to Growing Old* (1994) might not yet be that common (although see Tony Walter, 1993), but will surely become increasingly popular. It can also be noted that the shorter-term future of healthcare in general is highly promising, if that is the right word. The fact that 'Healthcare is expected to be one of the fastest-growing industries over the next few decades' (David Budworth, 2001, p.7) is largely due to the baby boomers approaching old age. It is very likely that alternative healing will not only benefit from this fact but will also serve to take some of the strain off the NHS, thus helping reduce increases in income tax.

8 Bruce (1996, p.273) might be wrong to indicate that New Age spirituality is already a declining force, but unless there is replenishment of the face-to-face by the younger, the ageing cohort scenario would suggest that he could become right – albeit for reasons which he does not explore – in the nearish future.

9 And, it can be added, this picture is enhanced by Michael Corsten's (1999) research, an essay title, 'Ecstasy as "This-worldly Path to Salvation": the Techno Youth Scene as a Proto-Religious Collective' conveying the gist of his portrayal.

10 A survey of mental health workers in the USA (reported by Brian Zinnbauer *et al.* (1997)) found that 'they were second only to the New Age group in percentage of respondents who identified themselves as spiritual but not religious'(p.562).

11 Andrea Cheshire, an MA student at Lancaster University, is thanked for having visited all the high street shops in Kendal to arrive at this figure.

12 Including Further Education courses, Workers' Adult Education provisions, summer schools, continuing education and other lifelong learning courses put on by universities and colleges.

13 See King (2001). New Age spiritualities of life have moved a long way from that cultic milieu, discussed by Colin Campbell (1972), which has to face the 'disapproval and even outright hostility of the organisations representing cultural orthodoxy' (p.129).

14 As Callum Brown (2001) writes of Christianity, 'Since the 1960s, the churches have become increasingly irrelevant in the new cultural and ethical landscape' (p.191). The significance of the shift in importance of cultural transmission vehicles for the future of both 'religion' and 'spirituality' cannot be underestimated.

15 Cultural transmission does not, however, seem to have resulted in much face-to-face involvement among the under-forties. Whether the younger generation is more likely than their predecessors to try practices like meditation at home is more difficult to research.

16 The argument that New Age spiritualities of life have become well-suited for mid-life issues, in particular by providing low, easy threshold points of entry for spiritualities focusing on bodily issues or disease, is suggested by evidence from the Kendal Project. See also Anneke van Otterloo (1999) for very similar findings from the Netherlands.

17 On the basis of extensive research in the USA, Wade Clark Roof (1999) and Robert Wuthnow (1998) have found widespread evidence of 'spirituality' (as opposed to 'religion'), spirituality which is very much bound up with the subjectivities of the life 'within'; and 'spiritual growth', it is reported by Robert Owens Scott (2001), is sought by 'four out of five' in the USA (p.26). See also Heelas (2000a; 2002a); Campbell (forthcoming).

18 See Heelas (2002a) for further discussion; see also Heelas (1996; 2000a) on the role which the development of humanistic expressivism might play in 'pointing' to New Age spiritualities of life.

19 Colin Campbell's (forthcoming) 'easternization of the west' thesis will also become increasingly applicable, as will Thomas Luckmann's (1967) 'invisible religion' thesis.

20 Given that they are larger in number, it is even possible that this will boost the realm of face-to-face practice. Although it has been claimed that more youthful 'GenXers', defined by Donald Miller and Arpi Miller (2000, p.3) as those born between 1961 and 1981, are in the process of developing forms of religiosity or spirituality which will come to rival, perhaps displace, New Age spiritualities of life (Miller and Miller, 2000), there are as yet few, if any, signs of this in Kendal.

References

Argyle, Michael and Beit-Hallahmi, Benjamin 1975: *The Social Psychology of Religion*. London: Routlege & Kegan Paul.

Ashley, Martin 2000: Secular Spirituality and Implicit Religion: the Realisation of Human Potential. *Implicit Religion*, 3 (1), pp.31–49.

Barker, Eileen 1998: New Religions and New Religiosity. In Eileen Barker and Margit Warburg (eds), *New Religions and New Religiosity*. Aarhus: Aarhus University Press, pp.10–27.

Boseley, Sarah 2000: Peers Say NHS could Embrace Alternative Therapies. *The Guardian*, 29 November.

Brierley, Peter (ed.) 2001: *UK Christian Handbook. Religious Trends 3*. London: Christian Research.

Brown, Callum G. 2001: *The Death of Christian Britain*. London: Routledge.

Bruce, Steve 1996: Religion in Britain at the Close of the 20th Century: A Challenge to the Silver Lining Perspective. *Journal of Contemporary Religion*, 11 (3), pp.261–75.

Bruce, Steve 2002: *God is Dead. Secularization in the West*. Oxford: Blackwell.

Budworth, David 2001: The Brave in Aggressive Investing. *The Sunday Times, Money*, 11 November, p.7.

Campbell, Colin 1972: The Cult, the Cultic Milieu and Secularization. In Michael Hill (ed.), *Sociological Yearbook of Religion in Britain*. (Vol. 5). London: SCM, pp.119–36.

Campbell, Colin (forthcoming): *The Easternisation of the West*.

Chopra, Deepak 1994: *Ageless Body, Timeless Mind. A Practical Alternative to Growing Old*. New York: Harmony Books.

Collins, Sylvia 1997: Young People's Faith in Later Modernity. PhD, University of Surrey.

Corsten, Michael 1999: Ecstasy as 'This-Worldly Path to Salvation'. The Techno Youth Scene as a Proto-Religious Collective. In Luigi Tomasi (ed.), *Alternative Religions Among European Youth*. Aldershot: Ashgate, pp.91–124.

Coward, Rosalind 1990: *The Whole Truth*. London: Faber & Faber.

Gallup, George H. and Bezilla, Robert 1992: *The Religious Life of Young Americans*. Princeton: The George H. Gallup International Institute.

Gregoriadis, Linus 1999: Doctors Call for Better Regulations as More Turn to Alternative Cures. *The Guardian*, 24 August.

Harrison, Judy and Burnard, Philip 1993: *Spirituality and Nursing Practice*. London: Avebury.

Heelas, Paul 1996: *The New Age Movement. The Celebration of the Self and the Sacralization of Modernity*. Oxford and Cambridge, MA: Blackwell.

Heelas, Paul 2000a: Expressive Spirituality and Humanistic Expressivism. Sources of Significance Beyond Church and Chapel. In Steven Sutcliffe and Marion Bowman (eds) *Beyond New Age. Exploring Alternative Spirituality*. Edinburgh: Edinburgh University Press, pp.237–54.

Heelas, Paul 2000b: New Age Spirituality: Oppositional or Integrative? In Jeffrey Kaplan (ed.), *Beyond the Mainstream*. Helsinki: SKS, pp.43–55.

Heelas, Paul 2002a: The Spiritual Revolution: From 'Religion' to 'Spirituality'. In Linda Woodhead, Paul Fletcher, Hiroko Kawanami and David Smith (eds), *Religions in the Modern World*. London and New York: Routledge, pp.357–77.

Heelas, Paul 2002b: Work Ethics, Soft Capitalism and the 'Turn to Life'. In Paul du Gay and Michael Pryke (eds), *Cultural Economy*. London: Sage, pp.83–101.

Heelas, Paul and Woodhead, Linda 2001: Homeless Minds Today? In Linda Woodhead, with Paul Heelas and David Martin (eds), *Peter Berger and the Study of Religion*. London and New York: Routledge, pp.43–72.

Janssen, Jacques 1999: The Abstract Image of God. The Case of Dutch Youth. In Luigi Tomasi (ed.), *Alternative Religions among European Youth*. Aldershot: Ashgate, pp.57–82.

Jorgensen, Danny 1982: The Esoteric Community. *Urban Life*, 10 (4), pp.383–407.

King, Ursula (ed.) 2001: *Spirituality and Society in the New Millennium*. Brighton: Sussex Academic Press.

Kubiak, Anna (unpublished) New Age Culture in Poland. Manifestations, Milieu, Significance. Institute of Philosophy and Sociology of the Polish Academy of Sciences, Warsaw.

Lowendahl, Lena 2002: *Med Kroppen Som Instrument*. Lund: Religionshistoriska Avdelningen.

Luckmann, Thomas 1967: *The Invisible Religion*. New York: Macmillan.

Lynch, Gordon (unpublished manuscript): Is there a 'Clubbing Spirituality'?

McGuire, Meredith 1988: *Ritual Healing in Suburban America*. London: Rutgers University Press.

McSherry, Wilfred 1998: Nurses' Perceptions of Spirituality and Spiritual Care. *Nursing Standard*, 13 (2), pp.36–40.

Mears, Daniel and Ellison, Christopher 2000: Who Buys New Age Materials?, *Sociology of Religion*, 61 (3), pp.289–313.

Meek, James 1999: Alternative Health 'Leads to New Spiritual Awareness'. *The Guardian*, 25 October.

Miller, Donald E. and Miller, Arpi Misha 2000: Introduction. Understanding Generation X. In Richard W. Flory and Donald E. Miller (eds), *GenX Religion*. London: Routledge, pp.1–12.

Otterloo, Anneke H. van 1999: Selfspirituality and the Body. New Age Centres in The Netherlands since the 1960s. *Social Compass*, 46 (2), pp.191–202.

Robbins, Thomas 1988: *Cults, Converts & Charisma*. London: Sage.

Roberts, Andrew 2001: Charles is the Only One Standing in His Way. *The Sunday Telegraph*, 8 July.

Roof, Wade Clark 1999: *Spiritual Marketplace. Baby Boomers and the Remaking of American Religion*. Princeton, NJ: Princeton University Press.

Roof, Wade Clark and Gesch, Lyn 1995: Boomers and the Culture of Choice. In Nancy Tatom Ammerman and Wade Clark Roof (eds), *Work, Family, and Religion in Contemporary Society*. London and New York: Routledge, pp.61–80.

Rose, Stuart 1998: An Examination of the New Age Movement. Who is Involved and what Constitutes its Spirituality. *Journal of Contemporary Religion*, 13 (1), pp.5–22.

Scott, Robert Owens 2001: Are You Religious or Are You Spiritual?, *Spirituality & Health*, Spring, pp.26–31.

Sharma, Ursula 1995: *Complementary Medicine Today. Practitioners and Patients*. London and New York: Routledge.

Sharma, Ursula and Black, Paula (undated): The Sociology of Pampering: Beauty Therapy as a Form of Work. Centre for Social Research, University of Derby.

Starhawk, M., Nightmare, Marcha and the Reclaiming Collective 1997: *The Pagan Book of Living and Dying: Practical Rituals, Blessings and Meditations on Crossing Over.* London: HarperSanFrancisco.

Taylor, Charles 1991: *The Ethics of Authenticity.* London: Harvard University Press.

Walter, Tony 1993: Death in the New Age. *Religion,* 23 (2), pp.127–46.

Walter, Tony 1996: Developments in Spiritual Care of the Dying. *Religion,* 26 (4), pp.353–63.

Wuthnow, Robert 1998: *After Heaven. Spirituality in America Since the 1950s.* London: University of California Press.

York, Michael 1995: *The Emerging Network.* London: Rowan & Littlefield.

Zinnbauer, Brian J., Pargament, Kenneth I., Cole, Brenda *et al.* 1997: Religion and Spirituality. Unfuzzing the Fuzzy. *Journal for the Scientific Study of Religion,* 36 (4), pp.549–64.

Index